HISTORICAL DICTIONARIES OF ASIA, OCEANIA, AND THE MIDDLE EAST

Edited by Jon Woronoff

Asia

1. *Vietnam*, by William J. Duiker. 1989. *Out of print. See No. 27.*
2. *Bangladesh*, 2nd ed., by Craig Baxter and Syedur Rahman. 1996. *Out of print. See No. 48.*
3. *Pakistan*, by Shahid Javed Burki. 1991. *Out of print. See No. 33.*
4. *Jordan*, by Peter Gubser. 1991.
5. *Afghanistan*, by Ludwig W. Adamec. 1991. *Out of print. See No. 47.*
6. *Laos*, by Martin Stuart-Fox and Mary Kooyman. 1992. *Out of print. See No. 35.*
7. *Singapore*, by K. Mulliner and Lian The-Mulliner. 1991.
8. *Israel*, by Bernard Reich. 1992.
9. *Indonesia*, by Robert Cribb. 1992. *Out of print. See No. 51.*
10. *Hong Kong and Macau*, by Elfed Vaughan Roberts, Sum Ngai Ling, and Peter Bradshaw. 1992.
11. *Korea*, by Andrew C. Nahm. 1993. *Out of print. See No. 52.*
12. *Taiwan*, by John F. Copper. 1993. *Out of print. See No. 34.*
13. *Malaysia*, by Amarjit Kaur. 1993. *Out of print. See No. 36.*
14. *Saudi Arabia*, by J. E. Peterson. 1993. *Out of print. See No. 45.*
15. *Myanmar*, by Jan Becka. 1995. *Out of print. See No. 59.*
16. *Iran*, by John H. Lorentz. 1995. *Out of print. See No. 62.*
17. *Yemen*, by Robert D. Burrowes. 1995.
18. *Thailand*, by May Kyi Win and Harold Smith. 1995. *Out of print. See No. 55.*
19. *Mongolia*, by Alan J. K. Sanders. 1996. *Out of print. See No. 42.*
20. *India*, by Surjit Mansingh. 1996. *Out of print. See No. 58.*
21. *Gulf Arab States*, by Malcolm C. Peck. 1996.
22. *Syria*, by David Commins. 1996. *Out of print. See No. 50.*
23. *Palestine*, by Nafez Y. Nazzal and Laila A. Nazzal. 1997.
24. *Philippines*, by Artemio R. Guillermo and May Kyi Win. 1997. *Out of print. See No. 54.*

Historical Dictionary of Taiwan (Republic of China)

Third Edition

John F. Copper

Historical Dictionaries of
Asia, Oceania, and the Middle East, No. 64

The Scarecrow Press, Inc.
Lanham, Maryland • Toronto • Plymouth, UK
2007

SCARECROW PRESS, INC.

Published in the United States of America
by Scarecrow Press, Inc.
A wholly owned subsidiary of
The Rowman & Littlefield Publishing Group, Inc.
4501 Forbes Boulevard, Suite 200, Lanham, Maryland 20706
www.scarecrowpress.com

Estover Road
Plymouth PL6 7PY
United Kingdom

British Library Cataloguing in Publication Information Available

Library of Congress Cataloging-in-Publication Data

Copper, John Franklin.
  Historical dictionary of Taiwan (Republic of China) / John F. Cooper. — 3rd ed.
    p. cm. — (Historical dictionaries of Asia, Oceania, and the Middle East)
  Includes bibliographical references.
  ISBN-13: 978-0-8108-5600-4 (hardcover : alk. paper)
  ISBN-10: 0-8108-5600-X (hardcover : alk. paper)
    1. Taiwan—History—Dictionaries. I. Title.
  DS798.96.C67 2007
  951.24'9003—dc22

                                                                    2006029893

To Royce Wellington Copper

Contents

Editor's Foreword

The Republic of China, often referred to as Taiwan, has long aroused interest abroad and, on numerous occasions, serious concern. Earlier, much attention focused on Taiwan's extraordinary economic development. Observers wondered how such a small, densely populated, and initially poor country with virtually no natural resources could accomplish what it did. Indeed, the media portrayed Taiwan as an "economic miracle." Comments on the political system were far less flattering due to the authoritarian rule of the Kuomintang regime. However, a "political miracle" also occurred, and the country became one of the most democratic in the world, especially as compared to its archrival, the People's Republic of China. This rivalry, notwithstanding their rapid economic integration, has been expressed in political spats that often turn nasty and produce war scares. The Taiwan Strait remains one of the world's flashpoints, said by many to be the most dangerous.

Given the continuing interest in Taiwan and the momentous changes it has experienced recently, including a historic change of ruling parties when Chen Shui-bian won the presidency in 2000 and the KMT that had been in power for more than fifty years became the opposition, a third edition of the *Historical Dictionary of Taiwan (Republic of China)* is needed. The chronology charts the high points of its history, going back to a time when Taiwan had several names, up to the present. The introduction tells us more about the place, its inhabitants, and its different ruling political regimes. But the bulk of the information in this book is to be found in the dictionary, which includes several hundred entries on important persons; places and events; political parties and institutions; and major political, economic, social, and cultural aspects of the island country. This is obviously just a starting point, although a very substantial one; those who want to know more can consult the comprehensive bibliography that follows.

John F. Copper is the Stanley J. Buckman Distinguished Professor of International Studies at Rhodes College in Memphis, Tennessee. Far from being just an academic, he knows the region intimately, having lived in Asia for fifteen years, including six in Taiwan. Along with the first two editions of this volume, he is the author of numerous articles and papers and more than twenty books on Taiwan, China, and Asian affairs. Among the most recent—all of which focus on critical issues— are *Taiwan in Troubled Times*, *Taiwan: Nation-State or Province?*, *Consolidating Taiwan's Democracy*, and *Playing with Fire: The Looming War with China over Taiwan*. In addition to writing and lecturing, Dr. Copper has testified before the Senate Foreign Relations Committee and the House Foreign Affairs Committee. This third edition, substantially expanded as well as updated, provides an exceptional look at an exceptional country.

Jon Woronoff
Series Editor

Note on Chinese Terms

The Wade-Giles System of romanizing Chinese words, terms, place names, and people's names is generally used in this book. This is the system long used in Taiwan and is the system employed in romanizing Chinese in most historical works published in the West. The Pinyin System used in the People's Republic of China is accepted for words whose referent is a current place or name in China. Sometimes words will be romanized in two systems, indicating that they are spelled differently in different places. In some cases, persons' names are romanized using another system or from a dialect of Chinese rather than Mandarin. The author prefers to accept the spelling of the person's name that he or she uses, even though it is not standard. Some aboriginal words are used in this book, taking whatever spelling is used in Taiwan. The reader should note that family names come first in Chinese; given names come last and, in Taiwan, are hyphenated if there are two given names.

Acronyms and Abbreviations

ADB	Asian Development Bank
AIT	American Institute in Taiwan
APACL	Asian Pacific Anti-Communist League
APEC	Asia–Pacific Economic Cooperation (forum)
APPS	Association for Public Policy Studies
ARATS	Association for Relations across the Taiwan Strait
ASPAC	Asian and Pacific Council
BCC	Broadcasting Corporation of China
CAC	Campaign Assistance Committee
CAL	China Airlines
CBC	Central Bank of China
CBS	Central Broadcasting System
CCK	Chiang Ching-kuo
CCNAA	Coordination Council for North American Affairs
CDC	China Development Corporation
CEC	Central Election Commission
CEPD	Council for Economic Planning and Development
CETDC	China External Trade Development Council
CFL	Chinese Federation of Labor
CHT	Chunghua Telecom
CKS	Chiang Kai-shek
CLA	Council of Labor Affairs
CNA	Central News Agency
CNFI	Chinese National Federation of Industries
CPC	Chinese Petroleum Corporation
CRC	Central Reform Committee
CSC	Central Standing Committee
CSDP	Chinese Social Democratic Party
CTOC	Chinese Taipei Olympic Committee

CTS	China Television Service
CTV	China Television Company
CYC	China Youth Corps
CYP	China Youth Party
DPP	Democratic Progressive Party
DSP	Democratic Socialist Party
EPA	Environmental Protection Administration
EPC	Economic Planning Council
EPZ	Export Processing Zone
FAPA	Formosan Association for Public Affairs
FTV	Formosa Television Corporation
GATT	General Agreement on Tariffs and Trade
GIO	Government Information Office
ICDF	International Cooperation and Development Fund
IDF	Indigenous Defense Fighter
ITRI	Industrial Technology Research Institute
JCRR	Joint Commission on Rural Reconstruction
KMT	Kuomintang (or Nationalist Party)
MAC	Mainland Affairs Council
MOFA	Ministry of Foreign Affairs
MSA	Mutual Security Agency
NDIPA	National Democratic Independent Political Alliance
NP	New Party
NSB	National Security Bureau
NSC	National Science Council
NSC	National Security Council
NTU	National Taiwan University
NUC	National Unification Council
OCAC	Overseas Chinese Affairs Commission
PCT	Presbyterian Church of Taiwan
PFP	People First Party
PRC	People's Republic of China
ROC	Republic of China
SEF	Straits Exchange Foundation
STSP	Southern Taiwan Science Park
TAIP	Taiwan Independence Party
TCP	Taiwan Communist Party
TECRO	Taipei Economic and Cultural Representative Office

TIM	Taiwan Independence Movement
TMD	Theater Missile Defense
TRA	Taiwan Relations Act
TRAPP	Tangwai Research Association for Public Policy
TSEA	Taiwan Security Enhancement Act
TSU	Taiwan Solidarity Union
TTV	Taiwan Television Corporation
USAID	United States Aid to International Development
WTO	World Trade Organization
WUFI	World United Formosans for Independence

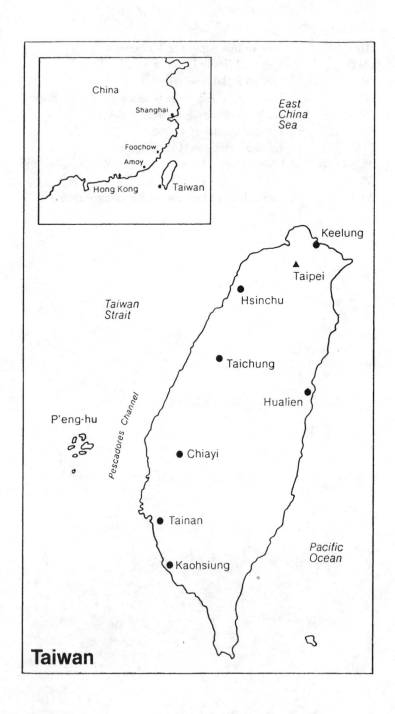

Taiwan

Chronology

c. 10,000 BCE There is human life on Taiwan.

206 BCE Taiwan is referred to in Chinese records as the "Land of Yangchow."

CE 239 Chinese emperor Wu sends an expeditionary force to Taiwan to explore the island.

607 First of three exploratory missions from China are sent to Taiwan.

c. 1000 Chinese settlements are present in southern Taiwan.

c. 1350 Mongol Dynasty ruling China sends a mission to the Pescadores, where a base is established.

1517 Sailors on a Portuguese vessel sailing to Japan spot Taiwan and call it "Ilha Formosa" (beautiful island). This is the first mention of Taiwan in Western history.

1622 Dutch forces capture the Pescadores and build a base from which Dutch ships can control traffic through the Taiwan Strait.

1624 The Dutch reach an agreement with the Chinese government to evacuate from the Pescadores in return for establishing settlements on Taiwan. This marks the beginning of Dutch colonial rule of Taiwan.

1626 Spanish forces seize Keelung and from there expand to control northern Taiwan.

1628 Japanese settlers leave Taiwan under orders from the Tokugawa Shogunate, Japan's military leader, as part of Japan's isolationist policies.

1642 Dutch forces capture major Spanish settlements in northern Taiwan, thereby consolidating control over the island.

1659 Cheng Ch'eng-kung, also known as Koxinga, operating from a base in Taiwan, sends forces to China in an effort to overthrow the Manchu Dynasty and reestablish the Ming Dynasty. They almost capture Nanking.

1662 Cheng Ch'eng-kung defeats Dutch forces, marking the end of Dutch rule and the beginning of the "Cheng Dynasty" in Taiwan.

1683 Cheng family rule of Taiwan ends; China's governance of Taiwan under the Manchu Dynasty begins.

1729 Emperor of China forbids immigration to Taiwan—under penalty of death.

1786 There is a major rebellion in Taiwan against Chinese rule.

1860 Several ports in Taiwan open to Western trade.

1874 Japanese punitive expedition is sent to Taiwan in response to aborigines killing Japanese sailors.

1884 Liu Ming-chuan becomes governor of Taiwan. French naval vessels attack port of Keelung.

1887 Taiwan is made a province of China.

1895 Treaty of Shimonoseki concludes Sino–Japanese War; Taiwan is ceded to Japan "in perpetuity." Unsuccessful attempt is made to form the Republic of Taiwan.

1924 Lin Hsien-tang presents twelve-point grievances to Japanese colonial government.

1928 First university is established in Taiwan.

1935 Taiwan experiences its worst-ever earthquake; more than three thousand die.

1938 Chiang Kai-shek announces his intention to take Taiwan back from Japan.

1941 Taiwan serves as a base for Japanese forces that attack the Philippines.

1943 At the Cairo Conference, the United States and the United Kingdom promise Chiang Kai-shek the return of territories "stolen by Japan," including Taiwan, to China after the war.

1945 **July** Allied forces at Potsdam reiterate the territorial provisions of the Cairo Declaration. **25 October** Taiwan becomes part of the Republic of China as a result of Japan's defeat in World War II.

1947 **28 February** A major rebellion breaks out against the rule of Nationalist Chinese governor-general Chen Yi; it is put down with force, and many Taiwanese are killed.

1948 **29 December** General Chen Cheng is appointed governor of Taiwan.

1949 The government of the Republic of China moves to Taiwan after its defeat on the mainland. Taipei becomes the provisional capital of the Republic of China. **10 December** Chiang Kai-shek flies from Chengdu to Taipei. **15 December** Wu Kuo-chen is named governor of Taiwan.

1950 **6 January** Taipei breaks diplomatic relations with the United Kingdom after the latter establishes formal ties with Peking. **March** Chiang Kai-shek resumes the presidency of the Republic of China. He names General Chen Cheng president of the Executive Yuan, or premier. **27 June** As a result of the outbreak of the Korean War, U.S. president Harry S. Truman sends the Seventh Fleet to the Taiwan Strait, blocking a planned invasion of Taiwan by Mao. **2 July** Popular election is held for Hualien City Council. **31 July** General Douglas MacArthur meets Chiang Kai-shek in Taipei. U.S. aid to Nationalist China, now on Taiwan, is resumed.

1951 **25 May** The Legislative Yuan passes the Farm Rent Reduction Act, limiting rent on farm land to 37.5 percent of the value of the crop, marking the first stage of Taiwan's land reform program. **9 September** Allied nations sign a peace treaty with Japan. China is not represented. Taiwan's status is not mentioned. **11 December** The Taiwan Provincial Assembly (provisional) is established.

1952 **28 April** A peace treaty is signed between the Republic of China and Japan. Some interpret this to legalize the transfer of Taiwan to the Republic of China. Some say this is not the case since such was not cited in the treaty. **31 October** China Youth Corp is formed.

1953 **10 January** The Legislative Yuan adopts the Land-to-the-Tiller Program—the second phase of land reform. The first four-year economic plan is announced. **12 April** Karl Rankin becomes U.S. ambassador to the

Republic of China. **27 September** Chiang Kai-shek extends the term of the National Assembly elected in 1947, until another National Assembly can be elected.

1954 January Fourteen thousand Chinese captured during the Korean War who refuse repatriation to the People's Republic of China arrive in Taipei. **11 March** The National Assembly approves the indefinite extension of the Temporary Provisions of the Constitution. **22 March** Chiang Kai-shek is reelected president for a second six-year term. Chen Cheng is reelected vice president. **4 June** Chiang Kai-shek appoints Yen Chia-kan governor of Taiwan. **3 September** Communist forces launch an artillery bombardment of Quemoy, the largest of the offshore islands held by the Republic of China. Washington pledges to help Taipei. **3 December** The U.S.–Republic of China Defense Treaty is signed in Washington, D.C.

1955 January The northernmost island of the Tachen Island group (held by Taipei) falls to People's Republic of China forces. All 720 of the Republic of China soldiers defending the island die. **26 January** The U.S. Congress passes the Formosa Resolution authorizing the president to use American forces to defend Taiwan, the Pescadores, and "related positions and territories." **3 March** Foreign Minister George K. C. Yeh and U.S. Secretary of State John Foster Dulles exchange ratification documents for the two countries' mutual defense treaty.

1956 28 March Taipei informs the Philippine government that the Republic of China claims sovereignty over the Nansha Islands. **7 July** The ground is broken for the construction of the East-West Cross Island Highway, the first modern road transversing the center of the island.

1957 3 May The Council of Grand Justices rules that the Legislative Yuan, the Control Yuan, and the National Assembly collectively will represent the Republic of China in international parliamentary organizations. **8 August** General Chou Chih-rou is appointed governor of Taiwan. **26 September** The first meeting of the Asian People's Anti-Communist League is convened in Taipei. **20 October** Chiang Kai-shek is reelected director-general of the Nationalist Party.

1958 23 August The second Offshore Island crisis begins with forces of the People's Republic of China firing on Quemoy. **13 September** U.S. president Eisenhower declares that the attack on Quemoy is preparatory to invading Taiwan and that the Formosa Resolution passed by Congress in 1955 applies to the present situation. **23 October** President Chiang Kai-shek and U.S. Secretary of State Dulles issue a joint communiqué reaffirming their solidarity and stating that Quemoy and Matsu are "closely related" to the defense of Taiwan. The communiqué also states that the use of force would not be the "principal means" to restore the freedom of the people of China.

1959 26 March President Chiang Kai-shek issues a special message to the Tibetan people supporting their aspirations in accordance with the principle of self-determination. **21 July** The Legislative Yuan revises the Conscription Law, stipulating that nineteen-year-olds are to be drafted for two years in the army or three years in the navy or air force. **7 August** The worst floods in more than half a century hit central and southern Taiwan. **15 August** Taiwan receives Nike-Hercules missiles from the United States.

1960 11 March The National Assembly adopts an amendment to the Temporary Provisions of the Constitution allowing the president and the vice president to exceed the two-term limit in Article 47 of the Constitution. **22 March** Chiang Kai-shek is reelected to a third term as president and Chen Cheng to a second term as vice president. **9 May** The East-West Highway is open to traffic. **18 June** President Eisenhower visits Taiwan. Prior to and during the visit, military forces of the People's Republic of China bombard Quemoy Island. **25 August** The Republic of China Olympic Team during games in Rome protests the fact that their athletes have to compete under the name "Taiwan." **6 September** Yang Chuan-kuang wins the silver medal in the Olympic games for his performance in the decathlon.

1961 27 October The United Nations General Assembly votes for the admission of Outer Mongolia. Taipei abstains after previously vetoing. **1 December** Taiwan's first nuclear reactor is put into operation.

1962 9 February Taiwan opens its first stock exchange. **14 March** Foreign Minister Shen Chang-huan announces that Taipei does not recognize Japan's residual sovereignty over the Ryukyu Islands. **22 November** General Huang Chieh is appointed governor of Taiwan.

1963 23 August Ambassador to the U.S. Tsiang Ting-fu signs the Nuclear Test Ban Treaty. **12 November** The 9th Party Congress of the

Kuomintang opens in Taipei. **16 November** Yen Chia-kan becomes premier.

1964   14 June Shihmen Dam is dedicated. **27 October** Treaty of Amity is signed with South Korea.

1965   1 July The United States officially terminates its economic aid to Taiwan. **31 July** the Republic of China and the United States sign an agreement on the status of U.S. military force in Taiwan.

1966   22 March The National Assembly elects Chiang Kai-shek to a fourth term as president. **3 December** The Kaohsiung Export Processing Zone is inaugurated. It is the first of Taiwan's export processing zones.

1967   1 February The National Security Council is formed, with Huang Shao-ku as its first secretary-general. **1 July** Taipei becomes a special municipality, with Henry Kao as its mayor. **28 July** The Executive Yuan extends the period of compulsory education from six to nine years.

1968   25 June Defense Minister Chiang Ching-kuo, Chiang Kai-shek's eldest son, is named vice premier. **24 August** Taichung's Golden Dragons baseball team wins Little League World Series.

1969   29 March The Kuomintang holds its 10th Party Congress.

1970   24 April Vice Premier Chiang Ching-kuo visits the United States; Taiwan independence advocates make an attempt on his life. **12 July** Chi Cheng breaks the women's record in the two-hundred-meter sprint in West Germany.

1971   24 August Construction on the North-South Freeway is started. **25 October** The Republic of China is "expelled" from the United Nations after the United States loses a General Assembly vote to make the matter of the China seat an "important question" requiring a two-thirds majority; the China seat is given to the People's Republic of China.

1972   28 February President Richard M. Nixon, during a visit to China, signs the "Shanghai Communiqué," which states that the United States "does not challenge" Peking's position that Taiwan is part of China. **21 March** The National Assembly elects Chiang Kai-shek to a fifth six-year term as president. **26 May** Chiang Ching-kuo becomes premier. **27 August** The Taipei Little League baseball team wins the World Series. **29 September** Japan severs diplomatic relations with Taipei.

1973   16 February Taipei revalues the New Taiwan dollar to NT$38 to US$1. **30 October** Tsengwen Dam and Reservoir, the largest in Taiwan, is inaugurated.

1974   26 January Premier Chiang Ching-kuo announces price adjustment plan to stabilize economy. **20 April** Taiwan–Japan flights by China Airlines and Japan Airlines are ended. **30 October** The first F-5E jet fighter made in Taiwan under a joint agreement with the United States comes off the assembly line.

1975   5 April Chiang Kai-shek dies. **6 April** Vice President Yen Chia-kan becomes president. **28 April** Premier Chiang Ching-kuo is elected chairman of the Central Committee of the Kuomintang.

1976   26 March Lin Yu-tang, Taiwan's best-known writer, dies. **17 July** The Republic of China Olympic Committee withdraws from the Montreal Olympic Games to protest its being forced to compete under the name "Taiwan." **31 October** Taichung Port is opened.

1977   3 June China Shipbuilding Corporation launches *Burmah Endeavor*, the world's third-largest vessel. **22 October** The first generator of Taiwan's first nuclear power plant is put into use.

1978   21 March Chiang Ching-kuo is elected president. Shieh Tung-min is elected vice president—the first Taiwanese to hold this office. **26 May** Former minister of economic affairs Sun Yun-suan is appointed premier. **30 June** The International Monetary Fund lists the Republic of China as the world's twenty-fifth-largest trading nation. **8 December** The Legislative Yuan passes a bill unpegging Taiwan's currency from the U.S. dollar. **15 December** President Jimmy Carter announces that the United States will derecognize the Republic of China and will establish diplomatic ties with the People's Republic of China. **17 December** Five thousand people stage a protest outside the U.S. embassy in Taipei because of the decision to move the embassy to Peking.

1979   1 January The United States officially grants diplomatic recognition to the People's Republic of China and breaks ties with the Republic of China. **10 April** The U.S. Congress passes the Taiwan Relations

Act into law. In it, the United States gives Taiwan security and economic guarantees and treats Taiwan as a sovereign nation-state. **17 June** Charles Cross assumes the post of director of the American Institute in Taiwan, which replaced the U.S. embassy. **1 July** Kaohsiung is elevated to the status of special municipality. **6 September** The cabinet announces its decision to extend the territorial waters of the Republic of China to twelve miles and to establish a two-hundred-mile economic zone. **10 December** *Formosa* magazine supporters organize a rally and parade in Kaohsiung to commemorate Human Rights Day, but also to protest policies that have caused Taiwan to become diplomatically isolated. The "Kaohsiung Incident" follows; more than one hundred people are injured, almost all of them police officers. Leaders of the protest are subsequently arrested. **17 December** Tsiang Yen-si replaces Chang Pao-shu as secretary-general of the Kuomintang Central Committee.

1980 1 January The U.S.–Republic of China Defense Treaty is terminated. **3 January** The U.S. government announces that it will resume arms sales to Taiwan that had been suspended for a year. **6 December** Seventy new members are elected to the Legislative Yuan, and seventy-six to the National Assembly in supplemental national elections. Many observers say it is the first competitive election in Taiwan at the national level and the beginning of democratic politics.

1981 18 February The government announces that it is planning to manufacture tanks, ships, and other sophisticated weapons. **29 March** The Kuomintang holds its 12th Congress. **3 April** President Chiang Ching-kuo is reelected chairman of the Kuomintang. **14 May** The first European Trade Fair in Taiwan opens at the World Trade Center in Taipei.

1982 12 May The Council for Agricultural Planning announces the second phase of land reform. **16 August** The United States and the People's Republic of China sign a communiqué in which Washington promises to decrease and ultimately end weapons sales to Taiwan. Taiwan expresses its dismay at the move.

1983 14 January The Legislative Yuan passes a revision to the Trademark Act to impose prison sentences on violators. **7 June** The Legislative Yuan passes the Firearms Control Act to place guns under strict control. **3 December** Taiwan holds its second competitive national election.

The Kuomintang wins a big victory, capturing fifty-two of seventy-one contested seats in the Legislative Yuan, leaving three to the opposition and three to independents.

1984   1 March The first domestically built jet training plane rolls off the assembly line. **21 March** President Chiang Ching-kuo is elected to another six-year term. Lee Teng-hui is elected vice president. **20 May** Former head of the Council for Economic Planning and Development, Yu Kuo-hua, is chosen premier. **2 June** Chiu Chuang-huan becomes governor of Taiwan Province. **20 July** The Legislative Yuan passes the Labor Standards Act.

1985   16 April Taiwan's first test-tube baby is born. **23 May** Hsu Shui-teh and Su Nan-cheng are appointed mayors of Taipei and Kaohsiung, respectively. **9 July** The last part of a transoceanic telecommunications cable linking Taiwan, Hong Kong, and Singapore is finished. **19 July** The Ministry of Defense announces that Taiwan has successfully tested a homemade surface-to-air missile named Sky Bow.

1986   1 April A new value-added tax is inaugurated. **23 April** Siamese twins are separated at National Taiwan University Hospital. **18 May** The Ministry of National Defense announces that the Sky Sword missile is successfully tested. **25 September** The Republic of China is readmitted to the Olympic Committee of Asia. **28 September** The Democratic Progressive Party, made up of opposition politicians, announces its formation. **15 October** Lee Yuan-tseh wins the Nobel Prize in chemistry. **6 November** The DPP holds its first assembly and releases a draft of its charter and platform. **6 December** The nation holds its first two-party election, with the Kuomintang competing against the DPP. The KMT wins.

1987   23 June The Legislative Yuan passes the National Security Law preparatory to ending martial law. **1 July** Lee Huan is appointed secretary-general of the Kuomintang. **15 July** The Emergency Decree, generally called martial law, is terminated. The National Security Law goes into effect. **1 August** The Council on Labor Affairs is created. **1 November** The Republic of China Red Cross announces that it is accepting applications from residents to visit relatives in China. **2 November** The Central Bank announces that Taiwan has US$70 billion in foreign exchange reserves—the largest in the world.

1988 **1 January** Regulations go into effect allowing new newspapers to publish and all papers to increase the number of pages printed. **11 January** The Legislative Yuan passes the Act on Assembly and Parades. **13 January** President Chiang Ching-kuo passes away from heart failure. Vice President Lee Teng-hui is sworn in as president—Taiwan's first native-born president. **27 January** President Lee Teng-hui is elected chairman of the Kuomintang. **9 March** The Council for Economic Planning and Development approves an NT$30 billion fund for assisting developing countries. **24 March** The Government Information Office states that Taiwan has never engaged in the development of nuclear weapons. **18 April** Mail from Taiwan begins going to China. **7 July** The Kuomintang opens its 13th Party Congress. The ruling party democratizes many of its rules and procedures and elects a majority of Taiwanese to its powerful Central Standing Committee. **28 July** The Executive Yuan approves regulations governing the importation of publications, films, and radio and television programs from China. **25 October** A comprehensive farmers' health insurance is started. **3 November** Taiwan allows people from China to come to Taiwan to visit sick relatives. **10 December** A prototype of Taiwan's first homemade jet fighter plane, called the Ching-kuo, is displayed in public.

1989 **20 January** The Legislative Yuan passes the Law on the Organization of Civic Groups, which allows new political parties and organizations to form. **29 January** The Legislative Yuan passes a new election law and the law on the voluntary retirement of senior parliamentarians. **17 April** Teachers and staff of public schools are allowed to travel to China for family visits. **20 May** Taipei proclaims its support for the Democracy Movement in China. **30 May** Lee Huan is appointed premier. **31 May** One million Taiwan students participate in a "hand to hand, heart to heart" rally in support of China's Democracy Movement. **4 June** President Lee Teng-hui issues a statement condemning the Tiananmen Massacre. **10 June** Telephone lines are opened to China. **11 July** The Legislative Yuan revises the Banking Act to end interest rate controls. **26 September** The Executive Yuan issues an order allowing prodemocracy students from China to settle in Taiwan. **2 December** The Democratic Progressive Party wins what is called a major upset victory in the national election, gaining a sufficient number of seats in the Legislative Yuan to propose legislation and to control district and city executive offices where 40 percent of the country's population resides.

1990   1 March The Executive Yuan approves direct trade with the Soviet Union and Albania. **21 March** President Lee Teng-hui is reelected president for a six-year term by the National Assembly in an uncontested vote, though Lin Yang-kang, a popular Taiwanese politician, and Chiang Wei-kuo, Chiang Kai-shek's second son, had challenged Lee. Lee meets with four thousand prodemocracy students who had occupied Chiang Kai-shek Memorial for six days and pledges democratic reform. President Lee promises, among other things, a National Affairs Conference. **20 May** Lee Teng-hui and Li Yuan-zu are inaugurated. Lee, in his address, announces opening channels of communication to China. **29 May** President Lee appoints General Hau Pei-tsun as premier, causing opposition protest. President Lee also announces amnesty for political prisoners. **21 June** The Council of Grand Justices rules that senior parliamentarians should retire by December 31. **4 July** The National Affairs Conference ends after suggesting popular elections of presidents and mayors of Taipei and Kaohsiung, and other reforms. Delegates to the conference include members of the ruling party, the opposition Democratic Progressive Party, and academics. **26 August** Taiwan wins the Little League World Series again. **11 October** The Ministry of Interior restates that Tiaoyutai Islands belong to Taiwan. **18 October** The Mainland Affairs Council is created. **21 November** The Straits Exchange Foundation is established.

1991   31 January The Executive Yuan approves the Six-Year Development Plan aimed at improving the nation's economic infrastructure at a cost over US$300 billion. Premier Hau says the plan will elevate Taiwan to the top twenty nations in the world in per capita income by the end of the century. **14 March** The Executive Yuan passes the Guidelines for National Unification. **22 April** The National Assembly passes the Additional Articles of the Constitution (constitutional amendments) and abolishes the Temporary Provisions. **30 April** President Lee Teng-hui declares the termination of the Period of Mobilization (or state of war with the People's Republic of China) effective May 1. **12 August** Two journalists from China arrive in Taiwan, the first such visit. **13 November** Taiwan joins the Asian-Pacific Economic Cooperation group, along with China and Hong Kong. **21 December** An election is held to pick a new National Assembly—the first national election that is not a supplementary election. The KMT wins and, according to some observers, gains a democratic mandate.

1992   28 February The official report of the "2-28 Incident" (in 1947) is released. **20 March** The new or Second National Assembly convenes to take up the task of amending the Constitution. Changes are made to give National Assembly members a four-year term instead of a six-year term, and increase its powers. The Control Yuan is slated to become a semijudiciary body rather than one of the nation's three parliamentary bodies. Amendments also make the provincial governor and county magistrate positions ones to be filled by direct popular vote. **16 May** Taiwan's sedition law (Article 100 of the Criminal Code) is revised, making it no longer a crime to discuss Taiwan's independence or Communism. **7 July** Interior Minister Wu Poh-hsiung announces that Taiwan's Black List would be reduced from 282 to 5 names. **16 July** The Legislative Yuan passes a statute decreeing that China is "one country, two areas" in regard to relations between Taipei and Peking, thereby recognizing laws in effect on the mainland and allowing Chinese Communist Party members to visit Taiwan. **31 July** The Taiwan Garrison Command is abolished. The Coastal Patrol Command is created to assume the role of control of the coastline and smuggling. **22 August** South Korea breaks diplomatic relations with Taipei and establishes ties with China—the last important Asian country to do so. **2 September** President George H. W. Bush approves the sale of 150 F-16 fighter aircraft to Taiwan. **29 September** Taiwan is granted observer status in the General Agreement on Tariffs and Trade as the "Separate Customs Territory of Taiwan, Penghu, Kinmen and Matsu." **24 October** The Mainland Affairs Council approves 158 categories of service industries that can invest in China. **1 November** Peng Ming-min, known as the father of Taiwan independence, returns to Taiwan after twenty-two years in exile in the United States. **7 November** The military administration of Kinmen and Matsu ends after forty-four years. **23 November** Formosa Plastics announces scrapping its plan to build a giant petrochemical complex in China. **30 November** U.S. trade representative Carla Hills visits Taiwan, the first such high official to do so in thirteen years. **19 December** Taiwan holds its first nonsupplementary Legislative Yuan election. The opposition Democratic Progressive Party wins fifty seats, increasing its representation from 14.4 percent to 31.1 percent in what is considered a stunning victory.

1993   4 January President Lee Teng-hui gives the first-ever state of the nation address to the National Assembly. Shouting and fighting over the issue of Taiwan independence follow his speech. **10 January** Thousands march in Taipei in support of Premier Hau Pei-tsun, who is expected to leave office soon. **4 February** Premier Hau and his cabinet resign, ending weeks of political uncertainty while setting a precedent for cabinet dissolution following a legislative election. **27 February** Lien Chan is sworn in as premier, the first Taiwanese to hold that office. **9 April** President Lee announces that Taiwan will actively seek participation in the United Nations while calling for international support for this effort. **27 April** The Koo-Wang talks between representatives of China and Taiwan begin in Singapore. **16 June** The Legislative Yuan passes a "sunshine law" requiring two thousand high government and public officials to make their financial records public. **10 August** The New KMT Alliance breaks with the ruling party and establishes the New Party. **16 August** The 14th Congress of the Nationalist Party reelects President Lee Teng-hui as chairman, Vice President Li Yuan-zu, former Premier Hau Pei-tsun, Judicial Yuan president Lin Yang-kang, and Premier Lien Chan as vice chairmen. **16 September** The Mainland Affairs Council issues the publication *There Is No Taiwan Question: There Is Only a China Question* in response to Beijing's white paper *The Taiwan Question and the Reunification of China.*

1994 **17 February** The first squadron of the locally made Indigenous Defense Fighters goes into service. **12 April** Cultural and educational exchanges with China are temporarily terminated because of the Qiandao Lake incident during which twenty-four tourists from Taiwan were murdered and robbed. **7 September** The U.S. government announces that the Republic of China's representative office in the United States can change its name to Taipei Economic and Cultural Representative Office, which is seen as an upgrading of Taipei's diplomatic status. **22 September** The UN General Assembly rejects a proposal on the Republic of China's membership in the United Nations. **3 December** The first popular election for governor of Taiwan province is held, and James Soong is elected. Elections for metropolitan city mayors are also held, after a hiatus of several years, and Chen Shui-bian is elected mayor of Taipei and Wu Den-yi mayor of Kaohsiung.

1995 **30 January** China's President Jiang Zemin offers an Eight-Point Proposal urging Taiwan to hold talks that might lead to reunification. **28 February** President Lee Teng-hui issues an apology to victims of the 28 February 1947 Uprising at the Taipei New Park. **1 March** The National Health Insurance program is formally put in place. **7 June** President Lee Teng-hui arrives in the United States where he gives an address at his alma mater, Cornell University. The visit is widely reported, and Lee wins considerable favorable publicity. Beijing, however, is angered by the visit. **21 June** China begins firing surface-to-surface missiles at targets in the East China Sea 140 kilometers north of Taiwan in response to President Lee's trip to the United States. **17 August** Control Yuan president Chen Li-an announces that he is a candidate for president. **21 August** Lin Yang-kang, vice chairman of the Nationalist Party, announces that he will be an independent candidate for the presidency. **31 August** President Lee Teng-hui announces that he will run for another term as president. **25 August** The DPP chooses Peng Ming-min as its candidate for the presidency. **2 December** 164 delegates are elected to the Legislative Yuan. The KMT suffers a defeat in the polls but hangs on to a majority. The Democratic Progressive Party makes gains, but a number of its well-known candidates lose. The New Party makes big gains. Observers say the election was influenced by China's missile tests.

1996 8 March China begins eight days of missile tests in the Taiwan Strait to intimidate Taiwan. **23 March** Lee Teng-hui and Lien Chan, respectively, are elected president and vice president with 54 percent of the vote. The election is reported as the first direct election of a chief executive in five thousand years of Chinese history. Elections are also held for the 334-member National Assembly. **5 June** President Lee reappoints Lien Chan to serve as premier. A number of Legislative Yuan members oppose the nomination because Lee had promised to appoint a new premier. **15 June** The Democratic Progressive Party convenes its 7th National Congress and elects a former chairman, Hsu Hsin-liang, as its new chairman. **4 July** The National Assembly convenes and elects Fredrick Chien as speaker. **18 July** The European Parliament passes a resolution backing the Republic of China's representation in international organizations. **24 August** The Republic of China wins the 1996 Little League World Series. **12 September** The Republic of China announces its policy on the Tiaoyutai Islands: absolute sovereignty, rational attitude, no need for cooperation with Beijing, and protection of fishing rights. **6 October** The Taiwan Independence Party is formed. **21 November** Taoyuan County Magistrate Liu Pang-you and seven other politicians are shot to death at Liu's home in what is reported as a gang political assassination. **27 November** South Africa announces that it will sever diplomatic relations with Taipei. **23 December** The National Development Conference opens. **31 December** Taiwan governor James Soong resigns after the National Development Conference recommends downsizing or abolishing the provincial government.

1997   28 February The day is declared a national holiday in memory of the 28 February 1947 Uprising. **2 March** The ship *Liana Feng* arrives in Kaohsiung, the first ship from China to call at a port in Taiwan in more than five decades. **28 March** The Tamsui line of the Taipei Rapid Transit System opens after ten years of construction. **14 April** The first two of the 150 F-16 fighter planes purchased from the United States in 1992 arrive. **4 May** A massive demonstration called "March for Taiwan" is held to protest the deterioration in social order. It is said to be the largest demonstration in Taiwan's history. **8 May** Minister of State Ma Ying-jeou resigns in protest over the Nationalist Party's weak efforts to deal with corruption; Minister of Interior Lin Feng-cheng also quits. **1 August** The Council of Grand Justices rules that legislators who engage in violence during legislative sessions will no longer be immune from arrest and prosecution. **25 August** The Nationalist Party holds its 15th Congress and reelects President Lee Teng-hui party chairman with more than 93 percent of the vote. **1 September** A new cabinet is sworn in with Vincent Siew the new premier. **30 September** The Committee on International Relations of the U.S. House of Representatives passes a resolution to include Taiwan in a theater missile defense system. **29 November** In elections for twenty-three city mayors and county magistrates, the Democratic Progressive Party wins twelve posts in a resounding victory. **31 December** South Africa severs diplomatic relations with Taipei, the last important nation to do so.

1998   2 January The Legislative Yuan approves a statute defining the Republic of China's territorial waters as twelve nautical miles from its shore. **10 January** A public opinion poll indicates that Chiang Ching-kuo is the most admired of the Republic of China's presidents. **21 February** Pope John Paul II formally appoints Bishop Paul Shan of Taiwan a cardinal. **1 May** In the largest labor rally ever, more than twenty thousand workers march in Taipei in protest of government labor practices. **28 May** The Legislative Yuan passes a bill giving compensation to victims of martial law. **30 June** President Bill Clinton, during a visit to China, states, "We don't support independence for Taiwan, or two Chinas, or one Taiwan, one China, and we don't believe that Taiwan should be a member in any organization for which statehood is a requirement." **30 July** Foreign Minister Jason Hu condemns violence against Chinese in Indonesia, especially the numerous rapes of Chinese women. **2 August** Lin Yi-hsiung is sworn in as the eighth chairman of the Democratic Progressive Party. A leftist group in the party lodges protests against outgoing party head Hsu Hsin-liang for advocating engagement with China. **2 September** An armored-car driver steals NT$49 million in the country's largest robbery. **4 September** The TAIEX (Taiwan's Stock Exchange) falls to a ten-year low as a result of the Asian economic crisis and a slump on Wall Street. **18 October** Koo Chen-fu meets with President Jiang Zemin of the People's Republic of China, marking the highest-level contact across the Taiwan Strait in nearly five decades. **5 December** President Lee Teng-hui uses the term "New Taiwanese" in an effort to play down ethnic differences in the context of an election campaign. **5 December** Elections for seats in the Legislative Yuan, the city councils of Taipei and Kaohsiung, and the mayorships of these two metropolitan cities are held. The ruling Nationalist Party wins a healthy majority in the Legislative Yuan while taking back the mayorship of Taipei, though it loses the Kaohsiung mayorship race. **21 December** Chao Shou-pu, former minister without portfolio, is appointed Taiwan's new governor. A twenty-plus member advisory council replaces the Taiwan Provincial Assembly.

1999 21 February The government announces new economic policies to stimulate the economy, including cuts in bank taxes and reserve requirements. **1 March** President Lee says China's missile threat forces Taiwan to upgrade its defenses and consider participating in theater missile defense. Poll shows that 85 percent of the population supports joining TMD. **8 April** President Lee calls for normalization of relations with China based on recognizing Taiwan as an equal. He rules out unification until China has adopted "social diversification and political democratization." **27 May** The Democratic Progressive Party chooses its presidential candidate for the March 2000 election, Chen Shui-bian. **7 June** President Lee Teng-hui announces a US$300 million aid package to help Kosovo war refugees. **9 June** President Lee Teng-hui, in an interview with the German radio company Deutsche Welle, declares that

Taiwan's relationship with China must be viewed as a state-to-state or special state-to-state one. **29 August** The Nationalist Party picks Vice President Lien Chan as its candidate for the March 2000 presidential election. Premier Vincent Siew is chosen as his running mate. **4 September** The Third National Assembly passes a constitutional amendment that extends the current terms of members from May 2000 to June 2002 and appoints all members on the basis of party proportional representation to the fourth National Assembly. **21 September** A 7.3 magnitude earthquake hits Taiwan, the worst in sixty years. More than two thousand people are killed, and over eight thousand injured. **13 November** Tokyo Governor Shintaro Ishihara visits Taiwan for three days, the highest Japanese leader to do so since 1972. **17 November** The Central Committee of the Nationalist Party ousts James Soong from the party for undermining party unity with his independent candidacy for president. **10 December** Chen Shui-bian announces that Annette Lu is his choice for vice presidential running mate. **13 December** A Nationalist Party member accuses James Soong of taking party money when he was secretary-general of the party.

2000   4 January Vice President Lien Chan announces that, if elected president, he will separate the Nationalist Party's ties with business by putting its assets in an independent trust. **1 February** The U.S. House of Representatives passes the Taiwan Security Enhancement Act by a vote of 341 to 70. China warns that relations with the U.S. will deteriorate if the bill becomes law. **21 February** China publishes a policy paper "ultimatum" saying that if Taipei refuses to negotiate unification within a reasonable amount of time, China will use military force against the island. **15 March** China's Premier Zhu Rongji warns Taiwan voters not to vote for the "candidate of independence" (meaning Chen Shui-bian) as this might "trigger a war." **18 March** Democratic Progressive Party presidential and vice presidential candidates, Chen Shui-bian and Annette Lu, are elected with 39.3 percent of the vote. This ends more than fifty years of Nationalist Party rule of Taiwan. **25 March** Former president Lee Teng-hui, after days of rioting and protest against him because Lien Chan lost the presidential election, resigns as chairman of the Nationalist Party. **29 March** Chen Shui-bian names Tang Fei as his choice for premier. **31 March** James Soong establishes the People First Party. **7 April** Vice President-elect Annette Lu, on a Hong Kong television program, states that Taiwan is "a remote relative and close neighbor" of China. **8 April** China's Taiwan Affairs Office describes Lu as the "scum of the Chinese nation." The *People's Daily* accuses her of leading Taiwan into the "abyss of war." **17 April** The United States announces an indefinite postponement of the sale of Arleigh Burke–class destroyers equipped with the Aegis system to Taiwan. **24 April** The Third National Assembly passes a constitutional amendment reducing its functions, including canceling its status as a standing body. **1 May** Premier-designate Tang Fei announces a new cabinet. Thirteen members are from the Nationalist Party and eleven from the Democratic Progressive Party, indicating that President Chen seeks to form a coalition government. **20 May** Chen Shui-bian and Annette Lu are sworn in as president and vice president respectively. President Chen uses conciliatory language in his inauguration speech, including announcing his "five noes" policy. **25 August** China's vice premier announces a "softer" definition of one China, stating that the "mainland and Taiwan are both parts of One China." **3 October** Chang Chun-hsiung becomes premier. **24 October** The Control Yuan recommends the impeachment of former navy commander in chief Admiral Yeh and two vice admirals in connection with corruption in a warship purchase from France. **27 October** Premier Chang cancels the partly built fourth nuclear power plant. The opposition is angered by the decision. **7 November** Opposition legislators move to recall or impeach President Chen Shui-bian, charging him with contempt of the Constitution, retrogression in relations with China, and incompetence in handling the economy (the stock market having lost 40 percent of its value since Chen's election). **12 November** Nearly twenty thousand of Chen's supporters demonstrate in Taipei in support of his cancellation of the fourth nuclear power plant.

2001 1 January The mini-three links between Quemoy and Matsu and China's Xiamen and Fuzhou ports are implemented. **1 February** The High Court drops embezzlement charges against James Soong filed during the 2000 election campaign. **14 February** Premier Chang announces resumption of work on the fourth nuclear power plant. **26 March** Taiwan-born Ang Lee's film *Crouching Tiger, Hidden Dragon* wins four Oscars: best foreign film, best art direction, best cinematography, and best original score. **1 April** The U.S. reconnaissance plane EP-3 collides with a Chinese fighter plane over the South China Sea while collecting information on new Chinese weapons that might be used against Taiwan. The damaged U.S. plane lands on Hainan Island; the plane and the crew are held by Chinese authorities, causing a major incident between the United States and China. **24 April** President George W. Bush announces a very large package of arms that Taiwan can purchase from the United States, including Kidd-class destroyers and submarines, but not ships equipped with the Aegis system. China expresses serious concern. **25 May** The government announces that the economy grew only 1.06 percent the first quarter, the worst performance in twenty-six years. **12 August** Former president Lee Teng-hui declares his support for the Taiwan Solidarity Union at its inaugural meeting, a party Lee helped form. The TSU announces it is sponsoring thirty-nine candidates in the December election. **26 August** President Chen lifts the US$50 million cap on investment in China. **23 September** The Nationalist Party revokes Lee Teng-hui's membership. **19 October** Taiwan announces boycotting the Asia–Pacific Economic Cooperation forum in Shanghai because China refused to accept its delegate, former vice president Li Yuan-zu, saying he is "too political." **1 December** In the election of Taiwan's Fifth Legislative Yuan, the Democratic Progressive Party wins 87 of the body's 225 seats, making it the largest party in the legislature. The Nationalist Party wins 68 seats in a major setback. The People First Party wins 46, and the Taiwan Solidarity Union 13. It is a victory for President Chen Shui-bian but does not give his bloc, pan-green, a majority in the legislature.

2002 1 January Taiwan becomes the 144th member of the World Trade Organization. **21 January** Yu Shyi-kun is appointed premier. **24 January** China's vice premier says he would welcome a visit by officials of the DPP. **28 February** The U.S. National Archives releases tapes from the Nixon presidency documenting Kissinger's promise to China that the United States did not support Taiwan's independence and that the United States would withdraw two-thirds of its troops once the Vietnam War ended. **9 March** The *Los Angeles Times* discloses a classified Defense Department document that talks about the development of new nuclear weapons and targets and mentions possible military confrontation over Taiwan. **30 March** The government raids *Next* magazine offices and seizes 160,000 copies of the recent issue that reports on the government's $100 million fund for intelligence and diplomatic activities. Journalists claim harassment. **10 April** Taipei District Court rules in favor of Vice President Lu, who had sued the *Journalist* magazine for reporting that she had leaked information about President

Chen's alleged sex scandal in 2000. **25 May** A China Airlines plane carrying 206 passengers and 19 crew members breaks up in the air and crashes into the Taiwan Strait. There are no survivors. **21 July** President Chen Shui-bian assumes the chairmanship of the Democratic Progressive Party at its 10th National Congress. **3 August** President Chen calls for legislation for a referendum on Taiwan's independence, saying, "Each side is a country." **5 August** Chinese officials say a declaration of independence by Taiwan would lead to "disaster" and would harm Taiwan's economy, which is increasingly dependent on China. **19 September** First Lady Wu Shu-jen delivers a speech at a reception for her at the Senate Russell Office Building in Washington, D.C. **4 November** China signs a free trade agreement with ten Association of Southeast Asian nations leading to the creation of a free trade area by 2010; Taiwan is not included in the plan. **7 December** Ma Ying-jeou and Frank Hsieh are elected mayors of Taipei and Kaohsiung respectively.

2003   5 February A high official in China states that accepting the one-China principle is no longer required for Taiwan to establish trade, shipping, and postal links. **18 April** Lien Chan, head of the Nationalist Party, and James Soong, head of the People First Party, announce they are forming a joint ticket to run in the March 2004 election, with Lien as the presidential candidate and Soong the vice presidential candidate. Polls show they lead President Chen by eight points. **23 April** Taiwan announces its first mass infection of SARS. **30 April** Taiwan reports 451 cases of SARS, including 78 listed as probable. **5 July** The World Health Organization announces Taiwan is removed from the list of areas affected by SARS after eighty-four die. **3 August** President Chen calls for legislation on referendums and declares, "There is one state on each side of the Taiwan Strait." China warns of "splittist forces" in Taiwan. **21 August** Taiwan signs its first-ever free trade agreement—with Panama. **1 September** Republic of China passports are issued with "Taiwan" in Roman script on the cover. **23 October** Madam Chiang Kai-shek, Soong Mayling, dies in New York at the age of 106. **7 November** President Chen formally declares that he will seek reelection and states that he will make the question of whether Taiwan should declare independence a central issue in the campaign. China responded with the bitterest comments in several years. **14 November** Taipei 101, the tallest building in the world, opens. **28 November** The Legislative

Yuan passes the Referendum Act allowing citizens to vote on issues of national or local importance but bars referendums on the issue of sovereignty and disallows the president or cabinet from calling a referendum, though they allowed an exception in the case that Taiwan is threatened by a foreign power. **7 December** President Chen announces that he will call a national referendum to coincide with the presidential election on 20 March 2004. **9 December** U.S. President George W. Bush reiterates America's one-China policy and expresses opposition to President Chen's willingness "to make decisions unilaterally to change the status quo."

2004 **16 January** President Chen discloses the content of referendums to be voted with the March presidential and vice presidential election: Should Taiwan strengthen its missile defense system if China refuses to withdraw its missiles targeted on Taiwan? Should Taiwan set up a "peace interactive network" to build consensus between people on both sides of the Taiwan Strait? U.S. Secretary of State Colin Powell warns both China and Taiwan against trying to unilaterally resolve their differences. **19 March** Both President Chen and Vice President Lu, while campaigning in Chen's hometown of Tainan, are shot. The assailant is not caught. The opposition levels charges that the event was staged. **20 March** President Chen and Vice President Lu win reelection by a very small margin—fewer than thirty thousand votes, or less than a 0.2 percent margin. Both referendums fail to get enough votes to pass. **21 March** Demonstrations, some violent, are held in Taiwan's major cities, led by the opposition that claimed Chen had "stolen" the election. The High Court orders ballot boxes sealed pending a recount. **7 April** Lien Chan files a suit with the High Court to have the March election nullified. **11 April** Forensic expert Henry Lee states that Chen and Lu were actually shot, but he does not rule out that the attack was staged. He says the crime scene was not preserved. About three hundred thousand demonstrators protest the election near the Presidential Palace; one hundred are injured. **23 August** The Legislative Yuan votes for a bill containing constitutional changes, including reducing the size of the legislature from 225 to 113, changing the electoral system from a multimember district, and changing the single-vote system to a single-member, two-vote system. The KMT and DPP both support the changes. **23 September** President Chen signs the Truth Commission Act (to investigate the March 19 shooting of the president and vice president), though he says it is unconstitutional. **25 September** Premier Yu states publicly that Taiwan would be safe if it could respond to a Chinese missile attack by returning a rain of missiles on Chinese cities like Shanghai. He suggests a balance-of-terror situation like the Cold War. **25 September** Thousands march in Taipei against the government's proposed arms budget. Lien Chan calls for big cuts, allocating more money to social welfare, and for a more pragmatic policy toward China. President Chen states that 610 Chinese missiles are targeting Taiwan. **4 November** The High Court rejects the petition of Lien Chan and James Soong to nullify the results of the March election. **11 December** Pan-green fails to win a promised majority in the legislative election; the media reports it is a setback. Pan-blue keeps its majority and even enhances its control of the legislature with the victory of several friendly independents. Analysts say President Chen overestimated the appeal of Taiwan independence. Others say the United States expressing anger with Chen may have had an impact. **14 December** Chen Shui-bian resigns as chairman of the Democratic Progressive Party, apologizing for the party's legislative election loss. **16 December** Laina Chiang, wife of Chiang Ching-kuo, dies at the age of eighty-eight.

2005   25 January Frank Hsieh becomes premier. **19 March** Taiwan's police announce they have a prime suspect, Chen Yi-hsiung, in the attempt to assassinate President Chen Shui-bian and Vice President Annette Lu. He reportedly blamed Chen for the poor economy and committed suicide shortly after the attack. Many people do not believe the police account. **26 March** Hundreds of thousands of people attend a rally to protest China's recently enacted Anti-Succession Law stating that China will use military force against Taiwan if it declares independence. **26 April** Nationalist Party chairman Lien Chan visits China and talks to President Hu Jintao. A joint communiqué is signed that mentions promoting cross-strait negotiations, economic exchanges, and international activities. Lien is treated almost as a visiting head of government. **5 May** James Soong visits China; he is given high-profile treatment. **7 June** The National Assembly ratifies a group of constitutional reforms approved by the Legislative Yuan in August 2004 that would terminate the National Assembly and transfer its power of impeachment to the Judicial Yuan, reduce the number of seats in the legislature from 225 to 113, and increase the length of its term to four years to match the term of the president and vice president. **18 August** China and Russia for the first time hold joint military exercises, aimed at fighting terrorism, extremism, and separatism (meaning Taiwan independence). **21 August** Thai workers help build Kaohsiung's rapid transit system riot over poor living conditions, embarrassing both local and national governments in Taiwan. **7 September** President Chen vows to abolish the death penalty in Taiwan "so that Taiwan can become a country founded on human rights." However, polls show that 80 percent of the public supports keeping the death penalty. **9 September** Premier Hsieh announces Taiwan's first cloned goat. **15 September** Vice Foreign Minister Michael Kau criticizes the United Nations for "political apartheid" after Taiwan's thirteenth bid for membership is turned down. **16 September** The Supreme Court upholds the results of the March presidential election and rejects opposition parties' pleas to have it declared null and void. **7 October** A *United Daily News* poll registers Chen Shui-bian's popularity at 25 percent, the lowest since he became president. In the same poll, 56 percent of respondents said they were dissatisfied with the DPP, while 61 percent said the DPP had lost its core values and 49 percent said the party was corrupt. **25 October** The Legislative Yuan passes the National Communications Commission bill, which will make the commission the highest media watchdog agency, taking over that responsibility from the Government Information Office. **21 November** Chen Che-nan, former secretary-general to President Chen Shui-bian, and twenty-one others are indicted for corruption in the Kaohsiung mass rapid transit construction scandal. **3 December** The Nationalist Party wins big in municipal elections; the DPP gets only six seats of twenty-three posts contested. Corruption is seen as a major cause of the DPP setback.

2006 1 January President Chen, in his New Year's address, promises a new Constitution and talks of risks of doing business in China, prompting a stock market sell-off. **10 January** Robert Tsao, chairman of United Microelectronics Corporation, is indicted for making illegal investments in China. **13 January** The legislature slashes the government's budget by NT$36.5 billion (or 2.3 percent), including money for arms purchases. **17 January** Frank Hsieh resigns, taking blame for the December election defeat. **18 January** Yu Shyi-kun is elected chairman of the DPP. **20 January** Direct flights to and from China for the Lunar New Year allow people to make the trip more easily. **20 February** The

February 28 Memorial Foundation publishes a report on the 2-28 Incident saying that Chiang Kai-shek was the "chief culprit." Ma Ying-jeou warns President Chen against abolishing the National Unification Council and urges him to stop the "power struggle" and work for the people. **27 February** President Chen announces disbanding the National Unification Council and ending the National Unification Guidelines. The Department of State calls on Chen to "correct the record" and affirm that the status quo is not changed. **7 March** Ang Lee is the first Asian to win an Oscar for directing the movie *Brokeback Mountain*. **13 March** The family of Chen Yi-hsiung, the alleged shooter of the president and vice president, say they were coerced by police to give testimony. Chen's widow says he is innocent. **20 March** Nationalist Party head, Ma Ying-jeou, visits the United States and talks to high officials there. The visit is given considerable publicity in the United States. **4 May** The United States allows President Chen only a stopover in Anchorage or Honolulu on his trip to Latin America, the lowest-level treatment for a Taiwan leader in more than a decade. **26 May** Dr. Chao Chien-ming, President Chen's son-in-law, is arrested on charges of insider trading. **1 June** In the context of declining popularity, below 20 percent in most polls, President Chen says he will delegate authority on domestic affairs to the premier. **2 June** Ma Yung-cheng, secretary to President Chen, resigns from office amid corruption charges. **13 June** The Legislative Yuan votes on a bill to recall President Chen Shui-bian.

Introduction

Taiwan is a leaf-shaped (upside down) island 370 kilometers (230 miles) in length and 137 kilometers (85 miles) wide, located 153 kilometers (95 miles) off the east coast of southern China. It is the largest piece of territory under the jurisdiction of the "nation" known officially as the Republic of China, or in the past often called Nationalist China. Other areas under the Republic of China's jurisdiction include several islands or island groups near Taiwan, such as the Pescadores (west of Taiwan); Orchid Island and Green Island (to the east); the "Offshore Islands," or the Quemoy and Matsu groups, which are just off the coast of China; plus some islands or islets in the South China Sea. The Republic of China has also laid claim to the Tiaoyutai islets (*Senkaku* in Japanese, and *Diaoyutai* as spelled in China) north of Taiwan, which are thought to be the site of undersea oil deposits and are in contention between China and Japan.

The word *Taiwan* (actually two characters in Chinese that mean "terraced bay"), the origin of which is unclear (possibly once the name of a city in the southern part of the island), in recent years has been used increasingly as a substitute for the term "Republic of China." It is employed by some to suggest that the territory controlled by the Republic of China is not really part of China (except perhaps the Offshore Islands) but rather is another China, or that the separation between China and Taiwan is, or should be, viewed as a permanent reality, meaning that Taiwan should be regarded as an independent, sovereign nation-state. Those people say that the Republic of China is not a legitimate government and that the name "Republic of China" should be changed to "Republic of Taiwan." Many people in Taiwan and elsewhere now use the term "Taiwan" rather than "Republic of China" simply because it is shorter and easier to remember, or they use the two terms interchangeably. Officials of the government of the Republic of China often

1

use the term "Republic of China on Taiwan" or "Republic of China, Taiwan" or some other variant.

The Western word for Taiwan was *Formosa*, which is still in use, though less frequently. Some in Taiwan and elsewhere in Asia say that the term *Formosa* should be discarded since it is a foreign word and recalls Taiwan's colonial past. Others, however, especially advocates of Taiwan's independence, like to use the term to suggest that Taiwan is not a "Chinese place" and should not be thought of as historically or otherwise connected to China. Alternatively, it is used for its literal meaning ("beautiful"), suggesting that Taiwan is a place of scenic beauty.

For many years, the government of the Republic of China claimed jurisdiction over not only the territory it ruled, but also all of China, as well as some territory that the government of the People's Republic of China did not control, such as Outer Mongolia. Most people in Taiwan did not take these claims seriously, even less so as time passed. Meanwhile, the government of the People's Republic of China claimed (and still does) Taiwan, as well as all other territory governed by the Republic of China. Taiwan is said to be a province of China—Taiwan Province. The Offshore Islands are deemed part of Fukien (Fujian in China) Province. Most people in Taiwan disagree; many, in fact, say this claim is a myth.

Taiwan and China may someday reconcile their differences, at which time Taiwan will presumably become part of China. Certain trends, such as trade, investment, and the large number of people traveling between Taiwan and China, suggest that this is a real possibility. The transition might see the creation of a "Greater China" federation, confederation, or commonwealth. However, political trends—meaning democratization in Taiwan and not in China (or at least at a much slower rate there) and the fact that Taiwan's population increasingly identifies itself as Taiwanese, not Chinese, and does not support unification at least in the short run— suggest otherwise. In any event, China does not support a federation, confederation, commonwealth, or other such ideas.

Chinese leaders in the People's Republic of China reject Taiwan's legal separation and vow that they will resolve the "Taiwan issue" by military force if necessary. In fact, Chinese leaders have and continue to assert that China's People's Liberation Army will attack Taiwan if it declares independence, builds or acquires nuclear weapons, allows foreign military bases on its soil, or experiences serious instability. They have also spoken of a time frame within which Taiwan must negotiate or China will employ military force to take the island. In 2005, China's legislature, the National People's Congress, passed a bill called the "Anti-Succession Law" that formalized this policy. Some say this law makes it virtually impossible for present or future leaders to "allow Taiwan to go free."

The United States government, while it espouses a policy of one China, demands that the "Taiwan issue" be resolved peacefully and according to the wishes of the people of Taiwan. Moreover, it is apparently bound by law (the Taiwan Relations Act) to guarantee Taiwan's security. As a matter of fact, many say that America's policy, which does not support formal independence but supports Taiwan's right to choose its future and promises to protect it, is contradictory. Or the United States may be seen to support the status quo, however untidy or ambiguous. Still, many believe that U.S. relations with a rapidly growing and possibly threatening China will influence America's Taiwan policy, though it is uncertain whether America's cooperation, or conflict, with a "rising China" will be the dominant trend. Some say the United States will eventually give in to China's demand that Taiwan be reunified. Others say that America has a vital national interest in Taiwan's remaining separate from China, and because of this, in addition to the fact that Taiwan is a democracy and is highly regarded by the American public (and China isn't), Washington will keep its promises to Taiwan.

Although Taiwan appears to be a pawn in big power politics, and either America or China, or the two together, will decide its fate, domestic opinion and politics in Taiwan may play a role and may even be decisive. Most citizens in Taiwan oppose unification with China in the short run (though most say they prefer the status quo over any other choice), and a separate national identity is growing in Taiwan. Yet most favor continued, if not increased, commercial ties with China and view Taiwan's economic prosperity as linked to China's. Thus, it is difficult to predict where Taiwan will go in the future if its population is to decide the issue. Political trends say one thing, economic trends another. The international community in principle favors Taiwan's right to choose because it supports the idea of self-determination and because Taiwan is a democracy with a good human rights record. On the other hand, China has been quite successful in isolating Taiwan diplomatically by pressuring most countries to eschew political ties with Taiwan and by keeping Taiwan from retaining or gaining membership in most important international organizations, including the United Nations and its affiliated bodies.

LAND AND PEOPLE

Taiwan is surrounded by more than a dozen islands or island groups that are considered connected to it geologically, though the Pescadores in the Taiwan Strait to the west is the only group of significant size. Orchid Island and Green Island off Taiwan's southern east coast may be seen as "connected to" Taiwan, but not the Quemoy and Matsu groups, just off the coast of the mainland. The islands controlled or claimed by Taipei in the South China Sea are not geologically tied to Taiwan.

Taiwan lies between the Ryukyus, the chain of islands extending southward from Japan's main islands and which are part of the Japanese nation, to the north and slightly east of Taiwan, and the Philippines, to the south. To the east of Taiwan is the Pacific Ocean; to the west is the Taiwan (or Formosa) Strait; to the northwest lies the East China Sea, and to the southwest, the South China Sea. The Bashi Channel separates Taiwan from the Philippines.

Some geologists say that Taiwan was once part of the Asia mainland or what is now China. Others dispute this view because of its volcanic soil (not found in China) and instead argue that Taiwan is geologically part of a long chain of islands separate from the Asian continent that extend from Alaska, through Japan and Taiwan, to the Philippines and farther south. These geologists contend that there was no mainland connection, or that if there ever was one, it is very far removed in time. It may be that volcanic activity caused Taiwan to separate from China at some time in the distant past and that therefore both of these views are true. All of this would not be considered very relevant except that the argument of whether Taiwan is, or should be, part of China is an intense one, and even geological evidence is cited by both sides to prove their view.

Taiwan is very mountainous; mountains, in fact, cover more than two-thirds of the island. A central range of mountains stretching from north to south, but closer to the island's eastern coast than its western shore, divides the island. Yu Shan (Jade Mountain) is the island's highest peak, reaching more than 3,952 meters (13,000 feet) above sea level. There are few good harbors on the eastern side of Taiwan. On the western side of the island lies a plain that is home to most of the population and where most of its tilled land is found. Taiwan's rivers originate in the mountains, are generally short, and are not navigable. The Tamsui River, which flows past Taipei and on to the Taiwan Strait, is an exception, though large ships cannot use the river.

Rainfall is plentiful, averaging over 254 centimeters (100 inches) a year. The east coast receives more rain than the west, and the mountains receive more than the lowlands. October through March is the rainy season in the north; the south gets more precipitation from April to September. Winds are periodic and seasonal, not continental or strong. Taiwan experiences no cyclones or tornadoes; however, it suffers very severe typhoons in the late summer and early fall. The typhoons that hit Taiwan are among the strongest in the world and do considerable wind damage and often cause severe flooding.

Taiwan is traversed by the Tropic of Cancer, just below the middle of the island. The climate of Taiwan is therefore subtropical and, in the very southern part of the island, tropical. Proximity to the ocean also moderates the climate. On the other hand, temperatures throughout the island vary considerably with elevation. In fact, snow falls in the high mountainous areas and occasionally at some lesser elevations to the north in the winter. Generally, however, temperatures are moderate to hot. The island's average temperature is twenty-one degrees centigrade (seventy degrees Fahrenheit).

The surface area of the Republic of China is 36,320 square kilometers (13,814 square miles), of which slightly over 10 percent is water (mostly ocean territory). This makes Taiwan slightly smaller than the U.S. states of Maryland and Delaware combined, or about the size of Holland. If Taiwan were made part of China, it would be its second smallest province (after Hainan).

The soil in Taiwan is generally rich in the lowlands but leached and acidic at higher elevations. This, in addition to changes in elevation, accounts for the wide variety of trees and other flora on the island. Crops that are cultivated on Taiwan's flat land at lower altitudes do well because of the good soil, plentiful rainfall, and lots of sunshine. Rice is the staple crop, and there are two or three harvests a year. Farmers grow a wide variety of vegetables and fruits, the latter having the reputation for being the tastiest in the world.

Taiwan has few natural resources. However, early in its history, coal and some other minerals were commercially important. Waterpower was critical to the island's economy in the recent past. Good soil also contributed to a strong agricultural sector of the economy; however, farming has declined markedly in importance to Taiwan's economy in recent years. Petroleum and gas exploration have not yielded any meaningful finds. Many now say that the nation's only resource of any consequence is its human talent.

The population of the Republic of China was just over twenty-three million in 2005. Nearly all of the nation's citizens reside on the island of Taiwan. The population of the Pescadores is around 150,000; Quemoy is home to 50,000 people, and Matsu about 8,000 (though there is a sizable number of military personnel stationed on Quemoy and Matsu). Considering its small geographic size, this makes the Republic of China the second most densely populated nation in the world after Bangladesh (excluding, of course, the city-states and mini-states). There are around 3,885 people per square kilometer (1,500 per square mile). Taking cognizance of the fact that most of the island of Taiwan is mountainous, the Republic of China has more people per unit of flat land than any small, medium-size, or large nation in the world.

In 1940, Taiwan's population was 5.8 million. An influx of people after the Nationalist Chinese regime was defeated by the Communists on the mainland, along with a rapid rate of increase for more than two decades thereafter, caused the population to grow rapidly. As a result, in 1964, the government established a birth control program. Subsequent years saw the population growth rate fall precipitously due to government policies and the very rapid urbanization fostered by the nation's successful industrialization. In the 1980s, Taiwan's birthrate fell to below the world's average. In fact, the current population replacement rate has been below par for two decades. Assuming little or no immigration, the Republic of China's population is projected to peak at about twenty-six million around the year 2020 and decline after that.

Although very crowded, Taiwan is not said to have a population problem. There was concern four or five decades ago, but this changed because of a falling rate of population growth and the nation's robust economy. In fact, there is now a shortage of labor due to the low birthrate. This has resulted in problems caused by importing labor from other countries. Another serious problem that is anticipated is aging. Life expectancy is now 77.3 years — 76.3 years for males and 80.3 years for females. These figures represent dramatic changes from the recent past and suggest high social welfare and medical costs in the future.

Taiwan's population can be divided into four ethnic groups. The aborigines, or the island's earliest inhabitants, are considered to be of Malay or Polynesian origin, based on their languages and culture. They constitute less than 2 percent of the population. There are two groups of early Chinese immigrants or "Taiwanese." The Hakka came from south China, mainly from Kuangtung (Guangdong or Canton) Province near Hong Kong, though some migrated from Fukien Province. The second, the Fukienese — Min Nan or Hoklo — came from Fukien Province directly across the Taiwan Strait. Together they represent 85 percent of the population, with the latter outnumbering the former by two or three to one. The fourth group is made up of Chinese who moved to Taiwan after World War II, mostly in 1949 when the Communists defeated the Nationalist Chinese armies. They hailed from various parts of China but came disproportionately from the coastal and southern provinces. In total, they constitute just under 15 percent of the population. They are referred to as Mainland Chinese, or "mainlanders."

The aborigines came to Taiwan in prehistoric times. Currently most live in the mountains, although originally two separate groups could be identified: mountain and lowland tribes. There are a number of different aboriginal groups, but there are said to be less than a dozen major ones. The aborigines speak languages or tribal dialects that resemble Malay rather than Chinese. However, their languages or dialects are mutually unintelligible, and their common language is Chinese. Many still live by hunting and fishing, though many aborigines are now working in other occupations, especially those associated with tourism. They are poorer than the rest of the population, and their birthrate is lower.

It is uncertain when the first Chinese took up residence in Taiwan. It may have been as early as the sixth century AD. However, probably most Chinese on the island at that time were fishermen who stopped on the island to repair their boats or nets, merchants who traded with the aborigines, and pirates who used places on the island as hideouts. By AD 1000, there were a number of Chinese communities in western Taiwan. Most of these early permanent Chinese immigrants engaged in fishing, farming, and trading. The Hakka, who probably came earlier, resided more in the southern part of the island. Today there are still Hakka-dominated areas in Taiwan. Hakkas speak the Hakka dialect of Chinese in addition to Taiwanese (a derivative of the Fukien dialect) and Mandarin Chinese. Hakkas are, in a number of ways, culturally distinct from other Chinese. Today, many Hakkas are in politics, and many work in local police organizations and the railroads.

The Fukien Taiwanese, or Hoklo, began to settle in Taiwan nearly a thousand years ago, but most migrated in the fourteenth through the seventeenth centuries. In the latter centuries, they forced most of the Hakka population to move inland and took the island's best farmland. They also controlled the island politically when it was not governed by outside powers. The Fukien Chinese or Taiwanese are now dominant in agriculture, business, and local and national politics. Because of the years of separation from China, and as a result of greater contact with other peoples and countries, along with a fifty-year period of Japanese colonial rule before World War II, their culture is also unique. They speak Taiwanese, which is derivative of the dialect spoken in southern Fukien Province.

The Mainland Chinese are called latecomers. Most were government or ruling party officials or soldiers. In the early years after 1949, they monopolized government employment and jobs in education and lived primarily in the large cities, especially Taipei. Since they hailed from all parts of China, they speak various dialects, in addition to Mandarin Chinese. Today many also speak Taiwanese.

There has been a history of "ethnic" (perhaps better called subethnic, or provincial in the case of the three groups of Chinese) friction between and among the four groups residing in Taiwan. The aborigines battled both groups of early-arrival Chinese, or Taiwanese, when the latter migrated to the island, and for a long time thereafter. In addition, the Hakka and Fukien Chinese also fought and have long harbored hostilities toward each other. After World War II, both of these groups espoused ill feelings toward the Mainland Chinese. Ethnic identification and hatred, however, have waned in recent years with urbanization, prosperity, and a common outside threat from China, though it at times seems worse due to democratization (especially during election campaigns). Ethnic tension increased after Chen Shui-bian was elected president in 2000.

In terms of religions or religious beliefs, the population of Taiwan is quite eclectic. Also, most people report adhering to more than one religion. The aborigines practice nature worship and various sacrifices. Most Chinese—65 percent according to a recent poll—adhere to some Chinese folk religion. But Chinese immigrants also brought Confucianism, Taoism, and Buddhism to Taiwan, and most of the population reports being followers of one or all of these "religions." (Many, however, view Confucianism more as an ethical system providing guidelines for personal interaction rather than a religion, and Taoism is said to be more a philosophy than a religion.) The Dutch introduced Protestant Christianity to Taiwan, while the Spanish brought Catholicism, and the Japanese brought Shinto to the island.

Buddhism has seen an increase in followers in Taiwan in recent years, with 15 percent of the population reporting to be converts. In all, there are one million "pure" Buddhists. There are many Confucian temples, even though Confucianism's main influence is in education and politics. There are also Taoist temples honoring China's earliest religion or philosophy. Taoism has merged with other religions and in Taiwan has adopted many of the practices of local folk religions. After making gains in the 1950s and 1960s, the number of Christians has remained about the same in recent years: Protestants count their numbers at just over 420,000, and Catholics number over 300,000. Among Protestants, the Methodist Church at one time had an advantage in seeking converts because Chiang Kai-shek was Methodist. The Methodist Church still attracts many Mainland Chinese. The Presbyterian Church, which was active in Taiwan earlier and which was, and is, more politically involved than other religions (especially in favor of Taiwan's independence), has, in contrast, attracted Taiwanese.

EARLY HISTORY

Anthropological studies reveal that there was human life on Taiwan ten thousand years ago, and probably earlier (some say much earlier). Whether or not these very early inhabitants were ancestors of the island's aboriginal population is uncertain. So are the origins of the aborigines. It has long been assumed that all or most of the aborigines came to Taiwan from Southeast Asia. Various cultural similarities suggest this. In addition, the aboriginal languages are classified as Malay based on grammatical structure and the fact that as many as two-thirds of the words in some of them are similar to those of Malay. However, this does not rule out the possibility that they came from the southern part of China, which was not at that time culturally Chinese and was populated by people who later migrated to Southeast Asia. On the other hand, certain evidence suggests that some tribes may have migrated from the north—North China or possibly even Japan. South Asia and other places have also been mentioned. Recently, yet another theory has been advanced: that Taiwan's aborigines or their ancestors populated Taiwan much earlier than thought, and they migrated from Taiwan to other parts of the region rather than the other way around.

Anthropologists say that in prehistoric times the human population of Taiwan was quite evenly distributed throughout the island and that the early residents lived by hunting, fishing, and some shifting agriculture. Their political and social systems were tribal in structure, with land held in common. Lineage and customs varied among the various tribes.

Little is known of Taiwan's early history because the aborigines did not develop a written language. There is mention of Taiwan in early Chinese historical records, but there are few details. Very early Chinese records do not even give Taiwan's precise location, and the names used for the island are inconsistent. Also, Taiwan was identified as an area "beyond the pale of Chinese civilization" and therefore not a place of interest to China. Clearly the island did not benefit in any meaningful sense from China's early historical or cultural development.

In the third century AD, the Chinese government sent a ten-thousand-man expeditionary force to Taiwan, ostensibly to explore the island, but no follow-up mission was sent. If the purpose of the effort was to make Taiwan Chinese territory, the idea was soon forgotten. After that, Taiwan was seldom mentioned in Chinese court documents or in Chinese historical records for the next 1,200 years, though there were some other government-sponsored visits to the island.

Later, Chinese began to visit the island: fishermen as a stop-off place, merchants to trade, and pirates to avoid capture by government authorities or to find "prizes" among ships traveling in the area. After Chinese began to permanently migrate to Taiwan from areas on the mainland across the Taiwan Strait, China learned about Taiwan from those who visited the island and from relatives of migrants, but information concerning Taiwan and its people was kept mostly in local record books or in family histories. Few Chinese who went to Taiwan to live returned to China, since much of the time it was unlawful for them to leave the motherland, and the punishment for doing so was death. In addition, they usually migrated for economic reasons, and when they found good land or other opportunities to improve their livelihood in Taiwan, they did not want to return to China. Furthermore, not many of those who did return had any contact with the government far off to the north in Peking.

In the fifteenth century, the famous eunuch and navigator engaged by the Ming court, Cheng Ho, reported to the emperor that he had "discovered Taiwan." Since many Chinese already lived there and the island is visible from the mainland, this was, of course, not literally true. Still, it was the first mention of the word *Taiwan* in Chinese history. On the other hand, reports about Taiwan and the people residing there were not complimentary, explaining at least in part why the Chinese court at this time showed no real interest in the island.

When the Mongols ruled China (from 1280 to 1368), a military mission brought the Pescadores under control; however, the Mongols made no effort to extend their control to Taiwan. Hakkas in the south and Japanese pirates in the north occupied some of the coastal areas of Taiwan at this time. Fukienese were also residing on the island. The aborigines controlled the interior of the island and constituted the majority of the population.

In the thirteenth and fourteenth centuries, Chinese from various parts of China (but chiefly the Amoy area of southern Fukien Province) began to migrate to Taiwan in large numbers. Thus Fukienese became the dominant group among the local Chinese population. Japanese pirates at this time still held control over some of the northern part of the island, and Chinese pirates occupied some ports in the south. When the first Westerners arrived, Chinese, numbering twenty-five thousand at most, were the main population on only a small portion of the island.

THE PERIOD OF WESTERN COLONIALISM

In 1517, a Portuguese ship sailing through the Taiwan Strait on the way to Japan sighted Taiwan, and in the ship's log were recorded the words

Ilha Formosa, meaning "beautiful island." Formosa thus became the Western term for Taiwan. The Portuguese, however, did not lay claim to Taiwan or try to colonize it; nor did other Western countries at this time. In 1593, Japan, under the rule of Toyotomi Hideyoshi, made a weak and ill-fated attempt to colonize Taiwan.

In 1622, Dutch forces captured the Pescadores. They used their military presence there to control ship traffic through the Taiwan Strait and to harass Portuguese vessels traveling to and from Japan. The Dutch tried to wrest Macao, on the China coast, from the Portuguese, but failed. Subsequently, in 1624, Dutch representatives signed a treaty with China, which gave Holland posts on Taiwan and other rights in exchange for Dutch forces withdrawing from the Pescadores. The Dutch then established a settlement in southern Taiwan and built three forts, including Fort Zeelandia, the most famous, near the present-day city of Tainan.

In 1626, Spanish soldiers seized the port of Keelung in northern Taiwan and established control of an area down the west coast to a short distance from Tamsui. Two years later, in 1628, the Japanese government ordered the evacuation of Japanese traders and pirates as part of Japan's new isolationist policy; thus Spanish control spread. Nevertheless, in 1642, Dutch garrisons subjugated Spanish forces. Shortly after, the Dutch suppressed a Chinese rebellion with the help of the aborigines and established jurisdiction over the entire island, though their de facto control did not extend very far inland.

The Dutch East India Company forthwith gained exclusive rights to commercial operations in Taiwan and ruled most of the island as a colonial enterprise. The company's officials leased land and agricultural tools to the peasants and introduced oxen to till the rice fields. They also dug new wells, conducted land surveys, introduced cash crops such as sugar, and romanized the aboriginal languages. They built large forts or castles and introduced the residents of Taiwan to opium, which the Chinese population mixed with tobacco for smoking. During the early years of Dutch control, the Chinese population was estimated at thirty thousand; the aborigine population was probably several times larger. The Dutch population was but a few thousand.

At this time, the Manchus, or Manchurians, threatened the Ming Dynasty in China from the north. Before the Ming finally collapsed in 1644, Emperor Sze Tsung appointed Cheng Chi-lung, a Fukienese merchant-pirate of Hakka origin operating from a base in Taiwan, to train and rebuild remnant Ming naval forces to protect the dynasty. Cheng, with a fleet of three thousand vessels, won some battles but did not succeed in his given mission, and the Manchus finally captured and executed him.

Cheng's forces, however, survived. His son Cheng Ch'eng-kung, also known by the name Koxinga and whose mother was Japanese, inherited his father's sailors and fleet. The latter Cheng welcomed Chinese immigrants who fled to Taiwan to escape Manchu rule. He recruited them and built a larger army and expanded his already strong navy. With twelve thousand vessels and 120,000 soldiers, he battled the Manchus for more than a decade, trying to restore the Ming Dynasty. At one point, he nearly captured the city of Nanking.

In 1661, after at least temporarily abandoning his efforts to overthrow Manchu rule in China, Cheng Ch'eng-kung decided to launch an attack on the Dutch strongholds in the southern part of Taiwan. From his bases in the north, Cheng sailed down the coast with 30,000 men to do battle with the 2,200 Dutch soldiers and 600 Dutch farmers. After a nine-month siege, the Dutch negotiated an agreement whereby they would evacuate, and in so doing they ended their colonial rule of Taiwan.

After he defeated the Dutch, Cheng sent representatives to the Philippines to meet with the Chinese population there in hopes of rallying them to the cause of overthrowing the "foreign" Manchu Dynasty in China. Fearing a rebellion, Spanish officials in the Philippines ordered the suppression of Chinese political activities, killing ten thousand Chinese residents in the process. The Spanish then sent a message to Cheng that they had killed all Chinese residing in the Philippines. Cheng vowed revenge, but he died of a mysterious ailment (some say of a heart attack after hearing news of the fate of the Chinese in the Philippines) before he could retaliate against the Spanish as he swore to do. Cheng's demise occurred at the young age of thirty-eight, yet he had a major impact on Taiwan's history and is regarded as a national hero.

Before his premature death, Cheng Ch'eng-kung established a Ming-style government on Taiwan. He imported and nurtured Chinese culture, which he admired. He adopted the Chinese legal and political systems, recruiting the best available scholars and advisers. Cheng's court was located at Fort Zeelandia, which became a cultural and commercial center, with nearby Anping prospering as a port city. However, Cheng's political support came from Taiwan's rich land-owning families, and the social structure and economy in Taiwan differed from China's in important ways. In fact, Taiwan's political and social systems were feudal, similar to Japan's, unlike the bureaucratic imperial system in China. Thus Taiwan in some ways became sinofied, and in some other ways it did not.

In many respects, Cheng brought progress to the island. He encouraged Chinese across the Strait to come to Taiwan, setting in motion a wave of immigration that soon brought a significant increase in the Chinese population in Taiwan. Fearing Cheng's military, the Manchu government forced the evacuation of coastal areas, depriving many families of their livelihood in the process, thus forcing many more people to flee to Taiwan. Meanwhile, Cheng Ch'eng-kung promoted foreign trade with Japan, the Philippines, Indochina, Siam, and the East Indies. Taiwan's ports became busy and its population quite cosmopolitan.

Upon Cheng's death, his son, Cheng Ching, operating from a power base in Fukien Province, vied with his uncle in Taiwan for the right of succession. Cheng Ching defeated the armies of his uncle and became the recognized ruler of Taiwan's Chinese population. He subsequently led several unsuccessful military expeditions against the Manchus, trying to fulfill his father's dream of restoring the Ming Dynasty. He died in Taiwan, like his father, at a young age.

Another struggle for secession, this time a much more destructive one, followed Cheng Ching's death, partly because he bequeathed the throne to an illegitimate son. Many of his subjects, even loyal ones, refused to recognize this son as their ruler. The Manchu government in China immediately took advantage of the situation. Peking first sent a naval force to the Pescadores and destroyed the Cheng government's fleet there. In 1683, Manchu troops landed on Taiwan and, not encountering much resistance, brought to a close just over two decades of Cheng family rule over Taiwan—a period when Taiwan was self-governing.

TAIWAN UNDER CHINESE RULE

From 1683 to just before the beginning of the twentieth century, China governed Taiwan. However, it did so reluctantly, seeing Taiwan as important to China only for strategic reasons. Chinese officials, including the emperor, did not otherwise view Taiwan as valuable to China and did not see it as a place of culture and civilization, which defined China. Throughout most of this period, Taiwan was administratively a part of Fukien Province.

Officials sent to Taiwan were generally China's worst. Many were sent as a form of punishment. Corruption was rampant. Harsh and inhumane punishments were meted out for minor crimes. As a consequence, social and political unrest and opposition to official authority became commonplace; in fact, Taiwan became known as a "place of rebellion." In one revolt in the mid-1800s, twenty thousand soldiers sent from China were killed. Peking responded with punitive vengeance, further alienating much of the population. Most people on the island came to hate the government of China as a result of its oppressive rule and its regular use of military force to resolve problems. Officials in Peking continued to refer to Taiwan as a "frontier area," suggesting that they did not regard it as part of China.

Peking banned women from going to Taiwan, thus creating a Chinese society in Taiwan that was overwhelming male. This added to the frontier nature of Taiwan and the prevalence of violence. It also precipitated frequent "intermarriage" with aboriginal women, leading to the argument today that Taiwanese are not Chinese but are rather "mixed-race" people. Secret societies grew in Taiwan and took on a life of their own at this time.

The argument that advocates of Taiwan's independence make today that China "colonized" Taiwan is based on this history. It is further supported by the fact that Peking sent garrisons from China to Taiwan, and when it recruited local militia, it did so from the aboriginal population, not trusting the local Chinese. Also, very few local Chinese took the imperial civil service examination, and few, perhaps none, who passed were assigned to service in Taiwan. This suggests that China treated Taiwanese as an underclass and perhaps not as Chinese because Taiwan was not a "civilized place."

While it suffered from incompetent and unenlightened Chinese rule during this period, agriculture did well in Taiwan—so well that parts of China became dependent on food from Taiwan. Food was shipped to Japan as well. In 1714, three Jesuits were commissioned by Peking to produce a map of Taiwan in order to plan infrastructural improvements. Also, some efforts were subsequently made to spur commerce in Taiwan. But these were exceptions to Peking's usual policy of neglect.

Meanwhile, foreigner powers' trade interests in East Asia grew, and with it the desire to establish a presence in Taiwan. When problems arose, Western governments sought the redress of their grievances from Peking, especially for the killing of their subjects. Consistently, the response was that China bore no responsibility for Taiwan, thus repudiating, in the minds of Westerners, any claim of sovereignty over the island. In contrast to the growing notion that Taiwan was not claimed by China and thus was not legally part of China at this time, culturally, Taiwan became more and more Chinese. One must also note that China did not espouse the idea of nationhood, as was then common in the West, but instead viewed China as defined by its culture and civilization. The Chinese government also experienced opposition to its rule elsewhere, which it dealt with in similar ways to the troubles on Taiwan.

In the 1800s, several Western powers showed an interest in colonizing Taiwan, or at least in establishing some kind of permanent presence on the island. In fact, in the 1840s, the Chinese government suspected that the British planned to make Taiwan a colony. In 1854, Commodore Oliver Perry appealed to the U.S. government to establish a presence on Taiwan. Later, Townsend Harris, the U.S. representative in Japan, recommended that the U.S. government try to purchase the island from China and use it as a coaling station. Washington, however, did not follow this advice. A bit later, after acquiring the Ryukyu Islands, Japan also showed an interest in colonizing Taiwan.

Realizing that this constituted a threat to China, Peking sent more competent officials to rule Taiwan. Liu Ming-chuan became the most well known. In August 1884, after improving the island's defenses, he beat back a French attempt to seize the port of Keelung. The next year, Liu was appointed governor, and, upon his advice, Taiwan was made a full-fledged Chinese province. Under Liu's governorship, the infrastructure and both economic and political conditions improved. But his efforts were too late; Japan had already taken an interest in Taiwan and soon found an opportunity to bring the island under its control.

UNDER JAPANESE RULE

In 1894, China and Japan went to war. China lost, and in the surrender agreement, the Treaty of Shimonoseki signed in 1895, Peking ceded

Taiwan and the Pescadores to Japan. The transfer was "in perpetuity," and the Western powers, though reluctant, treated Japan's colonial acquisition as legal.

The Chinese population of Taiwan was split over the transfer of ownership of the island to Japan. Some favored it, feeling that Japanese governance could be no worse than the corrupt and cruel Chinese rule they had suffered under for more than two centuries. Many felt that Japan might be able to deal with the vexing problem of rival warlords, rampant crime, and other problems. Opponents pushed for independence and managed to proclaim the "Republic of Taiwan"—Asia's first republic. But this turned out to be a short-lived affair. The fate of Taiwan was decided by the formidable Japanese military presence and the absence of any foreign power to oppose Tokyo's intentions. Japan's rule of Taiwan thus became a fait accompli.

Another factor helped Japan gain control over the island: Peking, in a formal and public ceremony in Taiwan, turned over the reins of government to Japan, signaling to the population of Taiwan that China had no interest in keeping Taiwan and would not help those on the island who wanted to resist Japanese rule. Thus Japan quickly consolidated its control over the population of the island, and opposition to Japanese rule faded, though there was scattered opposition to Japanese rule for the next three years.

Tokyo had to formulate policies with little experience in governing a foreign territory, for Taiwan was Japan's first colony. In any case, the Japanese first sought to establish law and order, which they did very efficiently. The Japanese colonial government issued decrees, which were, in effect, criminal laws, and they enforced these laws harshly, including using capital punishment with considerable frequency. Some felt the Japanese were cruel, but most were thankful that warlordism, crime, and other problems were largely eradicated and that social stability had returned to the island.

Political and social tranquility laid the groundwork for economic development. The top economic priority for the Japanese colonial government was agriculture. Japan introduced new breeds of rice and better farming and harvesting techniques. Taiwan's agriculture soon showed signs of marked improvement. By the 1920s, Taiwan's population enjoyed a higher per capita consumption of meat, vegetables, and fruit than any place in China, and higher than some parts of Japan. Surplus food was sent to Japan, especially rice and sugar.

Building a transportation infrastructure was also given high priority. When Japanese colonial rule began in 1895, Taiwan had forty-eight kilometers (thirty miles) of railroads. By 1905, it had ten times that, and work was in progress to more than double that amount. Roads and harbors were improved and new ones built. As a result, domestic and foreign commerce increased rapidly. In 1903, Taiwan was electrified, making it the first area outside of Japan proper to take this step into modernity. Meanwhile, communications facilities were built or upgraded. Many diseases were eradicated, and others were reduced in terms of the number of people affected, making Taiwan the most disease-free area in Asia outside of Japan. Tokyo also undertook progressive social reforms. Education was improved; as a result, illiteracy was reduced markedly. Technical skills were improved, and the public's knowledge of commerce and world events increased. Superstitions were in large part eliminated. Binding women's feet was banned, and differences between rich and poor diminished.

However, Japanese colonial administrators, many of them high-ranking military officers, did not prepare Taiwan for democracy or self-rule. Tokyo's policies deliberately discouraged students from studying law or politics or any of the social sciences. They instead studied the physical sciences, engineering, and medicine. The best students went to Japan for higher education, precluding a student movement led by the "best and the brightest." Tokyo forced everyone to learn Japanese, meaning that Chinese (neither Mandarin nor the local dialects) was not taught in school; as a consequence, both the Chinese language and culture in Taiwan devolved. Japanese policies generally helped Taiwan develop economically and in some ways socially, but they were authoritarian and oppressive.

Japan ruled with the help of a local aristocracy or landowning class, which supported Japanese policies in return for favors, mostly economic ones. Japanese officials were generally honest and treated the local population well, but they did not consider them equal to Japanese. Thus they were generally condescending in their attitudes, which was reflected in their style of governance.

After World War I, Tokyo prohibited foreign enterprises from operating on the island. This had a positive effect on Taiwan's economy, with Taiwan developing many new industries: textiles, cement and other building materials factories, a chemical industry, and more. In the 1930s, Taiwan even began to build heavy industries.

Since Japan was concerned more about Taiwan's economic health and progress than other matters, colonial officials did not focus much attention on the aborigines. Japanese authorities found them difficult to control, though they successfully kept them from obtaining guns and thus reduced their threat to the Chinese (and Japanese) population. They also stopped them from practicing headhunting. The aborigines, however, stubbornly resisted Japanese control, and even into the 1940s exercised de facto control over much of Taiwan's mountainous areas.

During World War II, Taiwan served as Japan's "unsinkable aircraft carrier" in East Asia. The Japanese military used Taiwan as a beachhead for its expansion into Southeast Asia, including Japan's invasion of the Philippines. Taiwan's new industries supported Tokyo's war machine, and the island provided Japan with sizable quantities of food. The Japanese army built bases in Taiwan and trained soldiers there. Tokyo recruited soldiers among the Chinese community in Taiwan, even using some in units fighting in China. Some, in fact, participated in the atrocities committed against Chinese in Nanking and elsewhere.

Toward the end of the war, the United States contemplated invading Taiwan, but Washington gave up the plan when it found no good maps of Taiwan and, more importantly, calculated that the population would probably fight with the Japanese against American soldiers. U.S. forces, therefore, skipped Taiwan and invaded Okinawa. Hence, with the exception of U.S. planes bombing oil storage areas and some factories, Taiwan suffered relatively little damage during the war.

In 1943, at the Cairo Conference, the United States (with the United Kingdom concurring) promised Chiang Kai-shek that Taiwan and other territories "stolen by Japan" would be returned after the war. This pledge was reiterated in the Potsdam Agreement in July 1945. Japan's loss of Taiwan was considered part of the terms of the surrender, and in the fall of 1945, the Japanese colonial government departed, along with a number of Japanese businessmen and some farmers. In all, they constituted one-eighteenth of the population. Their exit left a serious vacuum in Taiwan in the realms of political administration, business management, and more.

Taiwan's legal status, however, was not discussed in the surrender agreement. One might infer that legal transfer was made to the Republic of China, though there were no formal documents to support this. In any case, Chiang Kai-shek forthwith sent military forces and government officials to Taiwan to replace the departing Japanese. The people of Taiwan generally welcomed both the end of Japanese colonial authority and the coming of Nationalist rule of Taiwan, though some discussed alternatives such as independence, a United Nations trusteeship over Taiwan, or a special relationship with the United States.

UNDER CHIANG KAI-SHEK

On 25 October 1945, Nationalist Chinese officials assumed political governance over Taiwan, and it thence became part of the Republic of China. Although the population generally applauded this, they soon became disappointed or worse. Taiwan was not made a province as expected. Nor did the Nationalists give a high priority to establishing democratic practices or institutions. Instead, Taiwan was placed under military rule. Ch'en Yi, a friend of Chiang Kai-shek's, was appointed governor and supreme commander with the same kind of near-absolute power that the Japanese colonial rulers had exercised. Soldiers and administrative officials from China were sent to Taiwan. They could not speak the dialects of Chinese spoken in Taiwan, and many despised the Taiwanese, perceiving that they had been "Japanized" or were traitors for serving in the Japanese military that Chinese on the mainland so intensely hated. The Nationalist government was preoccupied with a civil war on the mainland with the Communists and felt that the people of Taiwan should understand this and should be willing to accept sacrifices.

Taiwanese witnessed the economy deteriorate badly due mainly to what they considered gross mismanagement and corruption. With the economic decline, health standards deteriorated, causing epidemics of cholera and bubonic plague. Rumors spread that Nationalist soldiers brought these illnesses. Public works and the education system fell into disrepair. Bribery was rampant. Many Mainland Chinese claimed property based on squatters' rights, a concept not well known in Taiwan, while others looted factories in order to send materials needed in the war effort to the mainland. All of this evoked serious resentment on the part of the local population, which came to view government officials as carpetbaggers.

"Ethnic" hostility between the local Chinese or Taiwanese and the Mainland Chinese intensified. In this milieu, in February 1947, when police killed a woman selling black-market cigarettes on a Taipei street, a mob formed. Police fired into the crowd. This triggered open rebellion, an event now known as *er er ba*, or 2-28, for 28 February, when it started.

The hated Governor-General Ch'en Yi was in large measure blamed for the incident due to his inflexibility and his subordinates' venality, mistreatment of the local Chinese, and indifferent attitude toward local problems. He treated the rebellion as Communist inspired, which it was not. The melee saw Fukien Taiwanese beat and kill Mainland Chinese and anyone who could not speak Taiwanese, including some Hakka. Chiang Kai-shek sent troops to restore order. The troops used brute force against unarmed civilians, killing thousands, including many of Taiwan's best and brightest.

As a result of this incident, Chiang Kai-shek temporarily turned his attention to problems in Taiwan. He removed Ch'en Yi (and later ordered him executed). He made Taiwan a province and canceled military rule. He appointed more Taiwanese to political positions of importance. He ordered other reforms. But considerable lasting damage had already been done.

During the next two years, Nationalist Chinese forces suffered defeats throughout the mainland of China at the hands of Mao Zedong's armies. In the fall of 1949, the government and the military of the Republic of China fled to Taiwan. Taiwan thus became the Nationalists' base of operations, from which they hoped to regroup, counterattack Mao's forces, and "liberate" China (which they would rule again). But this was not to happen soon, and maybe not at all. As a result, Taiwan became synonymous with the Republic of China. The government of the People's Republic of China ruled the mainland, and Taiwan and China were once again separate.

In the meantime, the United States abandoned Chiang Kai-shek, and it appeared that Mao's People's Liberation Army would soon besiege Taiwan and make it part of the People's Republic of China. But when the Korean War started in June 1950, America changed its view of Mao and his Communist regime, and President Harry S. Truman ordered the U.S. Seventh Fleet into the Taiwan Strait to block the pending invasion and save the island. Taiwan thereafter assumed a center-stage role in the Cold War, representing "free" China, which was aligned with the West against the forces of Communism. The U.S. military presence, which soon grew on the island, made Taiwan secure, allowing its government to concentrate on domestic matters. There were, in fact, serious issues to attend to: the influx of 1.5 million Mainland Chinese worsened relations between them and the Taiwanese, the infrastructure was in disrepair, social and other services were lacking, and the economy needed immediate attention. In short, conditions in Taiwan were bad.

Taiwanese and the Mainland Chinese who governed the island soon realized that they had to put their differences behind them if they were to succeed in reconstruction efforts and launch a successful economic development program. The government proved that it was serious about rebuilding the infrastructure and fixing the economy, which it did effectively. It earned praise for this, especially for a highly successful land reform effort launched in 1950, a program that is to this day viewed as a model by scholars and officials of developing nations. With the help of U.S. aid advisers, land reform laid the groundwork for increasing agricultural productivity and subsequently for Taiwan's industrialization.

With American encouragement, Chiang Kai-shek nourished some democracy in local government, where Nationalist officials served as mediators between political factions. Democratization at the level of the national government, Chiang said, had to be delayed while the people were prepared for it. Chiang cited Sun Yat-sen, who had advocated a "period of tutelage" before full democracy could be realized. A political opposition, including new political parties that might compete with the Nationalist Party, or Kuomintang (KMT), was thus not allowed to develop. Rationalizing this, ethnic problems were potentially divisive, and many felt that Taiwan needed a strong government to prevent chaos and promote economic development.

Chiang also justified authoritarian rule by the fear of a military conflict with the People's Republic of China. Certainly there was tension with China. In 1954, and again in 1958, fighting broke out between the two sides over the Offshore Islands. Chiang regarded these islands, especially Quemoy and Matsu, as critical to his dream of reconquering the mainland. However, after U.S. officials repeatedly made it clear that Washington did not support actions that might involve the United States in a war, Chiang declared that recovering the mainland would be mainly political.

Chiang subsequently sought to "defeat" Communism by developing Taiwan economically and making it a showcase of his rule and capitalism. In ensuing years, he put Taiwan on the road to sustained rapid economic growth. He was so successful, in fact, that in 1964, when the United States decided to end its foreign aid to Taiwan, Taiwan's economy took off on its own. Economic growth soon was so rapid that the island became one of the fastest-growing economies in the world. Moreover, growth with equity benefited nearly all of the population. The result was the development of a large middle class, more contact with the outside world (since economic growth was propelled by foreign trade), and the need for democratic institutions to sustain the modernization process.

In ensuing years, support for Chiang's desire to liberate China (which was never supported with enthusiasm by the Taiwanese population) waned with the growing realization that the People's Republic of China was not going to collapse and that Taipei had little hope of recovering the mainland without a global war and the help of the United States. And American leaders did not like the thought of going to war with China (having experienced that in Korea), especially since it might expand into a U.S.–Soviet conflict. Stalemate resulted.

Taipei, however, was given a respite in dealing with the growing feeling in the United States and elsewhere that China had to be admitted into the world community and that Taiwan should no longer represent China in the United Nations and other international organizations. The Great Proletarian Cultural Revolution thrust the Chinese leadership into a power struggle in the mid- and late 1960s, and a self-imposed isolationism followed. At the same time, Washington-Peking relations deteriorated as a result of the United States escalating the Vietnam War in 1964.

But before long, both factors diminished in importance, and the United States and the People's Republic of China, in a new global political climate, sought rapprochement. In America's case, Richard Nixon was elected president in 1968 with a mandate of getting out of the Vietnam War "with honor." To do that, Nixon needed Peking's help. The new president also perceived that a different (meaning better) relationship with China was desirable for other reasons, especially in light of the Soviet Union engaging the United States in an arms race. The People's Republic of China had meanwhile begun to view the United States differently, even more so following a border war with the Soviet Union on the Ussuri River in 1969, after which Soviet military leaders clamored for aggressive action against China to prevent it from becoming a full-fledged nuclear power (China having tested an atomic bomb in 1964).

In the fall of 1971, Mao's government was admitted to the United Nations, and Chiang's government was expelled. The next year, U.S. president Nixon traveled to Peking where he toasted Mao and other Chinese leaders and set in motion a process of reconciliation between Washington and Peking. The United States needed cordial relations with the People's Republic of China to offset the Soviet Union's growing military power and influence in Asia. Peking needed Washington for the same reason. Thus they built a new relationship. This brought an end to the Nationalist Chinese claim to represent China in a world once clearly polarized into Communist and democratic blocs.

In April 1975, Chiang died. His dream of deposing Mao and removing the Communists from power in China was not realized. However, he could claim success in modernizing Taiwan and making it a model of economic development. The population of Taiwan by this time was enjoying prosperity, and Chinese throughout the rest of the world praised and admired Taiwan's "economic miracle." Political change in the direction of democracy had also begun.

UNDER CHIANG CHING-KUO

The death of Chiang Kai-shek marked the end of an era and the beginning of a new one. Although Yen Chia-kan became president in 1975 according to a provision in the Republic of China's Constitution whereby the vice president becomes president in the event that the president dies, Chiang Kai-shek's son, Chiang Ching-kuo, wielded considerably more political power. From his position as premier and head of the ruling Nationalist Party, CCK, as he was fondly called, had in fact already assumed many of his father's responsibilities after the latter's health had begun to deteriorate in the early 1970s.

Chiang Ching-kuo worked with Yen Chia-kan, or more accurately, the latter accepted CCK's dominance and served as an interim president. They did not compete. In March 1978, the National Assembly elected Chiang Ching-kuo president. President Yen had earlier declared that he would not be a candidate; CCK was thus the only real choice.

Chiang chose Shieh Tung-min, a Taiwanese, as his vice president and Sun Yun-suan, a mainlander and a talented technocrat, to be premier. In May, after his inauguration, CCK picked seven new cabinet members, all reformists.

One of the hallmarks of CCK's leadership was the incorruptible, "man of the people" image he built by forcing government officials to respond to public demands and complaints and by his frequent talks with workers and peasants. Another was his success (actually begun in 1972 when he became premier) in bringing more Taiwanese, who constituted 85 percent of the population, into the government and the Nationalist Party. In fact, CCK made the percent of Taiwanese in government and the party nearly equal to their portion of the general population. Another goal of the "younger Chiang" administration was good and democratic government. CCK promoted political reforms and accelerated the process of democratization of the national government. He announced stringent anticorruption policies. People knew he was serious when he jailed some of his close friends and relatives for graft or bribery. Similarly, CCK made efforts to improve Taiwan's human rights record, which, while not bad by global standards, still hurt the nation's image.

In mid-1978, President Chiang Ching-kuo called for an election in December that he promised would be open, competitive, and more important than any in Taiwan's history. It was to be the beginning of democracy at the national level in Taiwan. But President Jimmy Carter, on 15 December (a few days before the election), announced that the United States would grant formal diplomatic recognition to the People's Republic of China effective 1 January 1979, and that the American embassy in Taipei would be closed and the U.S.–Republic of China defense treaty canceled. Taiwan's government suffered a serious blow to its pride and its legitimacy as a result. CCK put the military on alert, closed the stock market, and canceled the election.

In early 1979, in order to fill the void left by President Carter's sudden decision, the U.S. Congress passed into law the Taiwan Relations Act (TRA). The president signed it in April. In essence, the TRA restored to Taipei its sovereignty in Washington's eyes by allowing it access to U.S. courts, by according its diplomats privileges normally granted only to the representatives of sovereign nation-states, and by keeping trade and investment ties on track. The TRA also guaranteed the sale of "defensive weapons" to Taiwan and pledged that U.S. military forces would remain in the area to ensure Taiwan's security. Some observers commented that the TRA's security provisions were broader (mentioning, for example, blockades) than the defense treaty Washington had with Taipei that was terminated on 1 January 1980. Officials in Taiwan liked the TRA but did not want to declare so publicly because the document did not use the country's official name, the Republic of China.

America's severing diplomatic ties with Taiwan prompted a number of other nations to follow suit. Both encouraged opposition groups in Taiwan to make stronger demands for reform and democratization. They, not to mention many in the government (including CCK himself), perceived that Taiwan had to move faster toward adopting a democratic political system in order to fend off Beijing's (the new spelling of Peking) claims that Taiwan belonged to the People's Republic of China. They perceived that the United States and the international community would probably support, especially if it democratized, Taiwan's right to choose its future—separate from or as a part of China, whichever it desired (but, for the short run, certainly separation). Democratization thus meant survival.

But some opposition groups wanted to move more aggressively in the pursuit of democracy and freer and more open politics. On 10 December 1979, Human Rights Day, demonstrators in the southern city of Kaohsiung organized a parade that quickly turned confrontational. The public, which had generally supported the opposition's views, took the government's side because of the violence it engendered and the fear of chaos that might benefit Beijing. In the wake of the incident, the government sought out those responsible and jailed them, some on charges of sedition.

But that resolved the crisis only temporarily. Taiwan needed a more democratic political system. Thus, agreements were subsequently worked out between the opposition (more moderate leaders) and Nationalist Party officials. Included were rescheduling the election canceled in 1978, new election regulations, and gentlemen's agreements to the effect that candidates could campaign freely but would not advocate Communism or Taiwan's independence, in order to make the next national election a more open and meaningful one.

As it turned out, the December 1980 election was a watershed event in the political modernization process in Taiwan. While there was no official opposition, independent candidates collectively known as *tangwai* (or "outside the party," meaning outside the ruling Nationalist Party) behaved like a political party. Its candidates criticized the government and the Nationalist Party in candid and harsh language. The new open political atmosphere in fact flabbergasted many citizens who observed the campaign. It was the first ever competitive national election in Taiwan or in any Chinese nation.

Another election in 1983 confirmed that free electoral contests were now an integral part of Taiwan's political system. The next year, in 1984, CCK was reelected to another six-year term. This time he picked Lee Teng-hui as his vice president. Like Shieh Tung-min, Lee was Taiwanese; but Lee was younger and U.S. educated, and he was seen by many as a more serious politician and a potential future president. In fact, Chiang's choice engendered speculation that he had chosen his successor, a political question that had loomed beneath the surface of Taiwan's politics for several years because of CCK's declining health.

In March 1986, following a Nationalist Party meeting, CCK ordered the formation of a high-level, twelve-member committee to study four "sensitive questions": martial law, the ban on forming new political parties, rejuvenating the elected organs of government, and strengthening local government. Dealing with these four issues came to constitute CCK's "design to make Taiwan a real democracy," which became his paramount goal during his final years.

But the opposition beat him to the draw on one of the questions—new political parties. In September, independent politicians met and announced the formation of the Democratic Progressive Party. CCK ordered government officials not to take action against them for violating the law banning new parties since it was soon to be rescinded. As a result, the Democratic Progressive Party ran against the Nationalist Party in the December 1986 national election in what was the first two-party election in Chinese history. The DPP fared well, but the Nationalist Party did better, giving the ruling party confidence that it could win in competitive elections against a recognized and organized opposition party.

In July 1987, the government announced the termination of martial law. Since martial law had not been fully in effect in the sense that Taiwan did not have military rule, ending it had little immediate impact. The psychological effect, however, was important. The move also had some bearing on the legal system, and it enhanced press freedom. Most

importantly, canceling the martial law decree gave Taiwan good publicity abroad. The Western media lauded Taiwan for taking a major step on
its way to becoming a democracy.

CCK died on 13 January 1988. In recent years, according to public
opinion surveys, CCK ranks the highest among Taiwan's favorite presidents. He left a legacy of reform, democracy, clean government, and
continued miraculous economic growth. Still, some of his goals were
yet to be realized, and the reforms he had accomplished had to be kept
in place. Those tasks were left to his successor.

UNDER LEE TENG-HUI, I

When Chiang Ching-kuo died, Vice President Lee Teng-hui became
president. He did not, however, inherit CCK's leadership of the party.
An emergency meeting of the ruling Nationalist Party was called, and
Lee, on a temporary basis only, was granted CCK's mantle of party
leadership. In the meantime, some members of the "old guard" (including Madame Chiang Kai-shek) colluded in an effort to block Lee from
wielding real political power, or at least to dilute his political authority.
They were troubled by the prospect of a transition of power to a Taiwanese president. On the other hand, Lee was CCK's chosen successor
and was seen as fiercely loyal to the Nationalist Party; he therefore had
the support of many party members, but especially Taiwanese.

Another crisis meeting followed, which resulted in Lee winning the
leadership reins of the party permanently. A motion to have a rotating
party leader was voted down. Those in favor of Lee, notably James
Soong, who was then deputy secretary-general of the ruling party, cited
CCK's intentions and the "wrong signal" an effort to undercut Lee's authority would send to investors in the stock market, foreign countries,
and even Beijing (which might take advantage of the situation).

Being Taiwanese (though of the Hakka minority), Lee's leadership in
some ways weakened and in other ways accentuated "ethnic" politics.
Clearly it marked the transition from a Mainland Chinese–dominated
government and ruling party to Taiwanese-dominated ones. Yet Lee's
holding the top position of executive leadership did not dampen opposition politics. The demand for democracy was growing. And various
interest groups had already learned that they could accomplish political

goals through protest politics. On 20 May 1988, farmers demonstrated in Taipei, leading to mass riots lasting seventeen hours and resulting in widespread property damage and injury to five hundred people. At this time, street demonstrations in Taiwan were occurring at a rate of 150 per month. Taiwan, in fact, had entered a new era politically, or so it seemed. President Lee had to contend with this.

At the Nationalist Party's Thirteenth Congress, held in July, Lee was officially elected chairman of the KMT. Democratization permeated the atmosphere. More delegates were chosen by primaries or other democratic processes. These delegates were not so docile and demanded the authority to choose a Central Committee from delegates they nominated rather than from Lee's list. They also made known their feelings about top party leaders, sometimes causing embarrassment to those who were not accustomed to criticism anywhere, much less in public. But Lee was popular, and the democratization processes in large measure worked to his benefit. The new Central Standing Committee (where real decision-making power lies in the party) was chosen, and for the first time it included a majority of Taiwanese.

The KMT not only democratized itself, suggesting that it planned to be the dominant political party in Taiwan for the foreseeable future, but it also made promises to further democratize the government, deal with social problems, and adopt a coherent policy toward the mainland. Regarding the latter issue, visits, trade, and investment were already extensive and seemed to offset political trends that were separating Taiwan more and more from China.

Soon after the Party Congress, Lee picked a new cabinet. It too was a Taiwanese one (meaning a majority of its members were Taiwanese). Later, Lee chose the popular Lee Huan to be premier when the less popular, but effective and loyal, Yu Kuo-hua stepped down. Meanwhile, Lee devoted considerable attention to improving ties with the military (where his political base was weak) and to the problem of acquiring the sophisticated weapons needed to defend the nation.

Because of Washington's promise to Beijing in 1982 to gradually reduce and ultimately end its arms sales to Taiwan, Taipei made plans to purchase military technology and build its own fighter plane. This plane, the Indigenous Defense Fighter, or IDF, was put on public display in December 1988, signaling that the Republic of China planned to defend its sovereignty in the face of leaders in Beijing continuing to assert that they would resolve the "Taiwan issue" by military force if necessary. President Lee gained increasing support from the military as a result.

On 20 May 1989, Taiwan officially proclaimed its support for the Democracy Movement in China. Taiwan, however, did nothing overt to help the movement. In June, after authorities in Beijing used the military to clear out demonstrators from Tiananmen Square, slaughtering students and many others in the process, international pressure on Taipei to negotiate with the People's Republic of China diminished markedly. By comparison, the Nationalist Party and the Republic of China's government looked good. There was no shooting of students on the streets of Taipei; instead, democratization was proceeding apace. In fact, the Tiananmen Massacre became a watershed event for Taiwan. Seldom after this was the appellation "pariah nation" used in reference to Taiwan; that opprobrium had been passed to Beijing.

That year, 1989, was also an important time for another reason. The opposition Democratic Progressive Party scored a major victory in the Legislative Yuan election late in the year. Its election success was built to some degree on the worldwide wave of democratic reform that made voters in Taiwan see the opposition party in a different, less radical light. Views about Taiwan's separation from China, which seemed more reasonable in the context of the Tiananmen Massacre, also helped the Democratic Progressive Party. Democratic Progressive Party leaders had likewise learned how to campaign and win votes. Its "victory" (called that because of major gains it made in seats in the legislature) was in fact so impressive that many, especially its leaders, predicted that the ruling Nationalist Party might be voted out of office soon—if only the system were made democratic by expelling members of the elected bodies of government that were frozen in office after the government moved to Taiwan in 1949 or were appointed to fill vacancies in these representative organs of government.

President Lee and his ruling party accepted the challenge and subsequently backed new laws to retire old members or "elder parliamentarians" in the elected organs of government and to reform these bodies so that they would represent citizens of Taiwan, not China. This was to be done in the name of democracy, though some saw it as supporting a hidden "splittist" (from China) agenda. Other observers, however, pointed out that an independent Taiwan, which a two-China policy suggested, was not realistic since it was not in consonance with Washington's one-China policy (though one might argue otherwise when looking at the

Taiwan Relations Act as opposed to the Normalization Agreement made by President Carter with the People's Republic of China).

President Lee was to some extent blamed for the Nationalist Party's "defeat" in the 1989 election. He was chided for having promoted confusing policies and was accused of not being able to fill CCK's shoes. As a result, he was challenged in the spring of 1990 when the National Assembly met to select a new president or renew Lee's tenure. In the end, President Lee dealt successfully with the challenge and was elected to a new six-year term (when Lin Yang-kang and Chiang Wei-kuo dropped out of contention), with Li Yuan-tzu as his running mate.

In March 1991, Lee promised to hold a "National Affairs Conference" to debate constitutional issues and other matters that related to the nation's political future. He then announced an end to the state of war with the Communists, thereby de facto recognizing the legitimacy of the government of the People's Republic of China. The "Temporary Provisions" were also ended, giving citizens broader civil and political rights guaranteed in the Constitution.

Notwithstanding the ascendancy of hard-line leaders and a shift to the left politically in China after Tiananmen, cross-strait trade and investment ties were kept on track and grew to the tune of billions of dollars in each category. Reporters and scholars from China were allowed to come to Taiwan, including even those with Chinese Communist Party connections. Proliferating links with China reflected the end of the Cold War and other watershed changes going on throughout the world. Many in Taiwan also perceived that economic blocs were replacing political-military blocs as the basis of a new world order and that relations with China thus had to change. This seemed to offset the trend in Taiwan toward separation from China.

In December 1991, after the Nationalist Party had made concerted efforts for some years, including making changes in the Constitution and employing various means to persuade the "elder parliamentarians" to step down, an election was held for a new, or "second," National Assembly. The Democratic Progressive Party, having created a divisive controversy by putting Taiwan independence in the party platform, which split the party and alienated a sizable number of voters, did not perform well at the polls. The Nationalist Party won, giving it, according to some observers, a "democratic mandate" and public support for its policies it had never before had.

In early 1992, the National Assembly made further revisions to the Constitution but did not resolve the issue of whether the nation should have a directly elected president or not. The Control Yuan was made a semijudicial body, and other reforms were instituted, such as making the provincial governor and mayors of Taipei and Kaohsiung elected officials. The infamous "Black List" was reduced to just a few names, and the Taiwan Garrison Command was dismantled.

In midyear, Taiwan lost formal diplomatic ties with the last important country in East Asia—South Korea. But it compensated for this to some degree with diplomatic accords with several new, albeit small, countries. More importantly, in the context of China acquiring new, sophisticated weapons, Taiwan was able to make purchases of top-of-the-line fighter planes abroad, including F-16s from the United States, thus maintaining some semblance of a balance of forces in the Taiwan Strait. In November, U.S. trade representative Carla Hills visited Taipei, giving the impression of improving U.S.–Taiwan relations, Hills being the first cabinet official to visit Taiwan in thirteen years.

That December, Taiwan held its first nonsupplemental legislative election—to some observers, its most important election ever. The Nationalist Party was split due to the New KMT Alliance faction, led by Jaw Shao-kang advocating a firmer one-China policy than did President Lee and the majority of members of the ruling party. Meanwhile, the DPP had regrouped after its defeat in the December 1991 election, was less divided, and was prepared to compete strongly in the election contest. Vastly improving its position in both the popular vote column and in seats in the new Legislative Yuan, the DPP celebrated victory after the election and talked once again of becoming the ruling party in the near future.

UNDER LEE TENG-HUI, II

Early in 1993, Premier Hau Pei-tsun resigned along with his cabinet, setting a precedent for cabinet dissolution following a legislative election. Hau's departure—some said his sacking by President Lee—however, also signaled a serious polarization in Taiwan politics along ethnic (Taiwanese versus Mainland Chinese) lines. On 10 January, before Hau stepped down, ten thousand protestors took to the streets and called for him to remain in office. Also, some three hundred thousand signed a petition to this effect. Nevertheless, President Lee replaced Hau with Lien Chan, thus making the premiership as well as the presidency Taiwanese. President Lee also picked a new cabinet.

Meanwhile, the new Legislative Yuan began exerting more political clout, passing laws that forced top government officials to disclose their personal finances, cutting presidential office budget requests selectively, and scrutinizing more carefully many government policies. Legislative Yuan members also exercised more authority in their respective parties. This inaugurated a new era of much greater legislative power.

At this time, President Lee experienced much stronger opposition from Mainland Chinese in the Nationalist Party and found it more and more difficult to maintain party unity. In August, before the Nationalist Party convened its Fourteenth Party Congress, several members of the New KMT Alliance, the heart of the Non-Mainstream faction of the Nationalist Party (a conservative wing of the party that advocated stronger allegiance to Sun Yat-sen's teachings, a one-China policy, etc.), announced their departure from the KMT and their decision to form the Chinese New Party.

Some observers said that President Lee was glad to get rid of opposition within the party. The ruling party nevertheless remained split between Mainstream and Non-Mainstream factions that generally reflected ethnicity as well as policy toward China. Still, President Lee was reelected party chairman by the first secret ballot in the party's history, with 82.5 percent of the votes cast (though over three hundred delegates defaced their ballots in protest of Lee's leadership).

Lee also encountered major difficulties in dealing with Beijing. Growing ill feeling toward China, which Lee seemed to encourage, was expressed openly in March 1994 when twenty-four tourists from Taiwan were murdered there in a robbery incident that implicated the military. Beijing first called the matter an accident and then apprehended and immediately executed three young men for the crime in what appeared to be a cover-up to the public in Taiwan. Relations across the Taiwan Strait soured, and Taiwan cut investments on the mainland, while public opinion polls showed the highest support ever for independence.

In the fall, the U.S. government notified the Republic of China's representative in Washington that the United States had decided to allow a name change in Taipei's representative office to Taipei Economic and Cultural Office and would permit its diplomats to visit U.S. government offices, except the Department of State and the White House, on official business. Observers saw this as an upgrading of U.S.–Taiwan relations, which the Clinton administration made under pressure from Congress.

In December, Taiwan held its first election for the governor of Taiwan Province and the first for a number of years for the mayors of its two metropolitan cities, Taipei and Kaohsiung (these offices having been made appointed positions in 1964 and 1976, respectively). The Nationalist Party's candidate, James Soong, was elected governor with President Lee Teng-hui's help. He won by a sizable margin in a campaign that saw ethnicity become an issue (Soong being Mainland Chinese). The KMT's Wu Den-yih won handily in Kaohsiung, which had been a Democratic Progressive Party stronghold. The DPP's Chen Shuibian, however, won the mayorship of Taipei, which was an embarrassment for the KMT. Also, the DPP and the New Party did well in the Taipei City Council race.

In January 1995, Jiang Zemin, president of the People's Republic of China, issued an eight-point proposal for the peaceful reunification of Taiwan with China. The proposal, while both tough and conciliatory, mainly generated a sense of cautious or skeptical optimism in Taiwan regarding relations with the mainland. This feeling was not to last for long though.

In June, President Lee visited the United States where he spoke at the graduation ceremony of his alma mater, Cornell University. The United States had heretofore been unwilling to give Lee a visa; the Clinton administration, however, succumbed to congressional pressure on this matter. The visit was reported on very favorably in the Western media, drawing attention to Taiwan's dearth of official diplomatic representation and to China's efforts to isolate Taiwan diplomatically. The visit was applauded at home and helped to promote Lee's policy of trying to enhance Taipei's international visibility, though Lee drew criticism for being provocative and possibly damaging U.S.–China relations.

Beijing's reaction was quick and hard. Chinese Communist Party leaders bitterly criticized Lee, calling him a traitor, among other harsh and uncomplimentary names. In July, the People's Liberation Army conducted military exercises at home and missile tests in the Taiwan Strait to intimidate Taiwan. Leaders in Beijing were ostensibly angry because they had been lied to by being told by the Department of State that Lee would not be granted a visa; they also saw the visit as mirroring a U.S. policy of containing China and playing the "Taiwan card." Meanwhile, on 28 February, President Lee apologized to victims of the *er er ba*—the 28 February (1947) "uprising"—at a ceremony held at Taipei New Park where a monument commemorating the tragedy was built by the government. This did not endear Lee with Chinese leaders in Beijing either.

In December, the Republic of China held its second nonsupplemental Legislative Yuan election. The campaign was conducted under the shadow of continued People's Liberation Army missile tests, which caused the Taipei stock market to fall and precipitated a run on visas to leave the country. The ruling Nationalist Party lost a significant number of seats, with the New Party making the most gains. Observers linked the election results to Beijing's successful efforts to hurt President Lee's party. The Nationalist Party barely held on to its majority in the legislative branch of government; in fact, this election inaugurated what some called "coalition politics" due to the gains of the other parties and the KMT's subsequent lack of sufficient discipline to control party votes.

On 23 March 1996, Taiwan held the first direct election ever for its president and vice president—a contest that was dubbed "a first in 5,000 years of Chinese history." President Lee Teng-hui represented the ruling Nationalist Party; Peng Ming-min (the "father of Taiwan independence") was the Democratic Progressive Party's candidate; Chen Li-an, who resigned from the KMT, ran as an independent with a female running mate; and Lin Yang-kang ran as an independent but was backed by the New Party with former premier Hau Pei-tsun as his running mate. President Lee and Lien Chan won with 54 percent of the popular vote. The campaign and the election were impacted by additional and even more threatening People's Liberation Army missile tests, this time with live warheads, forcing the temporary closing of two of Taiwan's major ports. The United States responded by sending two aircraft carrier battle groups to the area, the largest U.S. military presence in the area since the Vietnam War, resulting in what many said was a dangerous face-off between the United States and China. Some observers expected war.

In December, a National Development Conference was held in Taipei to debate important political questions facing the nation along with constitutional issues precipitated by the country's extremely rapid democratization. Major constitutional revisions were recommended, including one to eliminate or drastically reduce in size the provincial government. At the same time, promises were made to 302,000 provincial government employees that they would be hired elsewhere. Being the largest landowner, in addition to operating a number of banks and other businesses in Taiwan, provincial government assets were immediately a subject of attention and speculation. Governor James Soong tendered his resignation, which amplified the crisis. Critics said that President Lee sought to reverse the democratic process, give himself more political authority, and promote Taiwan's separation from China.

The return of Hong Kong to the People's Republic of China on 1 July again underscored Taipei's strained relations with Beijing. President Lee rejected China's "one country, two systems" formula for reunification, declaring that Taiwan was different from Hong Kong in that Taiwan possessed sovereignty and could defend itself. The public in Taiwan supported Lee. Chinese officials spoke of Taiwan as the "last territory to be liberated" and pledged that they would do that.

In August, the KMT's Fifteenth Party Congress met in Taipei. President Lee won an even bigger vote than at the Fourteenth Congress to remain party chairman. James Soong, who had meanwhile become (according to the press at least) Lee's enemy, visited the United States during the meeting but received the highest number of votes cast for membership on the party's Central Standing Committee. Lien Chan, at this juncture, stepped down as premier (keeping his position as vice president); Vincent Siew became premier.

In November 1997, the KMT suffered a serious setback in local elections for country magistrates and city mayors to the opposition Democratic Progressive Party, but did well in subsequent local elections and in the election of the Legislative Yuan, the Taipei and Kaohsiung mayorships, and city councils in December 1998. In the meantime, the Taiwan Provincial Government was drastically downsized, and in December 1998 the Provincial Assembly was abolished as well as the governorship.

During 1999 there was widespread speculation whether Lee would run for another term. It was not clear if the time he served as Chiang Ching-kuo's replacement counted toward the two-term limit or not. Anyway, Lee decided he would not run again.

Looking back, Lee's presidency was as eventful as it was controversial. Taiwan came to be seen as a genuine democracy as a result of Lee's pushing democratic reform. For that, he has been called Taiwan's "Mr. Democracy." He oversaw needed constitutional changes and kept the economy on track, even during the "Asian meltdown" in 1997 and 1998. However, ethnic relations, corruption, and relations with China worsened while he was president.

THE CHEN SHUI-BIAN ERA, I

On 18 March 2000, Chen Shui-bian, representing the opposition Democratic Progressive Party, was elected president, ending the Nationalist Party's more than fifty-year governance of Taiwan. Some called it the "consolidation" of Taiwan's democracy. Others said the Taiwanese majority now ruled Taiwan, not the Mainland Chinese minority (because the DPP was a Taiwanese party). Scholars said President Chen represented a "fourth generation" of leaders and spoke of more change and reforms to come. Clearly this was a momentous event, and Taiwan was going to be a different place for it.

How did this happen? Early in the campaign, former governor James Soong led Chen and Vice President Lien Chan (the other two candidates) in the opinion polls by a wide margin. But President Lee Teng-hui, who had come to dislike Soong intensely, did not want him to get the party's nomination and so orchestrated giving it to Lien. Thus, Soong was forced to run as an independent. A Nationalist Party official then released documents showing that Soong had siphoned party money into his own and relatives' bank accounts when he was party secretary-general. Soong, considered more honest than most politicians and lacking a party organization and money, was hurt badly by the charges, and his poll numbers fell.

Lien was not able to exploit Soong's predicament, and the conservative vote split. Chen ran a very clever and spirited campaign, taking advantage of (and exacerbating at times) ethnic ill feelings while provoking China in order to stimulate local nationalism that worked to his favor. Late during the campaign, it was rumored that President Lee perceived that Lien could not win, and because he secretly wanted Chen to be president, he diverted KMT funds to the DPP. Lee Yuan-tzu, head of

Academic Sinica and a Nobel Prize winner in chemistry, along with a number of noted businessmen, jumped on Chen's bandwagon as the voting neared, which also made a critical difference in Chen's chances of winning the election. Ironically, China also helped Chen; Chinese leaders created a backlash by warning Taiwan's voters not to cast their votes for the "candidate of independence" (meaning Chen).

After the election, Soong formed the People First Party (PFP). He and Lien (who became head of the Nationalist Party after Lee was forced to resign because he was blamed for the election defeat) put their differences behind them and joined forces to block President Chen's agenda in the Legislative Yuan. This was easy to do since Chen's party held only one-third of the seats. So Chen resigned from his party and tried to govern as a nonpartisan, populist president. For his premier, he picked Tang Fei, from the Nationalist Party. Most of the members of the cabinet were drawn from other parties than the DPP. But Lien and Soong argued that Chen did not have a mandate, having won less than 40 percent of the popular vote, and that he therefore should not have the broad powers of previous presidents. Chen retorted that he had won the election and was duly elected president and that his challengers opposed democracy.

The opposition also took the position that Taiwan's political system was a parliamentary one and used that to try to marginalize Chen. According to the Constitution, the system was a mixed parliamentary, presidential, and cabinet one, but more parliamentary. However, it had worked as a presidential system before this. Neither side would compromise on this fundamental constitutional question, much less on other issues at hand, and Taiwan's politics became extremely bitter and divisive. Making the situation worse, many in the Chen administration concentrated on settling scores with the previous government and with ethnic groups other than their own. Matters came to a head six months after Chen's inauguration when he canceled a nuclear power plant under construction (Taiwan's fourth) that had been approved by the previous government. The opposition impeached him. The effort did not succeed, however, due to the difficulty in carrying out the process. In the interim, Premier Tang Fei (who supported the plant) stepped down, breaking the record for a premier serving the shortest time in office. The public supported the plant, causing Chen's popularity to plummet. But the opposition's also declined. Pundits at this time said that Chen and his party didn't know how to rule and that the opposition didn't know how not to.

As a result of the severe political gridlock that followed, as well as doubts in the business community about the government's ability to run the country and manage the economy, and apprehension about future energy sources, Taiwan fell into recession. The next year, Taiwan's citizenry witnessed negative economic growth of 2 percent and unemployment that many thought was not possible. The opposition boasted of their past record in promoting growth and condemned Chen for "ruining their economic miracle." They also noted that Chen had caused relations with China to deteriorate by his support of Taiwan's independence and that the China market was the key to Taiwan's economic recovery, with its economy booming and with trade and investment opportunities across the Taiwan Strait burgeoning.

Chen contended that Taiwan's economic downturn was caused by a global recession, especially in high-tech products (which Taiwan's economy depended on), and by KMT and PFP obstructionism. He said that if his party won a majority in the legislature at the end of the year, he would be able to do something, including putting economic growth back on track. By provoking tension with China while appealing to local nationalism and to his ethnic group, and by organizing vote allocation (so that the voting base could be divided equally, enabling weaker DPP candidates to win), the DPP did very well at the polls and became the largest party in the legislature. In the meantime, former president Lee organized a new political party, the Taiwan Solidarity Union (TSU), to entice former KMT members who had supported him or had favored his localization policies to join his party. Lee then pledged his party's support to Chen. The two parties became known as pan-green (the color of the DPP's flag). Meanwhile, the KMT and PFP working in tandem became known as pan-blue (for the KMT's flag). Pan-green did well at the polls but did not attain a legislative majority. Thus the bitter political standoff continued.

The TSU became more supportive of Taiwan's independence as Chen and the DPP took more moderate positions while trying to rule the country. The two pan-green parties also disagreed over Taiwan's growing investments in and other commercial relations with China, with President Chen listening to the pleas of the business community that favored the contacts. The pan-blue parties also had their differences over the PFP's poaching of KMT members and over how to oppose DPP rule. Personalities also divided them. But for the most part, Taiwan was divided politically along a fault line between the two blocs. Occasionally they cooperated and there was some hope of revising Taiwan's odd electoral system that encouraged vote buying and other forms of corruption, cutting the size of the legislature, and several other reforms.

Meanwhile, pan-blue made political hay of Chen's foibles: getting his son into a legal job in the military despite his test scores being too low; his wife's alleged insider trading in the stock market; and, most sensational of all, Chen's alleged tryst with a female aide. The latter made more headlines than it would have otherwise because information about the affair was said to have come from Vice President Lu. She denied it, sued the magazine that reported it, and won. Still, the damage was done, and it underscored her dissatisfaction with being marginalized in the Chen administration.

The Chen government's upside was that it looked well in managing relations with the United States. The George W. Bush administration treated Taiwan much better than the Clinton administration had, and it promised a huge weapons package for Taiwan; and the president, the first lady, and other members of the Chen administration made well-publicized trips to the United States. This, however, was probably more the product of Washington's positive outlook toward Taiwan than clever policies or astute diplomacy on Taipei's part. After all, the new regime experienced a serious problem of a lack of talent to run foreign affairs and encountered serious difficulties with the military (with a number of officers, including pilots, resigning in protest of President Chen's independence views) and the intelligence and security agencies (where there were some highly publicized defections to China). The U.S. military and the intelligence community lamented the weakening of Taiwan's capabilities in these realms, which they considered important assets to the United States.

In late 2002, Ma Ying-jeou was reelected mayor of Taipei, propelling him to the status of a blue-team or Nationalist Party star. Pan-blue, however, lost the mayoral race in Taiwan's second metropolitan city, Kaohsiung; there, Frank Hsieh won reelection.

In July 2003, in the context of continued strained relations between the Chen administration and the People's Republic of China and of Beijing's recent successful efforts to further isolate Taipei diplomatically, President Chen declared publicly that Taiwan was prepared to "go its own way." He followed this with a speech on 3 August, in which he declared that Taiwan and China were two countries on each side of the strait. China reacted with anger to what it considered to be secessionist talk and confirmation that Chen was a true supporter of independence.

Meanwhile, in the spring of 2003, Taiwan was hit hard by the SARS (severe acute respiratory syndrome) epidemic. At first, the Chen administration was criticized for what many called its dysfunctional response and a needless feud between the president and Taipei mayor Ma. China, however, soon became seen as an ogre for blocking the World Health Organization from doing anything in Taiwan and for continuing to nix Taiwan's membership. This, and the fact that proposed "links" between Taiwan and China were not materializing, caused cross-strait relations to deteriorate further.

Referendums became a big issue in anticipation of the 2004 presidential election. A provision for such was in Taiwan's Constitution, but the process had never been defined and required legislation to do so. President Chen wanted to attend to that, but the opposition perceived this to be a ruse to promote independence. The effort was given considerable impetus when, in September, Lee Teng-hui organized a mass rally to "rectify Taiwan's name," suggesting that the island "nation" separate legally from China. Lien and Soong, seeing that the public favored some action on the referendum issue and that the United States was not going to restrain Chen on the matter, pressed their own version of a referendum law. They also shifted their views, stating that the Republic of China has its own sovereignty and that unification and independence are both alternatives for the people of Taiwan. Pan-blue, which controlled the legislature, passed a referendum law, but not one to Chen's liking. It, observers said, "bird caged" pan-green on the issue.

The economy, after seeing some recovery in 2002, continued to perform better in 2003. However, there remained unresolved questions about economic linkages with China and about Taiwan's industrial sector "hollowing out" due to many factories closing and moving to the mainland.

THE CHEN SHUI-BIAN ERA, II

In early 2004, President Chen and Vice President Lu ran for reelection. In the meantime, Lien Chan and James Soong agreed on a common

ticket to defeat them. Lien and Soong calculated that if each could gar-
ner the same portion of the popular vote they received in 2000, they
would win easily. They had split the conservative vote before; now they
would not. Chen's record in office, especially his managing of the economy; scandals; and difficulties with the United States and China constituted handicaps for the incumbent president. The opinion polls, the odds
calculated by those betting on the election, and the movement of the
stocks of companies linked to one camp or the other indicated a pan-
blue victory.

However, on 19 March, the day before the voting, President Chen
and Vice President Lu were both shot while campaigning in Tainan in
southern Taiwan. The incident generated a large sympathy vote facilitated by pan-green's accusing the KMT in collaboration with China of
the "assassination" attempt, especially focusing this tactic on southern
Taiwan, which is more ethnically Fukien Taiwanese and where the population is less educated and less cosmopolitan. Chen and Lu won by a
very small margin.

Pan-blue cried foul, saying that the election had been stolen by the
"staged" shooting, by pan-green's "underhanded" campaign, by Chen's
ordering the military and police (which favored pan-blue) to remain at
their posts so they could not vote, and by election officials who mis-
handled votes in favor of pan-green. Lien and Soong organized massive
protest demonstrations after the election, paralyzing Taipei and other
major cities for days. Pan-blue meanwhile asked for a recount and an
investigation of the shooting.

Pan-blue seemed to have a case. Chen and Lu were not wearing bul-
letproof vests, as they had been earlier in the day. The shooting took
place in Chen's hometown, and police did not cordon off the area after
the event; a child, not the police, found the bullet casings. Chen and Lu
did not go to the nearest hospital but rather one owned by Chen's friend.
DPP officials told the press that a bullet was in Chen's body when it was
inside his coat. And President Chen did not announce that his wound
was only superficial until that night.

Chen calculated that the postelection furor would pass and that Lien
and Soong would become seen as disruptive and as poor losers. He also
knew that pan-blue would have to look for new leaders, and that would
work to his advantage. Indeed pan-blue officials worried that they had
little chance of getting a new election or of having the results of the

election changed, and they had to get ready for the year-end legislative election or suffer another defeat. Many wanted Taipei mayor Ma Ying-jeou or Legislative Yuan speaker Wang Jin-pyng to take over leadership of the Nationalist Party.

Meanwhile, the U.S. State Department declined to send Chen and Lu a message of congratulations, seeing the election as perhaps tainted, and angry with both for not heeding Washington's advice not to provoke China during the campaign. After the election, Theresa Shaheen, director of the American Institute in Taiwan office in the United States, without State Department approval, sent a formal letter congratulating the president and vice president for their election, and for that she was fired (though technically she resigned). Elsewhere, the Pentagon was getting increasingly irritated over Taiwan's not purchasing weapons allocated in 2001 and thus not fulfilling its responsibilities for its defenses and relying too much on the United States (which the election drew attention to since President Chen put the issue to a referendum that lost).

China expressed its disapproval of President Chen and, contrary to what some in the Chen administration said, namely that China would now have to deal with Chen, continued to shun him. Beijing also further augmented its military forces across the Taiwan Strait, in particular with missiles targeted at Taiwan, and maintained its policy of isolating Taiwan by keeping Taipei out of various international organizations and pressuring as many countries as possible not to deal with Taiwan. The Chen administration could do little about either.

Leading up to the December 2004 legislative election, the United States appeared to adopt a "preemptive" policy to keep pan-green from creating tension with China, which Washington found distracting in view of its preoccupation with the Middle East, and unwanted in view of needing China's help in dealing with terrorism, nuclear proliferation, North Korea, and other foreign-policy problems. Going into the informal campaign period, no doubt as a warning to the Chen administration, Secretary of State Colin Powell stated publicly that Taiwan does not possess sovereignty. Pan-green leaders were taken aback, though Powell retracted the gist of what he said later.

As the election approached, Washington kept the pressure on the Chen administration, responding very quickly and critically to his calls for a referendum, a new constitution, and other facets of an independence policy. Beijing kept pretty much silent, not wanting to succor

Chen and pan-green as it had done in the past. The economy was doing better, but uncertainties, especially generated by large investments in China by Taiwan's businesses and exploding trade (with China now the largest destination of Taiwan's exports) did not help pan-green. Residual doubts about the shooting and Chen's legitimacy, social instability, and a host of other problems helped pan-blue win the election. It was a shocking setback for pan-green since President Chen hoped to have a majority in the legislature for the first time. Also, he and other pan-green leaders had loudly predicted that they would win. The loss also represented to some a turnaround for pan-blue after a string of pan-green victories, and it made Chen a lame duck to many observers.

Shortly after the election, as a measure to counter President Chen's support of Taiwan's independence, China's parliament passed a law, the Anti-Succession Law, saying that if Taiwan declared independence, China would employ nonpeaceful measures against the island. This appeared to make it difficult for Chinese leaders, present or future, to take a moderate line on Taiwan. Taiwan strongly opposed the law. The United States expressed dismay at the law but did not seem to be that concerned. European countries spoke against it, but China did not seem to care.

In the spring, both Lien Chan and James Soong made very publicized trips to China where they met top Chinese leaders. The Chen administration tried to label the visits as proof that the two wanted to "sell out" Taiwan. This did not work, as, according to public opinion surveys, the public favored the two going. The business community also did, as it had become increasingly weary of Chen provoking trouble with China, which affected commercial relations across the Taiwan Strait.

In mid-July 2005, Taipei mayor Ma Ying-jeou was elected chairman of the Nationalist Party after Lien Chan announced his retirement. Ma, well educated (Harvard Law degree), good-looking, articulate, and widely known for his honesty, won 70 percent of the vote. His victory helped unify the party and gave it hope for regaining the presidency from the Democratic Progressive Party in 2008.

In December, pan-blue won a huge victory in local magistrate and city council elections. President Chen, who had fallen badly in the polls before the election, did not help his party. Divisions within the Democratic Progressive Party, disagreements with their ally the Taiwan Solidarity Union, serious corruption, charges of abusing civil liberties (especially of foreign workers and foreign wives), perceptions that DPP had undermined press freedom, and a public feeling that pan-green did not know how to govern or manage the economy were also contributing factors.

Subsequently, President Chen reorganized his cabinet and tried to stir up nationalist sentiments by pushing the independence issue again. This did not work. More serious charges of corruption in the Chen administration, including the jailing of his son-in-law and indictments of some of his close aides, not to mention rumors that he and his wife were profiting personally from his presidency, further tainted the Chen administration. It was uncertain whether he could shed that image and how he would rule until he would leave office in 2008.

TAIWAN'S ECONOMIC DEVELOPMENT

Taiwan is known throughout the world as an economic success story, evoking the appellation the Taiwan "economic miracle." Indeed, the country's economic growth from the mid-1960s to 2000, but especially during the first part of that period, was phenomenal as judged by the fact that few if any nations have ever performed so well over such an extended period of time. And Taiwan did this, according to many economists, "against all odds." Thus Taiwan's accomplishments are worthy of study.

When Europeans first arrived in East Asia and shortly after visited Taiwan, the aborigines were engaged in hunting, fishing, berry picking, and some farming. Taiwan was also the base of operations for Chinese and Japanese pirates who engaged in trade with other places in the region. The Dutch, who colonized the island in the seventeenth century, brought oxen and farm implements, created a cash economy, and increased commerce and trade. During the short period of self-rule that followed, economic progress continued. Under Chinese control for the next two-plus centuries, Taiwan's agriculture sector expanded, and significant amounts of rice and sugar were exported to the mainland, though otherwise the economy did not show much progress. Toward the end of the Chinese period, however, successful efforts were made to improve Taiwan's infrastructure and make the economy more productive. Under Japanese rule for a half century prior to the end of World War II,

Taiwan became a modern economy, and the island was more prosperous than any part of East Asia, save Japan.

Nationalist Chinese rule of the island under Governor Ch'en Yi in 1945 saw gross mismanagement of the economy. Ch'en and his corrupt and incompetent officials sought to build a government-dominated "socialist" system. Due to this and the fact that there was a civil war on the mainland and resources from Taiwan were appropriated for that effort, the economy collapsed. The situation became even grimmer in 1949 when Chiang Kai-shek's armies were defeated by the Communists, and Nationalist soldiers and others who could fled to Taiwan along with the government and the party. The number totaled nearly two million. Taiwan was already crowded, and its economy could not easily absorb the influx of people. In fact, because of this, together with a very unfavorable land-to-population ratio, an absence of natural resources, a shortage of capital, and a discredited government, economists viewed the prospects for economic development as dim and even labeled Taiwan a "basket case" with little or no hope of economic growth and prosperity in the foreseeable future.

With the onset of the Korean War in June 1950, the United States decided to protect Taiwan. Washington resumed economic aid, and Taiwan's hapless economic situation changed a bit. U.S. military assistance made it possible for the government to divert funds that were allocated to the armed forces into economic reconstruction. The huge pool of administrative talent that came from China in 1949, sincere efforts by Chiang Kai-shek to reform the ruling party and the government, and the desire of the population to put the economy in a growth mode facilitated economic stability and modest growth.

Soon after, land reform made a major contribution to economic progress. Rent reduction, the sale of public lands to farmers, and a "land to the tiller" law (which forced landlords to sell land to the farmers who used it) made the agricultural sector more efficient and more productive. Agricultural production, in fact, increased by an impressive 14 percent annually in the 1950s. As a result, farmers provided investment capital and released labor for Taiwan's industrialization.

Rapid growth in Taiwan's industrial sector subsequently made the economy "take off," notwithstanding the termination of economic assistance by the United States in 1964. During the late 1960s and 1970s, factories were set up or expanded at such a rate that by 1977 the nation's industrial index was twenty-eight times what it had been in 1950, making the Republic of China again the most industrialized nation in East Asia after Japan. This growth was due to increases in labor productivity, privatization, a high savings rate coupled with large infusions of foreign investment capital, a solid infrastructure, and sustained exporting efforts that took advantage of the international marketplace and the global division of labor (after a short period of an import substitution policy), as well as to intelligent planning by the government and the cooperation of the business community.

A number of key industries can be identified that particularly facilitated the country's industrialization and economic growth. Textiles were the most important early on. Small appliances and sporting goods were two other important ones. Electronics, telecommunications, machine tools, and optical machines followed, along with chemicals, metals, and even steel and shipbuilding. Information products later became a major part of the economy; in fact, Taiwan became the largest producer in the world of keyboards, screens, and other computer parts.

Overall economic growth was very impressive. Taiwan witnessed 8.2 percent average annual increases in the gross national product in the 1950s, and 9.2 percent in the 1960s. In spite of the oil crisis, which hit Taiwan hard in 1973, its economic development for the decade of the 1970s was better than 10 percent. In the 1980s, it was 8.2 percent. Over a period of thirty years, Taiwan recorded more years of double-digit annual growth than any nation in the world. For a decade and a half, Taiwan's economic expansion was double Japan's and more than triple that of the United States. This was not all: uniquely (usually not accompanying growth using the capitalist model), Taiwan experienced improved income equity. Nearly all citizens benefited from Taiwan's economic growth; in fact, income equality soon exceeded that in the United States and Japan. Unemployment, meanwhile, fell from traditionally very high levels to below 2 percent, and Taiwan's foreign exchange position (due to export surpluses and high savings rates) gave it the number-one ranking in the world.

All of this afforded Taiwan a reputation for successful economic development that other countries sought to emulate. Economists and leaders of underdeveloped countries began to examine the keys to Taiwan's economic success. What were the things they noticed? Welcoming foreign capital was a hallmark of Taiwan's economic strategy, including establishing export-processing zones for that purpose. Engaging heavily in foreign trade, notably with Western capitalist countries, was another—thereby refuting dependency theory. Small, family-owned businesses; a high savings rate; privatization; low taxes; business-community-government cooperation; astute and helpful government planning by officials who believed in a free market; large investments in education, research, and development; a strong work ethic; and social stability and low crime rates were all seen as important elements of Taiwan's success.

For several reasons, Taiwan was an even more attractive model of economic growth than the other "Asian tigers"—South Korea, Hong Kong, and Singapore. Hong Kong and Singapore were city-states and too small for their economic development experience to have relevance to most underdeveloped nations. South Korea's growth was built on very large industries, which other countries could not easily copy. Thus Taiwan's economic experience was more widely studied.

While Taiwan experienced slower growth in the 1990s (natural, as its economy became a modern one), it was not hit hard by economic crises that have affected other countries in East Asia. In fact, in 1997, some observers praised Taiwan's economic planners for avoiding the so-called East Asia meltdown and offered this as further proof of the Taiwan economic miracle.

However, in 2001 Taiwan's economy saw a serious economic downturn. This was caused in large part by political paralysis after Chen Shui-bian was elected president and a fight with the opposition that ensued over a nuclear power plant. Meanwhile, the global economy, especially the market for high-tech goods, declined. As a consequence, Taiwan experienced negative growth of 2.18 percent, while unemployment rose to 4.60 percent (5.17 percent in 2002), both unprecedented in recent times.

Taiwan began to recover the next year, with growth reaching 3.59 percent. The GNP increased at a faster rate of 6 percent in 2004, but it dropped to 3.6 percent in 2005, attributed mainly to a decline in investment. Meanwhile, many of Taiwan's premier industries were "hollowing out," with most moving part or all of their operations to China. China by this time had become Taiwan's main destination for investment capital and exports, and with political relations being less than cordial, this presented Taiwan's leaders with a dilemma. Taiwan also witnessed considerable managerial and other talent going to China as well. The government sought to make Taiwan an "Asian hub" or "gateway to China," but Shanghai was increasingly becoming the center of economic action in Asia. Beijing also kept Taiwan out of various regional plans for an economic bloc that might lead to an Asian common market. High labor costs in Taiwan and local opposition to importing foreign workers added to Taiwan's economic woes.

Still, Taiwan's economic fundamentals, such as infrastructure, quality of workers, research and development, competitiveness, transparency, and the like, remained good and indicated that Taiwan's economic future should be propitious. Indeed, many of the factors that explained Taiwan's outstanding performance in the past were still present. Yet Taiwan was not the "economic miracle" it had been, and a return to that kind of growth did not seem likely.

TAIWAN'S DEMOCRATIZATION

Though not occurring as early as its phenomenal economic development, Taiwan has also experienced highly praiseworthy political modernization. Few observers, either in Taiwan or elsewhere, refer to Taiwan's political system as authoritarian anymore. The government of the Republic of China is now seen as a democracy, though some might say it is yet to be consolidated insofar as the democratization process happened so fast, and it has evoked changes that require adjustments and accommodations that are still in progress.

There are generally two views about Taiwan's democratization. One is that it occurred somewhat gradually (though fast compared to other nations) and for a host of reasons. A second is that it happened rather quickly in the mid-1980s due mainly to the appearance of a true opposition political party, the Democratic Progressive Party, and the end of martial law. There is also disagreement about the importance of various forces that engendered democratic change, and about who deserves the most credit for democracy's success (namely whether it happened from the bottom up or from the top down). In any case, the leaders of many developing countries and scholars in both the West and the Third World have seen this process as a model and have even spoken of it as a "political miracle." Indeed, it took place in the face of adversity (a state of war with the People's Republic of China), without a contributing colonial experience (unlike most other democratizing countries), and during a short period of time (unlike most Western democracies).

In addition to Taiwan's being lauded and emulated for its democratization, the process has had other implications. Taiwan's democratization contradicts the idea of one China, or at least unification in the short run, since the political gap between Taiwan and the People's Republic of China has become wider, and many nations of the world support Taiwan's separation based on the fact that it is a democracy and the People's Republic is not. In other words, it would neither be right nor supportive of democracy, which is viewed as the "wave of the future," to destroy Taiwan's accomplishments by forcing Taiwan to become part of China. This presents a special problem for the United States. The United States encouraged and helped (some even say coerced) Taiwan to democratize, yet the United States espouses a one-China policy and finds the "Taiwan issue" a major obstacle in pursuing better relations with Beijing.

This being said, the factors contributing to Taiwan's democratization, as well as important milestones in the process and the special contributions of certain individuals, need to be noted. They all help to understand why Taiwan became a democracy and the implications and lessons to be learned from its success in that process.

Taiwan's geography, say some scholars, is an important factor in its becoming a democratic nation. Taiwan is an island nation with secure frontiers, conditions common to other nations that have become democracies. It is also cut into pieces by mountains, a situation that lent itself to the growth of a feudal culture and a political system that seemed to impede the implanting of the Chinese bureaucratic system on the island. In modern times, feudal systems have made the transition to democracy easier than other systems.

History has also played a role. Taiwan was populated largely by immigrants; the newcomers were individualistic and were willing to try new ways of doing things, including governing themselves. Taiwan then witnessed Western colonial rule (which brought to its people some democratic ideals), self-rule, rule by China, and Japanese colonial rule. Not all of these experiences encouraged democratization, but perhaps the variety of them did. Meanwhile, Taiwan experienced contacts with other peoples in East Asia through trade. All of this made Taiwan quite cosmopolitan and its population more desirous of various freedoms that are either associated with democratic systems or are essential to democratic politics.

The United States played a special role in Taiwan's democratization beginning in 1950. President Truman ordered the U.S. Seventh Fleet to the Taiwan Strait to shield the island from an invasion by Mao's forces. The United States, from that juncture on, became Taiwan's protector. It hardly seems a coincidence that elections were held immediately after Taiwan was secure. America meanwhile encouraged Taiwan's leaders to establish a democratic system. American economic and military assistance also played a role. Both afforded U.S. advisers leverage over the government and the ruling Nationalist Party. Later, after economic assistance ended, Washington's influence remained considerable because arms sales and access to the American market were vitally important to Taiwan. The Taiwan Relations Act, written into law by the U.S. Congress in 1979, contained a provision specifically calling for improved human rights in Taiwan, implying that the United States expected further and faster democratization of its political system. In short, U.S. demands for Taiwan to democratize were a major motivating factor in Taipei's decisions to reform the government, introduce a competitive political party system, end martial law, and much more.

This is not to say that Taiwan's political leaders did not otherwise have cause to democratize. They did. They brought with them from China a democratic constitution that was in large measure based on the U.S. Constitution. It contained the framework for representative institutions, civil and political rights, and elections. Whereas the "Temporary Provisions," or amendments, to this Constitution nullified many of its democratic provisions for some time, there was never any serious attempt by any top leader or official in Taiwan to scrap the Constitution and establish some other kind of political system. Thus the system was an aspiring democracy that was, in reality, authoritarian; but the framework was there for a democracy, and some parts of it in fact worked. As other factors gradually created the impetus for political modernization, the Constitution made the process of democratic change easier.

The Republic of China's ideology or political philosophy also had this effect. Although ancient Chinese thought, including ideas from Confucius and the other early sages, emphasized good government and concern for the welfare and support of the people, the teachings and writings of Sun Yat-sen were more directly relevant. Sun advocated a U.S-style republican political system. He advocated democratization in stages, perceiving that the Chinese people had to be prepared for democracy before it could be implemented. His blueprint, some say, prevented Taiwan from trying to adopt "people's rule" precipitously, as many other developing nations unwisely did. Sun also sought to nourish nationalism and expressed concern about the livelihood of the people. Clearly his political philosophy, which was read by nearly everyone in Taiwan in school or in some other situation, was instrumental in nurturing a democratic political culture.

Another early factor was land reform. In 1950, the government embarked on a program to restrict rents on farmland, to put land into the hands of the farmers who tilled the land, and to facilitate the growth of agriculture through market mechanisms. Taiwan's land reform program succeeded eminently, and as it did it broke the bonds between the peasants and landlords and thus created the basis for local democratic politics. In this connection, some have argued that Taiwan attained democracy "from the bottom up." If this is true, then land reform must be accorded an important place in laying the groundwork.

Similarly, the Nationalist Party, or Kuomintang, undertook to reform itself as soon as it and the government moved to Taiwan. Party leaders realized that they had made serious mistakes that caused them to lose the hearts and minds of the people in China and that they had to rid the party of corruption, nepotism, and other bad traits that would block its effective governance and impede it from winning popular support in Taiwan. The Nationalist Party reformed. And it continued to exercise concern and vigilance lest it lose the confidence of the people. Party leaders also took the view that it was their duty to implement democracy in Taiwan and that, because of factionalism and undemocratic trends in local politics, they had to take the initiative. Thus they argued for "democracy from above." And while their viewpoint contradicted that of many local leaders who said democracy in Taiwan "seeped up," both in fact happened.

The role of Taiwan's economic miracle cannot be overestimated. It contributed to the rise of a democratic political culture and a democratic polity. Many Western scholars have argued that economic growth creates a middle class, promotes urbanization, and facilitates broad educational improvements and many other prerequisites necessary for democracy to work. Taiwan's very rapid growth created these conditions quickly. Growth with equity helped even more. The fact that Taiwan's transition to democracy happened at just the time when the per capita income grew to the point that Taiwan was no longer poor clearly cannot be written off as an unrelated circumstance.

More specifically, according to various opinion polls, the fact that by the 1980s most people identified themselves as middle class can be linked to growth in political participation and civic responsibility. Economic growth fostered this. The same goes for urbanization, which was probably faster in Taiwan during the 1960s and into the 1970s than in any country in the world. This engendered the need for political institutions that responded to the needs and political interests of the new city dwellers. These institutions helped make democracy function. Likewise, advances in education created a population that favored democracy and was prepared to make it work through enlightened participation.

Some also suggest that Taiwan democratized because it had a democratizer. Although Chiang Kai-shek and some other early leaders talked about democracy and laid some of the groundwork, especially economic growth, it was Chiang Ching-kuo who accomplished the most. He rooted out corruption and favoritism. He recruited Taiwanese into the government and the ruling party when they occupied few such positions. He insisted that government agencies respond to public demands and suggestions. He ordered the government to reform. Many say that he gave Taiwan democracy by edict; others contend that he did it by example and was the only person who was sufficiently respected and powerful enough to push the system away from its authoritarian character, and he did exactly that.

Some likewise attribute such a role to Lee Teng-hui, both as Chiang Ching-kuo's successor and as the leader who continued and in many ways furthered his democratization program. Lee oversaw the transition from Mainland Chinese to Taiwanese rule, an important change if Taiwan were truly to be a democracy. He restructured government and made the legislature represent its constituency and the president be a directly elected official. He did much more.

Meanwhile, the rise of an opposition party, first in the form of the *tangwai* (meaning "outside the party" but referring to anti–Nationalist Party independents who gradually organized) and then as the Democratic Progressive Party, was a major contributing factor to Taiwan's democratization. Party competition is said to be a sine qua non for competitive elections and thus for democratization. The DPP, unlike earlier political parties, provided electoral competition. The success of the DPP also pushed Taiwan toward a two-party system, which many say is the best form of party system for democracy. It also did other things. The DPP promoted the participation in politics of many who were, by choice or not, disenfranchised. Its members became active debaters in the parliamentary bodies of government, and the party pushed, often successfully, for democratic reform. Considering its impact and the fact that Taiwan seemed to take a big step forward in the democratization process in the 1980s, it may be justified to say that the DPP played a huge role in Taiwan's becoming a democracy.

Terminating martial law, which was done in 1987, was also a watershed event. Martial law had not only symbolized an antidemocratic government but in many ways had institutionalized it. When it was ended, most people felt that something important had happened. Civil liberties could be exercised, for the Constitution provided such guarantees. The legal system subsequently changed, and so did the media.

Finally, elections have played a central role in Taiwan's transition to democracy. Local elections attracted voter participation in the political system in the 1950s. National elections did so in the 1980s and after. A two-party election in 1986; "victory" (big gains in the popular vote and in seats) by the opposition party in 1989; nonsupplemental or plenary elections in 1991 and 1992 (to the National Assembly and the Legislative Yuan, respectively); and a direct election of the president and vice president in 1996 have been widely acclaimed as pushing Taiwan forward along the path of democratization and (by at least 1996) as making Taiwan a full-fledged and genuine democracy. Last but not least, Chen Shui-bian's election in 2000 is said to have finalized the democratization process.

Chen's presidency, however, brought political gridlock and divisiveness. In fact, it appeared that Taiwan's democratization had become challenged. Perhaps Taiwan had to learn the hard knocks of democratic politics. In any event, it appears that it has. Clearly democratization has meant a lot to Taiwan. Many say it is a "new country." Many say its democratization means that Taiwan should decide its future the same way it picks its leaders, and that it will pick independence. Others say it is a model that China will follow and that cross-strait relations will change. In any event, democratization has been a momentous factor in Taiwan's recent history.

The Dictionary

1992 CONSENSUS (CHIU-ER KUNG-SHIH). A verbal agreement reported to have been reached between **Taipei** and Beijing representatives in November 1992 to the effect that both sides accepted the one-China principle, but each would use its own definition of "China," and that the political problems regarding the meaning of China should not interfere with talks on practical matters. The "consensus" paved the way for the historic **Koo-Wang talks** in Singapore in 1993.

In its first white paper on the **Taiwan** issue published in August 1993, Beijing seemed to violate the agreement when it claimed that there was but one China, whose government is in Beijing, and that Taiwan was an inseparable part of China. It justified this by saying that the "consensus of 1992" applied only to cross-strait relations or dealings between the **Straits Exchange Foundation** and the **Association for Relations across the Taiwan Strait**. In ensuing years, Beijing also seemed to deny the consensus when it stated that Taiwan was part of the People's Republic of China. In 2002, President Chen Shui-bian said no consensus had been reached and there was only a **"spirit of 1992,"** but he asked China to resume talks on that basis. This angered both China and **pan-blue**. Chen noted that there was nothing in writing to prove there was any agreement. He suggested that the two sides had simply agreed to disagree.

President Chen proposed **"three acknowledgments and four suggestions"** as a substitute for the consensus. **Lien Chan**, Su Chi, **Ma Ying-jeou**, and others said that a consensus had indeed been reached and castigated Chen for saying there hadn't. In his **National Day** speech in October 2005, President Chen broached the idea of a "cross-strait code of conduct" and said he was ready to return to dialogue with China on the basis of the consensus. This issue is still contentious.

– A –

ABORIGINES. Called *shan bao* (mountain compatriot) or, more recently, *yuan chu min* (indigenous people) in Chinese, this is the general term for the people who inhabited **Taiwan** prior to the migration of Chinese to the island. There are said to be between eight and twelve main tribes of aborigines (eleven recognized in Taiwan's legal system). The **Ami** is the largest. There is disagreement among experts concerning the place of origin of the aborigines. One theory, the oldest, is that they came from Southeast Asia, probably from the Malay Peninsula area or Indonesia, or alternatively the Philippines. The vocabulary and grammatical structure of the aboriginal languages are very close to Bahasa, the language spoken in Indonesia, Malaysia, and Brunei. Many cultural traits, such as tattooing, identical names for father and son, rule by the old, head-hunting, spirit worship, and indoor burial, probably came from Southeast Asia. These cultural characteristics differ markedly from those found in other parts of Asia, including China, Japan, Korea, India, and elsewhere. Some prehistoric materials found on Taiwan resemble those in China, but these artifacts do not connect with what was mainstream Chinese culture; instead, they are similar to things found among the early non-Chinese people in South China, some of whom migrated to Southeast Asia and possibly Taiwan. Thus the aborigines may have lived in what is now South China before Chinese civilization reached there. Another view is that the various tribes came from different places and that one or more hailed from the north, either north China or Japan. This view is based on certain myths, as well as other evidence. A more recent theory based on DNA evidence is that the links to Southeast Asia, to the Maoris in New Zealand, and to the people of Polynesia stems from the aborigines in Taiwan having gone to these places; thus Taiwan is the origin or contributor rather than the recipient.

In any case, the aborigines constituted a majority of the population in Taiwan until sometime in the nineteenth century and controlled more than half of Taiwan's surface area into the twentieth century. By the end of World War II, however, they constituted less than 2 percent of the population. Currently they number less than 450,000, and their birthrate is below the average in Taiwan. Many aborigines have been assimilated; in fact, it is said that 70 to possibly more than 80 percent of Taiwanese have aboriginal blood (justifying, some say, the contention that Taiwanese are not Chinese). The lowland aborigines have for the most part been assimilated; the mountain aborigines have not been. Most of the latter reside in the mountainous areas of central or eastern Taiwan. Many have lost their language and culture, and those who haven't remain out of the mainstream of society in Taiwan. Most aborigines engage in farming or fishing or make a livelihood from tourism. A large number receive government welfare or subsidies, reflecting the fact that their incomes in general are below average.

Various social problems such as unemployment, alcoholism, and drug use are prevalent among aboriginal tribes. In recent years, aborigines have founded organizations to enhance their political influence and to deal with their problems and their minority status. Serious efforts are being made by some of these groups as well as the government to protect aboriginal languages and cultures, though this contradicts their integration into Chinese society. *See also* ALLIANCE OF TAIWAN ABORIGINES; ATAYAL; BUNUN; KETAGALAN; PINGPU; YAMI.

ACADEMIA HISTORICA (KUO SHIH KUAN). Established in Nanking when the Nationalist government was on the mainland, Academia Historica was started anew on **Taiwan** in 1957. Organized under the **Office of the President**, it is responsible for preserving documents and conducting research on modern Chinese history, especially the Republican period. It also keeps the archives and records of the Office of the President, the **Executive Yuan**, provincial and local governments, and some other official government organs and agencies. It holds over 7.5 million publications and documents, including the **Republic of China**'s **Constitution**. In 2001, Academic Historica began the digitalization of many documents.

ACADEMIA SINICA (CHUNG-YANG YEN-CHIU-YUAN). Considered the **Republic of China**'s top research institution, Academia

Sinica was established in Nanking in 1928 and moved to **Taiwan** (Nankang, about an hour outside of **Taipei**) in 1949. Its basic missions are to conduct research—done by its institutes, of which there are twenty-five—and direct and coordinate research in various institutions and universities in Taiwan. Academia Sinica is a government organization under the **Office of the President**, though in most respects it is considered an independent research organization. The most important body of the organization is the Assembly of Members or "Academics," elected by Chinese scholars of reputation and distinction. The assembly helps choose new members and plans national policy on research and **education**. In 1990, Academia Sinica decided to become a degree-granting institution. **Li Yuan-tseh** was appointed its president in 1993.

ACER GROUP INC. (HUNG CHI). Taiwan's leading computer manufacturing firm and one of the nation's best-known and most highly respected companies. In 1986, the company produced a 32-bit computer before IBM accomplished this feat. In 1992, it integrated a personal computer with consumer electronic technology to produce a multimedia PC called "Acer PAC." By 1997, Acer was the world's seventh-largest computer maker, turning out five million personal computers a year. The company is known in Taiwan for its large **investments** in research and development (5 percent of income) and its unique Chinese democratic-style management. Stan Shih is the founder and current chairman of Acer. Acer publishes the popular magazine *The Third Wave*.

AGRICULTURE (NUNG YEH). In the past, agriculture was the mainstay of Taiwan's **economy**. In fact, historically 90 percent of Taiwan's exports were agricultural goods. Farming was successful due to Taiwan's rich, volcanic soil and plentiful rainfall, so it was the pursuit of most of those who immigrated to Taiwan from China. **Land reform** in the 1950s made Taiwan's agricultural sector more productive and was a boon to farmers. Growth in the agricultural sector in the 1950s was an impressive 14 percent annually, and the sector provided half of the country's foreign exchange earnings and 40 percent of capital accumulation. Greater efficiency in the agriculture sector helped the economy overall, and especially Taiwan's **industry**, by creating a demand for farm machinery and other goods and by releasing labor to the industrial sector of the economy.

In the 1960s, however, agriculture became a declining sector of the economy. Productivity increases were only 4.5 percent, declining to 3 percent in the 1970s and 2 percent in the 1980s and early 1990s. Agriculture continues the slide, many say seriously. The main problems have been high production costs, small farms (1.64 hectares per household in 2003), and Taiwan's accession to the **World Trade Organization** (which requires Taiwan to reduce tariffs in many areas, most importantly on agricultural goods). In fact, Taiwan's exports are now only 2 percent agricultural products, while it imports large amounts of food—more than it exports. Meanwhile, agriculture has come to account for only around 2 percent of the gross national product. The farm population has declined from around 40 percent of the total in 1975 to just over 10 percent now, while less than 20 percent of farmers' income comes from agricultural activities.

Rice, which was the main crop grown by Taiwan's farmers, is in decline, as it cannot compete with foreign rice in price. Sugarcane and tea growing have decreased, as has raising livestock. Aquaculture has been growing. Farmers growing vegetables and fruits are doing better than other farmers since foreign competition is less threatening. Still, agriculture does not have a good future in Taiwan and will likely continue to shrink as a portion of the economy. Farmers' incomes have declined, though this has been offset to some degree by their engaging in farming only part time and by the increasing value of their land. The government has helped farmers adjust to foreign competition, but this is mainly in the form of developing new crops or moving into other professions. *See also* TRADE.

AKASHI MOTOJIRO. Governor-general of **Taiwan** from 1918 to 1919. Under his rule, Taiwan became regarded as a "home territory" of Japan.

ALLIANCE OF TAIWAN ABORIGINES (T'AI-WAN YUAN-CHU-MIN LIEN-MENG). An organization formed in 1984 to represent and enhance the political power of **aborigines**. Some say it was the first civil rights or minority rights organization in Taiwan.

AMERICAN CHAMBER OF COMMERCE IN TAIPEI (TAI-PEI MEI-KUO HSIANG-HUI). Known to most people as AmCham, it is the main organization representing U.S. business interests in **Taiwan**. AmCham publishes the magazine *Topics*, which assesses the local business climate and U.S. and other foreign operations in Taiwan. It also publishes an annual white paper on the Taiwan business environment that in recent years has strongly recommended greater economic ties with China.

AMERICAN INSTITUTE IN TAIWAN (AIT) (MEI-KUO TSAI T'AI HSIEH-HUI). A nonprofit organization incorporated in the District of Columbia in the United States in 1979, its purpose was to supplant the formal organizations, including those in the Department of State, that maintained diplomatic and other relations between the United States and the **Republic of China**. Headquartered in Roslyn, Virginia, it has field offices in **Taipei** and **Kaohsiung**. The heads of the branch offices (the main one being in Taipei) have often been drawn from the Foreign Service, though they assume leave status when at their post. The budget for AIT is a line item in the Department of State's budget, and it receives operating and other instructions through the assistant secretary of state for Asian and Pacific affairs. U.S. employees working for AIT in Taiwan have "functional immunity," meaning they cannot be arrested or tried for acts carried out in connection with their jobs. AIT, in essence, functions as a U.S. embassy and consulate. The Republic of China's counterpart of AIT in the United States was the **Coordination Council for North American Affairs**, which took the name **Taipei Economic and Cultural Representative Office** in 1994.

AMI (AH MEI). A tribe of lowland **aborigines** once inhabiting the coastal area of eastern **Taiwan**, the Ami lived in large settlements, often of more than one thousand, and sometimes two thousand. The Ami had large families, generally ruled by women, with a clan frequently headed by a maternal uncle and the tribe led by the eldest man. They lived in huts constructed of bamboo, straw, reeds, and lumber. The Ami is the only tribe that has preserved pottery making. The Ami tribe is the largest aboriginal group; today the Ami constitute about one-third of the aboriginal population.

ANDO RIKICHI. The nineteenth and last Japanese governor-general of **Taiwan**. Ando, an army general, served from December 1944 to the end of World War II.

ANDO SADAYOSHI. Governor-general of **Taiwan** from 1915 to 1918, he, like his predecessor, was a soldier and was not trained to run a civilian government. He did not, however, rule brutally, as General **Samata Sakuma** had.

ANTI-SUCCESSION LAW (FAN FEN-LIEH KUO-CHIA FA). A law passed by the National People's Congress in China in March 2005 stating that China "in the event that the **Taiwan** independence forces should act under any name or by any means to cause the fact of Taiwan's secession from China, or that major incidents entailing Taiwan's secession from China should occur, or that possibilities for a peaceful reunification should be completely exhausted, that [the] state shall employ non-peaceful means and other necessary measures to protect China's sovereignty and territorial integrity." At the time it passed, many in Taiwan viewed the law as a threat, and there was public protest against it. The U.S. Congress also voiced opposition to the law, with some saying the law conflicted with Article 2 of the **Taiwan Relations Act**, which states that the United States would view any nonpeaceful effort to decide Taiwan's future as a threat to peace and security in the Pacific area. Observers said passage of the law reflected China's concern about President **Chen Shui-bian** moving Taiwan toward separation. Still others said it was China's response to America's Taiwan Relations Act and its often being cited by the United States during talks centering on Taiwan. Some said it was the product of a split between civilian and military leaders in China over the "Taiwan issue" or that it was passed to placate or please the military.

APOLLO **(WEN HSING).** A reformist literary periodical published from 1957 to 1965. **Li Ao** was a contributing writer for some time. *See also* MEDIA.

APPLE DAILY **(P'ING-KUO JIH-PAO).** One of the newest but most popular **newspapers** in **Taiwan** started by a joint venture between

Next Media in Hong Kong and several Singapore companies. Its reporting is considered more colorful but also sensational compared to Taiwan's other papers. *See also* MEDIA.

ARMED FORCES (CHUN TWEI). Taiwan did not have a meaningful independent military in the past under Chinese or Japanese rule. After 1945, the number of soldiers in Taiwan was fairly small, though it increased considerably in size in 1949, after which Taiwan's military was around 600,000 strong. The standing military was reduced in size to 500,000 in 1985, and it is now less than 350,000. The army is much larger than the other two branches of the service, accounting for around 60 percent of military personnel.

The Military Service Act makes males at the age of eighteen liable for military service, though the draft does not necessarily require regular military service, and it may be gotten rid of in the future. In 2004, the Ministry of National Defense announced that it was aiming at an all-volunteer military. The next year, the length of service was reduced to one and a half years. In 2004, the military accounted for 16.39 (24.5 in 1995) percent of the national budget and 2.5 (3.69 in 1995) percent of the gross national product, both figures having decreased appreciably in recent years.

In the earlier years after 1949, the military's paramount mission was to reconquer the mainland, but this gradually changed to defending the island and other territories belonging to the **Republic of China**. China is Taiwan's sole enemy, and it is a formidable one, and for that reason Taiwan's military must rely on the United States for help in the event that it is attacked. The United States was committed in the **United States–Republic of China Defense Treaty** and, according to many observers, is now by the **Taiwan Relations Act**. In the past, Taiwan's biggest worry was maintaining air superiority over Taiwan and the **Taiwan Strait**. More recently it has to provide a defense against China's increasing number of missiles. Taiwan has put considerable money into missile defense, but many feel this is futile.

Thus there has been talk of attaining deterrence capabilities against China in the form of weapons of mass destruction. It has been reported on numerous occasions in the past that Taiwan was building a nuclear weapon, and in the 1980s the United States stopped the most advanced nuclear weapons project by kidnapping one of its nuclear scientists, after which it put pressure on Taipei to desist, and the government said it did. In recent years, there has been talk of needing and building weapons to bomb cities in China and even the Three Gorges Dam to counter the Chinese missile threat.

The morale of the military has been considered good, but after **Chen Shui-bian** became **president**, a number of Air Force officers resigned in protest over his support of independence, and now morale is questioned.

ART (YI SHU). The earliest art forms in **Taiwan** consisted of aboriginal wood carving and weaving and was reflected also in architecture. During the Chinese era, folk art, temple art, wood-block painting, and puppetry were popular, in addition to Chinese painting and calligraphy. During the Japanese period, impressionism (which came from France through Japan) was popular, as well as art that reflected Taiwan's uniqueness and its natural beauty. After World War II, Chinese painting, especially ink painting, landscapes, and calligraphy (which **Chiang Kai-shek** liked) became popular. In the 1960s, abstract art became popular, and in the 1970s, nativist art. Recently, art in Taiwan reflects a multitude of themes and is expressed through plastic art, ceramics, and seal (chops) carving. The **National Palace Museum** is a repository of both art from China and that produced in Taiwan. Art festivals and art galleries have meanwhile flourished.

ARTICLE 100 (HSING-FA YI-PAI T'IAO). A provision in the **Republic of China**'s criminal code dealing with domestic criminal violence, which states, "If any person behaves as if he or she intends to destroy the national polity, steal or take over national property, use illegal means to change the nation's constitution, or actually carries out these intentions, then that person has committed a crime of domestic criminal violence." This was frequently used by the **Taiwan Garrison Command** to arrest, charge, and imprison critics of the government. Even after **martial law** was terminated, this provision was kept and was said to discourage political protest and free speech. In 1991, **Jaw Shau-kong** and others called for its revision since it undermined constitutional protections of freedom of thought and speech. Many **Democratic Progressive Party** leaders said it should be abolished.

In 1992, it was revised such that if there is no violence or threatening behavior, there can be no punishment for causing domestic upheaval. Several dissidents were immediately released from prison after the revision was passed into law. Some said its revision created a new era of political freedom in Taiwan.

ASIA AND THE WORLD INSTITUTE (YA-CHOU YU SHIH-CHIEH-SHE). A nonprofit think tank located in Taipei with interests in both domestic and global affairs. **Han Lih-wu** founded it in 1976.

ASIAN DEVELOPMENT BANK (ADB) (YA-CHOU K'AI-FA YIN-HANG). Established in 1967 with its headquarters in Manila, the **Republic of China** was a founding member along with a number of other Asian nations, plus Belgium, the United Kingdom, Italy, the Netherlands, Switzerland, the United States, and West Germany. After Taipei lost its membership in the World Bank and the International Monetary Fund, the ADB became the most important international organization in which Taiwan participated. In 1983, the People's Republic of China asked to join and demanded that the Republic of China be expelled. Taipei, however, was in a stronger position to resist Beijing's demands than in other international organizations inasmuch as it was a founding member and because the organization was established after the government of the Republic of China moved to Taiwan. Also, Taiwan donated considerable money to the bank. Finally, Washington supported Taipei's remaining in the ADB. In fact, in November 1983, the U.S. Congress passed an amendment to an appropriations bill stating that it was "the sense of Congress" that Taipei should remain a member. Chinese officials in Beijing at the time accused the United States of trying to create **two Chinas**.

In May 1985, the U.S. Senate passed another resolution stating that the Republic of China should not have to change its name to stay in the ADB, but the White House did not act accordingly. In fact, ADB officials decided that the name Republic of China could not be used and instead adopted the title "Taipei, China." Officials in Taiwan complained that the change was made without their permission and protested. In subsequent meetings, Taiwan's officials attended under that title but used the name "Republic of China" on signs and in other places. Some regarded this as evidence of Taiwan's diplomatic revival and the success of its **pragmatic diplomacy**. Others saw it as a precedent for dealing with the issue of two Chinas. In early 1989, Finance Minister **Shirley Kuo** attended an ADB meeting in China, the first time a government official from Taiwan attended any high-level meeting there. Some observers at the time predicted this would set a precedent for further Beijing–Taipei contacts in a formal setting, but that did not happen. In recent years, there have been disputes over the representative Taiwan sends (China complaining that it should not send a "political" person), but Beijing's and Taipei's officials continue to meet at ADB meetings.

ASIAN PACIFIC ANTI-COMMUNIST LEAGUE (APACL) (YA-T'AI FAN-KUNG LIEN-MENG). Originally founded in June 1954 in South Korea by **Chiang Kai-shek**, Syngman Rhee, and Elpidio Quirino under the name the Asian People's Anti-Communist League, it constituted a response to the need for a regional alliance against the threat of Communism. Its name was changed in 1984. From eight original chapters, it expanded to thirty-four, including some in Middle Eastern countries. The secretariat, originally in Saigon, moved to Taipei. The organization sponsored conferences and publications. In 1979, it established the Asia Youth Anti-Communist League, which subsequently in 1986 changed its name to Asia Youth Freedom League. APACL later evolved into a global organization, the **World Anti-Communist League**.

ASIA–PACIFIC ECONOMIC COOPERATION (APEC) (YA-T'AI CHING-CHI HO-TSO HUI-YI). A regional organization, sometimes called a forum, established to promote economic ties among Asian countries. The **Republic of China** joined in 1991 as "Chinese Taipei" along with the People's Republic of China and Hong Kong. APEC is one of the few important governmental international organizations to which Taiwan belongs and is unique for being one where representatives of Taipei and Beijing meet. Membership in APEC is said to have facilitated Taiwan's joining the **World Trade Organization**. In recent years, there have been disputes with China about whom Taiwan could send to APEC meetings and other matters.

ASIA–PACIFIC REGIONAL OPERATIONS CENTER (YA-T'AI YING-YUN CHUNG-HSIN). A plan approved by the government of the **Republic of China** in January 1995 and supported by President **Lee Teng-hui** to turn Taiwan into a regional business center or hub for large companies. At first the emphasis was on telecommunications and manufacturing. The idea reflected Taiwan's economic orientation toward the Pacific Rim region as a competitor with the North American Free Trade Association and the European Union. The plan envisioned six subcenters: for manufacturing, telecommunications, financial services, air transportation, sea transportation, and media services. The **Council for Economic Planning and Development** was to be responsible for the planning and coordination of the projects, though operations centers are handled by the Ministry of Economic Affairs, the Ministry of Transportation and Communications, the Ministry of Finance, the **Central Bank of China**, and the **Government Information Office**. In March 1995, the Council for Economic Planning and Development established the Coordination and Service Office for the Asia–Pacific Regional Operations Center to attract international companies to take advantage of the opportunities provided by the center.

In fact, several large global corporations have expressed a strong interest in Taiwan or have set up or expanded operations there. President **Chen Shui-bian** has supported the idea of making Taiwan a commercial hub for foreign companies doing business elsewhere in East Asia. But he has not gotten any cooperation from China to do this; rather, Chinese leaders are promoting Shanghai as the area's business center.

ASSOCIATION FOR PUBLIC POLICY STUDIES (APPS) (KUNG-KUNG CHENG-TSE YEN-CHIU-HUI). A political association of opposition politicians, which, in the spring of 1986 under **You Ching**'s leadership, began to organize branches and behave like a political party. Some saw it as a further step in a process whereby the *tangwai* became a de facto political party. APPS's precursor organization, the Association of Tangwai Elected Officials for the Study of Public Policy, was formed in 1984 and changed its name to broaden its base of support. In 1986, some **Nationalist Party** officials and government leaders called for banning APPS, but that did not happen.

ASSOCIATION FOR RELATIONS ACROSS THE TAIWAN STRAIT (ARATS) (HAI-HSIA LIANG-AN KUAN-HSI HSIEH-HUI). A semiofficial organization connected to the government of the People's Republic of China established in December 1991, ARATS is responsible for conducting "negotiations" or talks with Taiwan, particularly with its "counterpart" the **Straits Exchange Foundation**, on a variety of nonmilitary issues. In November 1992, the two organizations agreed that each side could assume its own view of the one-China principle. (*See* 1992 CONSENSUS.) Subsequently, in 1993, the **Koo-Wang talks** were held in Singapore. **Wang Daohan** headed the organization until his death in 2005.

ASSOCIATION FOR TAIWAN INDEPENDENCE (TU-LI T'AI-WAN HUI). An organization founded in 1967 by Taiwanese living in Japan, it advanced the idea of Taiwan's independence. It also advocated socialism. It was founded by **Shih Ming**.

ASSOCIATION FOR THE STUDY OF CHINA'S LOCAL SELF-GOVERNMENT (CHUNG-KUO TI-FANG TSE-CHIH YEN-CHIU-HUI). An organization formed in 1958 by Taiwanese politicians to reform what they charged were corrupt electoral politics in Taiwan. The organization was not approved by the government. In 1960, a number of its members joined **Lei Chen** to form the **China Democratic Party**.

ASSOCIATION OF TAIWANESE CULTURE (T'AI-WAN WEN-HUA-HUI). An organization of Taiwanese political activists formed in 1921 that sought to oppose Japanese rule. However, the membership split due to disagreements among nationalists, reformists, and socialists who subsequently went in different directions. Some members of the association left and founded the **Party of Taiwanese People**, which emphasized social reform through lobbying rather than class conflict.

ATAYAL (TAI YA). One of the high-mountain **aborigine** groups in Taiwan, which until recent times had been warlike and practiced head-hunting.

ATOMIC ENERGY COUNCIL (YUAN-TSE-NENG WEI-YUAN-HUI). A cabinet-level agency founded in 1955 and attached to the **Executive Yuan**, it is empowered to deal with safety regulations, protection from radiation, and radioactive waste disposal; to conduct research in nuclear science; and to probe sources of nuclear energy.

AUGUST 23 BATTLE (PA-ER-SAN PAO-CHAN). The battle between Nationalist and Communist forces, which started the second Offshore Islands Crisis in 1958. It began with an artillery bombardment of **Quemoy** from the mainland, which lasted for forty-four days.

AUGUST COMMUNIQUÉ (PA-YI-CH'I KUNG-PAO). An agreement between the governments of the United States and the People's Republic of China concluded on 17 August 1982, wherein the United States agreed not to maintain a "long-term policy of arms sales to **Taiwan**" and pledged that weapons sales would "not exceed, in either qualitative or quantitative terms, the level of those (arms) supplied in recent years," but reiterated its policy of a peaceful solution only to the Taiwan question. Some interpreted the communiqué as both dangerous and detrimental to Taiwan. Others said it was merely an effort on the part of the U.S. government to help Deng Xiaoping, who at the time was under fire from hard-line leftists who were making trouble over the "Taiwan question," charging that Deng had done little to bring about reunification and in the course of building close relations with the United States seemed to make "bringing Taiwan back into the fold" less likely.

Immediately after the agreement was negotiated, President Ronald Reagan said he assumed that China had made a pledge of seeking only a peaceful solution to the Taiwan matter. But Deng said he had not. The communiqué was not signed, and Department of State officials later said that it did not have standing in international law. Subsequently, U.S. arms sales to Taiwan continued and even at times increased, though U.S. officials said this could happen due to inflation and it did not violate the communiqué. Notwithstanding questions about the status of the agreement and charges that the United States was not fulfilling its provisions, U.S. officials cited the document as one of the three U.S. communiqués that served, together with the **Tai-**

wan Relations Act, as the formal underpinnings of America's China and Taiwan policy.

The August Communiqué was blatantly violated and, some said, nullified by President George H. W. Bush's decision in late 1992 to sell F-16 fighter aircraft to Taipei, and the Clinton administration's subsequent delivery of the planes and other weapons to Taiwan. On the other hand, neither U.S. nor Chinese officials said this, though both at times have suggested that the large U.S. arms sales to Taipei in 1993 and after contradicted or undermined the agreement.

In 1996, when China conducted missile tests in the Taiwan Strait, several members of Congress declared that the Taiwan Relations Act was to be regarded as having a higher status than this or any of the other communiqués and pushed for even more arms deliveries to Taipei. No effort, however, was made to nullify the communiqué. In 2001, after the EP-3 Incident, when President George W. Bush announced another large sale to Taiwan, the August Communiqué was mentioned, and many observers said it was violated. But again the governments of neither the United States nor China stated this.

Some say U.S. efforts (or policy) to maintain a force balance in the Taiwan Strait explains why the United States can sell large quantities of weapons to Taiwan and not undermine the communiqué. Others say that both the United States and China want to keep the communiqué and have no reason to repudiate it.

– B –

BANKING (YIN-HANG CHIEH). Banking and finance in Taiwan are under the control of the **Central Bank of China** (CBC), which took over general management and control functions over banking in 1961 and requires banks to keep a minimum of legal and cash reserves with it, issues notes and is in custody of the nation's gold and foreign currency reserves. It also controls the credit market, the nation's currency value, foreign **investments**, and much more. Coinciding with Taiwan's rapid economic development, banking grew and prospered, including both local and foreign banks. In the early 1990s, regulatory liberalization saw the number of local banks increase rapidly, after which the government encouraged mergers. Taiwan's efficient and transparent banking industry was given credit for the nation's not being influenced by the "Asian meltdown" in 1997, which adversely affected some other countries in the region.

BASHI CHANNEL (PA-SHIH HAI-HSIA). Channel separating Taiwan and the Philippines, about 230 miles wide at its narrowest point.

"BLACK LIST" (HEI-MING-TAN). A list of persons barred from leaving or entering the **Republic of China**. The government long contended that the list was kept for national security reasons and was legal according to Article 3 of the **National Security Law**, which states that persons suspected of endangering national security or social stability will not be allowed to leave or enter the country. Opposition politicians claimed that the list was composed chiefly of opponents of the government or the ruling party, including political dissidents, and was not useful as a security measure. They also pointed out that the U.S. Department of State's human rights reports frequently cited and condemned the black list, giving the numbers each year of people affected by it. Controversy over the black list diminished in the late 1970s and early 1980s as it was cut in size and as its use declined in importance. In July 1982, Interior Minister **Wu Poh-hsiung** said the number on the list had been reduced from 282 to 5. The black list is still used, but now it includes only the names of people living in other countries involved in criminal activities who are *persona non grata* in the Republic of China.

BO YANG (1920–). Pen name for Kuo Yi-tung, a journalist and writer who was arrested in 1968 after drawing an uncomplimentary cartoon of **Chiang Kai-shek** that depicted a conflict between him and his son **Chiang Ching-kuo**. At his trial, he was also accused of trying to obtain classified military information and of persuading a friend to remain in China rather than flee to Taiwan. He was convicted and sentenced to death. The penalty was later reduced to an eighteen-year sentence, of which he served nine. In 1986, he wrote the very controversial book *The Ugly Chinese People*, which was highly critical, many said insulting, of Chinese people. The book was banned in China but not in Taiwan. In 1992, Bo Yang said that the **Republic of China** was the freest society in Chinese history. President **Chen Shui-bian** appointed him a presidential adviser, but in 2004 he criticized Chen for forcing constitutional reforms that could kill the young democracy and said that the **Democratic Progressive Party** was responsible for the present political turmoil.

BREAKFAST CLUB (TSAO-TSAN-HUI). A group of **Nationalist Party** legislators and other leaders who in the late 1980s offered a more progressive alternative to ruling party policies. This party "faction," as some called it, was led by legislator **Jaw Shau-kong**. It was later replaced by the **New KMT Alliance**.

BROADCASTING CORPORATION OF CHINA (BCC) (CHUNG-KUO KUANG-PO KUNG-SZU). Established in 1950, BCC grew from a few stations to 33 broadcasting networks and 177 stations by 1985. It became the largest broadcasting system in Taiwan, with one-third of Taiwan's radio frequencies and ten television channels. BCC sponsored Voice of Free China and Voice of Asia programs that were broadcast in Chinese and a number of other languages in short and medium wave to China and overseas. In 1996, the **Legislative Yuan** passed the Central Broadcasting System Statute that merged BCC's Voice of Free China with the **Central Broadcasting System**. *See also* MEDIA.

BROTHERHOOD ASSOCIATION (LAO-KUNG LIEN-MENG). A grassroots labor organization formed in the late 1980s from nine small **labor unions**, mostly in the chemical and fiber industries in northern Taiwan. It was Taiwan's first labor federation not affiliated or associated with the **Nationalist Party**.

BUNUN (BU NUNG). One of the high-mountain **aborigine** groups in Taiwan that resides mainly in the central part of the island. Until recent times, the Bunun tribe had been warlike and had practiced headhunting. The tribe was known for its extraction of certain teeth as a sign of social identity and adulthood.

– C –

CAIRO DECLARATION (K'AI-LUO HSUAN-YEN). A proclamation issued following the Cairo Conference in 1943 attended by

President Franklin Roosevelt, Prime Minister Winston Churchill, and President **Chiang Kai-shek.** The declaration stated that "territories Japan has stolen . . . such as Manchuria, **Formosa**, and the **Pescadores** would be returned to their rightful owners." Soviet leader Joseph Stalin accepted these provisions at the subsequent Teheran Conference, and the parties confirmed the agreement at the Potsdam Conference in July 1945. Some say the Cairo Declaration was the legal basis for the **Republic of China**'s claim to Taiwan or, by extension (meaning a successor government), the People's Republic of China's claim—though the latter interpretation is not seen as having a strong legal standing. Independence advocates argue that since the Cairo Declaration was simply a wartime statement and furthermore was not signed, it did not legally transfer Taiwan to the Republic of China, and therefore Taiwan's legal status was, and is, undecided.

CAMPAIGN ASSISTANCE COMMITTEE (HOU-YUAN-HUI). An organization of opposition political candidates who were active in or participated in national elections in 1980, 1983, and 1986, and through which non-KMT candidates endorsed and assisted fellow opposition candidates. This made it possible for *tangwai* politicians to have some of the advantages of belonging to a political party. Thus some called *tangwai* at this time a proto–political party. Others said it was an illegal organization, since there was a ban against forming new **political parties**.

CATHAY FINANCIAL HOLDINGS (KUO-T'AI CHIN-OU KUNG-KU KU-FEN-HSIEN KUNG-SZU). Taiwan's largest business financial holding by assets, valued at US$66.8 billion in 2004. It serves over ten million customers. Cathay Life Insurance, which is part of the group, is Taiwan's top life insurance company. The company also owns considerable expensive real estate.

CC CLIQUE (CC-PAI). A powerful faction in the **Nationalist Party**, active both before and after its move to Taiwan in 1949. "CC" refers to the two Chens: **Chen Li-fu** and **Chen Kuo-fu**.

CENTRAL ADVISORY COMMITTEE (CAC) (CHUNG-YANG P'ING-YI WEI-YUAN-HUI). An elite group of members of the

Nationalist Party chosen at a meeting of the **Party Congress** every four years. This body serves to advise the party on a variety of issues, but it is often seen as a party organization for retaining elder members and former party leaders. In 1996, the number of members of the CAC was increased to 286. In 2005, the CAC supported **Wang Jyn-ping** over **Ma Ying-jeou** for chairman of the party, thinking that Ma was too young and that he advocated too much reform.

CENTRAL BANK OF CHINA (CBC) (CHUNG-YANG YIN-HANG). An organ of the central government attached to the **Executive Yuan** that is responsible for regulating **banking** operations and maintaining monetary stability. It also governs money supply and interest rates. In 1992, it set up its first overseas office in New York, mainly to acquire financial information. After 1994, CBC approved most foreign exchange derivative products. In late 1995 and early 1996, CBC took measures to protect the NT dollar and wedded it to the U.S. dollar at a rate of 27.5 to 1, though during the subsequent "Asian meltdown" it allowed the NT dollar to float downward a bit. After 2001, CBC took an accommodative monetary stance to stimulate domestic demand in the face of low growth. It cut the discount rate twenty-five points in mid-2003 to stimulate the **economy** after the SARS epidemic.

CENTRAL BROADCASTING SYSTEM (CBS) (CHUNG-YANG KUANG-PO TIAN-T'AI). A large radio broadcasting organization with short- and medium-wave transmitters, which broadcasts to both Taiwan and China about political, economic, social, educational, and other issues. CBS broadcasts mainly in **Mandarin**, but also in several Chinese **dialects**. In 1996, CBS merged with the Voice of Free China, which was part of the **Broadcasting Corporation of China**. *See also* MEDIA.

CENTRAL COMMITTEE (CHUNG-YANG WEI-YUAN-HUI). A 232-member body of the **Nationalist Party** that makes decisions when the **National Party Congress** is not in session. It was originally chosen through secret ballot by delegates to the National Party Congress at meetings held every four years. Its functions include the execution of National Party Congress resolutions, administering party affairs, appointing and training party cadres, and enforcing party discipline. In reality it is considered more powerful than the National Party Congress, but since it usually meets only once a year in plenary session, it is not the center of power in the ruling party. It "elects" (from a list of people recommended by top party leaders) a **Central Standing Committee**, which is widely regarded to be the center of authority and is made up of Taiwan's most powerful political leaders. In recent years, picking Central Committee members has been more open and democratic. The **Democratic Progressive Party** is organized in a similar way to the Nationalist Party and also has a central committee. Thus, the term now refers to either party's body.

***CENTRAL DAILY NEWS* (CHUNG-YANG JIH-PAO).** A newspaper in Taiwan formerly owned and operated by the **Nationalist Party**. It was founded in China in 1922 and moved to Taiwan in 1949. During the 1950s and 1960s, it was Taiwan's dominant paper. Its circulation later declined appreciably due to democratization, which brought more **media** competition to Taiwan. In 2003, it shifted its emphasis from news and general interest items to culture and **education**.

CENTRAL ELECTION COMMISSION (CEC) (CHUNG-YANG HSÜAN-CHU WEI-YUAN-HUI). Formed in 1980, the CEC is an organ of the central government attached to the **Executive Yuan**, with responsibility for supervising national and local elections. This includes screening candidates, determining qualifications for office, recalling elected officials, and drafting or amending election laws. The **Public Officials Election and Recall Law** delineates its functions. The CEC is headed by a chairman. Members called commissioners are nominated by the **premier** and are approved by the **president**, and they serve for a six-year term. The CEC's activities and rulings during election campaigns have often been controversial and have frequently been criticized by candidates. The CEC also has the function of announcing referendums.

CENTRAL NEWS AGENCY (CNA) (CHUNG-YANG T'UNG-HSÜN-SHE). Taiwan's oldest and largest news agency and its only national and international news service, CNA was founded in China in 1924 and moved to Taiwan in 1949. Prior to 1973, when it became a private corporation, it was both owned and operated by the **Nationalist Party**. In 1996, CNA was reorganized and became a state-run corporation. It operates twenty-four hours a day and maintains a number of overseas offices and overseas correspondents. CNA began computerized Chinese-language transmissions in 1983, and English transmissions in 1984. CNA provides audiovisual news services to local radio and cable television stations. It also provides news over the Internet to Chinese and English-language **newspapers** daily. It has recently established CNAvista.com, a portal to 1.2 million pictures taken over a period of eight decades. CNA also publishes a monthly magazine, *CNA News Show*. In the absence of diplomatic ties with many nations of the world, it functions as a quasi-official link between the **Republic of China** and some other countries. *See also* MEDIA.

CENTRAL REFORM COMMITTEE (CRC) (CHUNG-YANG KAI-TSAO WEI-YUAN-HUI). Formed in July 1950 to overhaul the basic structure of the **Nationalist Party** in the wake of the Nationalist defeat by the Communists, its main goals were to get rid of factionalism in the party, restore control over the **Legislative Yuan** and the **Control Yuan**, and improve party discipline. The CRC was composed of sixteen young, well-educated, and able Nationalist Party members who were loyal to **Chiang Kai-shek**. Their work on party reform was generally successful.

CENTRAL STANDING COMMITTEE (CSC) (CHUNG-YANG CH'ANG-WU WEI-YUAN-HUI). A thirty-three-member top decision-making organ of the **Nationalist Party**, which many long regarded as made up of the most powerful and influential leaders in Taiwan; thus it was seen as the nation's most important center of political decision-making power and authority. The Central Standing Committee (earlier called the Central Executive Committee) functions for the **Central Committee** when it is not in session, though it is not controlled to any great extent by the latter. The CSC meets weekly. The chairman of the Nationalist Party picks sixteen of its members; members of the Central Committee choose seventeen. In the 1980s and 1990s, some analysts said that the CSC had lost power to or has been "captured" by party-state economic bureaucrats and technocrats, as evidenced by the fact that it had had little to do with the formulation of commercial policies, regulation of the **economy**, and some other important policies that require a high degree of specialized or technical knowledge. Those who challenged this view said that it was the force behind democratization both in the party and in the government, and its members were highly qualified and did not reflect entrenched interests since it was elected every year.

The 1988 Central Standing Committee was for the first time composed of a majority of Taiwanese; some saw this as significant and as reflecting the transfer of political power from **Mainland Chinese** to **Taiwanese**. The 1993 and 1997 Central Standing Committees gained an even larger proportion of Taiwanese. In 2005, newly elected party chairman **Ma Ying-jeou** changed the process of choosing the CSC to election by the **Party Congress** rather than the Central Committee.

The **Democratic Progressive Party** also has a Central Standing Committee, though it is composed of ten members. It functions in a manner similar to the Nationalist Party's CSC.

CHANG, CARSON (1887–1969). Considered the primary author of the **Constitution** of the **Republic of China**, he was influenced by the American founders' political ideals, the organization of the Weimer Republic, and of course **Sun Yat-sen**'s teachings and writings.

CHANG CHUN-HSIUNG (1937–). **Premier** from October 2000 to February 2002, Chang began his political career with **Chen Shui-bian** and **Frank Hsieh** and the team of lawyers that defended the *Formosa* magazine dissidents arrested after the **Kaohsiung Incident**. He subsequently founded the Ordinary Citizen Legal Service Center. Chang was a legislator from 1983 to 2000, first as an independent and then as a member of the **Democratic Progressive Party**. He was a founding member of the DPP. He served as presidential secretary-general before becoming **premier**. During his premiership, he came under attack from the opposition for supporting the cancellation of Taiwan's fourth nuclear power plant. After he stepped down from the office of premier, he served as the DPP's secretary-general from July 2002 to February 2005. In June 2005, after the death of **Koo Chen-fu**, he was appointed chairman of the **Straits Exchange Foundation**.

CHANG CHUN-HUNG (1938–). Chosen secretary-general of the **Democratic Progressive Party** in 1988, Chang was a well-known opposition political figure. He had been editor of the magazines *The Intellectual* and *Taiwan Political Review*. He was jailed from 1979 to 1987 for his involvement in the **Kaohsiung Incident**. He was a founding member of the DPP. Chang subsequently was appointed a DPP at-large legislator and served as vice chairman of the **Straits Exchange Foundation**. In recent years he has often been critical of his party.

CHANG HSIAO-YEN. *See* CHIANG HSIAO-YEN.

CHANG TSAN-HUNG (1936–). Founder of the U.S.-based **World United Formosans for Independence**. Chang was sentenced to prison in 1976 for masterminding a letter-bomb attack, which blew off the hand of **Shieh Tung-min**, then Taiwan provincial governor. After his release from prison, he successfully took up a political career. During the **Legislative Yuan** and metropolitan mayor and city council elections in 1998, as mayor of Tainan, he had a referendum put on the ballot regarding Taiwan's independence that caused considerable controversy and upset leaders in the People's Republic of China. Chang is currently a DPP member of the Legislative Yuan.

CHANG YUNG-FA (1927–). Chairman of the **Evergreen Group**, his personal wealth is put at over US$1 billion. In 1989, he established the **Institute for National Policy Research**. Chang was a major supporter of **Chen Shui-bian** in 2000 and after, and for that he was warned by Chinese leaders that he was doing business in China and supporting Taiwan's independence, which would not be tolerated. He was later at odds with President Chen about business ties with China that he felt Chen was obstructing.

CHAO YAO-TUNG (1916–). Minister of economic affairs from 1981 to 1984 and concurrently chairman of the **Council for Economic Planning and Development** and minister of state from 1984 to 1988, Chao had considerable influence on Taiwan's economic policies. Chao also helped found the **China Steel Corporation**. He is often said to have been one of the brains behind Taiwan's economic miracle.

CHEN CHENG (1907–1965). A general in the Nationalist Chinese military and a **Chiang Kai-shek** loyalist, Chen was sent to Taiwan in 1948 to fortify the island in preparation for the Nationalist retreat. In December of that year, he was appointed the third governor of Taiwan under the rule of the **Republic of China**. He served as **premier** from 1950 to 1954, and from 1958 to 1963. In 1954, he was elected vice president of the Republic of China. Chen was considered the most powerful official in Taiwan in the 1950s and 1960s after Chiang Kai-shek. He is credited with Taiwan's successful **land reform** and the country's early economic modernization. He is the father of **Chen Li-an**.

CHEN KUO-FU (1891–1951). A high-ranking official in the **Nationalist Party** and a very close associate of **Chiang Kai-shek** for many years, Chen opposed many reforms proposed by members of the Nationalist Party before it moved to Taiwan and after. *See also* CC CLIQUE.

CHEN LI-AN (1937–). Son of **Chen Cheng** and long regarded as one of Taiwan's young and promising politicians, Chen served as president of the **Control Yuan** from 1993 to 1995, having been minister of national defense from 1990 to 1993, minister of economic affairs from 1988 to 1990, chairman of the **National Science Council** from 1984 to 1988, and deputy secretary-general of the **Central Committee** of the **Nationalist Party** from 1980 to 1984. In 1996, he left the Nationalist Party and ran for **president** as an independent against **Lee Teng-hui** and two other presidential candidates, but especially against Lee. He ran on a platform of clean government. He was known as a devout Buddhist and won sympathy or support from many people for that reason. His vice presidential running mate was **Wang Ching-feng**. Chen won 9.97 percent of the popular vote—fourth among the four presidential candidates. Chen subsequently "retired" from politics.

CHEN LI-FU (1900–2001). A close associate of **Chiang Kai-shek**, he held a number of top positions in the **Nationalist Party** and the government prior to 1949. He served as minister of state from 1948 to 1950. *See also* CC CLIQUE.

CHEN SHUI-BIAN (1951–). The nation's **president**, Chen was born in Tainan in humble conditions. He excelled in school and attended **Taiwan National University**, where he graduated first in his class in its school of law. Chen was elected mayor of **Taipei** in 1994, previously having served as a member of the Taipei City Council from 1981 to 1985, and a member of the **Legislative Yuan** from 1989 to 1994. He lost a bid for reelection to the Taipei mayorship in 1981 to **Ma Ying-jeou**, but this may have been fortuitous, as it gave him time to prepare to run for the presidency in 2000.

Early on, Chen strongly supported democratic reform and Taiwan's independence. In 1980, as an attorney, he defended **Annette Lu**, who was charged with helping organize the **Kaohsiung Incident**. He subsequently was convicted of slander and served a term in jail. In 1986, he was a founding member of the **Democratic Progressive Party**. He avoided formal ties with the two main factions of the DPP but was closer to the **Formosa faction**. In 1991, he founded the Justice Alliance "group" in the DPP, which was called another faction, though its members tried to avoid factionalism and in fact made efforts to patch up factional differences in the party.

In 2000, Chen was elected president running as the candidate of the Democratic Progressive Party. His presidency ended a long period of **Nationalist Party** rule and was described as a monumental and historical event. It was also said to mark the consolidation of Taiwan's democracy. But Chen won the election with less than 40 percent of the popular vote, and his party held only one-third of the seats in the Legislative Yuan. He therefore had to deal with divided government and a hostile and uncooperative opposition. He tried to rule as a popular president by instituting a coalition government, but he failed. A serious economic recession followed in 2001. Nevertheless, he helped the DPP win an election that year, and it became the largest party in the legislature (though not the majority party).

During his first term, Chen faced accusations that he did not know how to manage the **economy**, that he deliberately exacerbated ethnic tensions for political gain, and that he dramatically worsened relations with China by doing and saying things in support of Taiwan's independence. He also to a considerable degree alienated the United States. He experienced an alleged sex scandal and did not get along with his vice president. It was also widely reported that his wife made money through insider stock trading. The opposition accused him of being a "public relations president"; clearly he did change his views often, though his defenders said he could not do otherwise.

In 2004, Chen was reelected president, this time with the help of the **Taiwan Solidarity Union**. During the campaigning, it appeared (judging from opinion polls, bets on the election, and the up-and-down movement of stocks of companies close to the DPP or the opposition parties) that he would lose. But Chen and Vice President **Annette Lu** were both shot just hours before the voting, helping them win by a very thin majority. The opposition **pan-blue** argued that the shooting was contrived and that only by cheating (by keeping the military and police at their posts so they could not vote) did Chen win. Massive protest demonstrations followed the election. Chen denied these charges. The opposition called for a recount and challenged the election in court. Later that year, the DPP suffered a setback in the legislative election, and in 2005 it lost badly in a magistrates and city council election, causing some to say that Chen had become a lame duck president. Subsequently, scandals in which his close aides and his family were involved in corruption hurt his image and his presidency.

CH'EN YI (1833–1950). The first governor of Taiwan after it became part of the **Republic of China** following World War II, Ch'en was a Nationalist general who had gained **Chiang Kai-shek**'s confidence after joining him in 1927 during the Northern Expedition. Ch'en was governor before and during the 28 February 1947, or *er er ba*, uprising and the massacre that followed in March, and he is widely blamed for that incident. Afterward, Chiang Kai-shek recalled him to the mainland and gave him a nominal post. Ch'en was later made governor of Chekiang Province. However, because of his alleged connivance with the Communists and Chiang's conviction that he was responsible for the **February 28 Uprising**, Chiang had him arrested, and on 18 June 1950, Ch'en was brought before a firing squad in Taiwan and executed.

Ch'en is regarded by most historians and the majority of Taiwanese as a grossly incompetent leader who caused Taiwan's economic, social, and political situation to deteriorate after World War II, and who, due to his poor performance in office, precipitated the **er er ba** incident. Some historians, however, say that his failings resulted from his hiring corrupt subordinates and his not understanding the fact that Taiwan's population had absorbed Japanese culture during a fifty-year period as a colony of Japan, while he thought that he could sinocize the island quickly. In addition, he mistakenly tried to institute socialist policies in Taiwan and was more concerned about what was happening on the Chinese mainland than about events in Taiwan during his tenure as governor.

CHENG CH'ENG-KUNG (1624–1662). Also commonly known as **Koxinga**, Cheng was born in Japan to a Japanese mother. His father, Cheng Chi-lung, was a Chinese pirate who operated from a base in Taiwan but was later appointed by the Ming Dynasty emperor Sze Tsung to command remnant Ming naval forces in a last-ditch effort to prevent the Manchus from conquering China. Cheng Ch'eng-kung inherited his father's forces and recruited more until he had an army of one hundred thousand and an armada of three thousand vessels. He continued his father's mission, and from 1648 (four years after the Ming Dynasty fell) to 1658, he fought a number of battles against the Manchus in the hope of restoring the Ming. He nearly captured the city of Nanking at one point. After abandoning this effort, in 1661 he attacked the Dutch stronghold of **Zeelandia**. Following a prolonged period of fighting, both on land and at sea, the Dutch conceded defeat and concluded an agreement to leave, thus ending thirty-eight years of Dutch colonial rule of Taiwan.

Cheng Ch'eng-kung established a Ming-style government on Taiwan, including a Chinese legal system, a court, and scholars that he recruited as advisers. He also promoted Chinese culture. His political system, however, was more like a feudal system than a Chinese-style bureaucratic system. Cheng encouraged Chinese migration to Taiwan, thus markedly increasing the Chinese population. He promoted trade with Japan, the Philippines, and other areas of Asia and brought stability and prosperity to Taiwan. Still clinging to the goal of ridding China of Manchu rule, and in an effort to accomplish this, Cheng tried to enlist support from Chinese living in the Philippines. This angered the Spanish, who killed as many as ten thousand Chinese residents there. They then informed Cheng that they had exterminated all Chinese in the Philippines, causing, according to some accounts, Cheng to have a heart attack and die. According to other records, Cheng died of a mysterious ailment. In any event, he passed at a young age—thirty-eight.

Had he lived, he might have accomplished much more. Still, he had a greater impact on Taiwan's history than perhaps any other single person, and for that reason he is acclaimed as a hero in Taiwan. Cheng Ch'eng-kung, in fact, is regarded as a hero-god by many in Taiwan, and as a special leader among advocates of Taiwan's independence because he was the first to rule an independent Taiwan "state." They also applaud his enlightened and effective governance. Ironically, China has built temples to memorialize him contending that he "liberated" Taiwan from colonial rule, promoted Chinese culture, and made Taiwan Chinese. Even Japan lauds Cheng's accomplishments, which they say came from the martial spirit inherited from his Japanese mother. His son, **Cheng Ching**, assumed power after he died.

CHENG CHING (1642–1681). Cheng Ch'eng-kung's son, who, after his father's death, from a power base in Fukien Province, vied with his uncle on Taiwan for succession. He won and continued his father's reign in Taiwan and his father's mission of ridding China of the Manchus. Like his father, he failed in that effort, and again like his father, he died at a young age. Upon his death, in large part because of his efforts to install an illegitimate son as his heir, the Cheng family rule of Taiwan disintegrated. Subsequently, Manchu troops defeated his armies and took the island in 1683, making it a part of China.

CHENG HO (1371–1435). A Chinese eunuch admiral who sailed to Southeast Asia, South Asia, and Africa and perhaps beyond during the early 1400s. Cheng was shipwrecked in Taiwan in 1430 on a return trip from Southeast Asia and made contact with the **aborigines**, bringing back some of their medicinal herbs to China. The visit, some say, bolsters China's historical claim to Taiwan. Others argue otherwise, saying it was accidental. It was not followed by other visits to Taiwan, and China made no claim to Taiwan at the time. Some Chinese officials now compare Cheng's "seven voyages" that were peaceful in nature to China's present rise; others dispute this claim and say that Cheng's missions were military in nature and reflected China's strategic aims.

CHI CHENG (1944–). A former secretary-general of the Republic of China's Track and Field Association and former member of the **Legislative Yuan**, she broke or set a number of world records in women's track events in the 1970s.

CHIA SHAN PROJECT (CHIA-SHAN CHI-HUA). A secret air force base built in the mountains in eastern Taiwan near Hualien. Begun in the mid-1980s, it was partially completed in 1990 when information about the base, which could hide jet fighter planes and would presumably be a command headquarters in the event of war with the People's Republic of China, was made public.

CHIANAN IRRIGATION ASSOCIATION (CHIA-NAN TA-CHUAN HSIEH-HUI). The largest of fifteen irrigation associations in Taiwan, it supplies water for the municipality of **Tainan** and the county of Chiayi. Like some other irrigation associations, it was considered an interest group of some importance. *See also* CHIANAN IRRIGATION SYSTEM.

CHIANAN IRRIGATION SYSTEM (CHIA-NAN TA-CHUAN). A large irrigation project started by the Japanese in 1920 and finished in 1930, it directed water from the Tsengwen River into an artificial coral reservoir that was formed by a major dam. The system converted 275 square kilometers (68,000 acres) of poor land on the west coast of Taiwan into fertile farmland that could grow rice and sugar cane. It had a marked positive impact on Taiwan's **agriculture**. *See also* CHIANAN IRRIGATION ASSOCIATION.

CHIANG CHING-KUO (1909–1988). Chiang Kai-shek's eldest son and Taiwan's third **president**, serving from 1978 until his death in January 1988. Fondly known as CCK, he was sent by his father to the Soviet Union at the age of sixteen, where he studied at the Sun Yat-sen University in Moscow. Subsequently, when relations between the elder Chiang and Stalin soured, he became a virtual hostage. As a consequence, he suffered considerable hardship for a number of years in the Soviet Union. In 1937, he was allowed to return to China with his Russian wife and was given various political and leadership positions by his father to determine his leadership abilities.

After the government moved to Taiwan in 1949, he became director of the political department of the **Nationalist Party** and subsequently served in various other positions, including deputy secretary-general of the **National Security Council**, minister of state, deputy minister of national defense, deputy premier, and head of the **China Youth Corps**. In 1972, he became **premier** and from that office launched various kinds of reform measures, including an anticorruption campaign and an "affirmative action" program to recruit more **Taiwanese** into government and the ruling Nationalist Party. He subsequently appointed a Taiwanese provincial governor and vice president.

CCK also issued "guidelines" for democratization of the political system. He assumed more authority as his father's health deteriorated and particularly after his father's death in 1975. From 1975 to 1978, he was considered the **Republic of China**'s top leader—even though he was not the nation's president—by virtue of his being head of the ruling party and premier. He was elected president in 1978 and again in 1984. In 1986, CCK organized a task force to recommend political reforms that included lifting the ban on forming new **political parties**, ending **martial law**, and reorganizing the government's parliamentary bodies. The **Democratic Progressive Party** formed shortly after this announcement. Martial law was terminated the next year. Meanwhile, he established a system of rotating military officers to limit their influence in politics. In 1984, he chose **Lee Teng-hui** as his vice president and made him his de facto successor.

Chiang Ching-kuo was considered a quiet, austere, no-nonsense, man-of-the-people person, in many ways quite unlike his father. He is often regarded as the force behind Taiwan's economic success, at least sustaining it, and even more so behind its political modernization and democratization. (*See* POLITICAL MIRACLE.) In recent public opinion surveys, residents of Taiwan regard him as their best president.

CHIANG CHING-KUO FOUNDATION (CHIANG CHING-KUO CHI-CHIN-HUI). A foundation whose full name is the Chiang Ching-kuo Foundation for International Scholarly Exchange, it is headquartered in Taipei with a regional office in McLean, Virginia, in the United States. It was established in 1989 in memory of the late President **Chiang Ching-kuo** to promote the study of Chinese culture and society. Operating funds come from interest on an endowment provided by both private and public sources. The foundation provides grants to universities, institutes, museums, and individuals.

CHIANG HSIAO-YEN (1941–). Also known as Chang Hsiao-yen, John Chiang, and John Chang, he is a member of the legislature representing the **Kuomintang** (KMT). He was formerly secretary-general of the **Nationalist Party**, director of the cultural division of the Nationalist Party, foreign minister, and vice premier. Chiang is the illegitimate son of **Chiang Ching-kuo**. In early 2005, he changed his family name from Chang (his mother's surname) to Chiang.

CHIANG KAI-SHEK (1887–1975). President of the **Republic of China** when the **Nationalist Party** ruled China before 1949, and of **Taiwan** after that until his death in April 1975. Chiang was born in Chekiang Province and was named Jui-yuan by his grandfather and Chung-cheng by his mother. He later took the name Chieh-shih, which is written "Kai-shek" in Cantonese. Chiang Kai-shek's father died when he was nine, and his mother raised him. Chiang was married twice. His eldest son, **Chiang Ching-kuo**, was from his first marriage. He later married **Soong Mayling**; they, however, had no children. It was long assumed that he fathered another son, **Chiang Wei-kuo**, by a Japanese woman, though Wei-kuo stated just before his own death that Chiang was not his father.

Chiang received an education in China, but he also went to Japan at the age of nineteen to study. In 1908, while in Japan, he joined the Tung Meng Hui, a revolutionary organization led by **Sun Yat-sen** that overthrew the Manchu Dynasty in 1911. That event prompted Chiang to return to China, whereupon he assumed command of a military unit and quickly built a reputation as a military leader. He also cemented a very close relationship with Sun Yat-sen and soon won an important leadership position in the Nationalist Party.

After Sun Yat-sen's death in 1925, Chiang struggled briefly to become his successor. He succeeded, and in 1926 he launched the Northern Expedition from South China to expel the warlord government in Peking and unify the country, a task he accomplished in 1928. Chiang at that point became head of the Nationalist government and ruler of China. During the 1930s and 1940s, Chiang fought the Japanese and the Chinese Communists while trying to prevent China's disintegration. He managed to tie down a large number of Japanese troops during World War II but won few battles and got little credit for Japan's defeat. The reality was that Japan was defeated by the United States; for that reason, Chiang attained little glory from the war, which had caused his regime and China extreme hardship. Partly as a result, but due also to corruption among his followers and mistaken policies, the Communists defeated Chiang's armies and took control of most of China in 1949, at which time Chiang resigned from the presidency of the Republic of China.

He and many of his supporters in the Nationalist government, the Nationalist Party, and the military subsequently fled to Taiwan. In March 1950, Chiang returned to power, once again assuming the presidency of the Republic of China, which no longer governed China but only Taiwan, the **Pescadores**, and the **Offshore Islands**. It was Chiang's dream to recover China, or the mainland, from the Communists. The dream, however, faded with time because of the strength of Mao Zedong's military in the newly formed People's Republic of China and the viability of Mao's government, not to mention lack of support from the United States. Also, this goal never had much support in Taiwan from locally born Chinese or **Taiwanese**. Chiang himself seemed to revise, or perhaps give up, this hope when in the late 1950s he referred to the goal as "70 percent political" and focused more of his attention on Taiwan's economic development.

However, Chiang remained adamant about retaining the Offshore Islands notwithstanding Mao's efforts to seize them, which led to global crises in 1954–1955 and 1958. Chiang saw them as stepping-stones to return to China and as important symbols.

Throughout his life, but varying through time, Chiang had considerable political support in the United States in the form of the **China Lobby**, but there were also many who criticized him and blamed him for the "loss of China." His support abroad, especially his claim to be the legitimate ruler of all of China, began to wane in the 1960s, although his policies were given respite by the Cultural Revolution in China and the Vietnam War. After both ended, in 1971 the Republic of China lost the China seat in the **United Nations**. To many, this marked the end of Chiang's claim to represent China in international politics. Nevertheless, Chiang remained president of the Republic of China and head of the Nationalist Party until his death. Though criticized for his misrule of China during the 1940s, for his defeat in China at the hands of the Communists, and later for his authoritarian-style rule in Taiwan, Chiang is credited with launching and building Taiwan's economic development and with starting, though belatedly according to critics, its political modernization. Chiang groomed his son, Chiang Ching-kuo, to be head of the Nationalist Party, to be the nation's leader after his death, and to carry on his policies, even though **Yen Chia-kan**, who was vice president at the time, succeeded him as president.

Chiang is often compared to Mao Zedong, both being "first-generation" leaders of modern China. But in some ways they were opposites: Since his death, Chiang's image has improved based on the fact that his efforts to modernize Taiwan economically.and, to a lesser extent, politically were so successful. On the other hand, Mao became viewed as a tyrant who hurt China's development and committed untold human rights abuses.

CHIANG KAI-SHEK, MADAME. *See* SOONG MAYLING.

CHIANG KAI-SHEK INTERNATIONAL AIRPORT (CHUNG-CHENG KUO-CHI FEI-CHI-CH'ANG). Located at Taoyuan, it is the larger of Taiwan's two international airports. It serves **Taipei** and northern Taiwan. It was one of six major transportation projects completed in the 1980s.

CHIANG KAI-SHEK'S BIRTHDAY (CHIANG-KUNG YEN-CHANG CHI-NIEN-JIH). Celebrated on 31 October, this was formerly an official holiday in Taiwan.

CHIANG PENG-CHIEN (1940–2000). The first chairman of the **Democratic Progressive Party**, serving from 1986 to 1987, Chiang was previously a member of the **Legislative Yuan** from 1984 to 1987. He was also the founding president of the **Taiwan Human Rights Association**. Chiang later served as a member of the **Control Yuan**.

CHIANG PIN-KUN (1932–). Currently vice chairman of the **Nationalist Party**, he was formerly chairman of the **Council for Economic Planning and Development** and was minister of economic affairs from 1993 to 1996. He was long considered one of the country's top leaders in economic affairs and a person with a good political future. In early 2005, he made an unprecedented visit to China and talked to high party officials there.

CHIANG WEI-KUO (1915–1997). Also known as Wego Chiang, he was long regarded as **Chiang Kai-shek**'s second son (by a Japanese woman to whom Chiang Kai-shek was not married) and half brother of **Chiang Ching-kuo**. He was a general in the Army of the **Republic of China** and in 1986 became secretary-general of the **National Security Council**. In 1990, together with **Lin Yang-kang**, he (as a possible vice presidential candidate) presented a challenge to President **Lee Teng-hui**. However, he and Lin subsequently withdrew their candidacies, and the **National Assembly** voted for the reelection of Lee as **president**. In 1997, shortly before his death, he declared publicly that he was not Chiang Kai-shek's son but rather the son of a close friend of Chiang's.

CHIAYI. One of Taiwan's five largest cities administered by Taiwan Province, located in south-central Taiwan.

CHIEH YEN FA. Literally a command or warning of strictness. It is usually translated as "emergency decree" in Taiwan, but as "**martial law**" elsewhere.

CHIEN, FREDERICK (1935–). Also known as Chien Fu, he served as minister of foreign affairs from 1990 to 1996, as speaker of the **National Assembly** from 1996 to 1998, and as president of the **Control Yuan** until 2004. He had previously been secretary-general of the **Council for Economic Planning and Development** from 1988 to 1990, and prior to that he was the Republic of China's "unofficial ambassador" to the United States. He is best known for his role in the conduct of the nation's diplomacy for a period of more than two decades. He is also the author of several books and numerous articles and speeches on international and foreign affairs. In 2004, President **Chen Shui-bian** appointed him to head a committee to investigate the shooting of the **president** and vice president.

CHINA AIRLINES (CAL) (CHUNG-HUA HANG-KUNG KUNG-SZU). A government-owned domestic and international airline in Taiwan that was for a long time the only official **flag** carrier of the **Republic of China**.

CHINA DEMOCRATIC PARTY (CHUNG-KUO MIN-CHU-TANG). A political party founded in 1960 by **Lei Chen**, which was the first serious attempt to organize an opposition to the **Nationalist Party**. The formation of a new party being illegal at the time, the party was immediately shut down.

CHINA DEMOCRATIC SOCIALIST PARTY (CHUNG-KUO MIN-CHU SHE-HUI-TANG). *See* DEMOCRATIC SOCIALIST PARTY.

CHINA DEVELOPMENT CORPORATION (CDC) (CHUNG-KUO K'AI-FA KUNG-SZU). A holding company run by the **Nationalist Party** that was, and is, involved in a number of commercial enterprises. In 1997, it won a contract to build the **Taipei International Financial Center** in Taipei, which included building Taiwan's tallest building, **Taipei 101**. It is also said to be the venture-capital arm of the Nationalist Party that invests party funds in other countries and has been responsible for Taiwan's sizable capitalization of projects and loans in Southeast Asia. CDC also provided funding to political campaigns and candidates. **Liu Tai-ying** was long the chairman of

CDC. In the past, opposition politicians criticized the CDC for using money to buy votes and fix elections. In recent years, the CDC's financial resources have been diverted, taken, or lost, and it does not have the importance or influence it once had.

CHINA EXTERNAL TRADE DEVELOPMENT COUNCIL (CETDC) (CHUNG-HUA-MIN-KUO TUI-WAI MAO-YI FA-CHAN HSIEH-HUI). The principal organization in Taiwan established to facilitate cooperation between business and government, it also maintains trade offices abroad and promotes bilateral economic relations. It is a semiofficial organization. CETDC gathers trade information, conducts market research, and promotes Taiwan-made products. It helps foreign businesses and local governmental organizations in other countries (including state governments in the United States) establish offices in the **World Trade Center** in **Taipei** and generally improve trade relations with Taiwan.

CHINA LOBBY (CHUNG-KUO YU-SHUO T'UAN). An organization formed in the summer of 1940 by T. V. Soong, **Madame Chiang Kai-shek**'s brother, in an effort to get U.S. support for the **Republic of China** in the war against Japan. It later became known as a group of influential people in the United States, especially Republicans, who supported the Nationalist Chinese against the Communist Chinese, both before and after they fled to Taiwan. In the 1970s, it lost much of its influence, many say because its supporters in the United States had lost their political clout. Others said it was no longer needed in view of the fact that Taiwan had become popular in the United States due to its democratization. Sometimes the term is used now for U.S. businesses that support the People's Republic of China. *See also* CONGRESSIONAL TAIWAN CAUCUS.

CHINA NEWS. See TAIWAN NEWS.

CHINA POST **(CHUNG-KUO YU-PAO).** One of Taiwan's three major English-language **newspapers**. It is **pan-blue** in its leanings. *See also* MEDIA.

CHINA SHIPBUILDING CORPORATION (CHUNG-KUO TSAO-CH'UAN KU-FEN YU-HSIEN-KUNG-SZU). Taiwan's largest shipbuilding company and formerly one of Taiwan's largest state-owned companies, it produces both civilian and naval craft.

CHINA STEEL CORPORATION (CHUNG-KUO KANG-T'IEH KUNG-SZU). Taiwan's largest steel producer, formerly a state-owned company.

CHINA TELEVISION COMPANY (CTV) (CHUNG-KUO TIAN-SHIH KU-FEN YU-HSIEN KUNG-SZU). The second television network established in Taiwan, the **Broadcasting Corporation of China** was its major shareholder. It had, and retains, close ties with the **Nationalist Party**, which some critics charge controls its programs and its political views. It is now one of four major television broadcasters. *See also* MEDIA.

CHINA TIDE **(CH'IAO-LIU).** A reformist literary and political magazine that began publishing in the early 1970s, carrying articles on Taiwan's history, society, economic development, and international relations. It propagated what became known as the "native soil movement," which called for the restoration of a dying agrarian society and romanticized the lives of farmers, fishermen, and workers. Some of the contributors later joined the **Democratic Progressive Party**. The magazine also called for the reunification of Taiwan with China and showed sympathy toward the People's Republic of China. Some of its staff and supporters joined the labor movement in the mid-1980s and helped form the **Labor Party**. *See also* MEDIA.

CHINA TIMES **(CHUNG-KUO SHIH-PAO).** One of the three largest Chinese-language **newspapers** in Taiwan. The *China Times* organization also publishes the *China Times Weekly*, the *China Times Express*, and a number of other publications. In September 1995, the company went digital with the *China Times* website. The *China Times* is considered moderate but politically slightly to the left of its main rival, the *United Daily News*, and to the right of the *Liberty Times*. *See also* MEDIA.

CHINA TRUST (CHUNG-KUO HSIN-T'UO). Taiwan's largest private bank. In 2003, it merged with the Grand Commercial Bank, and in 2004 it bought Fengshan Commercial Credit Cooperative. China

Trust provides full **banking** services in Taiwan and operates in a number of foreign countries. *See also* KOO CHEN-FU.

CHINA YOUTH CORPS (CYC) (CHUNG-KUO CH'ING-NIEN FAN-KUNG CHIU-KUO-T'UAN). A nongovernmental but quite politically oriented organization, formed in Taiwan in 1952 by **Chiang Kai-shek** in response to the failures of the Nationalist government to attract and maintain the support of the youth in China during the war against the Communists. **Chiang Ching-kuo** served as director-general until 1973, after which **Lee Huan** and then Sung Shih-hsuan headed CYC. Its main functions during the early years were to administer reserve-officer training programs on college and university campuses and in high schools and to manage young peoples' organizations. After 1957, it began to focus more on youth work and to emphasize culture, sports, and recreational activities. In 1967, it expanded its functions to factories and towns and built youth activity centers. Since 1992, CYC has organized cultural and educational exchanges with China.

CYC operated a wire service and a broadcasting station and published journals. It had close ties to the **Nationalist Party**, and its leaders were both politically active and influential. In many of its projects and endeavors, it worked with the Ministries of Defense, Education, and Interior, as well as with the **Overseas Chinese Affairs Commission**. It was regarded as both an anti-Communist mass organization and a civic organization similar to the Boy Scouts.

CYC has changed considerably and has declined in importance since **Chen Shui-bian** was elected **president** in 2000, though not as much as many similar organizations.

CHINA YOUTH PARTY (CYP) (CHUNG-KUO CH'ING-NIEN-TANG). A political party that formed in China in 1923 and moved to Taiwan in 1949 after the Nationalist defeat. It was called an opposition party, though many felt it served as only a token alternative to the **Nationalist Party**. Before the formation of the **Democratic Progressive Party**, it was the larger of two minor parties in Taiwan. In 1960, two of its members were involved in forming the **China Democratic Party**. In 1982, **Taiwanese** members tried to wrest control of the party from **Mainland Chinese** party leaders but failed. In 1987, it held seven nonelective seats in the **Legislative Yuan** and forty-five in the **National Assembly**, but as a result of the 1989 election, it lost most of its Legislative Yuan seats. In recent years, the CYP has declined dramatically in visibility and importance and has become generally inactive.

CHINESE ASSOCIATION FOR HUMAN RIGHTS (CHUNG-HUA JEN-CHUAN HSIEH-HUI). A national human rights organization founded in Taiwan in 1979 by the efforts of **Han Lih-wu**. It was concerned with human rights problems in both Taiwan and China. A provincial section was established in 1985 in **Taichung**, and another branch was established in **Kaohsiung** in 1988. The organization sponsors seminars, legal consultations, and various publications. *See also* TAIWAN HUMAN RIGHTS ASSOCIATION.

CHINESE FEDERATION OF LABOR (CFL) (CHUNG-HUA MIN-KUO CHUAN-KUO LAO-KUNG TSUNG-HUI). An umbrella labor organization founded in 1950 and restructured in 1975, it controlled a number of local labor organizations nominally affiliated with it, including several national and local unions in Taiwan's **export processing zones**. The CFL was closely linked to the **Nationalist Party**, its president serving in the **Legislative Yuan** representing both the Nationalist Party and labor. Critics said that because of ties with the ruling party and the government and the fact that it received subsidies from the government, and because its representatives were from occupational unions with many owning businesses, the CFL was weak in fighting for labor rights. In recent years, especially since 2000, the CFL has been involved more aggressively in protecting labor rights in Taiwan, but it has also gotten into disputes over foreign labor and other issues.

CHINESE NATIONAL FEDERATION OF INDUSTRIES (CNFI) (KUNG-SHANG-YEH TSUNG-HUI). Established in 1948, it is one of the oldest, largest, and most influential interest groups in Taiwan. Since 1994, CNFI has organized frequent management forums. In recent years, it has focused on helping Taiwan's industries adjust to globalization.

CHINESE NEW YEAR (CH'UN-CHIEH). Also called Lunar New Year, this is the most important holiday of the year in Taiwan. It falls on the first day of the lunar year, usually in January or February using the solar calendar. Most people return home and eat and talk with relatives for several days.

CHINESE PETROLEUM CORPORATION (CPC) (CHUNG-KUO SHIH-YU HUA-HSUEH KUNG-YEH KAI-FA KU-FEN YU-HSIEN KUNG-SZU). A state-owned corporation founded in Shanghai in 1946 that moved to Taiwan with the Nationalist government, it is responsible for petroleum and natural gas exploration, importing, refining, and marketing. It is Taiwan's largest company measured by sales.

CHINESE SOCIAL DEMOCRATIC PARTY (CSDP) (CHUNG-HUA SHE-HUI MIN-CHU TANG). A political party formed in 1990 by **Ju Gao-jeng**, the CSDP was the third-largest party in terms of the number of candidates it nominated for the 1991 **National Assembly** election and was one of four parties to receive time allotted for television advertising during that campaign. However, receiving just over 2 percent of the popular vote, it failed to win enough seats to qualify for party-allocated national representatives. A left-of-center party advocating many of the tenets of European social democratic parties, the CSDP declined in subsequent years and disappeared from Taiwan's political scene. Its founder later joined the **New Party**.

CHINESE TAIPEI OLYMPIC COMMITTEE (CTOC) (CHUNG-HUA AO-LIN-P'I-K'E WEI-YUAN-HUI). An organization in Taiwan responsible for international amateur sports activities and liaison with the International Olympic Committee. It has exclusive powers to organize participation in the Olympic Games, the Asian Games, and other top national sports activities. CTOC has been involved in a number of feuds and controversies over the **Republic of China**'s status in international sports competition, especially the Olympic Games, because the People's Republic of China insists that the Republic of China cannot use its official name or the name "Taiwan." Rather, the term "Chinese Taipei" is used. Similarly, the Republic of

China **flag** cannot be shown but instead a "delegation flag" is used, and the country's national anthem is barred and supplanted with a "flag song." Many in Taiwan and elsewhere feel that this is unjust treatment.

CHINESE TELEVISION SYSTEM (CTS) (CHUNG-HUA TIAN-SHIH KU-FEN YU-HSIEN KUNG-SZU). Established in 1970 from a public education television network then operated by the Ministry of Education, it was co-owned by the Ministry of Education and the Ministry of Defense but was gradually privatized. It now broadcasts both educational programs and regular entertainment. It was the first station to broadcast in both VHF and UHF, the latter being used for educational programs. *See also* MEDIA.

CHING CHUAN KANG AIR BASE (CHING-CH'UAN-KANG K'UNG-CHÜN CHI-TI). A large air base in central Taiwan near **Taichung**, used by U.S. forces until their departure in the late 1970s. At the peak of U.S. involvement in Vietnam, there were ten thousand U.S. personnel on the base. In 1965, it was enlarged to accommodate large planes. While B-52s did not use the base, as some said Taipei had hoped, C-130s and other planes that were part of the U.S. Vietnam War did. The base is now used by the **Republic of China**'s Air Force.

CHING-KUO. *See* INDIGENOUS DEFENSE FIGHTER.

CHIOU I-JEN (1950–). Currently the secretary-general of the **National Security Council**, he was previously secretary-general of the **Office of the President** and secretary-general of the **Democratic Progressive Party**. Earlier in his career, he was a leader of the "new generation" faction of *tangwai* and later became a founding member and then deputy general director of the DPP. He helped organize a protest demonstration against **Formosa Plastics** in 1986 and also a farmers' protest on 20 May 1988 that was the largest public political demonstration up to that time. He was the leader of the DPP's more radical **New Tide faction** and a strong proponent of the view that Taiwan must become independent before it can democratize successfully.

CHIU CHUANG-HUAN (1925–). Chiu served as minister of the interior from 1978 to 1981, vice premier from 1981 to 1984, and governor of Taiwan from 1984 to 1990, and later as a senior adviser to the **president**. He was regarded for many years as one of Taiwan's top political elite.

CHUNG SHA. *See* MACCLESFIELD BANK.

CHUNGHSING NEW TOWN (CHUNG-HSING HSIN-TS'UN). The administrative center of the Taiwan provincial government, located near **Taichung**.

CHUNGHUA INSTITUTE FOR ECONOMIC RESEARCH (CHUNG-HUA CHING-CHI YEN-CHIU-YUAN). A think tank established in 1981 to study economic issues. Its publications on economic conditions and forecasts are widely cited in the press and elsewhere.

CHUNGHWA TELECOM (CHT) (CHUNG-HUA TIEN-HSIN). Created in 1996 when it was spun off from the Ministry of Transportation and Communications to be eventually privatized, it became Taiwan's largest telecommunications operator. A listing on the New York Stock Exchange and a share sale in August 2005 reduced the government's stake to less than 50 percent.

CHUNGLI INCIDENT (CHUNG-LI SHIH-CHIEN). A mass protest that led to violence in the city of Chungli in 1977, precipitated by reports of irregularities or cheating in vote counting, in particular involving the candidacy of **Hsu Hsin-liang**. An angry crowd overturned and burned cars and set fire to a police station. One person was killed, and several others were injured. The protest was anti-KMT and was the largest in scale since February 1947. Some observers say the incident was the beginning of a unified opposition movement in Taiwan. *See TANGWAI.*

CHUNGSHAN INSTITUTE OF SCIENCE AND TECHNOLOGY (CHUNG-SHAN KE-HSUEH YEN-CHIU-YUAN). One of the nation's foremost research institutes and one devoted to the development of advanced military equipment and weapons. Its scientists have engineered and built the **Hsiung-feng** I and II surface-to-air missiles, the **Tien-kung** surface-to-air missile, the **Tien-chien** I and II air-to-air missile, Taiwan's **Indigenous Defense Fighter**, and a number of other sophisticated weapons. The institute has a large facility at Lungtan in Taoyuan County.

CINEMA (TIEN YING). Japanese movies were shown in Taiwan during the period of Japanese rule. Under Nationalist rule they were banned, and instead Chinese movies made in Hong Kong and later locally produced and foreign movies, mostly American, were shown. Taiwan's movie industry grew in the 1960s and 1970s, and some of its **Mandarin** movies were shown in Hong Kong and elsewhere. In the mid-1990s, the industry began to decline, in part because the government lifted the quotas on the showing of foreign films in 1986. Still, Taiwan-made movies have won a number of awards. Ang Lee, who was born in Taiwan, is widely acclaimed for his award-winning movies made in the United States.

CIVIC ORGANIZATIONS LAW (KUNG-MIN TZU-CHIH-FA). Titled the Civic Organizations Law During the Period of National Mobilization for the Suppression of Communist Rebellion, this legislation was revised in 1989 to allow new **political parties** to form in a follow-up to President **Chiang Ching-kuo**'s statement in June 1986 that the ban on political parties would be lifted. Although the **Democratic Progressive Party** was already founded in 1986 and participated in the national election that year and was widely recognized as a political party, it and other new political parties did not become legal until 1989 when this law took effect. At that time, a host of other new political parties formed.

COASTAL PATROL GENERAL HEADQUARTERS (HAI-HSUN TSUNG-PU). Created in 1992 to control smuggling, illegal entry and exit, and infiltration, it is administratively under the Corps Area Command. It was established at the time of the dissolution of the **Garrison Command** and assumed some of its functions.

COASTAL REMOVAL POLICY (HAI-CHIN). Policy of the Manchu government of China established in 1660 to force the coastal residents of China adjacent to Taiwan to move thirty to fifty *li* (one *li* equals one-third of a mile) inland in order to prevent them from making contact with and supporting **Cheng Ch'eng-kung**. As a result of this policy, many people were forced to abandon their homes and their rice crops and yet were still taxed. The economic dislocation and hardship caused more migration of China's coastal population living near the **Taiwan Strait** to Taiwan.

COMMITTEE ON THE DISCIPLINE OF PUBLIC FUNC-TIONARIES (KUNG-WU YUAN CH'ENG-CHIEH WEI-YUAN-HUI). A committee of the **Judicial Yuan** that serves as a check on decisions made by the **Control Yuan** involving the impeachment and dismissal of public civilian officials.

CONGRESSIONAL TAIWAN CAUCUS (MEI-KUO KUO-HUI TAI-WAN LIEN-HSIEN). Also called simply the Taiwan Caucus, it was inaugurated in April 2002 by eighty-five members of the U.S. House of Representatives. The group was bipartisan and sought to "positively enhance and strengthen U.S. relations and cooperation with the government and people of Taiwan in accordance with the **Taiwan Relations Act**." Caucus members noted that U.S. policy calls for a peaceful, mutually acceptable resolution to the "Taiwan issue" and that it wants to deepen dialogue with the people of the island and their elected representatives. Several members referred to Taiwan as an "independent nation" and opposed China's claim to Taiwan. The U.S. Senate established a Senate Taiwan Caucus in September 2003. The Congressional Taiwan Caucus is now made up of more than 150 members and is the second-largest such organization in the House. One of its main tenets is that the people of Taiwan should decide the future of Taiwan, though it has not taken a stance favoring or opposing independence.

CONSENSUS OF 1992. *See* 1992 CONSENSUS.

CONSTITUTION (OF THE REPUBLIC OF CHINA) (CHUNG-HUA-MIN-KUO HSIEN-FA). Written in 1946 and promulgated on 1 January 1947 when the government of the **Republic of China** ruled the mainland as well as Taiwan, it was modeled in large part after the

U.S. Constitution, particularly inasmuch as it sets forth provisions for a republican form of government, though the government designed by this constitution is a mixture of a presidential, parliamentary, and cabinet system. Also, instead of three branches of government, the Constitution provides for five, adding branches that performed major government functions in ancient China. (*See* CONTROL YUAN; EXAMINATION YUAN.) It contains provisions for many of the civil and political liberties found in the U.S. Constitution's Bill of Rights and incorporates the political philosophy of **Sun Yat-sen**, especially his teachings found in *The Three Principles of the People*. However, some of its important provisions, especially its guarantees of civil and political rights, were for some time nullified or held in abeyance by the **Temporary Provisions** and by the declaration of **martial law**.

Critics who said the government of the **Republic of China** was not democratic did not usually attack the Constitution or advocate writing a new constitution but rather called for its full and complete implementation. Thus, abolishing the Temporary Provisions and ending martial law were their targets. Ending both, in fact, made the Constitution a democratic one and made the civil and political liberties provided in it meaningful. In recent years, amending the Constitution has also made the political system more democratic and has had a major impact on the organization and working of the political system, though many believe more changes need to be made.

CONSTITUTION DAY (HSING-HSIEN CHI-NIEN-JIH). Formerly an official holiday in the **Republic of China**. The date 25 December was chosen in some part to give foreigners working in Taiwan a vacation day to celebrate Christmas.

CONSUMER PROTECTION COMMISSION (CHING-FEI-CHE PAO-HU WEI-YUAN-HUI). A commission established under the **Executive Yuan** in 1994 to study and review policies on consumer protection.

CONSUMERS FOUNDATION OF THE REPUBLIC OF CHINA (CHUNG-HUA-MIN-KUO CHING-CHI-HUI). An independent organization founded in 1980 in response to consumer anger toward what they considered irresponsible actions by manufacturers, and to some, by the business community in general. In May 1981, the foundation began publication of the magazine *Consumer Reports*. The foundation has since evolved into a powerful interest group.

CONTROL YUAN (CHIEN-CHA-YUAN). One of the five branches of the central government and formerly one of three parliamentary or elected bodies of government, it was called the supervisory or oversight branch of government. It was patterned after the Censorate in the ancient Chinese system, which was designed to check on officials and bureaucrats and guard against corruption. It was constitutionally given the powers of impeachment, censure, audit, and consent (of presidential appointments). Members were elected indirectly for six-year terms by provincial and special city councils, as well as by Mongolian, Tibetan, and **Overseas Chinese** groups.

Early on, critics charged that the **Nationalist Party** controlled Control Yuan appointments and that it lacked **Taiwanese** members. Beginning in the late 1960s, this changed. However, Taiwan-elected members made excessive allegations of corruption and increased the public's distrust of the body. Because of this, some groups, especially the **Wisdom Coalition**, said that the more democratic **Legislative Yuan** could better handle its functions. Constitutional amendments passed by the **National Assembly** in 1991, 1992, and 1993 changed the Control Yuan from a parliamentary branch of government into a quasi-judicial organ of government. Its members are hence no longer elected but are rather appointed by the **president** with the approval of the National Assembly. Its original membership was 223. This number was reduced to 51 in 1991. In 1993, it became 29 strong.

The Control Yuan was also stripped of its power to approve the nominations of presidents and vice presidents of the **Judicial Yuan** and **Examination Yuan**, leaving it with only the powers of impeachment, censure, and audit. Its impeachment power, however, applies to all levels of government, including the president. Its monitoring authority comes from the Law on Discipline of Public Functionaries.

COOPERATIVE SYSTEM (HO-TSO SHIH-YEH). Based on the **Constitution**'s provision that "cooperative enterprises shall receive encouragement and assistance from the state," the government assists, generally through the social affairs department of the Ministry of Interior, both single-purpose and multipurpose cooperatives. The former are mostly to respond to economic issues: **agriculture, industry**, marketing, labor, transportation, public utilities, insurance, and so forth. The latter are community or regional cooperative schemes. Agriculture and the handicraft industries have especially benefited from cooperative arrangements. As of 1996, there were more than five thousand cooperative associations with a membership of seven million and with capital of around US$200 million.

COORDINATION COUNCIL FOR NORTH AMERICAN AFFAIRS (CCNAA) (PEI-MEI SHIH-WU HSIEH-TI'AO-HUI). An unofficial organization that represented the **Republic of China** in the United States in lieu of an embassy and consulates after the United States broke formal diplomatic relations in January 1979. CCNAA was headquartered in Taiwan, but its real operation was in Washington, D.C. (where it functioned as an embassy), and in other cities in the United States (where it functioned as consulates), including New York City, Chicago, Atlanta, Houston, Seattle, San Francisco, Los Angeles, Honolulu, Boston, and Miami.

CCNAA was divided into ten divisions: the Secretariat, which handled political and governmental matters; the Service Division, which took visa and passport applications; the Administrative Division, which handled housekeeping; the Public Affairs Division, which did congressional liaison work; the Telecommunications Division, which managed communications with the home office in Taipei; the Cultural Division, which did the equivalent work of a cultural attaché; the Information and Communications Division, which was responsible for press and public relations; the Science Division, which promoted scientific and technological cooperation with the United States; the Economic Division, which mainly dealt with U.S.–Taiwan trade and economic issues; and the Service Coordination Division, which took care of military matters. There was also an Investment and Trade Office (located in New York City) and a Procurement Service Mission in Washington, D.C. The former provided information and services to U.S. investors; the latter was responsible for purchasing weapons in the United States. CCNAA's counterpart organization in Taiwan was the **American Institute in Taiwan**.

In 1994, following a reassessment of U.S. Taiwan policy by the administration of Bill Clinton, CCNAA was renamed the **Taipei Economic and Cultural Representative Office**, which assumed all of the functions of CCNAA. This was considered an upgrading of Washington-Taipei relations inasmuch as the latter title signifies what nation the organization represents; CCNAA did not. AIT remained the counterpart organization in Taipei.

COUNCIL FOR CULTURAL PLANNING AND DEVELOPMENT (WEN-HUA CHIEN-SHE WEI-YUAN-HUI). Established in 1981 under the jurisdiction of the **Executive Yuan**, the council is responsible for developing Chinese culture and culture in general.

COUNCIL FOR ECONOMIC PLANNING AND DEVELOPMENT (CEPD) (CHING-CHI CHIEN-SHE WEI-YUAN-HUI). Created in 1977 to replace the **Economic Planning Council**, it is considered Taiwan's top economic planning organization. It approves projects that have government involvement, it coordinates the nation's financial and economic activities, and it studies local and global economic trends and problems. CEPD collects and assesses economic data and business indicators, providing this information to the government and to the public. It has eight departments: Overall Planning, Sectoral Planning, Economic Research, Housing and Urban Development, Financial Analysis, Manpower Planning, Performance Evaluation, and General Affairs. Recently the CEPD established **Free Trade Port Zones**. *See also* ECONOMY.

COUNCIL FOR INTERNATIONAL COOPERATION AND DEVELOPMENT (KUO-CHI HO-TSO FA-CHAN WEI-YUAN-HUI). Created in 1963 to adjust to the coming termination of U.S. economic assistance, its purpose was to attract foreign **investment** and loans and to help launch Taiwan's first **Export Processing Zone** near **Kaohsiung**. It was reorganized by **Chiang Ching-kuo** in 1969 and lost some of its most important functions. In 1972, the **Economic Planning Council** replaced it.

COUNCIL FOR U.S. AID (MEI-KUO YUAN-CHU WEI-YUAN-HUI). An organization established in 1948 to implement U.S. economic assistance programs, it was restructured in 1958 to design tax, finance, and **investment** plans and to regulate exchange rates. The council was replaced by the **Council for International Cooperation and Development** in 1963.

COUNCIL OF GRAND JUSTICES (TA-FA-KUAN HUI-YI). Established in 1948 and made up of fifteen grand justices appointed by the **president**, its members are top officials of the **Judicial Yuan**. In fact, the president and vice president of the Judicial Yuan are chosen from council members. Its major functions were interpreting the **Constitution** and unifying the interpretation of laws and ordinances. In 1958, when the Law of the Council of Grand Justices was promulgated, the Council of Grand Justices began making rulings on constitutional interpretations made by individuals. In the late 1980s, the council made some important decisions on tax law, nullifying some provisions of the tax code.

A very important and controversial decision was made by the Council of Grand Justices in June 1990: an interpretation of the Constitution to the effect that **senior parliamentarians**—those members of the **National Assembly** and the **Legislative Yuan** not elected by Taiwan's electorate—would have their tenure terminated by the end of 1991. The **Nationalist Party** and the **Democratic Progressive Party** had both tried to get them to retire, and a law had been passed earlier to force them to step down, but these efforts had proven unsuccessful. While there was strong opposition to the Council of Grand Justices' decision by the senior parliamentarians and by those who saw their retirement as undermining the nation's **one-China** policy, it was carried out and had a momentous impact on the nation's political system and democratization. Some other rulings have been important and controversial: for example, a 1994 ruling that laws favoring fathers in deciding issues relating to children are unconstitutional, a 2001 decision that the **Executive Yuan** did not follow proper procedures in terminating Taiwan's fourth nuclear power plant, a 2005 injunction on the nation's fingerprinting program, and a ruling that the **Truth Commission** was in part unconstitutional.

Council of Grand Justices members serve nine-year terms. The body meets two or three times a week and may call extraordinary meetings. An interpretation of the Constitution requires a three-fourths vote of members present; a single majority makes other decisions. Its opinions, interpretations, and dissenting views are published by the Judicial Yuan.

COUNCIL OF LABOR AFFAIRS (CLA) (LAO-KUNG WEI-YUAN-HUI). An organ of the **Executive Yuan** created in August 1987 to administer labor laws, regulations, and policies. The CLC also serves as an advocate for labor, protects workers' rights, supervises labor-management relations, and promotes better working environments. It oversees the Bureau of Employment and Vocational Training, the Bureau of Labor Insurance, the Institute of Occupational Safety and Health, the Labor Insurance Supervisory Committee, and two Labor Inspection Offices. One of the controversial functions of the Council of Labor Affairs in recent years has been the responsibility for retraining Taiwan's displaced and elderly farmers. Another has been the oversight of Taiwan's foreign laborers and giving help to foreign spouses.

COUNCIL OF PRESBYTERIAN CHURCHES (CHANG-LAO CHIAO-HUI). The most active religious organization in Taiwan, it long advocated Taiwan independence and for that reason was at odds with the **Nationalist Party** and the government before 2000. *See also* TAIWAN INDEPENDENCE MOVEMENT.

COYETT, FREDERICK (1615–1687). Dutch governor of Taiwan who fought **Cheng Ch'eng-kung**'s forces in 1661 and 1662 and finally surrendered, ending the period of Dutch colonial rule of Taiwan.

CULTURE SOCIETY (WEN-HUA HUI). An organization of Taiwanese formed during the Japanese colonial period. Its purpose was to strengthen the population's identity. Being apolitical, it survived the demise of its parent organization, the **Home Rule Association**.

– D –

DAI WAN. Literally "big bay" in Japanese. Japanese traders used this term for Taiwan in the fourteenth century. It is also a native word for **aborigines**. Some say that this is the origin of the term "Taiwan."

DEMOCRACY FOUNDATION (MIN-CHU CHI-CHIN-HUI). A **Nationalist Party** think tank formed in November 1990 by party election strategist John Kuan after a split with President **Lee Teng-hui**. The foundation, which had considerable financial backing from a number of Taiwan's businesses, represented a kind of faction in the party for a while that opposed Taiwan's independence.

DEMOCRATIC PACIFIC UNION (DPU) (MIN-CHU T'AI-P'ING-YANG LIEN-MENG). Founded in Taipei on 14 August 2005 at the initiative of Vice President **Annette Lu**, the DPU is dedicated to peace, prosperity, and democracy in the Pacific region. It is a nongovernmental organization, and its founding had support in twenty-five nations, including the United States and Japan. The DPU grew out of the Democratic Pacific Assembly founded in 2003, also formed by the vice president. Critics, however, said that it resembles the **Asian People's Anti-Communist League** and its successor organization, the **World Anti-Communist League**, insofar as it is anti-China, will promote government policies, and will probably waste taxpayer money.

DEMOCRATIC PROGRESSIVE PARTY (DPP) (MIN-CHU CHIN-PU TANG). Called Taiwan's ruling party after **Chen Shui-bian**'s election to the presidency in March 2000, the DPP was formed on 28 September 1986, composed mostly of *tangwai* politicians, many of whom had been political prisoners or well-known dissidents. It was the first viable opposition **political party** formed in Taiwan under the government of the **Republic of China**. In fact, not long after it was established, the DPP became regarded as Taiwan's major and only serious opposition party. It was founded illegally, since the **Temporary Provisions** banned forming new political parties; but inasmuch as President **Chiang Ching-kuo** had stated a few months earlier that new political parties would soon be allowed, the government did not take action against DPP leaders. The DPP competed openly against the **Nationalist Party** in the December 1986 election, winning over 20 percent of the votes for **National Assembly** and **Legislative Yuan** seats. Some observers said this was evidence that Taiwan had evolved into a two-party system; others, however, doubted it.

At its first party congress in November 1986, the DPP elected **Chiang Peng-chien** party chairman. Also picked were a **Central Committee** and a ten-member **Central Standing Committee**. While the chairman was to serve for only one year and the DPP leadership was supposed to be a collective one, the organizational structure of the party was Leninist. Some considered this quite ironic since its members had long been highly critical of this aspect of the Nationalist Party. The party immediately advocated reduced defense spending; political reform, such as ending the Nationalist Party's hold on political power; the retirement of **senior parliamentarians** (members of the National Assembly and the Legislative Yuan elected before the government moved to Taiwan) so as to make the political system truly democratic; a free press; the end of **martial law**; and more. Its platform supported the rights of **women**, senior citizens, children, workers, **aborigines**, farmers, and other disadvantaged people. The DPP also advocated expanded social programs that some said indicated it wanted a welfare state, though it argued that it could expand welfare benefits by simply increasing government efficiency and that it would not have to raise taxes. It railed against corruption, which it blamed on the Nationalist Party. It affirmed the country's anti-Communist policy but also called for self-determination for Taiwan so that its residents could decide the island's political future. The DPP party platform called for a "flexible **foreign policy**" and for Taiwan's readmission to the **United Nations**, but party leaders offered few serious suggestions as to how this might be accomplished.

During the early years, the DPP engaged in "street politics," organizing demonstrations, protests, and other forms of political expression. It also employed disruptive tactics and sometimes violence in Legislative Yuan sessions to draw press attention to its issues and demands or to block opposed legislation. Some regarded the party's activities as proof of democracy evolving in Taiwan; opponents saw the DPP as demeaning the democratic processes. In any event, experiencing considerable success over a period of time in electing its members to various offices in the local as well as national government, the DPP moderated its policies.

Almost from the onset of its founding, the DPP experienced factional problems and intraparty strife resulting from personal power struggles and differing views on some critical issues, especially the matter of Taiwan's independence. DPP leaders were also often at odds over the party's relations with the KMT. Some observers saw its problems as nothing unusual for a new opposition party; others have viewed them as casting doubt on the party's future.

In 1989, the DPP performed well in the Legislative Yuan election, prompting some pundits to predict that it would be in office soon, or when the senior parliamentarians retired. It performed poorly, however, in the first nonsupplemental election in 1991 after the non-elected senior parliamentarians stepped down, due to putting the issue of Taiwan's independence in its platform. Yet it did very well in the first nonsupplemental Legislative Yuan election in 1992. The DPP also performed quite well in elections in the mid-1990s, although it did not do well in the first direct presidential election in 1996. It performed surprisingly well in local elections in November 1997, prompting observers to predict that the DPP might win the presidential election in 2000, especially if the KMT continued to experience factional and other problems. It did less well in the Legislative Yuan election in December 1998 and lost the **Taipei** mayorship, which it had won in 1994.

Meanwhile, the DPP worked with the ruling KMT in various lawmaking efforts and in passing amendments to the **Constitution**, even though some party leaders had said the Constitution was archaic and should be replaced. This DPP-KMT cooperation, in fact, prompted some observers to see their mutual efforts as marking the beginning of coalition or cooperative politics in Taiwan. Others said that this was only a temporary strategy on the part of the DPP and would not last. DPP leaders, especially those in office, often angered the People's Republic of China with their independence stance and were assailed frequently by Beijing for trying to split China, even though the DPP's stance on independence gradually moderated. The DPP was at odds on this issue with the KMT as well.

After 2000, when Chen Shui-bian was elected **president**, the DPP became the ruling party, though it held only one-third of the seats in the legislature. Because it was not really ready to rule, and because the Nationalist Party did not choose to be a loyal opposition party and questioned both Chen's mandate and the presidential system of government, polarization and gridlock followed. President Chen gave up his position as head of the DPP and tried to rule as a nonpartisan president, but this did not work. After doing well in the 2001 legislative election and getting help from the **Taiwan Solidarity Union**, the DPP, though still lacking a majority, was able to govern somewhat more easily. It did become the Legislative Yuan's largest party at this time. Still, difficulties managing the **economy**, running **foreign affairs**, ethnic strife, and a host of other problems plagued DPP rule. President Chen nevertheless was reelected in 2004—albeit winning only, many said, because he and his vice president were shot just before the voting. The DPP did not perform well in the Legislative Yuan election that December and did poorly in an election for local executives and city councils late in 2005. Subsequently, the DPP lost some members in the legislature and declined to become the second-largest party in strength.

Unlike the Nationalist Party (which is mixed in membership), the DPP's membership is almost exclusively **Fukien Taiwanese**. Also different from the KMT, its leaders are almost all lawyers, political activists, and elected government officials. In early 2006, it was reported that the DPP had a membership of 530,000, but that only 230,000 had paid their party dues.

DEMOCRATIC SOCIALIST PARTY (DSP) (MIN-CHU CHIN-PU TANG). A **political party**, which formed in Shanghai in 1946 and moved to Taiwan in 1949, it was the smaller of two legal opposition parties, the other being the **China Youth Party**. DSP ideology resembled European democratic socialism. Members of the DSP for some time held a number of nonelected seats in the **Legislative Yuan** and **National Assembly**. With the growth and success of the **Democratic Progressive Party**, the DSP lost support and faded from the political scene.

DEN KOJIRO. The eighth governor-general of Taiwan under Japanese rule and the first civilian governor-general.

DIALECTS (FANG YEN). A term that refers to the different "languages" of the various provinces of China, and sometimes within the provinces, that are unintelligible to Chinese from other provinces or areas, though they are written in the same characters and can be understood in the written form by other Chinese. **Mandarin** Chinese, the national language in both the People's Republic of China and the **Republic of China**, derives from the Peking dialect. **Taiwanese, Hakka**, and a number of other Chinese dialects are spoken in Taiwan. Taiwanese comes from Southern Fukienese, or the Amoy Dialect, and is spoken widely throughout Taiwan. Hakka, which has no provincial base in China, is prevalent in **Hsinchu,** Miaoli, Taoyuan, Pingtung, and some other parts of the island. Both are spoken with different accents depending on the area of Taiwan. Teaching in public schools in Taiwan is in Mandarin. Television and radio programs are mainly in Mandarin and Taiwanese, though since 1989 Hakka is heard more frequently on radio and television. The **president**'s national addresses are given in Mandarin and dubbed in Taiwanese and Hakka. If the different dialects are considered separate languages, most residents of Taiwan are at least bilingual. In other words, most speak a dialect in addition to Mandarin Chinese.

DIAOYU ISLANDS. *See* TIAOYUTAI.

DOLLAR DIPLOMACY (CHIN-YUAN WAI-CHIAO). A term used to describe the **Republic of China**'s policy of granting economic assistance to some small Third World countries to ensure keeping formal diplomatic ties with those countries, or establishing such relations with Third World countries by using money as an incentive. The People's Republic of China and critics in Taiwan and elsewhere have criticized previous governments as well as the Chen administration for promoting dollar diplomacy. Both have denied that they "buy" diplomatic ties and accuse Beijing of doing this. *See also* INTERNATIONAL COOPERATION AND DEVELOPMENT FUND.

DOUBLE TEN DAY (HSUANG-SHIH-CHIEH). Meaning the tenth day of the tenth month, or 10 October, this is the **Republic of China**'s National Day. It commemorates the Wuchang Uprising staged by **Sun Yat-sen**'s followers in 1911, which ignited a nationwide revolt against the Manchus, or the Ch'ing Dynasty government, then ruling the mainland part of China. The establishment of the Republic of China followed the next year. Parades and other festivities are held on this holiday, and the **president** gives a formal public address on this day.

DUTCH EAST INDIA COMPANY. The de facto colonial government of Taiwan for nearly four decades prior to 1662, it ruled the island from its Asian headquarters in Jakarta. By 1650, the company controlled almost three hundred Chinese villages. It governed the island by dividing it into districts formally ruled by **aborigine** chieftains. Though the company maintained political control by force of arms, it also used proselytizing and economic leverage as means of control. The company brought new crops and farming techniques to Taiwan and exported large amounts of venison, deerskins, and sugar from Taiwan to both China and Japan. For some years, Taiwan was the company's second-most-profitable venture, drawing handsome revenues from both taxes and trade. The Dutch East India Company also brought progress to Taiwan by building roads and irrigation works, conducting surveys, and romanizing aboriginal languages.

– E –

EAST ASIA ASSOCIATION (TUNG-YA HSIEH-HUI). Taiwan's quasi embassy in Tokyo set up after Japan and the **Republic of China** broke diplomatic relations in 1972.

ECONOMIC COOPERATION ADMINISTRATION (CHING-CHI HO-TSO HUI-YI). A U.S. government organization established to provide economic assistance to the Nationalist government after it moved to Taiwan in 1949.

ECONOMIC MIRACLE (T'AI-WAN CHING-CHI CH'I). A term frequently used to describe **Taiwan**'s very impressive economic development after the mid-1960s, but also employed to recognize that Taiwan was able to do so well in promoting economic growth in spite of a bleak outlook in the late 1940s and 1950s. In 1949, when the Nationalist government moved to Taiwan, many economists described Taiwan's economic prospects in very pessimistic terms. Some even called Taiwan a "basket case" and opined that Taiwan had little hope to grow economically and that it would always be poor. The reasons usually given were Taiwan's lack of natural resources; its very bad population-to-land ratio; its lack of capital; and an inefficient, corrupt, and discredited government. Some also noted that Taiwan lacked technological skills, and its population was not well educated.

These evaluations proved wrong, and instead Taiwan grew very rapidly, averaging 10 percent annual growth (often called miracle growth) from the mid-1960s to the early 1980s, notwithstanding two oil crises that caused economic instability and slowed growth. This rate of growth made Taiwan the number-one-performing **economy** in the world during this period. Taiwan's economic growth subsequently slowed, but over a period of thirty-five years, it was still the best of any developing country in the world. Thus Taiwan succeeded against what appeared to be all odds. Also, while Taiwan attained very rapid growth, incomes were very equitable, which is often not the case using the capitalist model of economic development. The term "economic miracle" has also been used to describe the fact that Taiwan was not affected very much by the so-called Asian economic meltdown that began in July 1997. Taiwan's economy was not hurt by this phenomenon as were many other countries in East Asia.

Taiwan's economic success has been attributed to a number of factors, including **land reform** in the 1950s; U.S. economic assistance (which for some years was the largest to any country in the world not at war, but which, unlike aid to most other recipients, was used effectively, and when it was terminated, Taiwan's economy "took off"); an intelligent import substitution plan (which was wisely terminated after a brief period, as many countries have failed to do); export promotion policies; high rates of savings; privatization; improvements in **education** geared to create a better workforce; **export processing zones**; and intelligent government planning and oversight of a free market economy. (*See* FOURTEEN PROJECTS; TEN PROJECTS.)

Taiwan pursued economic growth based on free market, free trade principles and invited foreign **investment** while rejecting dependency theory. Many large state-owned or state-controlled industries, which in the early years were felt to be best kept in the public sector due to their vital connections to national defense, were privatized. Unionization was discouraged, crime was controlled, taxes were kept low, and economic freedom and opportunities were provided generously by the government. It was a clear case of promoting business and viewing economic development as rightly preceding political change. The Taiwan economic miracle is often said to be the basis for its political modernization and democratization. *See also* LI KWOH-TING; POLITICAL MIRACLE.

ECONOMIC PLANNING COUNCIL (EPC) (CHING-CHI CHI-HUA FA-CHAN HUI-YI). Established in 1973, the EPC became the successor to the **Council for International Cooperation and Development**. It was a smaller and less powerful body, but like its predecessor organization it was responsible for planning economic growth.

ECONOMIC STABILIZATION BOARD (CHING-CHI AN-CHUAN WEI-YUAN-HUI). Established in 1953 as a successor to the **Taiwan Production Board**, it was responsible for ensuring currency stability and promoting economic development, especially by helping Taiwan's fledgling industries.

ECONOMY (CHING CHI). From the mid-1960s to 2000, Taiwan was said to have experienced miracle economic growth, though that term applies more strictly to the initial twenty-five years. Growth slowed toward the end of the period, though it was still regarded as good when Taiwan avoided the East Asian meltdown in 1997. Soon after **Chen Shui-bian** was elected **president**, however, the economy collapsed, and in 2001 the country experienced negative growth of 2 percent and unemployment near 5 percent, both rates that few had ever seen or thought possible. The opposition blamed the Chen administration for gross mismanagement of the economy combined with antibusiness policies, such as its rejection of Taiwan's fourth nuclear power plant and its alleged disregard for future **energy** supplies. Chen blamed opposition obstructionism and the downturn in the world economy, especially the recession in information technology.

The economy rebounded in 2002 with growth in the gross national product (GNP) just over 3 percent. This did not meet the standards of pre-2001, however, and was far behind Taiwan's growth in the past. Growth dropped a bit in 2003 to 3.5 percent and rose slightly in 2004 to fall again to just over 4 percent in 2005.

The issue of **trading** with and investing in China was of paramount concern because of its political and strategic implications. A million people from Taiwan were living in and doing business in China, constituting more than 10 percent of the workforce. This included many people with talent. Accompanying this was **investments** going to China that probably totaled well over US$100 billion. This was at once hollowing out Taiwan's industrial sector and generating huge profits (most of which were reinvested). Meanwhile Taiwan's trade with China exceeded—and nearly doubled—its trade with the United States. China allowed a very large trade deficit with Taiwan, keeping Taiwan's economy healthy, to a large extent, many said, because most of the profits stayed in China in the form of investments in the expansion of plants. This situation made Taiwan's economy dependent on China's. This issue was hotly debated in the Chen administration, with some saying that this was the only way Taiwan's economy could grow (in agreement generally with the opposition), and others saying that it was destroying Taiwan economically and undermining its sovereignty while trashing any hope it has for political independence.

The **three links** were part of the discussion since a ban on direct transportation ties with China made trade, travel, and so on inefficient and obviously more costly than it should be. Indirectly related to the China issue was the increasing number of foreign laborers in Taiwan and the problems this caused for local labor and labor organizations, and in some cases in human rights matters when these workers were exploited and mistreated. Meanwhile, foreign investment in Taiwan fell in 2001 and dropped further in 2002, but it rose after that and stayed just below pre-2000 levels. Domestic investment fell but recovered in 2004. Foreign trade followed this pattern. Foreign reserves remained high, ranking Taiwan number three in the world. In global surveys, Taiwan's economy generally received good marks for the basics.

In addition to the issues relating to dealing with China economically, a rising public debt, an increase in inequity in incomes and wealth, declining public health and health care, intellectual property rights violations, and corruption were cited by observers as concerns. There was also apprehension about China linking up with the Association of Southeast Asian Nations (ASEAN) to construct a common market, possibly adding Japan, Korea, and India to encompass nearly half the population of the world in an Asian market organization, with

China demanding that Taiwan not be included. *See also* BANKING; INVESTMENT; TRADE.

In 2005, Taiwan's gross national product was US$355 billion, and its per capita income was US$15,676 (though it was no doubt higher than this as there was a significant underground economy). Gross national savings was 25.01 percent, unemployment was 4.13 percent, and inflation was 2.30 percent. Foreign exchange reserves stood at US$253 billion. *See also* ECONOMIC MIRACLE.

EDUCATION (CHIAO-YU). Education had long played an important role in Chinese society; in fact, it was the major determinant in social class standing, though before 1949 this was less true in Taiwan than in China. Prior to the Japanese period, the educated portion of the population was small. By the end of the period, 70 percent of children attended elementary school. More education contributed to more worldly and progressive attitudes, a greater desire for political participation, greater equality, and much more. The Japanese government encouraged college students to study in the hard sciences, engineering, and medicine and discouraged law and the social sciences. The Chinese classics and the Chinese language fell into disuse. The best students went to Japan.

After 1945, under Nationalist Chinese rule, mass education was continued. The **Constitution** mandated schooling for children up to the age of twelve, and for 25 percent of the national government's expenditures (even more for provincial and local governments) to go to educational and cultural pursuits. The focus of education was on training a quality workforce to help promote economic development and to build social consensus and unity. In 1968, compulsory education was increased from six years to nine. The Ministry of Education set standards and decided on textbooks that were made standard throughout the country. The ministry encouraged girls to get an education and emphasized the sciences. The academic calendar was adjusted to follow the U.S. system. The number of private schools increased rapidly after 1950 to meet the increasing demand for education. Now private schools account for about one-fourth of students below the college level and for more than half of college and university students.

The greater resources provided to improve education produced results: by the 1980s, compared with countries at the same level of development, Taiwan's quality of education, according to **United Nations** surveys, was six times higher, and Taiwan competed favorably with many developed countries (with twice as many college students per capita as the United Kingdom). Meanwhile, illiteracy was reduced to 2 percent of the population by 1990. Many of Taiwan's students went abroad for graduate study, mostly to the United States. Through the 1980s, Taiwan sent more students to the United States than any country in the world. It is said that many who returned brought with them ideas about democracy that greatly influenced Taiwan politically. This was especially true in view of the fact that in Taiwan, higher education is seen as an important qualification to run for political office. In the 1990s, 70 percent of cabinet members had studied abroad, and around 60 percent had obtained U.S. PhDs. **Lee Teng-hui**, **Lien Chan**, and **James Soong** were among those that got a PhD degree from a well-known university in the United States. Taiwan has also attracted a number of foreign students to study Chinese, and **Overseas Chinese** who want to get degrees in Taiwan's institutions of higher learning.

Critics in recent years have said that Taiwan's universities do not match the quality of the nation's primary and secondary education (which ranks Taiwan one of the top five nations in the world according to international surveys), and the universities have not improved in quality compared to others in Asia or the world due to excessive egalitarianism, the opening of too many colleges and universities, and lowered standards.

EIGHT-POINT PROPOSAL (CHIANG BA-TIAN). Points made in a speech by Jiang Zemin in January 1995 entitled "Continuing to Promote the Reunification of the Motherland." The speech did not contain new policies but rather was a reiteration of Beijing's policy (by Jiang Zemin as Deng Xiaoping's heir apparent) toward Taiwan. Jiang said that China would make Taiwan a special administrative region of the People's Republic of China. The proposal was apparently made because of concern about a shift in U.S. Taiwan policy in the form of the **Taiwan Policy Review**, the maturing of democracy in Taiwan, and a succession problem in China (Deng Xiaoping being old and ill at this time). Jiang blamed independence advocates in Taiwan and "foreign forces" that were trying to "split" Taiwan from China, and he viewed the two as connected. He declared that China would use military force to stop this, though he also said "Chinese should not fight Chinese."

The proposal in many ways seemed generous and conciliatory, stating that China did not intend to "swallow up" Taiwan and would allow it a "high degree of autonomy." However, to Taiwan's political leaders and its population, since the proposal denied the sovereignty of the **Republic of China**, it was not considered acceptable. President **Lee Teng-hui** responded with a "**Six Point Proposal**"—the first time Taipei ever responded directly to any PRC proposal.

EIGHTIES, THE (PA-SHIH NIEN-TAI). A monthly magazine founded and operated by **Kang Ning-hsiang** in the late 1970s, which advocated democracy and supported opposition causes. It was considered more moderate than *Formosa*. *See also* MEDIA.

ELDER PARLIAMENTARIANS. *See* SENIOR PARLIAMENTARIANS.

ELECTION COMMISSION. *See* CENTRAL ELECTION COMMISSION.

EMERGENCY DECREE. *See* MARTIAL LAW.

ENERGY (NENG YUAN). Ironically, given **Taiwan**'s current energy situation, the island attracted foreign ships in the past that needed coal. Its coal mines now have been worked out, and all that remains are small deposits that are too deep to mine profitably. Taiwan's last operating coal mine closed in 2001. In the early post–World War II period, waterpower from dams provided cheap electricity that facilitated the island's economic development. In the 1970s, Taiwan's energy situation became a serious problem because its economic development far outpaced its local energy production, and new sources of energy were not found. Air pollution and the cost of imported energy were related critical problems. From self-sufficiency, Taiwan's domestic production of energy fell to 12 percent in 1983 and is now only around 2 percent, with annual increases in usage now around 6 percent.

As a result of concern about energy, Taiwan has diversified its sources of energy and also the origin of its imports. Oil provides the largest portion of Taiwan's energy but has decreased from 62 percent of the total in 1983 to 51 percent in 2003. Meanwhile, coal increased from 18 percent to 33 percent, and natural gas from 4 to 8 percent (including the liquefied form). Hydropower fell from 3 to 1 percent, and nuclear from 13 to 8 percent. The industrial sector of the economy has been the big consumer of energy, though it has fallen in recent years to 57 percent in 2003. **Agriculture** has used less; transportation and residential use have increased. Taiwan consumes a considerable amount of petroleum in its plastics industries.

Taiwan imports most of its oil, nearly 80 percent, from several countries in the Middle East. Most of the rest comes from Southeast Asia. Its natural gas comes from Indonesia and Malaysia. Its coal is purchased from Australia, Indonesia, and China. To ensure supplies, Taiwan has its own oil tankers and keeps a considerable amount of petroleum stored.

ENLIGHTENMENT SOCIETY (CH'I-MENG SHE-HUI). An organization formed in Japan in 1918 by **Taiwanese** who sought a voice in the Japanese National Diet. The organization had some influence in Japan, but Governor-General Akashi did not allow it to establish branches or to publish in Taiwan.

ENVIRONMENTAL PROTECTION ADMINISTRATION (EPA) (HUAN-CHING PAO-HU-SHU). Elevated to cabinet-level status in August 1987 and renamed in 1988, the EPA sought to respond to and correct the increasingly bad environmental situation in Taiwan caused by the nation's rapid industrialization. Before the creation of the EPA, protection of the environment was handled by the Bureau of Environmental Sanitation in the Department of Health, and later by the Bureau of Environmental Protection. **Jaw Shau-kong** became the EPA's director in 1991 and very aggressively pushed for stricter environmental standards. The EPA has been responsible for passing a host of new environmentally friendly laws and for providing Taiwan with cleaner air and water. The EPA is the only organization of the national government whose sole concern is the environment. *See also* TAIWAN ENVIRONMENTAL PROTECTION AGENCY.

EP-3 INCIDENT (EP-SAN SHIH-CHIEN). A crisis resulting from the collision of a U.S. Navy reconnaissance plane (the EP-3) and a Chinese F-8 fighter plane over the South China Sea on 1 April 2001. The Chinese plane crashed, and the pilot was killed. The U.S. plane made an emergency landing at a Chinese Air Force base on Hainan Island; its crew was held, and the plane was inspected, both violating international law according to the United States. Furthermore, Washington said that the pilot had a reputation for "hot-dogging," and it was his fault the collision occurred. China said the U.S. plane should not have been spying on China, even though it was over international waters, and warned the United States about continuing such flights. The plane was said to have been collecting information on China's new weapons acquired from Russia that had implications for Taiwan.

The incident, especially China holding the crew for eleven days and examining the spy equipment on board, caused a serious deterioration in U.S.–China relations for a while and was said to have motivated the George W. Bush administration to agree to a large sale of weapons to Taiwan soon after the incident. The United States continued the flights despite Chinese warnings not to.

ER ER BA. Meaning 2-2-8 in Chinese and referring to 28 February of 1947, the term recalls a period of bloody repression in Taiwan by the Nationalist government that had taken control of the island two years earlier. On that date, **Taiwanese** spontaneously took to the streets to protest, or rebel (the terms used varies), following an incident in which the police detained a woman who was selling black-market cigarettes on the street. A crowd formed that scared the police, and they opened fire, killing and injuring several people. At this time, tensions had been building between Taiwanese and the Nationalist government because of months of misrule of Taiwan under the leadership of Governor **Ch'en Yi**, during which time the **economy** collapsed and social order disintegrated while soldiers looted and stole private property. Because of this, the Nationalist government, after being initially welcomed by Taiwanese after World War II, became seen as a vile, incompetent, carpetbagger government.

On 28 February, thousands of Taiwanese who were provoked into action by the incident took the opportunity to vent their anger against the government and assault **Mainland Chinese**. Many Mainland

Chinese—or frequently simply anyone who could not speak Taiwanese, including many **Hakka**—were beaten and killed. Military forces were brought in from the mainland, and the "rebellion" was suppressed with a vengeance, resulting in widespread killing. Many Taiwanese leaders were among those who died, and many more were imprisoned or executed after order was restored, causing some to say that a generation of the "best and brightest" Taiwanese was lost. Most Taiwanese subsequently remembered the incident with strong ill feelings. However, for many years it was taboo to discuss the incident, and little was said or written about it. With democratization, however, details of the event have been discussed and made public.

In February 1992, the government issued a detailed report of the incident based on formerly classified documents and put the number killed at between eighteen thousand and twenty-eight thousand. In February 1995, President **Lee Teng-hui** made a public apology on behalf of the government for the incident, and the **Legislative Yuan** passed a bill to pay compensation to victims' families. A monument was also established. In 1997, 28 February was made a national holiday. President **Chen Shui-bian** and **pan-green** politicians often evoke memories of the event as a means of provoking public ire against the **Nationalist Party** and **pan-blue**, and to rally their political base during an election campaign.

EVERGREEN GROUP (CHANG-YUNG CHI-T'UAN). Also known as Evergreen Marine Corporation, it is one of Taiwan's largest corporate groups. It was founded in 1968 and soon became the largest container shipping company in the world. In July 1991, it launched EVA Airlines, Taiwan's first private international airline. **Chang Yung-fa** is the chairman and a major owner.

EXAMINATION YUAN (KAO-SHIH-YUAN). One of five branches of the central government of the **Republic of China**, it has the responsibility of writing and administering civil service examinations used to recruit government officials; the employment and management of civil service personnel; and setting criteria for evaluating, promoting, and compensating government employees. By making it a separate branch of government, the framers of the **Constitution** wanted it to remain free of partisan political influence. Its high status is also attributable to the importance of civil service testing and recruitment in Chinese political culture and to the fact that it has a counterpart in the ancient Chinese system. Its president and nineteen members are appointed by the **president** with the approval of the **Legislative Yuan** for six-year terms. The Examination Yuan is made up of a council, a secretariat, the Ministry of Examination, the Ministry of Civil Service, and the Civil Service Protection and Training Commission.

EXECUTIVE YUAN (HSING-CHENG-YUAN). One of the five branches of the central government of the **Republic of China**. The Executive Yuan is considered the highest administrative organ of government and the most powerful branch of the government. It is made up of policy-making organs, executive organs (the cabinet), and subordinate organizations such as its Secretariat; the **Government Information Office**; the Directorate-General of the Budget, Accounting and Statistics; the **Council for Economic Planning and Development**; and the **Research, Development, and Evaluation Commission**. The most important organs of the Executive Yuan are the eight ministries: interior, foreign affairs, national defense, justice, finance, economic affairs, communications, and **education**.

The Executive Yuan is constitutionally responsible to the **Legislative Yuan**, but in many respects it acts quite independently. The head of the Executive Yuan is the **premier**, who is appointed by the **president**. Second in command is the vice premier. The premier performs the duties of the president in the event the president and vice president cannot (for a period up to three months), presents administration policy to the Legislative Yuan, countersigns laws and decrees, and requests the Legislative Yuan to reconsider resolutions. When **Chiang Kai-shek** died, his son **Chiang Ching-kuo** ran the government from the position of premier. After **Lee Teng-hui** became president, there developed some controversy about the role and powers of the premier, especially vis-à-vis the president. With Lee appointing new premiers, and with constitutional changes dealing with this issue, the president clearly emerged stronger. Under President **Chen Shui-bian**, the Executive Yuan has been weaker because the opposition holds a majority in the Legislative Yuan. *See also* EXECUTIVE YUAN COUNCIL.

EXECUTIVE YUAN COUNCIL (HSING-CHENG-YUAN HUI-YI). The guiding body of the **Executive Yuan**, it is made up of the **premier** (who is chairman), the vice premier, heads of ministries and commissions, and ministers of state. It meets every Thursday morning to discuss the finalization of bills, declarations, and treaties to be submitted to the **Legislative Yuan** for approval, in addition to matters of concern to one or more ministries or commissions. It is considered an important locus of power in the government of the **Republic of China**. *See also* EXECUTIVE YUAN.

EXPORT PROCESSING ZONES (EPZ) (CHIA-KUNG CH'U-KOU-CH'U). First established in **Kaohsiung** in 1966, with two more zones added three years later at **Taichung** and Nantze, their purposes were to attract foreign **investment** and export Taiwan-made products. They offered foreign businesses tax breaks and reduced regulations. Foreign companies were not allowed to sell their products in the domestic market; however, this policy was later softened. The EPZs were so successful that, by the late 1970s, they accounted for nearly 10 percent of Taiwan's exports. They increased exports, reduced unemployment, and upgraded the country's labor skills. From 1966 to 1988, Taiwan's EPZs emphasized labor-intensive manufacturing; from 1989 to 1997, capital-intensive manufacturing; and from 1998 to the present, technology and design work. Other countries, including China, have copied Taiwan's export processing zones. Many said they were successful because they combined an industrial complex with a free port. *See also* FREE TRADE PORT ZONES; TRADE.

– F –

F-5E. The designation given to an aircraft manufactured by Northrop Corporation of the United States together with several companies in Taiwan. It was for many years the backbone of the **Republic of China**'s Air Force. Taipei for some time asked the United States to sell it a more advanced plane, but the United States refused. (*See* FX.) The Republic of China then decided to build its own fighter plane. (*See* INDIGENOUS DEFENSE FIGHTER.) Subsequently, the United States decided to sell **F-16** fighter planes to Taiwan, and

France sold Taiwan the **Mirage 2000-5**. After that, the F-5Es were mostly withdrawn from service or used for training. *See also* ARMED FORCES.

F-5G. An aircraft built by Northrop Corporation of the United States that Taiwan considered buying to replace the **F-5E** but decided against in favor of the **FX**.

F-16. A high-performance fighter aircraft manufactured by General Dynamics of the United States, 150 of which the United States sold to Taiwan in 1992 for the stated purpose of maintaining a force balance in the **Taiwan Strait** following the purchase of a number of high-performance MiG aircraft from Russia by the People's Republic of China. Taipei wanted to purchase the more sophisticated F-16C/D model but was allowed to buy only the F-16A/B, though this plane was modified to meet Taiwan's defense needs and was armed with AIM-7 Sparrow air-to-air missiles, AIM-9 Sidewinder missiles, Maverick missiles, cluster bombs, and other advanced weapons. Delivery of the planes began in 1997. The F-16s are based in **Chiayi** and Hualien and, in combination with the **Indigenous Defense Fighter** and **Mirage 2000-5** aircraft, give Taiwan formidable air defense capabilities. *See also* ARMED FORCES.

F-20. A fighter plane, also called the Tigershark, which Northrop Corporation of the United States planned and built in prototype and intended to sell as an air defense plane. Taiwan seriously considered buying this plane. However, Northrop did not get sufficient orders elsewhere, with most nations favoring the **F-16**, and therefore did not produce the F-20. *See also* ARMED FORCES.

FAIR TRADE COMMISSION (KUNG-P'ING MAO-YI WEI-YUAN-HUI). Established in 1992 and made part of the **Executive Yuan**, this commission seeks to promote a fair trade system.

FAMILY PLANNING PROGRAM (CHIA-T'ING CHI-HUA). A nationwide campaign launched in 1964 to curb the **Republic of China**'s then very-high birthrate. It reflected an awareness of Taiwan's very dense population and the economic costs of population growth. The program was so successful that the birthrate dropped precipitously. By 1990, the government became concerned about a "population gap" and began to encourage an increase in the birthrate. Family planning meanwhile had begun to emphasize promoting genetic health and screening for chronic diseases.

FEBRUARY 28 UPRISING (ER-ER-BA SHIH-PIAN). *See* ER ER BA.

FEI HSI-PING (1916–2003). A guerrilla leader who fought against Japan during World War II and later became a high **Nationalist Party** official and member of the **Legislative Yuan** representing Manchuria. In the 1970s, he quit his post and resigned his party membership because of disenchantment with party and government policies. In the early 1980s, Fei advocated expanding basic freedoms and democracy. He subsequently became a founding member and leader of the **Democratic Progressive Party** (DPP). In 1988, however, he left the DPP because of its support for Taiwan's independence and in protest of the DPP's stance on the retirement of **senior parliamentarians**. Fei was one of the few **Mainland Chinese** DPP leaders.

FIVE NOES (WU BU). Pledge made by President **Chen Shui-bian** in his inauguration address in May 2000: no declaration of independence, no change of national title, no inclusion of the two-states theory in the **Constitution**, no holding of a referendum on reunification or independence, and no abolition of the **National Unification Council** or the **National Unification Guidelines**. Originally there were four; the last was added later. The promises were intended to allay suspicions in the United States (and possibly China) about Chen's support for independence. Later, critics said that he did not honor his pledge. On a number of occasions, Washington cited the five noes pledge when President Chen seemed to be violating one or more of them or advocating or moving Taiwan toward independence.

FIVE-POWER SYSTEM (WU-CHUAN CHIH-TU). The term used to describe the **Republic of China**'s five-branch political system. Three are similar to those in Western democracies: the **Executive Yuan**, the **Legislative Yuan**, and the **Judicial Yuan**. Two others, the

Control Yuan and the **Examination Yuan**, come from the traditional Chinese system. **Sun Yat-sen** devised this system of government.

FIVE PRINCIPLES (WU-TA YUAN-TSE). Cited by President **Chiang Ching-kuo** on 28 December 1978 to be the basis of future relations between Taiwan and the United States in the absence of formal diplomatic relations. The principles were continuity, reality, security, legality, and governmentality.

FLAG (KUO CH'I). The flag of the **Republic of China** was officially adopted in December 1928 following the Northern Expedition led by **Chiang Kai-shek**, which unified China, though it had been in use in south China before that. The flag is composed of a white sun on a blue background in the upper left one-quarter of the flag; the rest of the flag is crimson. The twelve points on the sun represent the two twelve-hour periods of the day and unceasing progress. The three colors on the flag represent **Sun Yat-sen**'s **Three Principles of the People**. Specifically, blue signifies brightness, purity, freedom, and a government of the people; white represents purity, honesty, selfness, and equality, or a government by the people; and red stands for sacrifice, bloodshed, brotherly love, and a government for the people. The opposition before 2000, now the ruling **Democratic Progressive Party**, has been critical of the flag since it is seen to represent China and not Taiwan, as Taiwan was not part of China at the time it was adopted. They have also noted that the **Nationalist Party**'s flag is identical to the top left one-quarter of the national flag, suggesting that Taiwan is still a party-state system. They have suggested changing the flag, but at the present this seems unlikely in view of the fact that they do not have the votes in the legislature to change the **Constitution** or in some other way adopt a new flag.

FLEXIBLE DIPLOMACY (T'AN-HSING WAI-CHIAO). The term used for Taiwan's shift in **foreign policy** stance in the late 1980s regarding dealing with nations and international institutions that have formal ties with the People's Republic of China. According to the precepts of flexible diplomacy, the **Republic of China** should not demand formal recognition or require the use of the term "Republic of China" in dealing with foreign nations or international organizations.

Some observers said the policy was adopted to deal with Taipei's diplomatic setbacks in the 1970s and 1980s. Others said it related to confidence on the part of government leaders in Taipei due to Taiwan's successful and widely lauded democratization. Still others said it reflected the reality of **two Chinas**. Many associate flexible diplomacy with President **Lee Teng-hui**, though it seems to have originated with President **Chiang Ching-kuo** and what was earlier called "practical diplomacy." In any event, in 1988, the **Republic of China** resumed participation in the **Asian Development Bank** as "Taipei, China."

In November 1988, when Saudi Arabia announced it would probably establish formal diplomatic relations with the People's Republic of China, Taipei declared that it would no longer insist on being recognized as the sole legitimate government of China. At this same time, a spokesman for the Ministry of Foreign Affairs said that Taipei "did not flatly reject" offers to establish relations with nations that recognize the People's Republic of China. In 1989, Taipei welcomed ties with Grenada and Liberia despite their formal diplomatic ties with Beijing. In 1990, the Republic of China applied to the General Agreement on Tariffs and Trade as the "Customs Territory of Taiwan, Penghu, Kinmen and Matsu." In 1991, the Republic of China joined the **Asia–Pacific Economic Cooperation** forum as "Chinese, Taipei." *See also* DOLLAR DIPLOMACY; PRAGMATIC DIPLOMACY; SUBSTANTIVE DIPLOMACY; VACATION DIPLOMACY.

FOREIGN POLICY (WAI-CHIAO CHENG-SHE). Throughout much of **Taiwan**'s history, its foreign policy was determined by the ruling authority and not by the people. That was the case when Taiwan was governed by Holland, China, and Japan. In 1945, Taiwan again became part of China, following which its external relations were determined in Nanking. After 1949, when the Nationalists were defeated and fled to Taiwan, they continued to stand for China in international affairs. Most Western countries maintained formal ties with Taipei on that basis; Communist bloc countries established embassies in Beijing.

For the next twenty-two years, Taipei held the China seat in the **United Nations**, including a permanent seat on the Security Council.

During that time, the **Republic of China** aligned with the Western bloc led by the United States and took a decidedly anti-Communist position in world affairs. The government regarded China as a country occupied by "bandit" Communists and vowed to liberate the mainland and govern it once again. The **Taiwan Strait** became an area of tension as a result. In 1954–1955, and again in 1958, the two sides fought over the **Offshore Islands**, with the United States helping Taiwan on both occasions. After the first crisis, Taipei signed a defense agreement with the United States called the **United States–Republic of China Defense Treaty**. Just after it was signed, the U.S. Congress added the **Formosa Resolution** to extend the treaty's provisions to the Offshore Islands.

Thus Taipei aligned even more closely with the United States, though it was not successful in getting the United States to overtly help it liberate China. Washington feared that this would lead to an expanded conflict and might bring the United States into war with the Soviet Union. Gradually, Taipei gave less attention to freeing China from Communism, as it knew it was not likely to succeed at this. It thus focused its efforts on economic development and "defeating Mao politically." Taipei nevertheless stuck to its one-China policy. In the early 1960s, it appeared that Taipei might change this policy, but the Cultural Revolution in China and the Vietnam War gave a respite to those who wanted to keep it.

In 1971, the United Nations General Assembly voted to give Beijing the China seat, and Taipei left the UN. This was followed by most nations of the world shifting diplomatic recognition from Taipei to Beijing and by Taiwan's expulsion from most political international organizations. This prompted Taipei to reevaluate its one-China policy and to consider keeping or establishing formal diplomatic ties with nations that recognized Beijing, though because China did not accept this, it was not successful. Taipei did, however, succeed in maintaining informal relations and **trade** links with most countries in the world.

The Republic of China experienced another setback in 1979 when the United States switched recognition to Beijing. One of the Republic of China's responses to dealing with this shock, and to Taiwan's increasing isolation and Beijing's concerted efforts to marginalize Taiwan so as to eventually absorb it, was to democratize and thus win favor from the United States and the international community. Taipei hoped to gain support for its right to chose its future and to remain sovereign and separate from China. Taipei also pursued various forms of informal diplomatic initiatives. Coinciding with these shifts in policy, public opinion began to influence foreign policy making more and more, and Taiwan was soon said to have a democratic foreign policy.

In 1991, President **Lee Teng-hui** announced that the Republic of China was ending the state of war with China, and with it any claim to territory governed by Beijing. This, however, was not seen as a friendly move in China, but instead as a move to create **two Chinas**, or one China and one Taiwan. Lee continued to say and do things suggesting that he supported Taiwan's legal and permanent separation from China, thus angering Chinese leaders in Beijing. Lee contended that he was forced to do this because of China's efforts to isolate and denigrate its status in international affairs and that he was determined to preserve Taiwan's sovereignty. Thus he parried China's proposals to unify Taiwan with China by demanding that Taiwan be considered equal with China in any negotiations, which Beijing rejected. He also said frequently that he had to consider the wishes of the people, Taiwan being a democracy, and most citizens did not want to join China as long as it was poor and Communist.

When the Soviet Union collapsed in 1991, Taiwan had to contend with a militarily more threatening China since Beijing was able to move much of its military south to areas adjacent to Taiwan; thus Taiwan did not enjoy a "peace dividend" from the end of the Cold War but rather witnessed a more tense and dangerous environment. The most challenging matter was China's missile buildup across the Taiwan Strait. China, in fact, conducted missile tests near Taiwan to intimidate the island's population in 1995 and 1996, the latter during Taiwan's first direct election of its **president**. This caused the United States to send aircraft carrier groups to the Taiwan Strait, and a face-off with China resulted.

President **Chen Shui-bian**, elected in 2000, also angered China with his support for an independent Taiwan. Initially the Chen administration enjoyed strong support from the United States. Chen lost that from deliberately provoking China for his own political benefit and from Taiwan not doing its share in helping the United States maintain security in the region. The Chen administration's foreign policy also faced a dilemma in pursuing Taiwan's independence while advancing wider commercial relations with China and found that it could do little about China's successful efforts to isolate Taiwan.

FORMOSA. The Portuguese word for "beautiful" (translated into Chinese as *mei-li-tao*) used in the West, sailors on a Portuguese ship being the first Westerners to see **Taiwan** and recording that term in their logbook. They called it **Ilha Formosa** or "Beautiful Island." It was for a long time, and to some extent still is, the Western word for Taiwan. Although it is a term associated with the period of Western colonial rule over Taiwan, it is often used by the advocates of independence to suggest that Taiwan should not be regarded as historically (or now legally) part of China, as the term "Taiwan" might suggest. Some use the term to depict Taiwan as a scenic place. *See* REPUBLIC OF CHINA.

***FORMOSA* (MEI-LI-TAO LI-K'AN).** A magazine launched in February 1979 by the **Formosa group**, a radical, antigovernment political opposition active in Taiwan at the time. *Formosa* followed the themes of an earlier magazine, the *Taiwan Political Review*, in calling for reform and democracy while criticizing the **Nationalist Party**'s "monopoly" political rule and economic growth with high social costs. It was also highly critical of what it considered the slow process of democratization in view of the country's lack of credibility internationally after U.S. derecognition of the **Republic of China** in January. It was banned after a short time, but it had considerable influence for several months at a watershed time in Taiwan's recent history. *See also* KAOHSIUNG INCIDENT (KAO-HSIUNG SHIH-CHIEN); MEDIA.

FORMOSA FACTION (MEI-LI-TAO HSI). For some time the larger of the two major factions of the **Democratic Progressive Party** (DPP) and generally regarded as the moderate wing or faction when compared to the **New Tide faction.** Though it was once a radical faction, it changed in the late 1980s when many of its members were elected to office or saw hopes of gaining political positions. The Formosa faction advocated self-determination (demanding that the national government reflect the fact that it ruled only Taiwan and some other small islands and not the mainland of China) rather than independence. It also generally advocated negotiations rather than street action as a tactic to gain political power domestically, in contrast to the New Tide faction.

In recent years, the Formosa faction has advocated more extensive **trade** and other commercial relations with the People's Republic of China, as well as negotiations with Beijing that set aside the issue of sovereignty and focused on economic, social, and technical issues. It also differed from the New Tide faction in pressing the view that the DPP should appeal to the middle class and the business community, rather than underprivileged groups, and that the DPP should abandon its socialist views. In October 1988, at the DPP's third congress, **Huang Hsin-chieh**, then head of the Formosa faction, was elected chairman of the party. The Formosa faction was subsequently headed by **Hsu Hsin-liang**. In the mid-1990s, the Formosa faction began to fall apart and was subsequently disbanded, with most of its members joining other centrist factions.

"FORMOSA GROUP" (MEI-LI-TAO CHENG-T'UAN). A group, sometimes called a "political action" body, organized by **Yao Chia-wen**, **Chang Chun-hung**, **Huang Hsin-chieh**, **Hsu Hsin-liang**, and **Lin Yi-hsiung** in 1979 to publish the *Formosa* magazine, to advocate democracy and Taiwan's independence, and to criticize the **Nationalist Party** for its authoritarianism and failed foreign policy among other things. Members of this group organized events that led to the **Kaohsiung Incident**.

FORMOSA PLASTICS GROUP (T'AI-WAN SUO-CHIAO KUNG-YEH YU-HSIEN KUNG-SZU). One of Taiwan's largest corporate groups, made up of Formosa Plastics Corporation, Nan Ya Plastics, and some other companies, it is also regarded as one of Taiwan's most financially sound enterprises. It is headed by **Wang Yung-ching**.

FORMOSA RESOLUTION (T'AI-WAN CHUEH-YI-AN). A resolution adopted by the U.S. Congress one month after the **United States–Republic of China Defense Treaty** was ratified, it authorized the U.S. president to "employ the Armed Forces of the United

States as he deems necessary for the specific purpose of securing and protecting **Formosa** and the **Pescadores** against armed attack . . . to include related positions." This extended the authority of the president to take action to help Taipei defend against an attack by the People's Republic of China on the **Offshore Islands** of **Quemoy** and **Matsu**. Congress repealed the resolution in 1974 in the context of improving U.S.–China relations.

FORMOSA STRAIT. *See* TAIWAN STRAIT.

FORMOSA TELEVISION CORPORATION (FTV) (MIN-SHIH). Taiwan's first fully private over-the-air television, which was approved by the government in 1996 and began broadcasting in June 1997. FTV became the fourth television provider that could be received islandwide. FTV stocks are owned by a large number of shareholders, reportedly more than ten thousand. Its sister station, Formosa News, broadcasts over cable. Although FTV officials say the station is unbiased and will not yield to any business or political interests, its board of directors is made up mainly of **Democratic Progressive Party** members or supporters. *See also* MEDIA.

FORMOSAN ASSOCIATION FOR PUBLIC AFFAIRS (FAPA) (T'AI-WAN-JEN KUNG-KUNG SHIH-WU-HUI). An organization formed in 1982 in the United States by **Taiwanese**, including **Peng Ming-min**, its purpose being to influence the U.S. government and world public opinion to support democracy, self-determination, and human rights in Taiwan. Headquartered in Washington, D.C., but also running chapters around the United States and in major cities in some other countries, it became known as an effective lobbying group. In 1986, FAPA succeeded in getting representatives Stephen Solarz and Jim Leach to sponsor a resolution calling for freedom of expression and association in Taiwan and the establishment of a fully representative government. Some say the debate initiated by FAPA prompted *tangwai* leaders in Taiwan to subsequently form the **Democratic Progressive Party**.

In recent years, FAPA has lobbied more on behalf of Taiwan's interests that are seen as being threatened by China, especially by Beijing's efforts to isolate Taiwan diplomatically, and the right of Taiwan's leaders to visit the United States, membership in the World Health Organization, U.S. weapons sales to Taiwan, and so on. FAPA works with members of the **Congressional Taiwan Caucus**. *See also* WORLD UNITED FORMOSANS FOR INDEPENDENCE.

FORMOSANS FOR FREE FORMOSA (T'AI-WAN-JEN TI TZU-YU T'AI-WAN). A proindependence group formed in 1955 by students in the Philadelphia area. It supported **Liao Wen-yi**, who promoted Taiwan independence in Japan. In 1960, it became the **World United Formosans for Independence**.

FOUR NOES. *See* FIVE NOES.

FOUR PHASES OF THE ROC THEORY (CHUNG-HUA MIN-KUO SZU-CHIEH-TUAN). A construct promoted by **Chen Shui-bian** in 2005 that sees four periods in the **Republic of China**'s history: one, from 1911 to 1949, when the Republic of China (ROC) and **Taiwan** were not related; two, from 1949 to 1988, or the "ROC moved to Taiwan" period; three, from 1988 to 2000, or the "ROC in Taiwan" era; and four, after 2000, which became "the ROC is Taiwan" phase. In his **Double Ten Day** speech in 2004, President Chen had put forth the idea that the ROC is Taiwan and Taiwan is the ROC. China objected, saying that this was "intended to project Taiwan's sovereignty internationally." The United States responded by saying that it "didn't perceive Taiwan as an independent country." Chen, when putting forth his theory, announced also that he had changed the name of his office to the **Office of the Presidency**, Republic of China (Taiwan)—adding the word Taiwan.

FOURTEEN PROJECTS (SHIH-SZU-HSIANG CHIEN-SHE). A group of large and very important infrastructure development projects started in 1985 as a sequel to the **Ten Projects** and the **Twelve Projects**. Most were scheduled to be completed in the early 1990s. Total cost was projected to be about $33 billion. Projects included the following: Expansion of **China Steel Corporation**, Power Projects (Taiwan's fourth nuclear power plant plus hydroelectric and thermal plants), the Oil and Natural Gas Project, Modernization of Telecommunications, Railway Expansion, Highway Expansion, the

Underground Railroad in **Taipei**, the Taipei Mass Transit System, Flood Control and Drainage Improvement, Development of Water Resources, Ecological Protection and Domestic Tourism, the Municipal Solid Waste Disposal Project, the Medical Care Program, and Community Development Projects.

***FREE CHINA FORTNIGHTLY* (TZU-YOU CHUNG-KUO).** A literary journal established in 1949 in China with Ministry of Education funding, which shortly thereafter moved to Taiwan. "Free China," a group associated with this publication, advocated constitutional democracy and ending one-party rule in Taiwan. The well-known intellectual **Lei Chen** managed the journal. Free China followers advocated Anglo-American liberalism, which **Hu Shih** had tried to promote. Hu was supportive of the group at first but withdrew that support when the leaders of Free China became involved with the **China Democratic Party**. The journal ceased publication in September 1960. Those involved with this publication were predominantly **Mainland Chinese** and are regarded by some to have established the first real opposition movement in Taiwan. *See also* MEDIA.

FREE CHINA JOURNAL. *See TAIWAN JOURNAL.*

FREE CHINA REVIEW. *See TAIWAN REVIEW.*

FREE TRADE AGREEMENT (FTA) (TZU-YU MAO-YI HSIEH-TING). An agreement that dramatically reduces or eliminates tariffs and other barriers to trade between nations. Taiwan signed an FTA with Panama in 2003 and Guatemala in 2005 and has pursued agreements with a number of other countries including Japan and the United States. Taiwan's leaders see FTAs as a means of promoting advanced economic development through trade and dealing with the fact that China effectively opposes Taiwan's participation in regional economic organizations.

FREE TRADE PORT ZONES (TZU-YU KANG-CH'U). Established by the **Council for Economic Planning and Development** in 2004 in the port of **Keelung**, and adding **Kaohsiung** Port in 2005, the zones are treated as "within the territory but outside the customs" of Taiwan. Enterprises in the zones have considerable autonomy in their economic activities, including dealing with foreign exchange and carrying on other financial transactions. In addition, goods can be moved freely within the zones and to and from other zones. Companies enjoy exclusions from tariffs, commodity taxes, business taxes, trade promotion fees, and so on. Within the zones, 40 percent of the employees can be foreign. According to various studies, the zones will facilitate value-added businesses. *See also* EXPORT PROCESSING ZONES; TRADE.

FUBON FINANCIAL HOLDINGS (FU-BANG CHIN-K'UNG). Taiwan's second-largest financial services group. It is run by **Tsai Wan-tsai** and family.

FUKIEN TAIWANESE. *See* HOKLO.

FX. Designation of two jet fighter planes—the F-16/J79 and the **F-5G**—which the United States considered selling to Taiwan in the 1970s. In December 1981, however, the Ronald Reagan administration decided against the sale because the planes were considered "offensive" weapons. Beijing had strongly opposed the sale.

– G –

GARRISON COMMAND (OR TAIWAN GARRISON GENERAL HEADQUARTERS) (T'AI-WAN-CH'U CHING-PEI TSUNG-PU). Created in 1950 to administer **martial law**, the Garrison Command was one of the main commands under the Ministry of Defense. It was also considered the most powerful security organization in Taiwan for a long time because of its authority over arrests and prosecutions for sedition, its responsibility for monitoring the mail, its carrying out of censorship, and its checking on overseas travel. Its powers were diminished by the termination of **martial law**, and it was finally disbanded in 1992. The **Coastal Patrol General Headquarters** was created to handle its responsibilities in controlling smuggling.

GERMAN FORMULA (TEH-KUO MO-SHIH). Said, in retrospect, to have been a policy objective of the United States in the late 1960s and early 1970s in negotiating with the People's Republic of China, meaning Washington sought to establish diplomatic relations with Peking and keep official diplomatic relations with Taipei. This goal, if it was U.S. policy, was never realized. The German formula meant **two Chinas**, or at least two governments, and for that reason there were many opponents on both sides of the **Taiwan Strait**.

The German formula more recently has been cited as a means whereby the People's Republic of China and the **Republic of China** might mend their differences and unification might be realized, whereby China would allow Taiwan to participate in international organizations and have a legitimate place in the international arena, in return for which Taipei might be willing to talk about some kind of federation. The rationale is that Beijing's efforts to isolate Taiwan diplomatically make Taipei more recalcitrant and unwilling to negotiate unification. The German formula, in fact (though the term is not used often), may be said to have been the policy of government leaders in Taipei prior to 2000.

In 1993, Taipei announced the goal of joining the **United Nations** General Assembly under the divided nations formula that allowed the two Germanys and the two Koreas to join. Some at this time said that the Republic of China had formally accepted the German formula. Less has been heard about the German formula since **Chen Shui-bian** became **president**. China never supported the German Formula. *See also* SINGAPORE SOLUTION.

GO SOUTH POLICY (NAN-HSIANG CHENG-TSE). A government-guided initiative or informal policy announced in 1993 and promoted by President **Lee Teng-hui** that encouraged Taiwan businesspeople to invest in Southeast Asian countries rather than in the People's Republic of China due to a fear that Taiwan was putting too much **investment** capital in the mainland and that Beijing would gain economic leverage over the **Republic of China** as a result. President Lee advocated this policy even more strongly in 1995 and 1996 in response to the missile tests Beijing conducted in the **Taiwan Strait** to intimidate Taiwan prior to a **Legislative Yuan** election and before Taiwan's first direct presidential election. This policy has led to political contacts between Taiwan's top leaders and high officials in some Southeast Asian countries and has therefore been condemned by China. In recent years, this policy has become seen as having failed due to Taiwan's large and increasing investments in China, though Lee Teng-hui and some top leaders in the **Democratic Progressive Party** still advocate it. *See also* GO WEST POLICY; NO HASTE POLICY.

GO WEST POLICY (HSI-HSIANG CHENG-TSE). A policy enunciated by some leaders in Taiwan saying that **investment** should be encouraged in the People's Republic of China rather than discouraged according to the **Go South policy**. The **Democratic Progressive Party** has generally opposed this view, though former DPP chairman **Hsu Hsin-liang** has advanced it. Many business leaders in Taiwan support it, though they seldom use this term.

GOTO SHIMPEI. The first civil administrator of Taiwan, in office from March 1898 to November 1906. He helped bring reform to Taiwan under Japanese rule.

GOU, TERRY. Chairman of **Hon Hai Precision Industry Company**, Gou was named in *Forbes*'s richest-people list in 2006 as ranking 147th in the world and number two in Taiwan. His net worth was put at US$4.3 billion.

GOVERNMENT INFORMATION OFFICE (GIO) (HSIN-WEN CHU). A government agency created after World War II when the Nationalist government ruled China. It was reestablished in 1953 in Taipei. It is attached to the **Executive Yuan**, and its job is to explain government policies to the press and disseminate information about the **Republic of China** abroad through its numerous overseas offices. In the past, under **martial law**, it censored the press; subsequently, its function was mainly overseeing the **media** and serving as the government's voice in making its policies known to the populace and in doing public relations work. Before **Chen Shui-bian** became **president**, he and the **Democratic Progressive Party** (DPP) pledged to expand press freedom, and some thought that the GIO would be disestablished or would at least see its funds and functions cut. But instead the

GIO flourished and was used to control the press by buying advertising only from friendly publications, by refusing licenses to unfriendly radio and television stations, and the like. Thus it became an issue of criticism by the new opposition, or **pan-blue**. Recently the GIO has been downsized, with many of its functions transferred to the **National Communications Commission**.

GRAND HOTEL (YUAN-SHAN TA-FAN-TIAN). A large hotel built in traditional Chinese architectural style, located on the Keelung River in the outskirts of **Taipei**, and owned by the Taiwan Friendship Society. **Madam Chiang Kai-shek** was an initiator of building the hotel in the 1950s and was part owner. It has been the site of many important diplomatic meetings and conferences over the years. U.S. president Dwight D. Eisenhower stayed there during his visit to Taiwan in the 1950s. In recent years, the hotel has not retained its special status due to the large number of competing top-notch hotels in Taipei and its somewhat out-of-the-way location, though it remains a popular place for foreign tourists.

GREATER CHINA (TA CHUNG-KUO). The idea that Hong Kong, Macao, **Taiwan**, and possibly Singapore constitute Chinese political entities and should form some kind of union, such as a federation, commonwealth, or regional organization. The extensive economic links among them that formed after Deng Xiaoping came to power in 1978 pushing free market reforms and encouraging foreign trade and **investment** in the People's Republic of China are seen as the basis for this. The end of the Cold War and proliferating contacts among these groups have also given rise to this notion. Since Hong Kong and Macao are now part of China, and since Beijing does not claim Singapore as its territory, the focus now is on Taiwan. A Greater China federation or other such concept has been seen as a solution to the dispute between China and Taiwan over Taiwan's status and has been cited in the context of growing trade between China and Taiwan and Taiwan's large commercial investments in China. The Chinese government has not expressed support for the idea though.

GREEN ISLAND (LÜ TAO). An island off the east coast of southern **Taiwan** about forty kilometers (twenty-five miles) from Taitung, it is

the location of a famous prison. From May 1951 to 1991, an estimated 20,900 inmates passed through the prison, including many
convicted under **martial law**. Over one thousand were reported to
have been executed. The prison was built as a high-security facility
during the Japanese era on what was then called "Fire Island." The
island was renamed in August 1949. The prison remains, though the
government has recently been trying to make the island a tourist at-
traction by encouraging the building of international-class hotels
there. Indeed, few places in Taiwan can compete with Green Island
for unspoiled beauty. The island is called Green Island for its green
mountains, which contrast markedly with the turquoise ocean around
it. The island is quite small, about six square miles, and has a population of around three thousand, most of whom engage in fishing.

GREEN TERROR (LU KUNG-BU). Term used by the opposition and
other critics of the rule of **Chen Shui-bian** and the **Democratic Progressive Party**, depicting it as a dictatorship and as reviving many of
the aspects of **white terror** that it long condemned, and also criticizing its policies favoring **Fukien Taiwanese** and discriminating
against other ethnic groups, especially **Mainland Chinese**. Actions
taken against the **media** and scholars who do not favor the Chen administration are also cited. Green refers to the **Democratic Progressive Party**'s color.

GUIDELINES FOR NATIONAL REUNIFICATION. *See* NA-
TIONAL UNIFICATION GUIDELINES.

– H –

HAKKA (K'E CHIA). The term designating one of the two major
groups of Chinese who migrated to **Taiwan** before the end of World
War II and subsequently populated the island. The Hakkas were probably the earliest Chinese to go to Taiwan in any numbers, migrating
there beginning as early as a thousand years ago, from South China,
mainly Kuangtung. The Hakka had been earlier displaced from North
China and had moved to various parts of China, though mostly in the
south, and for that reason they became known as "guest people"—the

literal meaning of Hakka. They also suffered from various kinds of discrimination in China, including being barred from taking the civil service examination for many years. Not long after they arrived in Taiwan, Fukien Taiwanese, or **Hoklo**, forced them from the best coastal farming areas.

Today, Hakka compose 10 to 15 percent of the population of Taiwan. The Hakka are culturally, linguistically, and in many other ways different from the Fukien Taiwanese and have a history of conflict with them, particularly before the arrival of the Nationalists. Hakka constitute a majority of the population in some areas of Taiwan, including Taoyuan, Miaoli, Taichung, and Pingtung counties. Most Hakka speak their own language in addition to **Taiwanese** and **Mandarin**. Many are active politically, holding jobs in the police systems, railroads, and other government agencies. Former president **Lee Teng-hui** is Hakka.

HAN LIH-WU (1975–1991). Minister of **education** from 1949 to 1950 and adviser to the **president** from 1950 to 1956, he subsequently served as ambassador to a number of countries. Han, however, is best known for his efforts in bringing many antiques and other national treasures from the mainland in 1949, and for that he was on China's "most wanted list" of Nationalist Chinese officials. Nevertheless, in Taiwan, and even in China, he has also been regarded as a hero for his actions, since Red Guards would have destroyed many of these priceless artifacts during the Cultural Revolution in China. The treasures he brought make up a large portion of those things on display in the **National Palace Museum**.

HASEGAWA, KIYOSHI. The governor-general of Taiwan from 1940 to 1944. Hasegawa was an admiral in the Japanese navy.

HAU PEI-TSUN (1919–). **Premier** from 1990 to 1993, Hau was an army general who had a long and distinguished military career, including serving as chief of the general staff. Hau was also a top official in the **Nationalist Party** and served as minister of defense from 1989 to 1990. His appointment to the premiership was opposed by the **Democratic Progressive Party** and others who felt that a military person should not serve in this office, though he soon gained public respect due to his success in cracking down on crime and social disorder. During his tenure as premier, Hau on many occasions disagreed with President **Lee Teng-hui**, this being characterized as a personal feud and a struggle for power between **Mainland Chinese** and **Taiwanese** by the **media**. A subsequent more Taiwanese-dominated government and a strengthening of presidential authority followed his resignation in 1993. In late 1995, Hau resigned his membership in the Nationalist Party, and in 1996 he was a candidate for vice president on a ticket with **Lin Yang-kang**. The two ran as independents but had support from the **New Party**. *See also* ARMED FORCES.

HEAVEN AND EARTH SOCIETY (T'IEN-TI-HUI). One of the largest and most famous of China's secret societies, it was reputed to have been founded by **Cheng Ch'eng-kung** in 1646 and had a close **Taiwan** connection. It had much stricter rules of secrecy than other triads: participants could not divulge information about their membership to anyone, including their family. The Heaven and Earth Society was responsible for organizing and leading many of the great rebellions during Ch'ing Dynasty rule, including those in Taiwan. To "oppose the Ch'ing and restore the Ming" was one of its avowed political goals.

HOKLO. Term for the **Taiwanese**, or the early Chinese inhabitants of **Taiwan**, who came from Fukien Province, speak that language, and claim that their ethnic origins and culture are from there, as opposed to the **Hakka**, who have a different culture and language. The majority, or around 70 percent, of the population of Taiwan is Hoklo.

HOME RULE ASSOCIATION (TZU-CHIH HSIEH-HUI). An organization that was founded and grew in **Taiwan** in the early 1920s during the period of Japanese colonial rule. Its members were active in both Taiwan and Japan. Its main tenet was the advocacy of home rule for Taiwan rather than assimilation. **Lin Hsien-t'ang** was an active member and led the organization for a number of years. The organization also worked for better treatment of Taiwan by the Japanese government and equal rights for **Taiwanese**. For a while it enjoyed considerable influence in Tokyo. In 1936, after the Japanese colonial government cracked down on the organization's activities in Taiwan and arrested some of its members, many left and joined **Chiang Kai-shek** or Mao Zedong in China. Some other members formed the Taiwan Proletarian Youth League, which had ties with the Japan Communist Party. The association had six associated or subordinate organizations, of which one—the **Culture Society**—survived.

HON HAI PRECISION INDUSTRY COMPANY (HUNG-HAI CHING-MEI KUNG-YEH KUNG-SZU). One of **Taiwan**'s largest and most profitable companies, it claims to be the largest electronics manufacturer in the world. In 2005, *BusinessWeek* ranked it the world's number-two information technology company. The company has operations in various places in the world. It employs one hundred thousand people in China. Its chairman is **Terry Gou**.

HOUSE OF LIN (LIN CHIA). A family "dynasty" founded by Lin P'ing-hou, who gained wealth and government position in the Ch'ing Dynasty government in China, and who migrated to **Taiwan** from Fukien Province in 1778. His son, Lin Kuo-hau, relocated the family to Pan-ch'iao in Taiwan, and the family subsequently became Taiwan's largest landholder. Kuo-hau had several successful sons, one of whom helped **Liu Ming-ch'uan** in his modernization efforts. The family was later co-opted by the Japanese but remained rich and powerful for some time. The Lins founded a sugar company in 1909 and the Hua Nan Bank in 1919. Today, the Lin home and garden, recently donated to the county of **Taipei**, are tourist attractions.

HSI SHA. *See* PARACEL ISLANDS.

HSIAO LIU-CH'IU. Literally meaning "Small Liu-ch'iu" or Small Ryukyus, the term was used in China, even as late as the sixteenth century, to refer to Taiwan. *See also* PAKKAN TAO.

HSIAOKANG INTERNATIONAL AIRPORT (HSIAO-KANG KUO-CHI FEI-CHI-CH'ANG). Located near **Kaohsiung**, it is Taiwan's second international airport.

HSIEH, FRANK (1946–). Also known as Hsieh Chang-ting (his Chinese name), Hsieh served as **premier** from 2005 to 2006. He started his political career as one of the attorneys who defended the dissident leaders who stood trial after the **Kaohsiung Incident**. Subsequently he served on the **Taipei City Council** from 1981 to 1988. Meanwhile, he became a founding member and one of the noted leaders in the **Democratic Progressive Party** (DPP). He founded the Taiwan Welfare State Alliance, a DPP faction or support group. In 1989, he was elected to the **Legislative Yuan**. In 1996, he ran unsuccessfully as the party's candidate for vice president with **Peng Ming-min**. In 1998, he ran for the position of mayor of **Kaohsiung** and won. From 2000 to 2002, Hsieh was chairman of the DPP. When he left the premiership in early 2006, he was at odds with President Chen.

HSINCHU. One of **Taiwan**'s five large cities administered by Taiwan Province, it is located on the west coast of the northern part of the island near the **Hsinchu Science-Based Industrial Park**.

HSINCHU SCIENCE PARK (HSP) (HSIN-CHU K'E-HSUEH KUNG-YE YUAN-CH'U). A 5,200-acre research and industrial park established in 1980 near the city of **Hsinchu** (about an hour from **Taipei**) and patterned after California's Silicon Valley. Sometimes called "**Taiwan**'s Silicon Valley," it was a first for Taiwan and was quite successful. By 1989, ninety-nine high-tech companies were operating there, generating revenues of over US$2 billion. By 1996, revenues had reached US$11.34 billion. U.S. **investment** in the park was said to be around US$1.38 billion, and trade between the park's industries and the United States was US$4.6 billion. By 2003, the park had an annual production value of US$36 billion, representing 12 percent of Taiwan's manufacturing output, and that year, companies in the HSP accounted for 5 percent of the world's integrated circuits. A number of companies in the park have offices in Silicon Valley in the United States, and companies from Silicon Valley have offices in the park.

HSIUNG FENG II-E (BRAVE WIND). Taiwan's locally built cruise missile, first tested in June 2005, that has a one-thousand-kilometer range. It was developed by the **Chung Shan Institute of Science and Technology**, though it seemed patterned after the U.S. Tomahawk cruise missile. Observers noted that the missile could strike cities in Southeast China and may give Taiwan a measure of deterrence in the face of a large number of Chinese missiles placed across the **Taiwan Strait** and targeted on Taiwan. In early 2006, *Jane's Defense Weekly* reported that Taiwan plans to build fifty by 2010, and five hundred after that. *See also* ARMED FORCES.

HSU HSIN-LIANG (1941–). Chairman of the **Democratic Progressive Party** (DPP) from early 1996 to 1998, Hsu was formerly a **Nationalist Party** official but in 1977 ran for magistrate of Taoyuan County as an independent when he failed to get the party's endorsement. He won a very controversial election amid rumors of Nationalist Party ballot-box tampering to prevent his victory that sparked public violence. (*See* CHUNGLI INCIDENT.) He fled to the United States in 1979 after continuous feuding with the government and the Nationalist Party. He remained "in exile" in the United States until 1988, during which time he established the **Taiwan Revolutionary Party** and wrote articles advocating urban guerrilla warfare in Taiwan to overthrow the government. In 1986, Hsu established the Taiwan Democratic Party in San Francisco and offered to make his party an overseas branch of the Democratic Progressive Party when it was established in September of that year.

In November 1986, Hsu tried to return to Taiwan but was refused entry. Supporters who had gone to the airport to meet him engaged in stone throwing, to which the police responded with water hoses and tear gas, creating a widely debated "incident." Hsu returned to Taiwan after **martial law** was lifted in 1987 and joined the DPP. As a DPP member, he was a radical but popular opposition politician. Later he mellowed, changing in particular his formerly radical views about political reform in Taiwan and independence. Subsequently, Hsu headed the more moderate **Formosa faction** of the DPP.

In 2000, failing to get the DPP's nomination, he ran as an independent for **president**. At that time, he withdrew or was forced from the DPP mainly over his views regarding Taiwan's independence, which he no longer supported. In the next few years, Hsu was very critical of **Chen Shui-bian**'s policy toward China. In 2004, after the controversial presidential election when Chen Shui-bian and **Annette Lu** were shot, Hsu formed the Taiwan Democracy School.

HU SHIH (1891–1962). A professor of philosophy at Beijing University who in 1917 launched a movement to promote a written vernacular Chinese. Hu engaged in a "war of pens" with leftist and pro-Communist writers in the years that followed. Hu was active in the **May the Fourth Movement**, which marked the beginning of Chinese nationalism. He was subsequently the **Republic of China**'s ambassador to the United States. Hu went to Taiwan with the Nationalist government and there became an advocate of democratic reform.

HUANG, PETER (1937–). Also known by his Chinese name Huang Wen-hsiung, he was a member of the **World United Formosans for Independence** who, in 1970, when **Chiang Ching-kuo** was visiting New York, attempted to assassinate him. Huang and an associate were arrested but then jumped bail. They were found guilty of attempted murder in absentia. Huang returned to **Taiwan** to become president of the **Taiwan Association for Human Rights**. President **Chen Shui-bian** appointed Huang a human rights adviser.

HUANG HSIN-CHIEH (1917–1999). Chairman of the **Democratic Progressive Party** (DPP) for three terms from 1988 to 1991, his rise in politics was through elections, beginning with city councilor and ending with his election to the **Legislative Yuan**. He was early on a member of the **Nationalist Party** but left disillusioned. In 1964, Huang supported independent **Kao Yu-shu** for **Taipei** mayor. He was one of the **Formosa group** leaders who was arrested after the **Kaohsiung Incident** and sentenced to jail. In total, he served more than seven years in prison. After his release, he became a major figure in the establishment of the **Democratic Progressive Party**; some say he was its "spiritual founder." He subsequently became a leader of the more moderate **Formosa faction** of the DPP before becoming party chairman.

In the summer of 1997, Huang accepted President **Lee Teng-hui**'s offer to serve as vice chairman of the **National Unification Council**, which critics in the DPP said contradicted the party's stance on independence and that Huang's membership in the DPP should be suspended. Huang argued that his position on unification had not changed and that in accepting this job he was working for the good of the nation. Huang later in life became viewed by many as a DPP elder statesman.

– I –

ILHA FORMOSA. Meaning "Beautiful Island" in Portuguese, these were the words written in the log of a Portuguese ship when the first Westerners saw **Taiwan** in 1590. *See also* FORMOSA.

INDIGENOUS DEFENSE FIGHTER (IDF) (CHING-KUO-HAO CHAN-CHI). Also called the **Ching-kuo,** the IDF is Taiwan's home-built high-performance, all-weather, multi-role jet fighter plane. Its construction began after the Ronald Reagan administration decided not to sell Taiwan the **FX** aircraft. In March 1986, it was revealed that General Dynamics Corporation had been licensed as a consultant to help in the effort, though this was not a "full service" role—meaning that the consultants could not design the plane but could find flaws in design and so advise Taiwan's engineers and scientists. Beijing viewed this as reneging on the **August 1982 Communiqué**, but the United States argued that it was a private arrangement and did not violate the agreement.

Taipei announced the completion of the aircraft in 1988. The first demonstration flights were conducted in October 1989. The first squadron of IDFs was commissioned in 1994, and a second in 1995. In April 1997, the 427th Wing, composed of seventy IDFs, went into service. Another wing of sixty IDFs was formed in 1999. The plane was intended to help **Taiwan** maintain its defenses against an attack by the People's Republic of China by denying it air superiority over Taiwan and the **Taiwan Strait**. It was also built so that Taipei would have to rely less on the United States for arms purchases. In fact, some have said that the IDF resolved the thorny issue between Washington and Beijing concerning U.S. arms sales to Taiwan, and also that it marked the beginning of Taiwan seriously getting into the business of manufacturing arms.

The plane, however, was built at a very high unit cost. Its future was, moreover, brought into question in 1992 when the United States changed its policy and agreed to sell Taiwan **F-16** fighter planes, after which France decided to sell **Mirage 2000-5** fighters; Taiwan contracted to buy 150 of the former and 60 of the latter. Subsequently, Taipei decided to build only 130 IDF planes after originally planning to build 250. IDFs are based in **Taichung** and **Tainan**. *See also* ARMED FORCES.

INDUSTRIAL TECHNOLOGY RESEARCH INSTITUTE (ITRI) (KUNG-YEH K'E-CHIH YEN-CHIU-YUAN). Established in 1973 to develop technology in **Taiwan**, ITRI is a nonprofit organization that transfers research to local companies, in some cases under contract. It is located in **Hsinchu**. Its projects are largely generic and are done under government supervision. They are categorized by **industry**, including eight at present: electronics, information, mechanical engineering, material science and technology, **energy** and mining, electro-optics, pollution abatement, and measurement technology. ITRI has made a number of technological contributions to Taiwan's technological modernization and can take credit for some research breakthroughs, including work on microchips and successful experiments with superconductivity. ITRI has about five thousand employees, mostly engineers.

INDUSTRY (KUNG YEH). Industry in **Taiwan** before the late years of the Chinese period consisted of cottage industry. The Japanese developed light industry in Taiwan and later some heavy industry, but most of that remained in Japan. In the late 1950s, Taiwan began to become an industrial country with the growth of factories, such as textiles and small appliances, around the big cities. During the 1960s and 1970s, industry's share of the gross national product grew at twice the pace of the United States and Japan during their periods of industrialization. This is usually accounted for by Taiwan's good infrastructure, excellent government planning, privatization, and a high rate of savings. U.S. economic assistance helped in the early stages, but not after 1965. Increases in labor productivity were important once industrialization got going.

The first important industry in Taiwan was textiles, that industry using natural products, mostly cotton, and utilizing Taiwan's cheap labor. The industry has been hurt by increasing labor costs and has shifted to synthetics and up-market production. Electrical equipment, electronics, small appliances, and consumer goods followed as Taiwan's industries became more capital intensive. Information products came next, especially computers and parts, as industry became more knowledge intensive. Taiwan became the largest producer of computer parts in the world, making more than 50 percent of the total world's consumption of many items. Taiwan also developed its own computer industry; **Acer** is the most well-known brand. It has also gotten into the production of semiconductors and related items in a big way. Meanwhile, Taiwan developed a steel industry, shipbuilding, plastics, petrochemicals, and pharmaceuticals.

Recently, much of the computer industry and many semiconductor factories have moved to China, creating concerns in Taiwan that its premier companies have left, "hollowing out" Taiwan. Design and software remain, however. Meanwhile, Taiwan's **economy** is becoming more service oriented. In 1986, industrial production accounted for nearly half of Taiwan's gross national product; in 2004, it was under 30 percent. In terms of the workforce, it peaked in 1987 at 42.8 percent; in 2004, it was 35.2 percent. Manufacturing constitutes 86 percent of total industrial production. Small and medium-size enterprises account for most of Taiwan's industry by the number of companies, almost 98 percent in 2003. They employed 78 percent of the workforces and accounted for 31.5 percent of sales and 18.1 percent of exports that year.

INSTITUTE FOR NATIONAL POLICY RESEARCH (KUO-CHIA CHENG-TSE YEN-CHIU-YUAN). Founded in 1988 by **Chang Yung-fa**, it is the nation's first and foremost private think tank involved in public policy research. The institute is pro–**Democratic Progressive Party**.

INSTITUTE FOR TAIWAN STUDIES (TAI-WAN YEN-CHIU-SUO). Policy research organization in the Chinese Academy of Social Sciences in Beijing. In recent years it has held meetings and talks with a sizable number of individuals and groups from **Taiwan**. A number of universities also have organizations with the same name, the most famous being at Xiamen (Amoy) University in Fujian Province.

INSTITUTE OF INTERNATIONAL RELATIONS (IRR) (CHENG-TA KUO-KUAN CHUNG-HSIN). Founded in 1953 as a government think tank, it is now affiliated with **National Chengchi University**. The IRR was considered **Taiwan**'s foremost think tank on Communist nations and international politics before 2000, holding frequent conferences, publishing books and journals, and having considerable input into the foreign-policy–making process. In recent years it has declined in stature and importance.

THE INTELLECTUAL **(CHIH-SHIH FEN-TZU).** A reformist magazine that began publication in 1968 and advocated major social and economic reform, political pluralism, and the realization of **Sun Yat-sen**'s **Three Principles of the People**. It was started and operated by a group of university professors, students, and younger **Nationalist Party** officials, many of the latter associated with **Lee Huan**. The tone of the articles carried in the magazine contrasted, according to some analysts, with **Lei Chen**'s intellectual elitism.

INTERNATIONAL COMMUNITY RADIO TAIWAN (ICRT). Taiwan's only English-language radio station. It replaced Armed Forces Radio Taiwan in 1979 when the United States broke diplomatic relations with Taiwan.

INTERNATIONAL COOPERATION AND DEVELOPMENT FUND (KUO-CHI HO-TSO FA-CHAN YIN-HANG). Established in March 1988 as the International Economic Cooperation and Development Fund with NT$30 billion (just over US$1 billion), it was designed to assist the economic development plans of friendly developing nations. Since then, its funding has been increased. Creating this aid-giving organization reflected **Taiwan**'s new prosperity and its large foreign exchange holdings. According to some, however, its purpose was to "buy" diplomatic relations, which it clearly managed to do, or at least influence, in some cases. *See also* DOLLAR DIPLOMACY.

INTERNATIONAL TECHNOLOGICAL COOPERATION PROGRAM (KUO-CHI K'O-CHI HO-TSO CHI-HUA). A technical aid program established in 1961 to assist the technological development of several African countries and to help keep or expand diplomatic relations with African and other Third World countries. It has since enlarged to include twenty-four nations. Through this organization, **Taiwan** has also offered technical courses for participants from seventy different countries.

INVESTIGATION BUREAU (FA-WU-PU TIAO-CHA-CHU). An arm of the Ministry of Justice sometimes called "**Taiwan**'s FBI," the Investigation Bureau is responsible for domestic law enforcement and counterintelligence work. In the past, it was under the jurisdiction of the **National Security Council**.

INVESTMENT (TOU TZU). During Dutch rule, the **Dutch East India Company** provided some investment capital that helped **Taiwan** develop, though a considerable share of profits was repatriated. Capital was generated locally through taxes on the farmers. Tariffs later were a source of revenue. China provided capital for infrastructure development during the later part of its rule, as did Japan when it ruled Taiwan. Following World War II, especially after 1950, the United States provided capital in the form of economic assistance. Later, Taiwan attracted private capital by offering foreign companies tax holidays and other incentives and through other probusiness policies in the **Export Processing Zones**. By the mid-1980s, Taiwan benefited from more than US$500 million in foreign investments yearly.

Personal savings meanwhile increased to 40 percent—the highest in the world. Business savings were also high—around 25 percent. Favorable interest rates, frugality, and optimism about Taiwan's future economic growth account for this. In 2003, Taiwan received US$3.6 billion in foreign investment. The major sources were the Virgin and Cayman islands, Japan, the United States, and Germany. In the meantime, Taiwan became a foreign investor and in 2004 invested US$4 billion in other countries including the Virgin and Cayman islands, Hong Kong, the United States, Panama, and Vietnam. The investment going to Hong Kong flowed into China, and the amount reported was probably only a fraction of the actual total. It is often said that Taiwan has invested US$100 billion in China; some say it is much more than that. It is controversial because it has resulted in some of Taiwan's best industries moving to China and a hollowing out of Taiwan's **economy**, while also helping China grow economically and militarily. *See also* TRADE.

ISSUES AND STUDIES **(WEN-TI YU YEN-CHIU).** A quarterly journal published by the **Institute of International Relations** that deals with China, **Taiwan**, and global affairs.

– J –

JAPAN INTERCHANGE ASSOCIATION (JIH-PEN CH'IAO-LIU HSIEH-HUI). Japan's quasi embassy in **Taipei**, similar in function to the **American Institute in Taiwan**.

JAPAN–TAIWAN PARLIAMENTARIANS' LEAGUE (JIH-BEN KUO-HUI YU-T'AI HSIAO-CHU). A low-keyed, loosely organized group of approximately three hundred members of the Diet in Japan that includes members of various parties but mostly the Liberal Democratic Party. Though it does not meet formally, or at least with regularity, and little is known about its workings, it has had considerable influence on Japan's relations with **Taiwan**, but also with the People's Republic of China. It is reputed to have influenced Japan's policy a number of times in favor of Taiwan. Sixteen members of the group attended President **Chen Shui-bian**'s inauguration in May 2000.

JAW SHAU-KONG (1950–). At one time one of the activist leaders of the **Nationalist Party**'s **Breakfast Club** and the **New KMT Alliance**, Jaw later became head of the **Environmental Protection Administration** (EPA). In 1992, he resigned from the EPA to run for a seat in the **Legislative Yuan** in its first-ever nonsupplemental election. He did not have the endorsement of the party and in running created difficulties for the KMT. But he won a large number of votes— more than any other KMT candidate. Thus the party did not punish him. However, in 1993, after continued feuds with the **Mainstream faction**, he left the ruling party to help form the **New Party**. In 1994, Jaw was a candidate for the position of mayor of Taipei representing the New Party. He beat the KMT's candidate but came in second to

Chen Shui-bian, the DPP's standard-bearer. Some charged at the time that KMT leaders, knowing their candidate would lose, had diverted votes to the DPP candidate to defeat Jaw. In 1996, Jaw nominally withdrew from politics to pursue a business career, which included taking the position of chairmanship of UFO Broadcasting Corporation. However, he has maintained an influential role in the New Party, and in 1998 he served as the party's campaign manager. In January 2006, Jaw was acquitted in a defamation suit filed by President Chen Shui-bian after Jaw said Chen had given the president of Panama a US$1 million birthday gift.

JOINT COMMISSION ON RURAL RECONSTRUCTION (JCRR) (CHUNG-KUO NUNG-TSUN FU-HSING LIEN-HO WEI-YUAN-HUI). Originally composed of two U.S. and three local commissioners, it planned, and to a large extent effectuated, **Taiwan**'s successful **land reform** program in the 1950s. It continued to operate after land reform was completed, creating farmers' associations and government programs to improve **agriculture**. Many of the commission's reports have been studied by economists and officials in other countries. **Lee Teng-hui** worked for JCRR for several years early in his career.

JU GAO-JENG (1954–). A former leader of the **Democratic Progressive Party** and a parliamentarian who became known as **Taiwan**'s "Rambo" because of his ostentatious and sometimes very aggressive and disruptive tactics in sessions of the **Legislative Yuan**. He left the DPP in 1990 after failing to get the party's nomination to run for a seat in the Legislative Yuan the previous year. He ran as an independent and was elected. Subsequently he formed the **Chinese Social Democratic Party**. In 1994, Ju ran as the **New Party**'s candidate for Taiwan provincial governor but was not elected. In 1995, he was again elected to the Legislative Yuan and became the New Party's whip, but in 1997 he was expelled from the New Party after internal disagreements. In 1998, he ran again for the Legislative Yuan as an independent but was not elected.

JUDICIAL YUAN (SZU-FA-YUAN). One of five branches of the national government of the **Republic of China**, it is similar in its organization and functions to judicial branches in Western political systems. It is composed of a **Council of Grand Justices**, three levels of ordinary courts, administrative courts, and a **Committee on the Discipline of Public Functionaries**.

– K –

KABAYAMA SUKENORI. Taiwan's first Japanese governor-general, serving from 1895 to 1896. He consolidated military control over the island and built an effective police force. He also launched civilian rule in **Taiwan**.

KANG NING-HSIANG (1938–). A well-known opposition **Taiwanese** politician who served on the **Taipei City Council** in the 1960s and won a seat in the **Legislative Yuan** as an independent in 1972. Together with **Huang Hsin-chieh** and others, Kang organized the *tangwai*. Kang also founded a number of publications, including the *Taiwan Political Review* and *The Eighties* and wrote a number of books. Early in his career, Kang was viewed as a radical, but he subsequently became a leader of the moderate opposition. He led the mainstream faction of the **Democratic Progressive Party** in the late 1970s, and after the **Kaohsiung Incident** he became, in the eyes of many observers, the DPP's most prominent leader (with the more radical leaders now in jail). In a few years, however, Kang lost his influence in the DPP. In 1983, **Chiou I-jen** called Kang an appeaser. In 1986, Kang was returned to the Legislative Yuan, though in 1988 the **Formosa faction** and the **New Tide faction** absorbed his faction. In 1993, President **Lee Teng-hui** appointed him to a position on the **Control Yuan**. In 1998, he joined the **Koo-Wang** delegation that visited the People's Republic of China, but he was snubbed while he was there. Kang served as vice minister of national defense under President **Chen Shui-bian** and in 2003 was appointed head of the **National Security Council**.

KAO CHUN-MING (REVEREND) (1929–). The secretary-general of the **Presbyterian Church of Taiwan** in the 1970s; in 1979, he was arrested for giving sanctuary to **Shih Ming-teh**, who masterminded the **Kaohsiung Incident**.

KAO YU-SHU (1913–2005). Mayor of Taipei from 1954 to 1957 and from 1964 to 1972, Kao, also known as Henry Kao, was one of the earliest successful **Taiwanese** politicians that was not a member of the **Nationalist Party**. He was the first popularly elected mayor in 1964, an event that inspired other Taiwanese to seek office as independent politicians and to support Taiwan's independence. Kao later joined the Nationalist Party and served as minister of communications from 1972 to 1976, minister of state from 1976 to 1989, and senior adviser to the **president** from 1989 to 2005.

KAOHSIUNG. Taiwan's second-largest city and its largest port, handling a large portion of the island's exports and imports. The **Republic of China**'s navy operates primarily out of Kaohsiung Port. Its shipbuilding companies are nearby. Kaohsiung was the site of Taiwan's first **Export Processing Zone** and had the distinction at one time of being one of the world's largest container ports. Kaohsiung is located in southwest Taiwan and has a population of a million and a half.

KAOHSIUNG CITY GOVERNMENT (KAO-HSIUNG SHIH-CHENG-FU). Similar to the **Taipei City Government**. It gained the status of a special municipality in 1979, with the reason given being that it was **Taiwan**'s biggest and most important port and its second-largest city.

KAOHSIUNG EIGHT (TSAN-YU KAO-HSIUNG SHIH-CHIEN SHIH-PA JEN). Eight defendants convicted in a widely publicized and controversial trial in March 1980, they were given sentences ranging from twelve years to life for their roles in the **Kaohsiung Incident**. They were **Chang Chun-hung**, Chen Chu, **Huang Hsin-chieh**, Lin Hung-hsuan, **Lin Yi-hsiung**, **Annette Lu**, **Shih Ming-teh**, and **Yao Chia-wen**.

KAOHSIUNG INCIDENT (KAO-HSIUNG SHIH-CHIEN). A widely publicized event that occurred in the city of **Kaohsiung** in December 1979 following an antigovernment protest demonstration parade that was organized by the **Formosa group**. It happened on, and the parade was intended to commemorate, Human Rights Day—

December 10. The demonstration led to an outbreak of violence, during which 183 police were reported injured, though only a few seriously. No demonstrator was hurt. Whether the demonstrators planned to attack the police or whether they panicked when the police tried to surround them is uncertain. If planned, whether the attacks were precipitated by gang members, using the occasion as an opportunity to get revenge against the police, or the Formosa group is not known. In any event, the demonstration followed the loss of diplomatic relations with the United States early that year, which caused the government to lose credibility; opposition activists thus tried to promote the rapid democratization of the political system, saying that only through democracy could **Taiwan** justify asking for support from the international community for keeping its sovereignty. They had considerable public support for promoting democratization. However, after the violence occurred, the public changed its view and sympathized more with the government. In fact, there was little public outcry when those accused of causing the violence, including a number of well-known political figures, were convicted and sentenced to prison. (*See* KAOHSIUNG EIGHT.) Subsequent to the Kaohsiung Incident, there were compromises made between the government and the opposition, and there were "gentlemen's agreements" about democratization. A tangible product was a new election law written for the December 1980 election, which became a watershed event in Taiwan's political development.

KATSURA TARO. Taiwan's second Japanese governor-general, who served in office only three months in 1896.

KEELUNG. A seaport on Taiwan's northern coast, often referred to as Taipei's harbor city.

KETAGALAN (KAI-DA-KE-LAN). A tribe of **aborigines** regarded by some scholars as the oldest inhabitants of **Taiwan**. The Ketagalan were **Pingpu** or plains-dwelling people of the island who resided on its west coast before the arrival of Chinese settlers. Like other Pingpu tribes, they were assimilated by the Chinese or driven into the mountains where they were absorbed by other aboriginal tribes. The Ketagalan are close to extinction now. The name "Ketagalan" also refers to the street in **Taipei** where the Foreign Ministry and the **Presidential Palace** are located.

KINMEN. *See* QUEMOY.

KMT. *See* NATIONALIST PARTY.

KOBAYASHI SEIZO. The governor-general of **Taiwan** appointed in the fall of 1936. He was a retired naval admiral, and his appointment, after seventeen years of civilian rule, signaled Japan's militarization and the coming war with China. Kobayashi renovated the **education** system in Taiwan during his four-year rule and made other improvements.

KODAMA GENTARO. The governor-general of **Taiwan** from February 1898 to April 1906. General Kodama also served as Japanese minister of war after 1900, leaving **Goto Shimpei** in de facto charge of the colonial government in Taiwan. *See also* KODAMA REPORT.

KODAMA REPORT (ER-YÜ PAO-KAO-SHU). A report allegedly written by General Kodama, governor-general of **Taiwan**, in 1901. The report contained a detailed plan of a Japanese attack on French possessions in Southeast Asia, using Taiwan as a base of operations. It was reprinted in a French publication, engendering controversy in France while straining Japanese and French relations. The Japanese government subsequently called it a fabrication. The report resurfaced in 1941, when U.S. intelligence officials noted that nearly all of the projects cited in it had been completed and that Taiwan was indeed used as a stepping-stone for Japan to expand southward.

KOMINKA (HUANG-MIN-HUA). The policy of assimilation practiced off and on by Japan vis-à-vis **Taiwan**, advocated by the political left in Japan. Its supporters opposed a policy of separate rule.

KOO CHEN-FU (1917–2005). Former senior adviser to the **president**, patriarch of the **China Trust Group**, and chairman of the Taiwan Cement Corporation and the Chinese National Association of Industry, Koo wielded considerable political and economic influence in Taiwan for a number of years, though he never held any official government position. Widely known as C. F., he was also the founding chairman of the Taiwan Stock Exchange. Koo garnered considerable press attention and public acclaim through several semiofficial political positions he held, the most important being the chairmanship of the **Straits Exchange Foundation**, where he engaged in negotiating various issues with Beijing in the early 1990s. (*See* KOO-WANG TALKS.) Koo was the son of **Koo Hsien-yung**. The Koo family fortune is valued at several billion U.S. dollars.

KOO HSIEN-YUNG (1866–1937). Born in Lukang, a port city on **Taiwan**'s west coast, he assisted the Japanese army in entering **Taipei** (then a walled city) shortly after the signing of the **Treaty of Shimonoseki** in 1895, during a time of intense debate concerning whether to fight the Japanese or allow them to take control of the island. Later, Japanese authorities gave him a position in the government's security apparatus and a monopoly over the salt trade, plus land in central Taiwan. Koo also got into sugar, manufacturing, retail trade, and land development and served as the director of a number of companies when Taiwan was a Japanese colony. Koo was very active politically, becoming the first **Taiwanese** to sit in the Japanese House of Peers. He also served on the governor-general's advisory council. He helped set up the Public Interest Society in 1923 and later became its president. He established the progressive *Taiwan Magazine* and the **Taiwan Youth Association** (in Tokyo). He was opposed by members of the **Home Rule Association**. **Koo Chen-fu** is his son.

KOO-WANG TALKS (KU-WANG HUI-TAN). Unofficial but important negotiations held in Singapore in April 1993 that were considered to have marked a breakthrough in relations between **Taipei** and Beijing. The meeting was unprecedented in many respects. **Koo Chen-fu**, head of the **Straits Exchange Foundation**, representing Taipei, and **Wang Daohan**, head of the **Association for Relations across the Taiwan Strait**, representing Beijing, led the talks on the two sides. Four agreements were signed. More meetings were anticipated, but they were not held due to anger on the part of the leaders of the People's Republic of China about **President Lee Teng-hui**'s visit to the United States in 1995. Another meeting, however, took place in October 1998 that resulted in some minor agreements.

KOXINGA. *See* CHENG CH'ENG-KUNG.

KU CHENG-KANG (1902–1993). A senior adviser to the **president** in the 1980s, he is also known as the founder of the **World Anti-Communist League**, which he headed for a number of years. He was also head of the **Asian Pacific Anti-Communist League**.

KUNG TEH-CHENG (1920–). A senior adviser to the **president**, he is also a seventy-seventh-generation lineal descendant of Confucius and is the only person in **Taiwan** who holds a hereditary title: Duke of Yen Sheng.

KUNINGTOU (KU-NING-TOU). A village located on the island of **Quemoy** where a bloody battle was fought between Nationalist and Communist forces in October 1949. Following a fierce artillery barrage, the Communist People's Liberation Army launched an assault using three hundred small craft (carrying seventeen thousand troops) against Quemoy. During a two-day siege, Nationalist forces killed eight thousand Communist troops and captured more than six thousand. Communist military units then gave up trying to capture the island, and it remained in Nationalist hands.

KUO, SHIRLEY W. Y. (1930–). An economist who published several books on **Taiwan**'s **economic miracle** and later became a prominent **Nationalist Party** and government official. In July 1988, she was the first woman to become a member of the **Central Standing Committee** of the Nationalist Party and almost at the same time was appointed minister of finance, becoming the first woman cabinet official. The next year, she attended the **Asian Development Bank** meeting in the People's Republic of China, the first time a high government official visited China on official business. In 1990, she was appointed head of the **Council for Economic Planning and Development**. After 1993, she served for several years as a minister of state.

KUO YU-HSIN (1908–1985). A well-known opposition leader who, following defeat in the 1975 national election, went to the United States. He later announced that he sought to run for the presidency against **Chiang Ching-kuo**, but he did not attain sufficient support to become a serious candidate.

KUOMINTANG (KMT) (KUO-MIN-TANG). Literally "Nation-Citizen Party." *See* NATIONALIST PARTY.

– L –

LABOR DISPUTES LAW (LAO-TSE CHENG-YI CH'U-LI-FA). A **Republic of China** law regulating labor-management problems. It was amended in June 1988 to extend the right to strike to any group of ten or more workers involved in a dispute, or two-thirds of the workforce of enterprises with fewer than ten employees, regardless of whether the dispute is in the public or private sector.

LABOR STANDARDS LAW (LAO-TUNG CHI-CHUN-FA). Passed in 1984 by the **Legislative Yuan**, this law, known as **Taiwan**'s "key labor law," defined the role of workers, employers, wages, and contracts while extending labor standards to many workers not previously covered. It also provided guarantees of minimum wages, regulated hours, vacation time, pensions, severance pay, pay equity, maternity leave, and occupational safety and health. Initially, the law covered about 40 percent of the nation's more than eight million workers. In May 1997, the law was extended to cover workers in financial organizations and some other occupations. In December 1996, the law was revised and extended to many workers not covered by the law. By early 1998, the Labor Standards Law covered over 57 percent of Taiwan's workforce. Although the law had a major impact in improving labor conditions, critics complain that it punishes violators with fines only and does not treat infractions as criminal offenses.

LABOR UNION LAW (KUNG-HUI-FA). A **Republic of China** law that regulates union organizing and limits unionization to firms with thirty employees or more. The Labor Union Law allows strikes only after a majority vote of affected workers supports it and if mandatory mediation fails. Critics say the law should be expanded and strengthened, and they note that it allows only one workers union to establish at the national level. In 2004, the government proposed changes that would bar teachers, civil servants, and employees of state-run companies from forming unions. The teachers, opposition parties, and other groups criticized this. *See* CHINESE FEDERATION OF LABOR.

LABOR UNIONS (LAO-GUNG HUI). Labor unions were late to develop in **Taiwan** and were traditionally weak and still are. The Nationalists viewed labor organizations as tools of Communist infiltration and subversion and brought organized labor under party control when on the mainland, and again in Taiwan when it was returned to China's control in 1945. In addition, under **martial law**, strikes were illegal. When martial law was ended in 1987, new unions formed to compete with the government-controlled **Chinese Federation of Labor**.

Soon there were over one thousand industrial unions and more than two thousand craft guilds. In late 1987, a political party, the Labor Party, formed to represent workers. In 1989, another, the Workers Party, organized. Both of these parties were too leftist in their views and thus failed to attract workers' support. The **Nationalist Party** claimed to represent labor, but many said it was too probusiness. The **Democratic Progressive Party** appealed to labor, but it was too focused on city street politics to attract workers' support. The fact that Taiwan has so many small, family-owned businesses was a hindrance to strong unions. On the other hand, recent laws make union membership required in factories that employ more than thirty workers (though civil servants, teachers, and workers in munitions plants are exempt).

The main benefit of union membership, though, is labor insurance; collective bargaining is not important, and the government usually handles safety matters. Thus union membership is high, around 40 percent of union-qualified workers (compared to around 13 percent in the United States and 22 percent in Japan), but it is not as important to workers as in other countries.

LAND REFORM (T'U-TI KAI-KE). Refers to three separate policies carried out during the period 1949 to 1953. The first was rent reduction, which set the rent limit on cultivated land at 37.5 percent of the annual standard yield of chief crops no matter what the actual harvest. (Landlords had previously collected about half of the crop in rent.) The law also included provision for rent relief in the event of crop failure or calamity. The second part mandated the sale of public farmland to farmers, mostly land previously owned by Japanese and confiscated by the Nationalist Chinese government after World War II. This land, amounting to 20 to 25 percent of **Taiwan**'s arable land, was sold to cultivator farmers during the period of 1948 to 1958. The third measure was the land-to-the-tiller program passed into law in 1953, which forced landlords to sell to the government any farmland in excess of 2.9 hectares of medium-grade paddy for a price equal to two and one-half times the annual yield. The government then sold it to tenant farmers. Around 22 percent of the private farmland in Taiwan changed hands as a result of this law. Land reform in Taiwan set the stage for rapid growth in the agricultural sector. More efficient farming subsequently released laborers to work in Taiwan's new factories, thus spurring industrial growth. Land reform also contributed to the end of feudalism in rural Taiwan, rapid urbanization, and the popularity of the **Nationalist Party** in the countryside. On the negative side, it caused instability in rural Taiwan for a while and is said to have cheated the landlords, who received payment in low-interest bonds. Taiwan's land reform program is widely regarded as one of the most successful, if not the most successful, in the world. Western scholars and Third World leaders still study Taiwan's experience in land reform. *See also* JOINT COMMISSION ON RURAL RECONSTRUCTION.

LAW ON CIVIC ORGANIZATIONS (KUNG-MIN TZU-CHIH-FA). A law passed by the **Legislative Yuan** in 1989 to regulate trade associations, social organizations, and political parties. The law's most important provision was to make forming new political parties legal (which was barred under the **Temporary Provisions**). It also put various civic organizations under the jurisdiction of the ministry of interior. The number of civic organizations, including political parties, proliferated after the passage of this law.

LEAGUE FOR THE RE-EMANCIPATION OF FORMOSA (T'AI-WAN TSAI-CHIEH-FANG LIEN-MENG). An organization founded in Hong Kong by **Liao Wen-yi** and Ms. Hsieh Hsueh-hong after the 28 February uprising or rebellion. (*See* ER ER BA.) The former advocated a **United Nations** plebiscite that would allow for self-determination and eventual independence; the latter advocated Communism. Liao later moved his faction to Japan. Hsieh went to the People's Republic of China.

LEE HUAN (1917–). A close associate of **Chiang Ching-kuo** for many years, he served as minister of **education** from 1984 to 1987, secretary-general of the **Nationalist Party** from 1987 to 1989, and **premier** from 1989 to 1990. He lost power following disagreements with President **Lee Teng-hui** in early 1990.

LEE TENG-HUI (1923–). The eighth **president** of the **Republic of China** and chairman of the **Nationalist Party**, both for twelve years from 1988 to 2000. Lee attended Kyoto University in Japan during World War II but returned to **Taiwan** to receive his BS degree from **National Taiwan University** in 1948. In 1953, he got an MA from Iowa State University, and in 1968, a PhD in agricultural economics from Cornell University. His first political job in Taiwan was with the **Joint Commission on Rural Reconstruction** in 1957. He subsequently served in several other positions before being appointed mayor of **Taipei**, serving in that position from 1978 to 1981, and governor of Taiwan Province from 1981 to 1984. Lee then became vice president under **Chiang Ching-kuo** from 1984 to January 1988, whereupon he became **president** following Chiang Ching-kuo's death. He was, in fact, picked by Chiang to be his successor. He also became acting chairman of the Nationalist Party upon Chiang Ching-kuo's demise, though some top officials in the party, including **Madam Chiang Kai-shek**, briefly challenged him. He was elected party chairman in July 1988 at the Nationalist Party's **National Party Congress**. He was reelected president by the **National Assembly** in May 1990 after a brief challenge by **Lin Yang-kang** and **Chiang Wei-kuo** and was reelected party chairman in 1993. In 1995, he made a widely acclaimed trip to the United States, the first Taiwan president to do so. The visit both angered and alienated leaders in China, who saw Lee at this point as supporting Taiwan's independence. In 1996, Lee was elected president for another term in the nation's first direct presidential election, winning over 54 percent of the vote in a four-way race. This election was widely reported on throughout the world because of missile tests conducted by Beijing to intimidate Taiwan and send a signal that Beijing would not tolerate Taiwan independence. In 1997, Lee was again reelected chairman of the Nationalist Party. In 1999, Lee upset officials in both China and the United States when he announced that Taiwan and China were separate states.

In 2000, Lee was pressured to step down as chairman of the Nationalist Party after its candidate **Lien Chan**, suffered an election defeat. Many party members perceived that Lee had helped Chen win. In 2001, Lee was instrumental in founding the **Taiwan Solidarity Union**, which joined the **Democratic Progressive Party** in the legislative election that year, the two parties being labeled **pan-green**. For that, the Nationalist Party expelled him. Subsequently, Lee became an open advocate of Taiwan's independence and often harshly criticized Lien Chan and **James Soong**.

Being the country's first **Taiwanese** president, Lee represented a transition from **Mainland Chinese** to Taiwanese rule, as well as an end of the "Chiang Dynasty," though Lee was also known for some time for his loyalty to Chiang Ching-kuo and for his determination to continue his reforms. For this, he was called Taiwan's "Mr. Democracy." Critics, however, say he was dictatorial and that he caused the Nationalist Party to become corrupt and the KMT to split—one faction forming the **New Party**. They say he oversaw the decline of the party in terms of public opinion and election defeats. He was assailed by some in the Nationalist Party for abandoning **Sun Yat-sen**'s principles and for his alleged stance in favor of Taiwan independence. Lee's defenders say he saved the Nationalist Party and was forced to take an independence view by China, and that what he did in that realm was both inevitable and good for Taiwan.

LEE YUAN-TSEH (1936–). President of **Academia Sinica** and national policy adviser to the **president**, Lee won the Nobel Prize in chemistry in 1986 and is regarded as one of Taiwan's foremost scholars. In 2000, during the presidential campaign, Lee strongly endorsed

Chen Shui-bian for president, which some say was decisive since it created a bandwagon effect. His support also suggested that President **Lee Teng-hui** favored Chen, since it was Lee Teng-hui who appointed Lee Yuan-tseh to the presidency of **Academic Sinica**, and the two were regarded as close friends. Lee is also known for his advocacy of reforms in **education**. In 2005, he apologized before the **Legislative Yuan** for the failure of his proposed reforms made ten years earlier, and he also expressed disappointment with Chen Shui-bian and the **Democratic Progressive Party**.

LEGISLATIVE YUAN (LI-FA-YUAN). One of the five branches of the central government and the highest legislative or lawmaking organ of government in the **Republic of China**. Its original duties were to hear reports from the **Executive Yuan** and make policy both on its own and on recommendations from the Executive Yuan, pass laws, confirm emergency orders of the **president**, hear reports on government policy, examine budget bills, consent to the nominations of the **premier** and other high officials, settle disputes among other organs of government, and propose constitutional amendments to the **National Assembly**.

Many of its members for some time were holdovers from elections on the mainland. Thus the Legislative Yuan was criticized as being undemocratic since most members did not represent the territory under the nation's control. In the 1980s, however, with new members elected in supplemental elections, **Taiwan**-elected members began to have more influence in Legislative Yuan sessions. In fact, they did more than their numbers suggested because of their vitality and their closer contacts with the populace. By the end of the decade, locally elected members, for these reasons and because **senior parliamentarians** often missed sessions or were not energetic, often dominated debates on important issues. However, after the **Democratic Progressive Party** (DPP) performed well in the 1989 election and gained political clout, its leaders charged that the system was undemocratic because the DPP could not become the ruling party even if it won every seat in an election due to the presence of the senior parliamentarians. Many **Nationalist Party** members agreed that the situation needed to be changed. Pressure thus increased on the senior parliamentarians to resign. In 1991, those not elected in elections held in

Taiwan agreed to step down in preparation for the election of a new Legislative Yuan in December 1992.

Since that time, the Legislative Yuan has been much stronger and has played a larger role in Taiwan politics. Democratization generally strengthened the Legislative Yuan, as did the Nationalist Party's weakening control over the legislature and the addition of more activist members through elections. The downside was that the Legislative Yuan became the site of protests, antics, fistfights, and other violence, though this has decreased in recent years. It suffered considerably from an image problem and lost some public confidence as a result. The Legislative Yuan has been at odds with the Executive Yuan and the National Assembly on various matters, the most serious being the powers assumed by each and their relationships in terms of political authority, resulting in frequent contention, bad publicity because of disruptions in conducting business, and frequent stalemates in passing laws. This has been much more serious since **Chen Shuibian** was elected president in 2000 and Taiwan has had a divided government, with **pan-green** controlling the executive branch of government and **pan-blue** controlling the legislative branch.

In the 1990s, the **Constitution** was amended in ways that altered the powers and the mode of conducting business in the Legislative Yuan. Now two members are elected from each district or special municipality, but where the population exceeds two hundred thousand, one member is added for each one hundred thousand, and where the population exceeds one million, another member is added for each 200,000 people. Three members represent lowland and highland **aborigines**, and six represent Chinese citizens abroad. Those representing aborigines or Chinese abroad are elected by party-list proportional representation. Thus, 176 of the total of 225 seats are filled through direct ballot; **political parties** are allocated the remaining seats. The Constitution was again amended in 2005 to reduce the size of the legislature to 113, thinking that a smaller number of legislators would reduce bureaucratism and corruption and increase the prestige of members. At the same time, the electoral system was changed, and the single-vote, multimember district system was abolished in favor of a two-vote system.

The Legislative Yuan is a unicameral body and conducts much of its business in committees. The Legislative Yuan holds two sessions each year: from February to the end of May and from September to the end of December. Members cannot be held responsible for opinions expressed or votes cast, nor can they be arrested, except in the case of very serious crimes. No member may hold concurrently another government post.

LEI CHEN (1897–1979). Mainland Chinese intellectual, writer, and high-ranking **Nationalist Party** official who, before the Nationalist government moved to Taiwan, was an assistant secretary-general to the People's Political Council. He was also minister without portfolio in the **Executive Yuan** and adviser to the **president** on national strategy. In **Taiwan**, Lei founded the journal *Free China Fortnightly* and wrote for and managed the journal for eleven years. He was associated with **Hu Shih** and other intellectuals as well as the **Republic of China**'s top political leadership. Lei, however, opposed the KMT's dominance in Taiwan's politics and its extraconstitutional powers, and the Republic of China's authoritarian political system. For this, he became controversial and made enemies. In 1960, shortly after founding the **China Democratic Party** (at a time when establishing new **political parties** was illegal), he was accused of harboring a Communist agent on his staff and was sentenced to ten years in prison for sedition. Critics of the government and many outside observers called the charges false. In 1988, opposition politicians protested when the army allegedly burned his prison memoirs.

"LETTER TO TAIWAN COMPATRIOTS" (CHIH T'AI-WAN TUNG-PAO SHU). Public letter sent by the Standing Committee of the National People's Congress of the People's Republic of China to officials in **Taiwan** proposing the establishment of **trade**, travel, and communications links while promising to "respect Taiwan's status quo, adopt reasonable and rational policies and methods, and refrain from causing Taiwan people to suffer." This letter was "sent" on 1 January 1979, the date that official diplomatic relations were established between the United States and the People's Republic of China. It was the first of many efforts by China, after the normalization of relations with the United States, to persuade Taipei to agree to talks aimed at reunification. It reflected what officials in Beijing thought was an opportunity, because of the severe blow to **Taipei** and a desperate situation for the government and the ruling **Nationalist Party** caused by U.S. derecognition, to negotiate unification of Taiwan on Beijing's terms.

LI AO (1935–). Perhaps Taiwan's most famous dissident writer, Li has published more than one hundred books, including two autobiographies. For some time, he was a contributor to *Apollo*, a reformist literary periodical. Li's writings were very provocative, and many were banned; he served more than seven years in jail or prison. With democratization, Li became popular and legitimate. In 2000, his novel *Fa Yuan* (Martyr's Shrine) was nominated for a Nobel Prize in **literature**. That same year, the **New Party** picked Li as its candidate in the presidential election. He was not serious about campaigning and spent most of his time satirizing and castigating the other candidates. He criticized **James Soong** but said people should vote for him as he was the least incompetent and corrupt. Recently Li has had a television show and continues to play the role of public commentator.

LI KWOH-TING (1910–2001). K. T. Li, as he was often called, was considered for some time, and is still so viewed, as the brains behind **Taiwan**'s economic takeoff and is thus called the "Father of Taiwan's **Economic Miracle.**" He served as minister of economic affairs from 1965 to 1969 and as minister of finance from 1969 to 1976. Li is the author of a number of books on economics and business that include an analysis of Taiwan's successful economic growth.

LI TSUNG-JEN (1891–1969). Leader of the Kwangsi faction of the **Nationalist Party** in the mid-1940s, he was elected vice president of the **Republic of China** in spring 1947. When it became clear that the Nationalists would lose the civil war to the Communists, **Chiang Kai-shek** resigned, leaving Li **president**. He was president when Nationalist forces fled to Taiwan and after, up until December 1949, when he had to abandon his temporary seat of government in Chengtu. The next day, **Taipei** was proclaimed the new temporary capital of the Republic of China. Li, however, went to the United States for medical help and remained there. His supporters fled to Hong Kong. Li met President Harry Truman in March 1950 to enlist support for a so-called Third Force (meaning neither the Nationalists nor the Communists). At the same time, he wrote to Chiang Kai-shek, protesting Chiang's resumption of the presidency, saying that without an election of the **National Assembly**, he had no legal grounds for this. Li subsequently hoped to go to **Taiwan** where he might play a potential role or influence America's China policy, but he never did.

LI YUAN-ZU (1923–). Former vice president and currently a vice chairman of the **Nationalist Party**, Li was close to both **Chiang Ching-kuo** and, subsequently, **Lee Teng-hui**. He served as minister of **education** from 1977 to 1978 and as minister of justice from 1979 to 1984. He was secretary-general to the **president** before he became vice president in 1990. His nomination for the vice presidency by Lee Teng-hui, however, caused controversy, as Li was not so well known and had not been considered a strong contender for that office. **Lien Chan** replaced him as vice president in 1996.

LIAO WEN-YI (1910–1976). Also known as Thomas Liao, he was one of the founders of the **League for the Re-emancipation of Formosa** that was formed in 1947 in Hong Kong and later moved to Japan. Liao also established a "provisional government of the Republic of Formosa" and was one of Taiwan's leading advocates of independence for some time, perhaps its most well-known advocate. By the late 1950s, however, most younger activists had abandoned him.

***LIBERTY TIMES* (DZ-YOUSHIH-PAO).** One of **Taiwan**'s three major **newspapers**, it is pro-**pan-green**.

LIEN CHAN (1936–). Vice president from 1996 to 2000 and chairman of the **Nationalist Party** from 2000 to 2005, Lien was twice a candidate for **president** (in 2000 and 2004). Earlier, Lien served as **premier** from 1993 to 1997, as governor of Taiwan province from 1990 to 1993, as minister of foreign affairs from 1988 to 1990, as vice premier from 1987 to 1988, and as minister of transportation and communications from 1981 to 1987. He was vice chairman of the Nationalist Party from 1993 to 2000. At age forty-five, he was the youngest minister ever in the government and the youngest member ever of the **Kuomintang Central Standing Committee**.

As premier for four and a half years from 1993 to 1997, Lien presided over considerable change in Taiwan: increased social pluralism (with advances in minority rights); an economic recovery (with budget deficits brought under control); and a universal health insurance program, which he introduced and which though popular was also very expensive and did not bring him much acclaim. During the latter years as premier and in the absence of a significant Nationalist Party majority, Lien faced a hostile **Legislative Yuan** that often opposed his programs. It was very difficult for him to deal with the Legislative Yuan on many issues and get legislation passed. After Lien was elected vice president in the nation's first direct election of the president and vice president, he remained premier; members of the legislature protested this and even on occasion blocked his entry into the Legislative Yuan, saying that he should not hold the two offices concurrently.

Though Lien is considered to have been successful in office, he has not fared very well in public opinion polls, and he lost two presidential bids. In 2000, he was third in the vote count following **Chen Shui-bian** and **James Soong**. In 2004, with James Soong on the ticket with him, he lost a very close election to incumbent president Chen Shui-bian that he and his supporters said was "stolen" by Chen using underhanded tricks including a "staged," or at least suspicious, shooting to generate sympathy votes, which arguably Chen needed to win. Lien contested Chen's victory in court and in other ways but did not win.

Lien is regarded as ethnically **Fukien Taiwanese** (after his father). However, he was born in Sian in Central China, and his mother is not Taiwanese. **Pan-green** depicted him as Chinese and pro-China and used the ethnic card against him in presidential election campaigns. Others say he bridged the gap between Taiwanese and **Mainland Chinese** and between Taiwan and China. He is rumored to have been involved in the **Taiwan Independence Movement** when he was young but to have changed his views on this subject. Lien's grandfather, Lien Heng, who wrote *A History of Taiwan*, which was widely read by students and others in the past, said he was loyal to both Taiwan and China. Lien married a Mainland Chinese, a former Miss China. When Lien left his position as chairman of the Nationalist Party in 2005, he said that his chief accomplishments were maintaining peace with

China and engineering the first democratic election of the chairman of the Nationalist Party.

LIN HSIEN-T'ANG (1881–1956). A member of the Lin family of Wu-feng in central Taiwan near **Taichung** that supported and aided **Liu Ming-ch'uan** when the latter was governor of Taiwan. The family became very wealthy in business, especially through trade with China and retailing. Lin later founded the Taito Trust Company under Japanese rule and was very influential politically. For some time, he opposed General **Sakuma Samata**'s harsh rule of Taiwan and supported a policy of assimilation. He was a spokesman for the Home Rule movement and advocated a democratic Taiwan under Japanese rule. *See also* HOME RULE ASSOCIATION.

LIN YANG-KANG (1927–). Long considered one of the nation's most charismatic and experienced **Taiwanese** politicians and one of its best campaigners, Lin was commissioner of the Taiwan Provincial Department of Reconstruction from 1972 to 1976, **Taipei** mayor from 1976 to 1978, governor of **Taiwan** from 1978 to 1981, and subsequently minister of the interior. He served as vice premier from 1984 to 1987 and as president of the **Judicial Yuan** from 1987 to 1994. Lin, together with **Chiang Wei-kuo**, challenged **Lee Teng-hui** for reelection in 1990, causing the **Nationalist Party** to suffer an internal split. He subsequently dropped his challenge, and the **National Assembly** elected Lee.

In 1996, after resigning his membership in the Nationalist Party, Lin again ran for the presidency, with **Hau Pei-tsun** on the ticket as his vice presidential candidate; he ran as an independent, though he had support from the **New Party**. During the campaign, Lin criticized Lee Teng-hui's authoritarian governing style and his provocative actions toward China, which he said caused a crisis in cross-strait relations. The Lin-Hau ticket received 14.9 percent of the popular vote and was third among four teams of candidates running for the presidency and the vice presidency.

LIN YI-HSIUNG (1941–). Elected the eighth chairman of the **Democratic Progressive Party** (DPP) in 1998, Lin began his political career when he was elected to the **Taiwan Provincial Assembly** in

1977. In 1979, he was arrested following the **Kaohsiung Incident** and was sentenced to twelve years in prison. Lin's mother and two daughters were murdered at that time, a crime that has still not been solved and for which accusations have been made that the Nationalist Party and security agencies of the government were responsible. Lin served over four years of his prison term, after which he spent time in the United States, the United Kingdom, and Japan. He returned to Taiwan in 1989, at which time he presented a draft of a basic law for an independent **Republic of Taiwan**.

In 1996, Lin unsuccessfully sought the DPP's nomination to run for **president**. As DPP chairman, Lin was considered a stronger advocate of Taiwan's independence than his two predecessors and was often called a "democracy fighter." Lin ran **Chen Shui-bian**'s successful campaign for president in 2000. Subsequently, Lin became less active in politics, though he was a strong advocate of political reform, including downsizing the **Legislative Yuan** and changing **Taiwan**'s electoral system. In 2004, Lin met Nationalist Party chairman **Lien Chan** and thanked him for working for these reforms. In early 2006, Lin quit the Democratic Progressive Party, apparently unhappy with its causing a worsening of ethnic relations in Taiwan.

LIN YU-TANG (1895–1966). Born in China, Lin became one of China's and, later, **Taiwan**'s most well-known writers and philologists. He supported the Nationalist revolution and subsequently served in an official position, but he gave that up to write in the late 1920s. He studied in the United States and Europe and wrote in English. His two most famous books were *My Country and My People* and *The Importance of Living*. Both were nonfiction and depicted the nature of Chinese thought and the character of the Chinese people to the West. He founded and edited several journals. He also devised a system for romanizing Chinese and wrote a widely used Chinese-English dictionary. In all, he wrote thirty-six books.

LITERATURE (WEN HSUEH). Literary pursuits were not traditionally popular in **Taiwan**, though there were some poets of note during the Chinese and Japanese periods. During the latter era, writing, except in the scientific fields, was discouraged. Early in the post–World

War II period, the government banned certain unwholesome themes in literature (such as pornography, homosexuality, nihilism, etc.) and sought to use literature for fostering national unity. The government and the **Nationalist Party** pushed the study of the Chinese classics and other traditional books with nationalistic themes. Otherwise, poverty, local culture, the differences between **Mainland Chinese** and **Taiwanese**, and Communism were popular themes. Most writers were young, and many were **women**. Later, romance and social problems became favorite topics.

Western influence was noticeable in the late 1950s and 1960s, introducing such trends as symbolism, surrealism, existentialism, Freudianism, and modernism. With democracy came political issues and Taiwan's sense of national identity, as well as pragmatism and realism. In the 1990s, multiculturalism and a proliferation of foreign travel brought a greater variety of themes into the literary works produced in Taiwan. After **Chen Shui-bian** was elected **president**, the government encouraged writing that looked at Taiwan's history and culture apart from China and ethnic literature. In 2001, the *Taiwanese Literary Yearbook* began publication, and in 2003, the National Museum of Taiwanese Literature opened in Tainan.

LIU, HENRY (1932–1984). Businessman and writer of a biography on **Chiang Ching-kuo**, Liu was murdered at his home in Daly City outside of San Francisco in October 1984. Some said the reason was the biography he wrote. Members of the local Bamboo Gang were arrested for the murder and implicated Wang Hsi-ling, who was the head of military intelligence in **Taiwan**. The incident had an adverse effect on U.S.–Taiwan relations, even causing a congressional committee to hold hearings and attempt to tie arms sales to Taiwan's untoward activities in the United States. Subsequently it was learned that Liu had been a triple agent (for the United States, China, and Taiwan) and that Wang sought retaliation against him for disclosing the names of agents working in China, allegedly resulting in some being captured and executed. Also, it came out during the trial that Wang had acted on his own, and the killing was not ordered or approved by a higher authority in Taiwan, and later that Wang had not specifically ordered Liu's killing but rather had told the Bamboo Gang to "get him."

LIU MING-CH'UAN (1837–1896). Sent by the Chinese government to rule **Taiwan** in 1884, Liu promoted needed and widely heralded innovation. He introduced a railroad and postal system, developed mines and harbors, and encouraged trade. He established **Taipei** as the capital of the island. He also established foreign-language schools and encouraged trade and other contacts with various places in Asia and with the West. Taiwan experienced progressive change and boomed economically under his leadership. In 1891, however, he returned to China before many of his plans were fulfilled, discouraged because of the Chinese bureaucracy's opposition to his reforms. Still, Liu is considered one of Taiwan's foremost reformers and is regarded as a national hero.

LIU TAI-YING (1936–). Chairman and CEO of the **China Development Corporation** and former chairman of the ruling **Nationalist Party**'s Business Management Committee during **Lee Teng-hui**'s presidency, Liu was the person responsible for the Nationalist Party's finances and its **investment** policies, and therefore wielded considerable political power. He was cited in the press for making contributions to political causes and to political parties abroad, and he was even mentioned in connection with the U.S. Democratic Party's fundraising scandal in 1996, though Liu denied giving any money, and no such charge was proven. Liu planned President Lee Teng-hui's trip to the United States in June 1995 that gave Lee favorable publicity in the United States and at home but caused strained relations with Beijing. In early 2003, Liu was arrested for suspected embezzlement and breach of trust. A number of other charges were cited at the time, as well as the fact that legal action had been initiated against him twice earlier and dropped, some said because of the influence of **Chen Shui-bian** and Lee Teng-hui.

LU, ANNETTE (1944–). Also known by her Chinese name Lu Hsiu-lien, Lu was elected vice president in 2000 and again in 2004 on the **Democratic Progressive Party**'s ticket with **Chen Shui-bian**. Lu is **Taiwanese**, born in northern Taiwan. She studied law at **Taiwan National University** and graduated in 1967. She went to the University of Illinois at Urbana-Champaign and Harvard University where she earned master's degrees. Upon returning to Taiwan, she joined the *tangwai* movement, and in 1979 she spoke at the rally that led to the **Kaohsiung Incident**. She was arrested and was sentenced to twelve years in prison for sedition. She served five years. She was elected to the **Legislative Yuan** in 1993 and as magistrate of Taoyuan County in 1997. Lu meanwhile became the spiritual (if not more) founder of the feminist movement.

After her election to the vice presidency, she was often at odds with President Chen Shui-bian and his top advisers over her role in the administration, which they considered should be of minimal importance. She disagreed and was usually visible and outspoken. She kept a hard position on Taiwan's separation from China when Chen did not, and she felt that growing economic ties with China endangered Taiwan's sovereignty. During the Chen administration's first term, there was speculation in the **media** that her office was the source of information about the **president**'s tryst with a female aide, but Lu sued the magazine that published the story and won. Leading up to the election in 2004, there was widespread speculation that she would not be kept on the ticket, but that did not prove true. The day before the voting, she and the president were shot, Lu in the knee. In December 2005, Lu was appointed acting chairperson of the Democratic Progressive Party and served for little over a month.

Lu has attained the highest rank in Taiwan's government of any female ever. She is viewed as being free of corruption and is considered a possible candidate for the party's nomination for president in 2008.

LUNAR NEW YEAR. *See* CHINESE NEW YEAR.

– M –

MA YING-JEOU (1950–). **Taipei** mayor and chairman of the **Nationalist Party,** Ma has long been considered one of **Taiwan**'s young political stars. Early on, he served as an interpreter for President **Chiang Ching-kuo**, following which he held a number of important positions in the government and in the Nationalist Party, including head of the **Research, Development, and Evaluation Commission** from 1988 to 1991, and vice chairman of the **Mainland Affairs Council**. He was concurrently minister of justice and minister of state from 1993 to 1996, and subsequently minister without portfolio. He gained a reputation for honesty and promoting clean politics when he headed the Ministry of Justice as a result of his arresting and indicting a large number of politicians for vote buying and other kinds of corruption. In May 1997, he resigned from government service in protest over continued corruption and crime. In early 1998, however, he reentered politics and ran for Taipei mayor as the Nationalist Party's candidate; he won that race against the then-popular **Democratic Progressive Party** mayor **Chen Shui-bian**. Ma was reelected Taipei mayor in 2002.

In 2005, Ma became the first popularly elected chairman of the Nationalist Party, defeating legislative speaker **Wang Jyn-ping**. He won without the support of the party's **Central Advisory Committee** (which included his father) because they felt he was too young and pushed party reform too aggressively. When Ma became chairman, he changed the process of electing the powerful **Central Standing Committee**, having it picked by the **Party Congress** rather than by the **Central Committee**.

Ma is considered the likely Nationalist Party candidate for **president** in 2008. **Pan-green** spokesmen attempt to use the fact that he is **Mainland Chinese** (though he notes that he was conceived in Taiwan and born in Hong Kong) against him and charge that he favors Taiwan's unification with China.

MACCLESFIELD BANK (CHUNG-SHA CHUN-TAO). Group of islands, called **Chung Sha** in Chinese, in the South China Sea claimed as territory of the **Republic of China**. *See also* PARACEL ISLANDS; PRATAS ISLANDS; SPRATLY ISLANDS.

MAINLAND AFFAIRS COUNCIL (MAC) (TA-LU WEI-YUAN-HUI). Cabinet-level body created in October 1989 at the request of President **Lee Teng-hui** to, among other things, draft rules to formalize contacts between **Taiwan** and China and plan, coordinate, evaluate, and in some part implement policy toward the mainland. Members of MAC include most cabinet ministers and related commissioners. In August 1997, MAC proclaimed "shared sovereignty, divided jurisdictions" as an idea to describe the situation between **Taipei** and Beijing following a press statement from the **Office of the**

President that talked about "pursuing the unification of China based on the reality of separate jurisdictions." MAC conducts frequent opinion polls on the attitudes of Taiwan's citizens toward China, unification, and a number of other issues. *See also* NATIONAL UNIFICATION COUNCIL; STRAITS EXCHANGE FOUNDATION.

MAINLAND CHINESE (WAI-SHENG-JEN). Also called "Mainlanders" (in Chinese, "outside province person"), this term refers to Chinese who migrated to **Taiwan** from China after 1945, though most went in 1949 at the time of the Communist victory over the Nationalists, plus their sons and daughters, even if born in Taiwan. Most were government officials or military personnel; some were businessmen. They hailed from various parts of China, but more came from the coastal provinces and south China. They speak **Mandarin** Chinese, the official language of both China and Taiwan, but most also speak their provincial **dialects**. Many younger ones and those born in Taiwan, especially outside of Taipei, now speak **Taiwanese**. Until recent years, they occupied the majority of positions in the government and in **education**. Their political power, as well as their social status, however, has diminished with democratization and Taiwanization. They make up about 15 percent of Taiwan's population.

MANDARIN (KUO-YU). The official language of both Taiwan and the People's Republic of China, and a derivative of the Peking dialect. Formerly it was the court language of China, but it came into widespread use in the early part of the twentieth century. However, it was not spoken much in **Taiwan** before 1945, when it was made the national language there by the government of the **Republic of China**. With its use since World War II in the **educational** system and elsewhere, it is now spoken by most of the population of Taiwan, although many residents also speak **Taiwanese** and **Hakka**.

In recent years, Mandarin—which is called *kuo yu*, or "national language"—has been influenced by English and some other foreign languages, as well as by popular culture in Taiwan. In the People's Republic of China, it is called *pu tong hua*, or the "ordinary language." There it has undergone change influenced by Communism and Communist ideology. Though Chinese in China do not understand some terms used in Taiwan and vice versa, residents of the two places can usually communicate without difficulty. In recent years, with greater contacts across the **Taiwan Strait**, the differences in Mandarin spoken in China and Taiwan have diminished.

Mandarin Chinese is the largest language in the world by number of speakers and is becoming a popular second language and business language among East Asians. For that reason, many in Taiwan who promote Taiwanese do not want to abandon the use of Mandarin.

MARTIAL ARTS (KUO SHU). A number of the Asian martial arts are taught and practiced in Taiwan. The Chinese martial arts, or *kuoshu* (meaning the nation's art or mastery), consist of twenty main forms, with *tai chi chuan* being the most common. The government supports *kuoshu* and helps **Taiwan**'s athletes participate in contests at home and abroad. Judo and karate (Japanese) and tae kwon do (Korean) are also popular.

MARTIAL LAW (CHIEH-YEN-FA). Initially put into effect by the Nationalist government in China in 1934, it was applied in **Taiwan** by executive order in December 1949. **Chiang Kai-shek** activated that order in January 1950. Subsequently, the **Garrison Command** was created to take charge of matters concerning the implementation of martial law rules, which included regulating foreign travel, overseeing emigration and customs, reviewing publications and broadcasts, and much more. Under martial law, ten categories of criminal offenses were handled in military courts. Though many martial law procedures (such as the Garrison Command's control over local administrative and judicial matters) were never implemented or were not applied in full, many felt that martial law nevertheless constituted a serious encroachment on civil and political liberties because it canceled important constitutional protections in the realms of basic civil and political rights, and it was used by the government and the ruling **Nationalist Party** to maintain tight control over the population and to preserve an authoritarian political system.

Many thus saw it as antithetical to the development of democracy. Others, however, argued that it was necessary and that by maintaining national security, it made Taiwan's miraculous economic growth, and even democracy, possible. Whereas public opinion polls taken during the time that it was in force indicated that a large majority of the population did not feel inconvenienced by martial law and that most favored keeping it, in October 1986, President **Chiang Ching-kuo** promised to terminate it, reasoning that it distracted from democratization and was not good for Taiwan's image abroad. Indeed, Western news reporters often cited it in a negative way, suggesting that it was a trapping of an undemocratic regime. Martial law was formally ended on 15 July 1987. *See also* CHIEH YEN FA.

MATSU (MA-TZU). One of the **Offshore Islands** that remained in Nationalist Chinese hands after 1949, it became a locus of international tension, in particular a dispute between **Taipei** and Beijing and involving the United States, in 1954–1955 and again in 1958. *See also* QUEMOY.

This name also refers to the most popular deity in **Taiwan**; Matsu was born in China in 963 and died in 991 at the age of twenty-eight, at which time she ascended to heaven. She was believed to have performed miracles during her life and after. The Chinese explorer **Cheng Ho** spread her cult to Southeast Asia and Taiwan. There are various Matsu shrines in Taiwan.

MAY 20, 1988, INCIDENT (WU-ER-LING SHIH-CHIEN). Massive street demonstrations were held on that date in **Taiwan**, organized by the **Democratic Progressive Party** and the **Labor Party** together with fruit and chicken farmers to protest the government's agricultural policies. Considerable chaos resulted, which was said at the time to reflect the ability of opposition **political parties**, especially the DPP, to use street politics or demonstrations to rally people to their causes.

MAY THE FOURTH MOVEMENT (WU-SZU YUN-TUNG). A mass protest that occurred in Peking in 1919 in response to China being "sold out" in the Treaty of Versailles that turned into a broad historical movement that is said to have been the beginning of Chinese nationalism. In 1949, many of its pro-Western leaders, such as **Hu Shih**, went to **Taiwan** and continued their advocacy and support of democratic change. The May the Fourth "group"—which was an offshoot and included **Lei Chen** and some other notables— is said to be the first significant advocacy group for democratization in Taiwan.

MEDIA (HSIN-WEN CHIEH). In **Taiwan** in the past, the primary means of communication were word of mouth and notices pasted on walls in public places. Radio and **newspapers** became common during the Japanese period. Five radio stations served one hundred thousand receivers by the mid-1940s. In 1993, there were 33 stations, and in 2001 there were 142. In the past, radio programs focused on cultural, dramatic, educational, and children's programs. In recent years, more time is devoted to **music**, talk programs, financial analysis, and traffic. Taiwan has both private and publicly owned radio stations. Broadcasts are in **Mandarin**, **Taiwanese**, **Hakka**, and English.

Television came to Taiwan in 1962 when the **National Educational Television** station went on the air. Other stations followed. The opposition complained that the government and the **Nationalist Party** controlled the television stations, and so it established **Formosa Television** in 1997. Public Television Service began operations the next year. Cable television became popular in the 1980s, though many broadcasting companies operated illegally by wiring up an apartment building or a number of buildings. The Cable Television Law was passed in 1993 to correct this and provide larger systems to viewers. More than 80 percent of the population has access to cable TV. *See also* CINEMA; NEWSPAPERS.

MEILITAO. Literally "beautiful island," this term is sometimes considered the Chinese translation of *Formosa*.

"MESSAGE TO COMPATRIOTS IN TAIWAN FROM THE STANDING COMMITTEE OF THE FIFTH NATIONAL PEOPLE'S CONGRESS." *See* "LETTER TO TAIWAN COMPATRIOTS."

MILITARY AID AND ADVISORY GROUP (MAAG) (CHUN-SHIH KU-WEN-T'UAN). Group of U.S. military advisers who helped rebuild Nationalist forces in **Taiwan** in the early 1950s and stayed on until Washington and **Taipei** broke diplomatic relations in

1979. The group grew from around four hundred in 1952 to several thousand in the 1960s.

MIN-CH'UAN. "People's Rights," or democracy. *See* THREE PRINCIPLES OF THE PEOPLE.

MIN-SHENG. "People's Livelihood." *See* THREE PRINCIPLES OF THE PEOPLE.

MIN-TSU. "People's Nationhood," or nationalism. *See* THREE PRINCIPLES OF THE PEOPLE.

MINI-THREE LINKS (HSIAO SAN-TUNG). Links between **Taiwan**, **Quemoy**, and **Matsu** islands established following passage of the Offshore Island Development Act in March 2000 and a legislative resolution calling for implementation of the mini-three links. The minilinks were launched in January 2001. They allowed people from Quemoy and Matsu to travel to China. Trade, mail services, and shipping were also allowed. Visits by citizens of China to the two islands were permitted, but the numbers were restricted. In 2003, the scope of the legislation was expanded to allow businesspeople from Taiwan to transit the islands on the way to China. It has long been assumed that the mini-three links might be a precedent for later "big links," meaning unlimited transport, **trade**, and postal links, but this has not happened. *See also* THREE LINKS.

MINNAN. Term that refers to the southern part of Fukien Province in China, from which most of the early Chinese immigrants hailed. It also refers to the Fukien Taiwanese and their language. *Minnan* is "**Hoklo**" in Fukienese or **Taiwanese**.

MIRAGE 2000-5 (HUAN-SHANG LIANG-CH'IEN WU). Sophisticated high-performance fighter aircraft sold to **Taiwan** by France in 1992. Taiwan decided to purchase sixty of these planes to augment its air defenses, even though it was building its own plane, the **Indigenous Defense Fighter**, and had been authorized to purchase 150 **F-16** fighter planes from the United States at the time. The deal caused friction between France and China. The Mirage 2000-5s are stationed in **Hsinchu** and are intended to provide high-altitude defense of the island together with the F-16s. *See also* ARMED FORCES.

MOUNTAIN PEOPLE. *See* ABORIGINES.

MUSHA REBELLION (WU-SHE SHIH-CHIEN). A joint **aborigine-Taiwanese** uprising in 1930 that resulted in the deaths of several hundred Japanese police and government officials. The rebellion was led by an aborigine named Moldanao.

MUSIC (YIN YUEH). The music of the **aborigines** consists of simple harmony, often performed together with dances. It is accompanied by melodic choruses and bells and other metal sounds. Drums, stringed instruments, woodwinds, and percussion instruments are used. Music often accompanies rituals and ceremonies that frequently last for several days. The following themes are most often found: harvest, daily work, love, and tribal legends. The Chinese brought classical Chinese music to **Taiwan** that was played in concert or that accompanied puppet shows or Chinese **opera**. The Japanese brought their music to Taiwan. Western classical and then Western popular music became popular in the 1950s and after. Classical Chinese music adopted some Western instruments and styles. Chinese popular music grew in the 1970s and after and remains popular, led by such singers as **Teresa Teng**. Today all kinds of music can be heard in Taiwan. *See also* OPERA.

– N –

NANSHA ISLANDS. *See* SPRATLY ISLANDS.

NATIONAL AFFAIRS CONFERENCE (KUO-SHIH HUI-YI). A "constitutional-style" meeting held from 28 June to 4 July 1990 in **Taipei** to discuss various political reforms, including the direct election of the **president** and the mayors of Taipei and **Kaohsiung**; the recomposition of the **National Assembly** and the **Legislative Yuan**; and relations between the **president**, the **premier**, and the cabinet. **Lee Teng-hui** called the meeting after students demonstrated in opposition to the undemocratic composition of the National Assembly in the spring. Participants included a cross-section of Taiwan's political figures and groups, even opposition politicians who had recently been released from jail. **Tsiang Yien-si** and **Shih Chi-yang** were the coconveners of the conference.

More than a hundred discussion meetings preceded the conference, with more than thirteen thousand people attending. These meetings produced a number of suggestions on political reform, including the termination of the **Temporary Provisions**, the retirement of **senior parliamentarians**, new policies toward China, and amendments to the **Constitution**. Most of the suggestions for reform were adopted in the following months. *See also* NATIONAL DEVELOPMENT CONFERENCE.

NATIONAL ASSEMBLY (KUO-MIN TA-HUI). Organ of the central government whose main functions as set forth in the **Constitution** (before it was amended) were to elect or recall the **president** and vice president and to amend the Constitution. As originally constituted, it met in regular sessions every six years. Extraordinary sessions could be called by a vote of not less than two-fifths of the delegates or by the president to discuss initiatives or referendum measures, to impeach the president or vice president, or when an amendment to the Constitution was proposed by the **Legislative Yuan**.

Like the Legislative Yuan and the **Control Yuan** (the other two elective bodies of government before the Constitution was amended), the National Assembly's makeup or representation was based on the claim that the government of the Republic of China represented "all of China" and thus had holdovers from the 1947 election frozen in office, or replacements hailing from the same province. Since supplemental elections had affected its membership less than they had affected the Legislative Yuan and the Control Yuan, as of 1989 it was still nearly 90 percent composed of members representing areas not under the control of the government. In 1989, as part of **Taiwan**'s democratization, a law was passed to rectify this situation, and delegates were offered retirement bonuses. Only a few, however, accepted the offer.

In 1990, the National Assembly met and tried to expand its powers and play a special role in the election of the **president**. This evoked public outcries and demonstrations in opposition, including thousands of college and university students staging sit-in protests. This provoked a political crisis. Debate about the role and powers of the National Assembly and other issues followed. (*See* NATIONAL AFFAIRS CONFERENCE.) Later, in 1990, the **Council of Grand Justices** ruled that the **senior parliamentarians** had to step down by the end of 1991, and they did. Thus, in December 1991, an election was held to elect a "new" National Assembly.

In 1992, the National Assembly made important changes in the Constitution. Subsequently, more amendments were passed, including provisions for the direct election of the president, which eliminated one of the major functions of the National Assembly. Later proposals were made to eliminate the National Assembly and to turn it into an electoral college similar to that in the United States, or to merge it with the Legislative Yuan, making that body a bicameral legislature. None of these proposals, however, was realized. In 1997, the National Assembly made additional changes to the Constitution, during which time there was heated debate over eliminating the provincial government. Friction also developed with the Legislative Yuan over the powers of each and their mutual relationship, in addition to other issues. Finally, the major parties got together and agreed that because the National Assembly had lost its main function—electing the president and vice president—it should became an ad hoc body to be formed by special election called by the Legislative Yuan.

In May 2005, a National Assembly election was called, and voting was done by party-list proportional representation. The ruling **Democratic Progressive Party** and the **Nationalist Party**, which had jointly sponsored several constitutional amendments, won the election. The **People First Party** and the **Taiwan Solidarity Union** did poorly. Voter turnout was very low. In June 2005, the National Assembly voted to abolish itself while turning over its functions to the Legislative Yuan. Thus, to impeach the president or vice president, the legislature must pass a resolution by a simple majority and then get the approval of two-thirds of members to pass. Then the resolution goes to the Council of Grand Justices to review it in Constitutional Court.

Before it ceased to exist as a standing body, the National Assembly voted to cut the legislature from 225 members to 113; to adopt a single-member district, two-vote electoral system for legislative elections beginning in 2007; and to extend lawmakers' terms from three to four years beginning at that time. Future constitutional amendments will be proposed by at least one-fourth of lawmakers, adopted by three-fourths present, and put to the voters in the form of a referendum in three months. An absolute majority of voters must cast ballots, and approval is by one-half of those voters.

NATIONAL CHENGCHI UNIVERSITY (CHENG-CHIH TA-HSUEH). Located in Mucha outside of Taipei, *cheng-ta*, as it is often called, is regarded as one of the nation's best universities. It specializes in politics, journalism, and several other fields. *See also* EDUCATION.

NATIONAL CHIANG KAI-SHEK CULTURAL CENTER (CHUNG-CHENG CHI-NIEN-T'ANG). A large center in **Taipei** that includes the Chiang Kai-shek Memorial Hall and Park and the National Concert Hall, built as a memorial to the late President **Chiang Kai-shek**. The hall was completed in 1980, the theaters in 1987. It has since become one of Taiwan's major **tourist** attractions. In March 1990, thousands of college and university students staged a sit-in demonstration there protesting the **National Assembly**'s effort to expand its powers. The students departed peacefully after having a meeting with President **Lee Teng-hui**.

NATIONAL COMMUNICATIONS COMMISSION (NCC) (KUO-CHIA T'UNG-HSUN CHUAN-PO WEI-YUAN-HUI). An independent body created by the **Legislative Yuan** in February 2006 mandated to regulate telecommunications, information, and broadcasting. The creation of the NCC followed a dispute when the **Government Information Office** (GIO) canceled the licenses of some television stations, according to **pan-blue** for political reasons, though there had long been sentiment on both sides that the GIO should not have so much power to control the **media**. The NCC will take over many functions of the GIO and some formerly exercised by the Ministry of Transportation and Communications. Critics of the NCC said they doubted that it would be nonpartisan.

NATIONAL DAY. *See* DOUBLE TEN DAY.

NATIONAL DEMOCRATIC INDEPENDENT POLITICAL AL-LIANCE (NDIPA) (CH'UAN-KUO MIN-CHU TU-LI CHENG-CHIH LIEN-MENG). Political "party" formed by a group of independent candidates prior to the 1991 **National Assembly** election. The NDIPA claimed to be made up of "nonparty" politicians, yet the alliance became one of four **political parties** that qualified for television time during the campaign, having nominated more than ten candidates. The NDIPA, however, got just over 2 percent of the popular vote, not enough to qualify for national seats allocated by party. Its platform was vague and its future uncertain after the election. It subsequently faded from **Taiwan**'s political scene. The NDIPA was founded by Kao Tse-min.

NATIONAL DEVELOPMENT CONFERENCE (KUO-CHIA FA-CHAN HUI-YI). A meeting convened in December 1996 to debate constitutional reform, economic development, and relations with the People's Republic of China following generally the format of the 1990 **National Affairs Conference**. The Ministry of Interior, the **Council for Economic Planning and Development**, and the **Mainland Affairs Council** provided working papers. Some 170 individuals participated, including members of the three main **political parties**, government officials, and scholars. President **Lee Teng-hui** called "consensus building" the most important objective of the meeting. However, the meeting evoked serious disagreement over a number of issues, in particular the recommendation to reduce, if not eliminate, the provincial and village parts of the **Republic of China**'s four levels of government. Also controversial was the plan to strengthen the presidency vis-à-vis the **Legislative Yuan**. The **Democratic Progressive Party** generally supported the ruling **Nationalist Party**, which presented the reforms. The **New Party** did not and boycotted the meeting.

Provincial governor **Soong Chu-yu** tendered his resignation over the issue of downsizing or eliminating the provincial government, though Premier **Lien Chan** did not accept it, and Soong remained on the job. Subsequent talks between Soong and President Lee, however, did not produce any visible compromise, and according to many observers the two became alienated after that.

Critics of President Lee said that his actions showed him to be less than a genuine supporter of democracy and that seeking to eliminate the provincial government revealed that he supported Taiwan independence. Supporters said that the overlap in government between the national and provincial governments was expensive and that eliminating one level of government would help resolve the serious problems of corruption, especially vote buying. Taiwan's political system did need revamping for these and other reasons, especially in view of the new reality of party politics and coalition government.

Some of the proposals coming out of the meeting were written into constitutional amendments proposed and passed later in the year and have had an impact on the political system. The political reforms discussed at the meeting overshadowed the debate about both economic policy and relations with the mainland, and few changes were made in the latter two areas as a result of the conference. *See also* CONSTITUTION.

NATIONAL GENERAL MOBILIZATION LAW. *See* MARTIAL LAW.

NATIONAL HEALTH INSURANCE (CHUAN-MIN CHIEN-PAO). A national program providing universal health care to virtually all citizens of the **Republic of China** that went into operation in March 1995. Prior to this, only 59 percent of the population had health insurance. The program incorporated health care coverage provided by thirteen existing plans and extended coverage to an additional 7.5 million people. The main beneficiaries were the elderly, children, students, and housewives. Participation in the program was made mandatory under the Health Insurance Law.

Employees paid 30 percent of the premiums, employers 60 percent, and the government 10 percent. People over age seventy and the disabled paid no premium. By 2004, 99 percent of the population was covered under the plan, it being mandatory for citizens residing in the Republic of China for more than four months, as well as for foreign nationals with an Alien Registration Certificate. The program pays 70 to 95 percent of costs for patients admitted to hospitals. The **Nationalist Party** promoted the plan and took credit for its implementation.

But the program soon became controversial due to increasing costs and disagreements over who would pay for it as well as overuse and abuses. Delays in treatment for many patients and scandals over doctors asking for additional payments for services also sullied the program, as did the fact that the quality of health care declined or remained low in many areas.

NATIONAL INDEPENDENT LABOR FEDERATION (CHUAN-KUO TU-LI LAO-TUNG TSUNG-HUI). Established in 1988 by the **Taiwan Association for Labor Movement**, its unions represent workers in the petrochemical and synthetic fiber industries. Its unions' members mostly support the **Democratic Progressive Party**.

NATIONAL MOBILIZATION LAW (CH'UAN-KUO TSUNG-TUNG-YUAN-FA). Formerly a law that regulated labor in **Taiwan** including a ban on strikes.

NATIONAL PALACE MUSEUM (KUO-LI KU-KUAN PO-WU-YUAN). Opening in 1965 and located in suburban **Taipei**, the Palace Museum is generally recognized as the best Chinese museum in the world. It contains artifacts and **art** objects from five thousand years of Chinese history, most of which were brought from the mainland in 1949 by Dr. **Han Lih-wu**. Its large five-story building also houses a library, a lecture hall, and research rooms. The library houses 640,000 items, of which only 1 percent can be displayed at any one time.

NATIONAL PARTY CONGRESS (CH'UAN-KUO TANG-TAI-PIAO TA-HUI). Theoretically the highest decision-making organ of the **Nationalist Party**. However, it meets infrequently and when not in session delegates power to its 210-member **Central Committee**, which in turn selects the thirty-one-member **Central Standing Committee** of the party, where real decision-making power resides. The **Democratic Progressive Party** also has a National Congress that meets annually and selects its thirty-member **Central Executive Committee** that picks a ten-member Central Standing Committee.

Important policies are announced at these meetings, though the policies are usually made in advance.

NATIONAL POLICE AGENCY (NAI-CHENG-PU CHING-CHENG-HSU). The nation's highest public security authority, rising to that status after the dissolution of the **Taiwan Garrison Command**, or Garrison Guard Headquarters, in 1992. It commands and supervises all police functions in the nation.

NATIONAL POLICY FOUNDATION (KUO-CHIA CHENG-TSE YEN-CHIU CHI-CHIN-HUI). Founded in 2000, it is one of Taiwan's most active think tanks. Many staff members are former **Nationalist Party** officials, and its views reflect those of the party.

NATIONAL SCIENCE COUNCIL (NSC) (KUO-CHIA K'O-HSUEH WEI-YUAN-HUI). An organ of the **Executive Yuan** that is considered the highest government agency responsible for planning scientific and technological development and setting relevant policies, recruiting experts, and funding research. It is composed of eight divisions: biological, agricultural, and medical sciences; natural sciences and mathematics; engineering and applied sciences; humanities and social sciences; planning, coordination, and evaluation; science education; program administration; and international programs. Heads of government offices dealing with science and technology, ministers without portfolio, the president of **Academia Sinica**, the secretary-general of the Executive Yuan, and noted scientists are members. The National Science Council holds conferences and advises the **president**. One of its current goals, it says, is to make **Taiwan** an innovation and R & D base.

NATIONAL SECURITY BUREAU (NSB) (KUO-AN-CHU). Established in 1954, the NSB is considered the highest intelligence organization in **Taiwan**. It directs and coordinates the nation's intelligence activities, both external and internal. The NSB is composed of six departments: Mainland Operations, Overseas Operations, Internal Security Intelligence, Research and Production, Communications, and Cipher, plus an Intelligence Staff Training Center and a VIP Security Task Force. In 1991, the NSB was put under the jurisdiction of the

National Security Council, which is controlled by the **president**. In 1993, the redefining of the National Security Council's missions resulted in narrowing its functions primarily to foreign intelligence work.

After 2000, the NSB suffered from disunity and morale problems due to its opposition to Taiwan independence and the fact that many of its employees viewed President **Chen Shui-bian** and the now-ruling **Democratic Progressive Party** as promoting formal independence from China. The Chen administration accused many NSB employees, especially **Mainland Chinese**, of being traitors. In response, the NSB reportedly leaked secret documents to China, and some of its top officials defected. In 2004, the NSB was ordered to give lie detector tests to employees working in the **Office of the President** to ensure their loyalty to President Chen but also, according to the press, to seal information that was feeding scandals involving the president and first lady.

NATIONAL SECURITY COUNCIL (NSC) (KUO-CHIA AN-CH'UAN HUI-YI). Established by a presidential order in 1967 as a special organ attached to the **Executive Yuan**, its status was altered and made more official in 1987 after passage of the **National Security Act**. Early in its history, the NSC controlled the **Taiwan Garrison Command**, the **National Security Bureau**, the **Investigation Bureau**, and other intelligence agencies that often operated beyond the law and represented the repressive side of **martial law** in Taiwan. Its status was changed in 1993 from that of an advisory body to the president to a constitutionally mandated organization made part of the Executive Yuan and subject to oversight by the **Legislative Yuan**. The Intelligence Committee of the Legislative Yuan approves its budget, though parts of it remain secret.

The NSC's responsibilities include helping to formulate defense and **foreign policy**, overseeing domestic security and counterintelligence, and making policy toward the mainland. Members of the NSC include a president (who is the NSC's chairman), vice president, secretary-general of the **Office of the President**, chief of the President's Military Staff, **premier**, vice premier, minister of defense, minister of foreign affairs, minister of finance, minister of economic affairs, chief of the general staff, NSC secretary-general, chairman of the National Reconstruction Research Committee, and chairman of the Committee for Science Development. The latter two organs are adjunct bodies of the NSC.

NATIONAL SECURITY LAW (KUO-CHIA AN-CH'UAN FA). A law passed after **martial law** was ended in July 1987 that its supporters said was needed to guarantee the nation's security. They also argued that the law was very similar to such laws in most other countries including Western democracies and was therefore not antithetical to democracy. Critics, however, including leaders of the **Democratic Progressive Party** who mobilized its supporters to protest and oppose the law, said that it was "old wine in new bottles," or martial law in disguise. Most controversial was a provision that disallowed an appeal of civilian cases tried by military courts under martial law. Complaints about the National Security Law diminished after **Chen Shui-bian** became **president** in 2000.

NATIONAL SECURITY REPORT NO. 48-1 (KUO-CHIA AN-CH'UAN PAO-KAO-SHU). A report presented to the U.S. National Security Council on 23 December 1949, which stated that "logistical support of the present Nationalist island regime cannot ensure its indefinite survival as a non-communist base. Failing U.S. military occupation and control, a non-communist regime on Taiwan will probably succumb to the Chinese Communists by the end of 1950." The report followed a Joint Chiefs of Staff assessment, which concluded that Taiwan's strategic importance did not justify overt U.S. military action to protect it, and a State Department memorandum stating that intervention would provide the Chinese Communists with a potent "ideological issue." The report served as the basis for a U.S. policy of reduced support to the Nationalist government on Taiwan, and subsequently to a policy of what some called the "abandonment of **Chiang Kai-shek**." This policy was discarded with the onset of the Korean War. National Security Report No. 48-1 became public with the publication of the Pentagon Papers in 1971.

NATIONAL SPORTS COUNCIL (T'I-YU WEI-YUAN-HUI). Established in 1997 within the **Executive Yuan**, this body seeks to promote and regulate sports.

NATIONAL TAIWAN UNIVERSITY (T'AI-WAN TA-HSUEH). Considered **Taiwan**'s top institution of higher learning and known as *Tai-ta*, it is located in Taipei. *See also* TAIHOKU IMPERIAL UNIVERSITY.

NATIONAL UNIFICATION COUNCIL (NUC) (KUO-CHIA T'UNG-YI WEI-YUAN-HUI). A government organization founded in October 1990 by President **Lee Teng-hui** to advise the **president** and conduct research and write policy statements. It is attached to the **Office of the President**, and the president is its chairman. The NUC's membership comprises thirty-two people from various fields who serve for one year. Members include representatives of the opposition parties, since the NUC seeks to forge a consensus among various parties and groups on the issue of China's reunification. In March 1991, the NUC promulgated a three-phase program for the unification of **Taiwan** with China, called the **National Unification Guidelines**. However, conditions were attached leading most analysts to think that unification would not be likely for some time—if ever. In the summer of 1992, the NUC engaged in a four-month-long debate on the definition of **one China**, opting for a policy of **one China, two areas** or **one country, two entities** in an effort to give the two sides equal status and to offer an alternative to Beijing's **one country, two systems** formula for reunification.

When **Chen Shui-bian** became president in 2000, he vowed not to abolish the NUC. (*See* FIVE NOES.) However, he did not call any meetings and in early 2006 announced that he would abolish it, a statement that drew criticism from China and the United States. In late February 2006, he said that it would "cease to function." Chen said the NUC was incompatible with Taiwan's democracy and cited China's intimidation of Taiwan.

NATIONAL UNIFICATION GUIDELINES (KUO-CHIA T'UNG-YI KANG-LING). A set of policies proposed by President **Lee Teng-hui**, adopted by the **National Unification Council**, and approved by the **Executive Yuan** in early 1991, according to which the **Republic of China** will be unified with the People's Republic of China in three phases: unofficial contacts through people-to-people exchanges and activities that benefit mutual understanding; opening

three links (postal, air and sea, and trade); and negotiations on unification based on political democracy, economic freedom, and social
equality. The country was presently said to be in the first stage, em-
phasizing "four exchanges"—tourist, academic, cultural, and
sports—though some links cited in phase two may be said to have already been established because of the large volume of **trade** and the
considerable amount of **investment** from **Taiwan** in China. Moving
from step one to step two was, according to its formulators, contin-
gent upon Beijing not denying Taiwan's status as a "political entity"
and its pursuing economic and political reforms, settling disputes
through peaceful means, and respecting **Taipei**'s rights in the international community.

The **Democratic Progressive Party** rejected the guidelines when
they were proposed and formalized. Some observers, however, said
that the formulation of this policy would not have any immediate impact, if any impact at all, and was President Lee's way of parrying
criticism that he supported Taiwan's independence, especially by opponents in the **Nationalist Party**.

The National Unification Guidelines were important for another
reason: they constituted a formal abandonment of Taipei's claim to
sovereignty and jurisdiction over territory ruled by the government of
the People's Republic of China. Some said Beijing did not reply to
this in a positive way because Chinese leaders saw the move as
legally separating Taiwan from China. The guidelines, on the other
hand, paved the way for increased contacts between the populations
of Taiwan and China. Reference was made to "one China," but also
to two political entities and unification based on parity. The idea of
two political entities was opposed by Beijing; one China was not.
When **Chen Shui-bian** became **president** in 2000, he vowed not to
abolish the National Unification Guidelines, but in early 2006 he
changed his position and announced that they had "ceased to apply."
See also NATIONAL UNIFICATION COUNCIL.

**NATIONALIST PARTY (KUOMINTANG, OR KMT) (KUO-MIN-
TANG).** Long Taiwan's dominant political party, and until 2001 its
largest party, the KMT traces its origins to several political organizations founded or led by **Sun Yat-sen**, including the Hsing Chung Hui

or the Society for Regenerating China, which he founded in November 1894 in Hawaii. The party, in fact, sees that occasion as its birth and on 24 November 1994 claimed to be more than one hundred years old. Sun's, and the party's, goals at that time were to end Manchu rule of China and unify China. Sun's followers staged a number of uprisings before one in October 1911 succeeded. Sun then became **president** of the newly formed **Republic of China**, but he stepped down almost immediately in order to prevent conflict and what some said might have been a civil war because his support was in south China, and a new leader, Yuan Shih-kai, was in control in the north. Though Sun advanced Western democracy American style and was a Christian, he did not enjoy strong support among Western countries that continued to deal with the government in Peking.

After Sun died, the party experienced a split between left and right factions. **Chiang Kai-shek**, leader of the rightist faction, won control of the party's leadership after a brief power struggle. In 1928, after the success of the Northern Expedition led by Chiang, the Nationalist Party ruled China. The Nationalist Party–led military, trying to completely unify the country, fought both the Japanese and the Communists in ensuing years. It moved to Taiwan in 1949 with the government of the Republic of China and the Nationalist military, following the defeat of Nationalist forces by Mao and his Communist forces.

Sun Yat-sen held the honorary title of president (tsung li) of the Nationalist Party; Chiang Kai-shek held the title of director-general (tsung tsai) and led the party until his death in 1975. **Chiang Ching-kuo** was elected chairman of the party after his father's death. **Lee Teng-hui** became acting chairman upon Chiang Ching-kuo's death in January 1988 and was formally elected chairman at the Thirteenth Party Congress in July 1988, again at the Fourteenth Party Congress in 1993, and once more at the Fifteenth Party Congress in 1997. **Lien Chan** was elected chairman in 2000 following the party's defeat in the presidential election, which party leaders as well as the rank and file blamed on Lee Teng-hui. **Ma Ying-jeou** was elected chairman in 2005.

The **National Party Congress** is theoretically the highest decision-making organ of the party, but it is too large to deliberate seriously on policy issues and therefore delegates power to its **Central Committee**.

Real power, however, resides in the thirty-one-member **Central Standing Committee**. Before 2000, the Nationalist Party was considered a mass party, with a membership of around 2.5 million members, or about 11 percent of the Republic of China's population. Its membership represented virtually all social classes and segments of the population. Though sometimes thought of as a party of **Mainland Chinese**, which it was during the early years of its role in **Taiwan**, its membership had become 70 percent **Taiwanese** by the early 1980s. In fact, some now claim that the Nationalist Party is the only large multiethnic party in Taiwan, the **Democratic Progressive Party** being almost exclusively composed of Taiwanese.

The party's work is carried out by several departments and commissions. Departments include Organizational Affairs, Social Affairs, Youth Activities, and **Women**'s Activities. There are commissions dealing with financial affairs, party history, and discipline. The party also operated a number of businesses. In fact, its vast holdings earned the KMT the reputation of being the richest **political party** in the world, and this among other reasons prompted the other parties in Taiwan to criticize the Nationalist Party for its use of money in buying elections and its unfair or illegitimate ties to many businesses. Since 2000, however, the KMT's financial position has deteriorated, and many no longer see it as a rich party.

Until the 1980s, typical of a one-party system, the Nationalist Party and the government were in many ways synonymous, and their functions to a large extent overlapped. With the growth of democracy and the formation of new, opposition political parties, this ceased to be the case. After 1995, the KMT has had to seek support from the Democratic Progressive Party or the **New Party** to pass legislation and write and pass constitutional amendments. Following its defeat in the 2000 presidential election, the KMT, together with the **People First Party**, became an opposition bloc that stymied many of the initiatives of President **Chen Shui-bian**. (*See* PAN-BLUE.)

The KMT long opposed Taiwan's independence but later played down unification with China, making it a long-term goal predicated on the support of the population in order not to be hurt at the polls due to the changing national identity in Taiwan. The Nationalist Party lost membership after its 2000 election defeat but has partially recovered in the last three or four years. In early 2006, it put its membership at 1.06 million.

NEW KMT ALLIANCE (HSIN KUO-MIN-TANG CHEN-HSIEN). A caucus group formed within the **Nationalist Party** in 1988, led by **Jaw Shau-kong**, which reflected the views of younger **Mainlander Chinese** and represented more progressive KMT members' views on a number of issues, such as democratization. Members alleged that President **Lee Teng-hui** had acquired too much power and supported **Taiwan**'s independence. The New KMT Alliance was considered more of a party faction than its predecessor the **Breakfast Club**. The New KMT Alliance supported the **Non-Mainstream faction** of the party. Most of its members joined the **New Party** in 1993, and soon after that, it faded from the political scene.

NEW MOVEMENT FACTION (HSIN CH'IAO-LIU HSI). *See* NEW TIDE FACTION.

NEW PARTY (NP) (HSIN-TANG). A **political party** formed in August 1993 at the time of the **Nationalist Party**'s Fourteenth Party Congress by members of the party's **Non-Mainstream faction**. It was originally called the Chinese New Party. The important founding members were **Jaw Shau-kong** and **Wang Chien-shien**. The NP criticized the KMT's performance in elections, its corruption, and what NP members considered KMT's weak stance (pointing especially to **Lee Teng-hui**) against Taiwan's independence. Its platform included stricter adherence to the teachings of **Sun Yat-sen**, social justice, and clean politics.

The NP was also organized differently from the Nationalist Party and the **Democratic Progressive Party**, stressing the leadership roles of those holding public office and more open and democratic decision-making processes. In the 1994 election, the NP did well in the **Taipei City Council** race, and **Jaw Shau-kong** garnered the second-largest number of votes for Taipei mayor, some saying at the time that the KMT had helped the DPP candidate win to preclude Jaw's victory. In 1995, the NP tripled its seats in the **Legislative Yuan**, and in 1996 it improved its position in the **National Assembly**. After that, it did not perform well in election contests. In the 2000 election, it got less than 1 percent of the vote.

Its bad performance at the polls was attributed largely to its taking a proactive stance on Taiwan's unification with China. The NP also suffered from its being a regional party (in the **Taipei** area) supported mainly by **Mainland Chinese**. Some said the party's procedural rules were too democratic and that it lacked discipline because its support came from intellectuals and younger people. For a while it was the only opposition party, other than the DPP, that competed seriously in **Taiwan** politics. The NP became part of the **pan-blue** bloc after **Chen Shui-bian** was elected **president**. In 2005, most of its members returned to the Nationalist Party.

NEW PEOPLE'S SOCIETY (HSIN-MIN-HUI). Also called the Taiwan Cultural Society, this organization was formed in 1920 in Japan by **Taiwanese** who sought a means to promote **Taiwan**'s cultural identity. **Lin Hsien-t'ang** was its president for a time. The organization published the magazine *Taiwan Youth*. The New People's Society opposed both assimilation by Japan and ties with China.

NEW TIDE FACTION (HSIN CH'IAO-LIU HSI). A faction of the **Democratic Progressive Party** founded by **Chiou I-jen**, whose members came mainly from the **Formosa group**, it was long considered the more extreme segment of the DPP, though also the best organized. Early on, it unequivocally advocated the independence of **Taiwan** and used street demonstrations as its main tactic for attaining this and other objectives. Its philosophical position was that there could be no democracy in Taiwan until it was formally independent of China, and that the DPP should regard itself as a "revolutionary party." Its members proposed the use of Philippine-style "people's power" to overthrow the government.

Its agenda also included changing the name of the **Republic of China** to the **Republic of Taiwan** and obtaining a new **Constitution**, **flag**, and national anthem. The New Tide faction also promoted the idea that Taiwan should be an operations center for multinational businesses, but it opposed more extensive **trade** and commercial relations with the People's Republic of China, stating that political talks with the PRC were as important as economic negotiations. It refuted the notion of interdependence as well as the idea of **Greater China**. The New Tide faction sought the support of farmers, workers, and students—the so-called deprived social groups—but with only limited success. In recent years, its views have moderated, and it has gained strength in the DPP to the point that it is now the only major or real faction in the party. *See also* FORMOSA FACTION.

NEWSPAPERS. While the publication of newspapers was quite restricted in the past (not only with regard to what they could say but their size as well), this began to change considerably before **martial law** was ended in 1987, and things changed dramatically thereafter. The termination of the Publication Law in 1995 helped further. There are now several hundred newspapers operating in Taiwan. The three major Chinese-language newspapers are the *China Times*, *Liberty Times*, and *United Daily News*. There are also three English-language papers published in Taiwan: *China Post*, *Taipei Times*, and *Taiwan News*. The *Asian Wall Street Journal* and *International Herald Tribune* are printed in Taiwan and are for sale in most hotels and many newsstands. Many other foreign newspapers are available. *See also* MEDIA.

NINE-POINT PROPOSAL (YEH CHIU-TIEN). A set of proposals directed at **Taiwan**, set forth in a speech by Ye Jianying, chairman of the Standing Committee of the National People's Congress in the People's Republic of China in September 1981. Ye suggested talks between the Chinese Communist Party and the **Nationalist Party**. His most important points concerned the establishment of trade, mail, and shipping ties; cultural and sports exchanges; and visits by relatives. He promised that after reunification Taiwan could keep its socioeconomic system and would enjoy a high degree of autonomy as a special administrative region of the People's Republic of China.

Officials in Taipei responded coolly, saying that it had "nothing to gain and everything to lose" if it accepted the proposal. They jeered at the offer of economic help, noting that Taiwan was rich and China was poor. **Taipei** responded with its **Three Noes Policy**. Leaders in Taiwan subsequently pointed out that the proposal included autonomy for the **Republic of China**'s **armed forces**, yet Chinese leaders sought to pressure the United States to end arms sales to Taipei. *See also* SIX-POINT SUPPLEMENT.

NITOBE INAZO. A Japanese agricultural specialist who was made director of the Bureau of Industry in **Taiwan** very soon after it was incorporated into the Japanese empire. He turned Taiwan's **agriculture** into a very efficient and productive part of the **economy**, developed new strains of rice, and encouraged trade in food commodities.

NO HASTE POLICY (CHIEH-CHI YUNG-JEN CHENG-TSE). Also called the "no haste, be patient strategy," it was a tenet of **Taiwan**'s **foreign policy** initiated by President **Lee Teng-hui** in 1995 following missile tests conducted by China's People's Liberation Army in the **Taiwan Strait** to intimidate Taiwan. Lee admonished businessmen at that time not to invest too much money in the mainland in view of strained relations between **Taipei** and Beijing. In 1996, after more missile tests further strained relations, Lee repeated this statement. In late 1997, speaking to a **National Unification Council** plenum meeting, Lee reiterated this policy and used the term "no haste, be patient" in dealing with China. In early 1998, Premier **Vincent Siew** said the policy was aimed at pushing Beijing to review and reconsider its irrational policy toward Taiwan. Chang King-yu, chairman of the **Mainland Affairs Council**, said that it was intended to restrict **investment** in high-technology industries, infrastructure projects, and some massive investment projects only. The policy was subsequently interpreted to prohibit investments of more than US$50 million and to ban financial involvement in infrastructure projects.

When **Chen Shui-bian** became **president**, he did not support the policy, some said because he wanted the support and contributions of Taiwan's business community. This put him at odds with others in the **Democratic Progressive Party**, including Vice President **Annette Lu** and his ally **Lee Teng-hui**. President Chen later made statements that seemed to support the policy. In October 2002, when China and Taiwan were about to be admitted to the **World Trade Organization**, Taipei announced a policy of "liberalization with effective management," though what this meant was unclear. The "no haste" idea remains, as do restrictions (though hardly very effective) on investing in China. *See also* GO SOUTH POLICY.

NOGI MARESUKE. Third Japanese governor-general of **Taiwan**, who served from 1896 to 1898. Though a lieutenant general in the Japanese army, Nogi brought civilian government to Taiwan and restricted the power and authority of the army there.

NON-MAINSTREAM FACTION (FEI CHU-LIU P'AI). A group of **Nationalist Party** members that opposed President **Lee Teng-hui**'s nomination of **Li Yuan-zu** as vice president in 1990. The group then briefly supported **Lin Yang-kang** and **Chiang Wei-kuo**, respectively, for **president** and vice president. Members of the group included important political figures such as **Chen Li-an** and **Hau Pei-tsun**. This group continued to exist after the challenge to President Lee failed, but not as a formal organization or faction. Members criticized Lee's accruing too much power and his support of **Taiwan**'s independence. In 1993, a number of members of the faction left the Nationalist Party and formed the **New Party**. Those who remained in the party continued to oppose many of President Lee's policies, especially his stand on independence. Its members were mostly **Mainland Chinese**.

NON-PARTISAN SOLIDARITY UNION (WU-TANG T'UAN-CHIE LIEN-MENG). A political organization with the status of a **political party** founded in June 2004 to prepare for the legislative election at the end of the year. Leaders said the group stood for a middle way but generally supported **pan-blue**. Their candidates won six seats in the **Legislative Yuan**.

NORMALIZATION AGREEMENT (CHENG-CH'ANG-HUA HSIEH-YI). A communiqué signed between the United States and the People's Republic of China in December 1978, which formalized diplomatic relations between the two countries as of 1 January 1979. On that date the United States severed relations with the **Republic of China**. In the agreement, the United States acknowledged the position of the government of the People's Republic of China regarding **Taiwan**: that there is but one China, and Taiwan is part of China. On the other hand, the agreement stated that the United States would "maintain cultural, commercial and other unofficial relations with the People of Taiwan." Congress was dissatisfied with the way the

Jimmy Carter administration treated Taipei in signing the Normalization Agreement and subsequently wrote the **Taiwan Relations Act** and passed it into law.

The Normalization Agreement was said to have represented a departure from ambiguity in U.S.–China policy and to have erected a policy in which the United States favored the People's Republic of China. It also had a marked negative effect on **Taipei**'s diplomatic situation, causing other nations to similarly break relations. And it likewise led the United States to terminate, after a one-year hiatus, the **United States–Republic of China Defense Treaty**.

– O –

OFFICE FOR PRIVATE INVESTMENT (SZU-JEN T'OU-TZU-CH'U). Established in 1958 within the USAID mission organization, it sought to encourage the development of private industry in **Taiwan** and the privatization of the **economy**. The Industrial Development and Investment Center and the China Productivity Center furthered its aims. *See also* INVESTMENT.

OFFICE OF THE PRESIDENT (TSUNG-T'UNG FU). The Office of the President consists of a secretary-general, advisers, military aides, **Academia Sinica**, **Academia Historica**, the **National Unification Council**, and, since 1967, the **National Security Council**. The First Bureau of the Office of the President is in charge of drafting and promulgating laws and decrees; the Second Bureau handles information and documents; and the Third Bureau is responsible for protocol, awards, honors, and the like. The Code Office takes care of telegraphic correspondence and national archives. The Office of the Guards is in charge of security. The Department of Public Affairs manages public relations. *See also* PRESIDENT.

OFFSHORE ISLANDS. Several island groups close to China that were, after 1949, or still are, controlled by the **Republic of China**, including **Quemoy**, **Matsu**, and some other islands. Communist forces did not capture these islands in 1949 when Mao Zedong defeated Nationalist forces on the mainland and established the People's Republic of China. The islands became an issue of international concern when the People's Liberation Army attacked Quemoy in 1954–1955 and again in 1958. After the first crisis, Washington and Taipei concluded the **United States–Republic of China Defense Treaty**, which subsequently covered the Offshore Islands via the **Formosa Resolution**, wherein the U.S. Congress gave the president discretionary authority to protect them.

For a number of years, Republic of China leaders considered the islands important to its plan to counterattack the mainland and liberate it from Communism. **Taiwan** kept one-third of its military forces on the islands for some years—against the advice of U.S. military advisers. Some small ones were abandoned. The Republic of China currently maintains jurisdiction over the islands, but tension over them has diminished. In fact, there are broad contacts between the islands and China. (*See* MINI-THREE LINKS.) Leaders of the **Democratic Progressive Party**, in order to separate Taiwan from China, have suggested that the islands are not part of Taiwan and should be abandoned, but they found that position unpopular and abandoned it.

ONE CHINA (YI-KE CHUNG-KUO). The idea or principle that China should not be split and that **Taiwan** is or should be a part of China for historical, cultural, political, and a variety of other reasons. Under **Chiang Kai-shek** and **Chiang Ching-kuo**, and for a while under **Lee Teng-hui**, the **Republic of China** proclaimed a one-China policy and said that *it* was the legitimate government of China, claiming territory under the jurisdiction of the People's Republic of China, plus Outer Mongolia and some other territory. Chinese leaders in Beijing also adhered to the one-China idea but claimed that one China meant the People's Republic of China and asserted that the Republic of China did not constitute a legitimate or sovereign nation. They still maintain this view, although they have veered somewhat from it at times to encourage **Taipei** to negotiate reunification.

Under Lee Teng-hui, one China came to refer to a historical or a cultural China and not to a Chinese nation-state, thereby allowing separate (at least temporarily) Chinese governments. (*See* ONE COUNTRY, TWO ENTITIES.) Later, China accused President Lee of not supporting the one-China principle. The **Democratic Progressive Party** opposed one China, saying so in its platform. (*See* ONE

CHINA, ONE TAIWAN.) The **New Party** strongly supported it but did not call for immediate action to unite the two parts of China. The **Nationalist Party** formally supported it, but many members as well as outside observers said that President Lee, especially after his statement in 1999, did not really support it. Opinion polls in Taiwan reflect low support for both separation, or independence, and unification; most people instead support the status quo. When **Chen Shui-bian** became **president** in 2000, he promised not to declare Taiwan independent, but in many ways he demonstrated that an independent Taiwan was his goal. **Pan-blue** has opposed independence and has seemed, therefore, to support one China—though that generally meant something that might happen in the future.

One China is said to be the policy of the United States and most other nations of the world. However, most nations have simply "taken note of" or "acknowledged" Beijing's claim to Taiwan rather than "recognizing" its sovereignty over territory governed by the Republic of China. Also, Washington adheres to a policy that the "Taiwan issue" must be settled peacefully and that Taiwan's future must be resolved according to the wishes of its residents, which many see as contradicting Washington's one-China policy.

ONE CHINA, ONE TAIWAN (YI-CHUNG YI-T'AI). The idea that **Taiwan** and China are separate, or should be, based on history, culture, language, and other differences, and that they are or should be legally and politically two states, both with sovereignty. Some who support this idea say that the **Republic of China** is synonymous with Taiwan and that this is both a legal and a practical reality. Others say that a **Republic of Taiwan** should be declared to realize the idea of one China, one Taiwan. More radical members of the **Democratic Progressive Party** espouse the latter position; most in the **New Party** oppose it strongly.

Some say this idea is, in fact, the policy of most nations of the world since they deal with Taiwan separately from China and support its right to choose its future because of its successful democratization and/or because they support the idea of self-determination. *See also* ONE CHINA.

ONE COUNTRY, TWO AREAS (YI-KUO LIANG-KE-DI-FANG). An idea for dealing with the situation of **two Chinas** that was passed in the form of a resolution by the **Legislative Yuan** in **Taiwan** in July 1992. *See also* ONE COUNTRY, TWO ENTITIES; ONE COUNTRY, TWO GOVERNMENTS.

ONE COUNTRY, TWO ENTITIES (YI-KUO LIANG-KE-CHENG-CHIH SHIH-T'I). A formula advanced by some in **Taiwan** in the 1990s for dealing with the situation of **two Chinas**, or the separation of Taiwan from China by using "creative ambiguity," referring to both sides as "political entities." Some say it originated because President **Lee Teng-hui** had earlier referred to the People's Republic of China as a political entity. *See also* ONE COUNTRY, TWO GOVERNMENTS; ONE COUNTRY, TWO AREAS.

ONE COUNTRY, TWO GOVERNMENTS (YI-KUO LIANG-FU). A formula advanced by some **Republic of China** officials to deal with the problem of the existence of **two Chinas**, or the separation of the Republic of China and the People's Republic of China. Those advocating the formula supported the sovereignty of the Republic of China but also the principle of **one China**. Both Beijing and most opposition politicians in Taiwan reject this concept or idea. Chinese leaders promote another formula. (*See* ONE COUNTRY, TWO SYSTEMS.) Most members and supporters of the **pan-green** parties take the position that Taiwan and China are equal political entities, each with sovereignty, and are separate—therefore such a formula does not apply. *See also* ONE CHINA, ONE TAIWAN; ONE COUNTRY, TWO AREAS; ONE COUNTRY, TWO ENTITIES.

ONE COUNTRY, TWO SYSTEMS (YI-KUO LIANG-CHIH). A formula advanced by leaders of the People's Republic of China to realize the reunification of China. The concept is attributed to Deng Xiaoping, although other Chinese leaders had talked about it before Deng first began to promote it in 1982, at which time it was put in China's constitution (though phrased somewhat vaguely). It was applied to the reunification of Hong Kong in July 1997, and Chinese leaders said at the time that it would be used as the basis for **Taiwan**'s incorporation.

Taipei rejected the formula, stating that it was an attempt to make the government of the **Republic of China** a local government under Beijing's control and take away its sovereignty. Officials in Taiwan added that it does not take into consideration Taiwan's history and its democratization. They also cited China's bad human rights record, pointing out that autonomous regions in the People's Republic of China, which Taiwan would become under the formula, are not positive examples of Beijing's rule, mentioning especially the bad situation in Tibet. President **Lee Teng-hui** personally rejected the formula, stating that Hong Kong and Taiwan are two very different places and that Hong Kong was formerly a British colony and was not self-governing or sovereign, unlike the Republic of China. He has also declared that Taiwan, unlike Hong Kong, is capable of defending itself. President **Chen Shui-bian** has also rejected the formula. *See also* ONE CHINA, ONE TAIWAN; ONE COUNTRY, TWO AREAS; ONE COUNTRY, TWO ENTITIES; ONE COUNTRY, TWO GOVERNMENTS; ONE COUNTRY ON EACH SIDE.

ONE COUNTRY ON EACH SIDE (YI BIAN YI KUO). On 3 August 2002, President **Chen Shui-bian**, speaking to a meeting of the World Federation of Taiwan Associations meeting in Tokyo, said that there is one country on each side of the **Taiwan Strait** and that **Taiwan** is neither a part of nor a province of another country. He further said that Taiwan's twenty-three million people have the right to decide their future and that this should be done through a referendum. He then suggested that a **referendum law** be passed. Upon hearing Chen's statement, China condemned what it called a "desinicization campaign." The George W. Bush administration also criticized Chen, having been generally tolerant of Chen's provocative statements up to this point. Observers said Chen made the statement to incite China and to energize his political base at home before the presidential election in March 2004, though he was indeed serious about a referendum law. Just before he used the phrase, China had persuaded Naru to break diplomatic relations with **Taipei** and establish ties with Beijing; thus Taiwan's further diplomatic isolation may also have motivated Chen to make his statement about one country on each side.

OPERA (KE CHU). The Chinese brought Chinese opera to **Taiwan**, and it has been one of the island's foremost and unique **art** forms. Peking Opera, with its emphasis on Confucian moral values such as filial piety, loyalty, and patriotism, and often containing acrobatics and battle scenes, is the most famous. However, opera performances are also done in the various **dialects** and represent provincial Chinese culture. **Taiwanese** opera, which has its origins in short songs from Ilan County and is influenced by aboriginal culture, became more popular in the 1960s, with many performances shown on television. Some consider puppeteering, which was popular in the past and in the early years after World War II, both from China and that which developed locally, a kind of opera. The government encouraged Western opera after World War II, but it did not draw large crowds. In recent years, Chinese opera has been influenced by new forms in China.

OPERATION CAUSEWAY. Invasion plan designed by U.S. Admiral Chester Nimitz in early 1944 based on a directive of the U.S. Joint Chiefs of Staff to investigate the feasibility of an invasion of **Taiwan**. Because of successes against Japanese forces in the Central and Western Pacific, together with doubts as to whether the Chinese residents of Taiwan would rise up and fight against the Japanese government and military, the plan was abandoned in October 1944.

ORCHID ISLAND (LAN YÜ). A small island off **Taiwan**'s southeast coast that is known for the orchids that grow on the hillsides. It is home to about three thousand **Yami aborigines**. In 1980, a controversial nuclear waste facility was built there.

OTA MASAHIRO. The governor-general of **Taiwan** appointed in early 1931 following the **Musha Rebellion**. His rule was a harsh one, and Home Rule leaders recalled him after little more than a year following numerous complaints.

OVERSEAS ALLIANCE FOR DEMOCRATIC RULE IN TAIWAN (T'AI-WAN MIN-CHU HAI-WAI LIEN-MENG). Formed by **Kuo Yu-hsin** in 1978, mainly from members of the **World United Formosans for Independence**, the organization advocated **Taiwan**'s separation from China.

OVERSEAS CHINESE (HUA-CH'IAO). Term originally referring to people of Chinese descent living outside of the **Republic of**

China, but more recently to Chinese not residing in either the People's Republic of China or the Republic of China. There are around forty million Overseas Chinese, around 80 percent of whom live in Southeast Asian countries. Most of the rest live in the United States. The majority hails from Kuangtung and Fukien provinces. Earlier the government in **Taiwan** considered the allegiance of Overseas Chinese, sometimes called "mothers of the revolution," very important because the Republic of China was created, in large measure, with their support and because of the past competition between Taipei and Beijing for recognition as the legal government of China. Taipei still considers the Overseas Chinese important for economic, public relations, and other reasons. (*See* OVERSEAS CHINESE AFFAIRS COMMISSION.)

Overseas Chinese representation in the Taiwan government is provided in the **Constitution** and specifically in an amendment added in 1991. Overseas Chinese previously served in the **National Assembly** and are currently in the **Legislative Yuan**. Overseas Chinese support for Taiwan has declined in recent years because China turned to free market capitalism under Deng Xiaoping, which provided **investment** and other economic opportunities for them in China. They have also expressed concern about provincialism and ethnic discrimination in Taiwan that grew after **Chen Shui-bian** was elected **president** in 2000.

OVERSEAS CHINESE AFFAIRS COMMISSION (OCAC) (HUA-CH'IAO WEI-YUAN-HUI). Established in 1926 as a commission of the **Executive Yuan**, the OCAC seeks to protect the welfare and interests of **Overseas Chinese**. Its work consists of helping students, getting passports and visas for Overseas Chinese, and running the Overseas Chinese News Agency and the Chung Hua Correspondence School. In recent years, more effort has been expended to bring in Overseas Chinese **investment** and to attract Overseas Chinese students.

OVERSEAS ECONOMIC COOPERATION FUND (HAI-WAI CHING-CHI HO-TSO CHI-CHIN). A fund established in 1989 as a foreign assistance program to help "friendly developing countries." The government appropriated NT$2.5 billion in fiscal year 1989 and

NT$3 billion in fiscal year 1990 for the fund. The fund was to have a total of NT$30 billion. By July 1991, ten countries had applied for economic assistance from the fund. Fund activities include making loans and grants and facilitating capital transfers. According to government guidelines, the People's Republic of China cannot apply to the fund. Many observers say the main purpose of the fund is to upgrade **Taiwan**'s diplomatic ties with Third World countries and influence some countries to grant diplomatic recognition to **Taipei**. *See also* TAIWAN INTERNATIONAL COOPERATION AND DEVELOPMENT FUND.

– P –

PAKKAN TAO. Literally "northern anchorage," this term was used by Chinese fishermen in the thirteenth century to refer to **Taiwan**.

PALACE MUSEUM. *See* NATIONAL PALACE MUSEUM.

PAN-BLUE (FAN-LAN). Term used for the opposition parties that became more unified following **Chen Shui-bian**'s victory in the presidential election in 2000, made up of the **Nationalist Party,** the **People First Party**, and also the **New Party**. Blue comes from the Nationalist Party's party color. Pan-blue is regarded as conservative, procapitalist, and opposed to Taiwan's independence, but also as more cosmopolitan and global. Its "founders" or original leaders were **Lien Chan** and **James Soong**. *See also* PAN-GREEN.

PAN-GREEN (FAN-LU). Term used for the **Democratic Progressive Party** (DPP) and the **Taiwan Solidarity Union** shortly after the latter was formed in 2001. Pan-green is liberal and supports **Taiwan**'s independence and is more provincial and nationalist. Green is from the party color of the DPP. It is led by and supports **Chen Shui-bian**. *See also* PAN-BLUE.

PAO CHIA (PAO-CHIA CHIH-TU). System of social organization and control used in ancient China and also in Taiwan. According to the system, each of ten households chooses a representative who meets with nine other similarly chosen representatives, that group also selecting a leader, and on and on. The system was abolished by Tokyo in 1895 when **Taiwan** became a Japanese colony. **Goto Shimpei**, however, revived it in 1898. It was used primarily as a means of facilitating police control by making each individual person responsible for those in his or her unit and subject to punishment for crimes committed by those people. Thus it incorporated the idea of collective responsibility and collective punishment for crimes. Under Japanese governance, it evolved into a means of political control and record keeping as well.

PARACEL ISLANDS (HSI-SHA CHUN-TAO). A group of islands, called Hsisha in Chinese, in the South China Sea claimed as territory of the **Republic of China**. *See also* MACCLESFIELD BANK, PRATAS ISLANDS; SPRATLY ISLANDS.

PARTY CONGRESS. *See* NATIONAL PARTY CONGRESS.

PARTY OF TAIWANESE PEOPLE (T'AI-WAN MIN-CHUNG-TANG). A **political party** formed in **Taiwan** in 1927 under Japanese colonial rule, which was the first-ever legal political party in Taiwan. It functioned, however, for only four years, until the governor-general banned it. It cannot be correctly called an opposition party, however, since it did not oppose Japanese rule. Nor did it help consolidate a fledgling political opposition in Taiwan, but rather it resulted in a split among **Taiwanese** political activists.

PENG MING-MIN (1923–). Known as the "father of **Taiwan** independence," when a professor at **Taiwan National University** in the mid-1960s, he began to agitate against the "Chiang clique." In 1964, together with two associates, he wrote and published a manifesto called the "Declaration of the Taiwanese Self-Salvation Movement," advocating Taiwan's independence. For this, Peng was arrested and incarcerated. Because he was well known in Taiwan and abroad (the youngest professor ever at Taiwan National University and having represented the country at a number of international conferences), he was not given more severe punishment. He served fourteen months in jail, after which he was placed under house arrest. In 1970, Peng fled the country and for the next three-plus decades lived in the United States. While in the United States, he founded the **Formosan Association for Public Affairs**. He also wrote the book *A Taste of Freedom* about his life and about the need for Taiwan to be independent.

Peng returned to Taiwan in 1992 and in 1994 joined the **Democratic Progressive Party**. He was viewed as a symbol of the past travails and sufferings of proindependence advocates. In 1996, he was nominated by the DPP to be its candidate for **president**, and he ran with **Frank Hsieh** as his running mate. He was defeated, receiving only 21.13 percent of the popular vote. Subsequently Peng's relationship with the DPP deteriorated, and he experienced increasing isolation in the party due to what many considered his lack of realism and his ultra–hard-line position on independence. Peng subsequently organized the Nation Building Association, which evolved into the **Taiwan Independence Party**. Peng's political influence waned dramatically after that.

PENGHU. *See* PESCADORE ISLANDS.

PERIOD OF NATIONAL MOBILIZATION FOR THE SUPPRESSION OF THE COMMUNIST REBELLION (TUNG-YUAN K'AN-LUAN SHIH-CH'I). Declared in 1948 based on the **Temporary Provisions** to the **Constitution**, which canceled many of the provisions guaranteeing individual rights and freedoms as well as limits on government power, it is now seen as the period when the **Republic of China** was staunchly anti-Communist and democracy was limited. President **Lee Teng-hui** terminated the "period" in May 1991, restoring the original rights in the Constitution and technically ending the state of war between the Nationalist government and the Communist government as far as **Taipei** was concerned. Beijing did not view this as a friendly gesture and did not reciprocate, because Chinese leaders viewed Lee's actions as further separating **Taiwan** from China.

PESCADORE ISLANDS (P'ENG-HU CH'UN-TAO). A group of islands or what might be called an archipelago off the southwestern coast of **Taiwan** in the **Taiwan Strait**. There are sixty-four islands in all, comprising 126 square kilometers in area. **Penghu**, the largest island, accounts for about half of the land surface of the archipelago and 70 percent of its population. The islands form a natural demarcation between the East China Sea and the South China Sea. The Pescadore Islands attracted the attention of Chinese fishermen in the twelfth century and were the first among islands around Taiwan, including Taiwan itself, to be settled by Chinese, which began at that time.

In 1622, the Dutch occupied the islands and intended to use them as a base to control ship traffic in the Taiwan Strait, but two years later they were forced to leave, though another interpretation is that they negotiated with the Chinese government and traded the islands for the island of Taiwan (though Taiwan was not really controlled by China). The Dutch, however, got control of the Pescadores again later. In 1895, the Pescadores, along with Taiwan and other surrounding islands, were transferred to Japan via the **Treaty of Shimonoseki**. They were returned to the **Republic of China** with Taiwan and other surrounding islands at the end of World War II.

PFG-2 (CHU-LI CHIEN-ER-HAO). The designation of **Taiwan**'s home-built missile frigate, also called the Perry Frigate, launched in October 1991. The navy ordered it from **China Shipbuilding Corporation** in August 1989. Its design follows the U.S. PFG-7, but it has greater offensive capabilities. It is to be used to defend Taiwan against an attack by China. *See also* ARMED FORCES.

PINGPU (P'ING-P'U). A name that refers to the plains-dwelling **aborigines** of **Taiwan** who were driven from the flatlands or were assimilated by the Chinese settlers after the latter began to populate the island. There were ten tribes of Pingpu aborigines. They lived in houses built on stilts and cooked food and ate pickled vegetables. They worshipped nature, ghosts, and their ancestors. **Women** were responsible for tilling the fields and weaving, and the eldest daughter in the family became the heir, her husband usually adopting her family name.

PO YANG. *See* BO YANG.

POLITICAL MIRACLE (T'AI-WAN CHENG-CHIH CH'I-CHI). A term used to describe the **Republic of China**'s rapid political modernization that began in the early or mid-1980s and which, according to most observers, turned **Taiwan** into a genuine or full-fledged democracy within a decade or two. Many called it a miracle because Taiwan had been widely regarded as a hard authoritarian dictatorship that resisted reform and was frequently labeled a pariah nation for that, but it was soon seen as a real, working democracy. The transition to a democratic system was made, moreover, without the benefit of a colonial experience that prepared Taiwan for the change, it was accomplished in a very short period of time compared to Western democracies, and it happened without bloodshed. It also occurred at a time when the nation was technically at war and was certainly under threat. Taiwan's experience is unique in these respects, and as a result it has been viewed as a model for other countries seeking to democratize. (*See* TAIWAN EXPERIENCE.) Taiwan's political modernization and transition to democracy were also more difficult, according to some scholars, because of the fact that its authoritarian control was built on the rule of a single party rather than the military, which could simply "return to the barracks." Party control of the **media**, judiciary, and the government bureaucracy was, in other words, difficult to break. Also, the military and security organizations had to be depoliticized and their ties with the party broken, and this was not an easy task.

The factors contributing to the Taiwan "political miracle" included **land reform**, which destroyed the feudal landlord-tenant ties and which fostered the development of local democracy; rapid economic growth with equity; urbanization (which led to the creation of interest groups); the growth of competing **political parties**; elections; enlightened leaders, especially **Chiang Ching-kuo** and **Lee Teng-hui**; pressure by the United States; and efforts by the government to build a better image in the international community in the face of efforts by the People's Republic of China to force Taiwan to negotiate reunification. The **Democratic Progressive Party** (DPP) defined the Taiwan political miracle to have happened more because of the advent of a genuine opposition political party, meaning the DPP. After **Chen Shui-bian** became **president** in 2000, many included the idea of a change of ruling parties; some, in fact, saw this as the main ingredient.

The Taiwan political miracle (or its democratization, which many say is synonymous) is often seen as the major obstacle to reunification with China. It is often cited by **Taipei** as the reason that Taiwan cannot unify with China, since the People's Republic of China has not democratized. *See also* ECONOMIC MIRACLE.

POLITICAL PARTIES (CHENG-TANG). Before 1986, **Taiwan** had a one-party system, although there were two token legal opposition parties before that: the **Young China Party** and the **China Democratic Socialist Party**. The political party system began to change in the late 1970s and early 1980s with the increasing number of independent candidates participating in elections, and later due to the formation of the *tangwai*—a loose organization of independent politicians. In September 1986, the *tangwai* evolved into the **Democratic Progressive Party** (DPP). The DPP, though still technically an illegal organization, challenged the **Nationalist Party** in the 1986 election.

After the lifting of **martial law** in July 1987, more parties formed, although they did not become formally legal until January 1989 with the passage of the **Law on Civic Organizations**. The DPP performed well in the December 1989 election, prompting some to say that a two-party system was evolving. Nevertheless, by the end of February 1990 there were more than forty registered political parties, which some said meant that Taiwan had a multiparty system. But, prior to the December 1991 **National Assembly** election, only four political parties had enough support to qualify for television time: the Nationalist Party, the Democratic Progressive Party, the **Chinese Social Democratic Party**, and the **National Democratic Independent Political Alliance**. The results of the election again suggested to many observers that a two-party system was evolving, as only the Nationalist Party and the Democratic Progressive Party did sufficiently well to win at-large delegates in the National Assembly. Others noted that, because of the KMT's large margin of victory and its better performance than in the 1989 election, the system was rather a one-party dominant system, or a mixture of that and a multiparty system. This view was reversed in favor of a two-party system after the **Legislative Yuan** election in 1992, when the DPP again performed very well.

In 1993, the **New Party** formed from the **Non-Mainstream faction** of the Nationalist Party and made a credible showing in the 1994 election and turned in an even better performance in the 1995 Legislative Yuan election. This prompted speculation that the political party system was a three-party system. That, however, was heard less after the 1996 presidential election and subsequent local elections, and especially after the 1998 Legislative Yuan and metropolitan mayoral races; the NP did poorly in all of these elections. After the 2000 presidential election, **James Soong** formed the **People First Party**. In 2001, former president **Lee Teng-hui** helped form the **Taiwan Solidarity Union**. As a result, Taiwan seemed to have a four-party system made up of two blocs, with the Nationalist Party and the People First Party in one bloc and the Democratic Progressive Party and the Taiwan Solidarity Union in another. *See* PAN-BLUE; PAN-GREEN.

Recent amendments to the **Constitution** that change the electoral system will likely result in the parties of the two blocs merging, or in the weaker ones dying and a two-party system evolving, although since forming a political party in Taiwan is easy, there no doubt will be other parties around in the foreseeable future.

POTSDAM DECLARATION (PO-SZ-TAN HSUEN-YEN). A formal agreement by the United States, the United Kingdom, and the Soviet Union in July 1945 (when Japan's defeat was imminent) that, among other things, confirmed the promise made in the **Cairo Declaration** that "**Taiwan** and other territories stolen by Japan" would be returned after the war. However, it was not stated in the declaration specifically to whom Taiwan was to be given. Rather this matter was to be resolved in a subsequent peace treaty. The Potsdam Declaration is frequently cited by those who argue that Taiwan belongs to the **Republic of China** and not the People's Republic of China (since the latter did not exist at the time), and also that it should not be independent. However, due to the fact that it was vague about Taiwan's future and didn't declare Taiwan's legal status, it is also cited by those who say that Taiwan's status is yet to be decided or who advocate an independent Taiwan.

PRAGMATIC DIPLOMACY (WU-SHIH WAI-CH'IAO). A new style of diplomacy practiced by the **Republic of China** and attributed to **Lee Teng-hui** soon after he became **president**, though some attribute it to **Chiang Ching-kuo**. It included efforts to reinforce formal diplomatic ties, establish substantive relations with nations with which the Republic of China did not have formal ties, establish ties with Communist nations, and obtain admission or readmission to international organizations. The assumption was that the fading of the Cold War provided new diplomatic opportunities and that the diplomatic war with the People's Republic of China was no longer a zero-sum contest. It was also the product of **Taiwan**'s successful democratization and the fact that Taiwan had a good reputation in the world community and could capitalize on this. It likewise mirrored Taiwan's considerable **investment** in and **trade** with the mainland and the possibility of improved political relations with Beijing.

Pragmatic diplomacy was originally undertaken, some say, as a response to charges by the opposition that the government was to blame for the Republic of China's loss of diplomatic relations and diplomatic status, and it in large part includes tenets of the **Democratic Progressive Party**'s **foreign policy** agenda. It has been criticized as lacking principles and as supporting Taiwan's separation from China, or a two-Chinas policy. *See also* DOLLAR DIPLOMACY; FLEXIBLE DIPLOMACY; SUBSTANTIVE DIPLOMACY; VACATION DIPLOMACY.

PRATAS ISLANDS (TUNG-SHA CH'UN-TAO). Located in the eastern part of the South China Sea, these small islands include territory claimed by the **Republic of China**, which maintains a small military force there. The People's Republic of China, Vietnam, the Philippines, Malaysia, and Indonesia also claim the islands. They are considered strategically located and may be important because they lie near vital shipping lanes, and their ownership is seen as the possible basis for claims to undersea resources in the vicinity.

PREMIER (HSING-CHENG-YUAN YUAN-CHANG). The president of the **Executive Yuan**, the premier is considered the highest executive leader in the government of the **Republic of China** and generally its second most important political figure after the **president**. When **Chiang Ching-kuo** was premier from 1975 to 1978, being also head of the ruling **Nationalist Party**, most regarded him as the nation's most powerful political leader rather than **Yen Chia-kan**, who was president, and the political system as more a cabinet or parliamentary one than a presidential one. Under President **Lee Teng-hui**, the **president** and the **premier** became locked in dispute, and the fact that the president could appoint the premier but could not fire him led to a minor constitutional crisis. It was resolved in practice when **Hau Pei-tsun** either stepped down at Lee's behest or left with the cabinet (both interpretations have wide acceptance) following an election of the **Legislative Yuan** in 1995. The relationship between the **president** and the premier was formally altered as a result of amendments to the **Constitution** passed in 1997, which strengthened the presidency and pushed the system toward a presidential one.

PRESBYTERIAN CHURCH OF TAIWAN (PCT) (T'AI-WAN CHANG-LAO-CHIAO-HUI). Established in 1865 by British and Canadian missionaries, the PCT soon built a large following. In the nineteenth century, its missionaries developed a system for romanizing the **Taiwanese** dialect or language. During the Japanese period, the PCT was suppressed because the colonial government believed it was involved in agitating among the **aborigines**.

The PCT was distrusted by the Nationalist Chinese government because of its sympathy with the **Taiwan Independence Movement**, and the church was often the target of investigations and repression, with some of its foreign missionaries being expelled from the country. In 1971, the PCT issued a "Public Statement on Our National Fate"; this document advocated self-determination in the wake of Taipei's expulsion from the **United Nations**. In subsequent documents, the PCT called for freedom of **religion** and human rights and called on the United States to protect **Taiwan**'s independence. In 1979, Reverend **Kao Chun-ming**, then the secretary-general of the PCT, was imprisoned for his role in helping **Shih Ming-teh**, one of the leaders sought by police after the **Kaohsiung Incident**.

Although appearing unified in its views, the PCT has sometimes suffered from internal divisions over differences between its Fukien Taiwanese membership and its aborigine membership. Critics of the PCT note that it is the only religious organization in Taiwan that is strongly involved in politics or takes an unequivocal stand on political matters. Church leaders reply that they have not supported any independence organization. However, **Thomas Liao** and **Peng Ming-min** were influenced by their association with the PCT. **Lee Teng-hui** is a member of the PCT, as is **Yao Chia-wen**, former head of the **Democratic Progressive Party**. *See also* RELIGION.

PRESIDENT (TSUNG-T'UNG). The highest official of the **Republic of China** according to the **Constitution**. The **National Assembly** formerly elected him or her for a six-year term with a two-term limit (exempted by the **Temporary Provisions**). The president is now elected by direct election for a four-year term. The first direct election was held in 1996. The president has the power to command the military forces, issue mandates, conclude treaties, represent the nation in foreign affairs, declare war or peace, effectuate **martial law**, grant amnesties, and make appointments—including the **premier**; the president, vice president, and grand justices of the **Judicial Yuan**; the president, vice president, auditor-general, and members of the **Control Yuan**; and the president, vice president, and members of the **Examination Yuan**. He or she also grants amnesty and commutations, appoints and removes civil service officers, and confers honors. The president may also intervene to resolve disputes between the **Executive Yuan** and the **Legislative Yuan**.

The fact that past presidents have been the leaders of the ruling party enhanced the president's power beyond what was constitutionally given, and this, plus the perceived need for a strong leader in Taiwan, made the political system in practice a presidential one—even though the **Constitution** sets forth a mixed presidential, cabinet, and parliamentary system (some say more the latter). Through both practice and constitutional change, the president is now head of what most people say is a presidential or semipresidential system of government, and the presidency is the locus of political authority. When **Lee Teng-hui** was president, democratization strengthened his presidency since he was a major force behind that process, though it also strengthened the Legislative Yuan, and the two were often in conflict. When **Chen Shui-bian** became president, he had to contend with the difficulty of divided government, and **pan-blue** leaders often argued for legislative supremacy and a parliamentary system of government. *See also* OFFICE OF THE PRESIDENT.

PRESIDENTIAL AND VICE PRESIDENTIAL ELECTION AND RECALL LAW (TSUNG-T'UNG FU-TSUNG-T'UNG HSUAN-PA-FA). A law passed by the **Legislative Yuan** in July 1995 after amendments were written to the **Constitution** that changed the method of electing the **president** to a direct system, leading to the first such election in March 1996. It states, among other things, that the presidential and vice presidential candidates may be nominated by any political party gaining at least 5 percent of the vote in the most recent provincial-level or higher election, or by collecting the signatures of at least 1.5 percent of the eligible voters in the most recent parliamentary election. In addition, the **Central Election Commission** must provide thirty minutes of national television time for each candidate and funding for national televised debates when two or more candidates agree to participate. *See also* PUBLIC OFFICIALS ELECTION AND RECALL LAW.

PRESIDENTIAL PALACE (TSUNG-T'UNG-FU). A large office building located in downtown **Taipei** built by the Japanese, which, during the colonial period, contained the offices of the governor-general and other high officials. It is now the site of the **president**'s office and some other important agencies of government. On **National Day**, 10 October, it is the scene of parades and celebrations and a presidential address.

PROVINTIA (JE-CHE-LAN-CH'ENG). A fort and town or city that became the capital of the Dutch colonial government in 1650. At one time there were six hundred Dutch officials living there, in addition to over two thousand troops. In Chinese, it was called *hung mao lou*, or the "edifice of red-haired barbarians." It was located at the present city of **Tainan**. *See also* ZEELANDIA.

PROVISIONAL AMENDMENTS FOR THE PERIOD OF MOBILIZATION FOR THE SUPPRESSION OF COMMUNIST REBELLION (TUNG-YUAN K'AN-LUAN SHIH-CH'I LING-SHIH TI'AO-K'UAN). A set of amendments promulgated by the Nationalist Chinese government on 10 May 1948, during the Chinese Civil War, that canceled or held in abeyance a number of provisions in the **Constitution**. The amendments remained in effect when the government moved to **Taiwan**. Commonly known as the "Temporary Provisions," the amendments expanded the emergency powers given to the **president** in articles 39 and 43 of the Constitution. They also permitted the president and vice president to exceed the constitutionally limited two terms in office and authorized the president to appoint members to the three elected bodies of government. They held in abeyance many of the political and civil rights guaranteed to individual citizens in the Constitution.

Critics of the Temporary Provisions felt that, while they were perhaps justified at one time, they should have subsequently been repealed and were an obstruction to constitutional government and democracy. The Temporary Provisions were altered three times, in 1960, 1966, and 1972, and were finally abolished in 1991.

PUBLIC LAW 96-8. *See* TAIWAN RELATIONS ACT.

PUBLIC OFFICIALS ELECTION AND RECALL LAW (KUNG-CHIH JEN-YUAN HSUAN-PA-FA). A new election law adopted on 14 May 1980 that laid the foundation for a competitive national election in December 1980. The law was the result of a series of meetings that involved government officials, scholars, the **media**, and others called after the **Kaohsiung Incident**. Compromises were made between the government and the ruling party on the one hand and opposition politicians on the other so that democratization would be possible without causing political instability. The election law was amended in 1983 and again after that. It contains a set of elaborate rules on conducting elections and electing officials. It also guarantees the impartiality of the **Central Election Commission**. Another set of laws was written specifically for a direct presidential election in 1996. *See also* PRESIDENTIAL AND VICE PRESIDENTIAL ELECTION AND RECALL LAW.

PUBLIC OPINION RESEARCH FOUNDATION (MIN-YI TIAO-CH'A CHI-CHIN-HUI). Founded in 1986 primarily to aid businesses in doing market research, it now conducts opinion polls on a variety of subjects and does frequent opinion surveys on political issues and leaders.

– Q –

QIANDAO LAKE INCIDENT (CH'IEN-TAO-HU SHIH-CHIEN). At a resort lake in Chekiang Province in China where, in March

1994, twenty-four tourists from **Taiwan** were murdered. The government of the People's Republic of China labeled the incident an accident and refused a request by the **Straits Exchange Foundation** to send representatives to accompany family members of the victims and to help deal with the matter. Chinese police then arrested three young men for the crime, and they were immediately executed. To relatives and the public in Taiwan, the handling of the matter was seen as a cover-up—for the military that had been involved in a robbery and mass killing. The incident resulted in a sudden and marked drop in Taiwan **investment** in China. Following the incident, the highest level of support for independence since opinion pollsters in Taiwan had first asked that question was recorded.

QUEMOY (CHIN-MEN). A small island (though the name also refers to a chain of islands) off the coast of China (called "Kinmen" in the local dialect of Chinese and in **Taiwanese**, and sometimes in English). In 1949, Communist forces failed to defeat Nationalist armies there and left the island in Nationalist hands. (*See* OFFSHORE ISLANDS.) Quemoy was subsequently heavily fortified by the Nationalists and became the main "stepping-stone" in their plan to counterattack and liberate the mainland. In September 1954, shortly after the Geneva Conference on Indochina, Mao ordered an attack on the island. The United States came to **Taipei**'s rescue, thus preventing the People's Liberation Army from taking the island. Three months later, Washington and Taipei signed the **United States–Republic of China Defense Treaty**. A month after this, a joint resolution of the U.S. Congress, called the **Formosa Resolution**, put Quemoy and some other islands not far away under U.S. protection by giving the **president** discretionary authority to protect them. In 1958, another assault was made on Quemoy, again resulting in U.S. action—including the placing of an atomic cannon on the island (though it had no nuclear shells). Peking backed down but shelled the island on alternate days after that until the United States granted diplomatic relations to the People's Republic of China on 1 January 1979. The Nationalist military originally stationed around one hundred thousand soldiers on the island. The United States advised that the number should be reduced, as they might be killed or captured in a major conflict. The cutback, however, didn't come for a long time.

As of mid-2005, there were reported to be ten thousand troops left. The local population is around sixty thousand. Links, called the **Mini-Three Links**, have recently been established between Quemoy and China, and in that way, indirectly, between China and **Taiwan**. *See also* MATSU.

– R –

REFERENDUM LAW (GONG TOU FA). A law passed in November 2004 and signed by the **president** the next month that clarified a provision in the **Constitution** that provided for referendums. President **Chen Shui-bian** and **pan-green** officials had talked about holding a referendum on writing a new Constitution and perhaps some other issues, including some that related to **Taiwan**'s independence—opposition politicians having long advocated holding a referendum to decide the nation's legal status and its relationship with China. The **Nationalist Party** had long opposed the idea, as **pan-blue** did now. But President Chen's proposals found considerable public support, and pan-blue did not want to be hurt at the polls. (There was a presidential election in March the next year.) So pan-blue proposed a referendum law of its own design that gave the **Legislative Yuan** and the people (not the executive branch of government) the right to initiate a referendum, with only the legislature entitled to call one on constitutional issues. Pan-green said it had been "birdcaged" and that democracy had been hurt by pan-blue's actions. Nevertheless, President Chen put two referendums on the ballot for the March election using the "defensive referendum" provision of the law. Pan-blue contended that this was illegal and protested, but Chen went ahead.

The United States criticized Chen's actions as provoking trouble with China. China condemned the referendums but did not take any overt action. The referendums asked if Taiwan should employ anti-missile weapons to deal with China's missiles aimed at Taiwan and if the government should try to negotiate with China to establish peace and stability in the region. Pan-blue advised voters to boycott the referendums, which many did, and neither passed. Referendums have been mentioned rather frequently since, but none has been put on a ballot.

RELIGION (TSUNG CHIAO). Taiwan is very diverse in terms of its religious organizations and practices. Its religions are generally not exclusivist, so most people adhere to more than one. Religion and politics do not connect closely, and there have been few feuds or conflicts based on religious belief, leading some observers to say that **Taiwan** may be the freest and most tolerant country in the world in terms of religion.

The **aborigines** historically practiced animism, nature worship, and various kinds of animal sacrifices. In addition, they combined ancestor worship with agrarian rites. Their belief systems were polytheistic, and they did not make a distinction between gods and spirits. Except for two groups, they did not have the concept of a creator-god. They also practiced headhunting for its religious meaning.

The Chinese brought Buddhism, Confucianism, and Taoism to Taiwan. The Dutch brought Protestantism, the Spanish brought Catholicism, and the Japanese brought Shinto. When the Communists took control of China in 1949, many religious organizations and their officials, including priests and ministers, fled to Taiwan.

The largest religions in Taiwan are Taoism (with 7,600,000 followers); Buddhism (5,486,000); Yi Guan Dao (791,000); Protestantism (605,000); and Catholicism (298,450). **Chiang Kai-shek** and **Chiang Ching-kuo** were Methodist, though not active practitioners. **Lee Teng-hui** is Presbyterian. The government recognizes twenty-six religions in Taiwan. There are 33,026 temples and churches in the country, the largest number by a big margin being Taoist. Religious organizations, as of 2003, operated 31 hospitals, 46 clinics, 26 retirement homes, and 32 institutions for the mentally handicapped, in addition to 112 monasteries, 14 universities, 5 colleges, 40 high schools, 11 elementary schools, and 359 kindergartens.

REPUBLIC OF CHINA (ROC) (CHUNG-HUA MIN-KUO). The term originally referred to the government established in China after the 1911 revolution inspired by **Sun Yat-sen** and which replaced the Manchu government or Ch'ing Dynasty. In 1945, Taiwan was incorporated into the Republic of China. In 1949, Mao Zedong's forces defeated the Nationalist Chinese armies on the China mainland, after which the government, its military forces, and the **Nationalist Party** fled to **Taiwan**. The government of the Republic of China and the

Nationalist Party, however, continued to claim to be the legitimate government of all of China, even though it ruled only Taiwan, the **Pescadore Islands**, the **Offshore Islands**, some other islands close to Taiwan, and some islands in the South China Sea.

Nationalist Chinese officials said they would liberate China from Communism and Mao's rule. This claim, however, became less credible over the years and was ended in principle in 1991 when Taiwan ended the **period of mobilization to suppress the Communist rebellion on the mainland** and acknowledged the People's Republic of China as a legal "entity." Even before that, most considered the Republic of China to consist only of the territory over which it had actual jurisdiction. In the 1990s, the term **Republic of China on Taiwan** became commonly used. Some other terms have also been used as substitute names for the Republic of China, such as "ROC, Taiwan"; "Taiwan, ROC"; and "Taiwan–ROC." **Chen Shui-bian** said he prefers "(ROC) Taiwan" to indicate that the two are synonymous, which many agree they are, though Chen's intent, many said, was to say that Taiwan was separate from China. Many proindependence groups in Taiwan meanwhile contended, and still argue, that the term "Republic of China" is illegitimate and should be replaced by the "**Republic of Taiwan**" or some other name. However, the nation's **Constitution** refers to the Republic of China, and it cannot be changed or replaced easily. Another problem is that the United States and many other countries oppose a name change.

The term "Republic of China" has been replaced by "Chinese Taipei" in the Olympics and the **Asia–Pacific Economic Cooperation** forum, and by "Separate Custom Territory for Taiwan-Penghu-Kinmen-Matsu" in the **World Trade Organization**. The country's name is a serious matter of dispute between **pan-blue**, which wants to keep the term "Republic of China" in some form, and **pan-green**, which wants to emphasize the name "Taiwan" or get rid of the "Republic of China."

REPUBLIC OF CHINA AMATEUR SPORTS FEDERATION (CHUNG-HUA-MIN-KUO T'I-YU YUN-TUNG TSUNG-HUI). An organization responsible for upgrading athletic skills and promoting sports activities among the public in **Taiwan**.

REPUBLIC OF CHINA ON TAIWAN (CHUNG-HUA MIN-KUO TSAI T'AI-WAN). The designation given to the **Republic of China** or **Taiwan** by President **Lee Teng-hui** in 1993. The term came into more official usage after that, though the title "Republic of China" remained. In 2003, Lee said he would like to remove the "Republic of China" part.

REPUBLIC OF CHINA PROFESSIONAL BASEBALL LEAGUE (CHUNG-HUA CHIH-PANG LIEN-MENG). Making **Taiwan** the sixth country in the world with a professional baseball league in 1990, the league has four teams and plays a season of games in **Taipei**, **Taichung**, and **Kaohsiung**.

REPUBLIC OF CHINA–UNITED STATES TRADE COMMITTEE (CHUNG-HUA MAO-YI HSIEH-HUI). An ad hoc cabinet-level committee that deals with economic issues, especially **trade**, between **Taiwan** and the United States.

REPUBLIC OF TAIWAN (T'AI-WAN KUNG-HO-KUO). Promoted by an independence movement that sought to resist Japanese rule over **Taiwan** after China had agreed to transfer Taiwan to Japan following the signing of the **Treaty of Shimonoseki**, it lasted only ten days. Ch'ing Dynasty rulers in China did not help or recognize it. After World War II, the term was used by advocates of Taiwan's independence for the nation they would like to create after either defeating the **Nationalist Party** at the polls or ending its rule by force. In 1989, **Lin Yi-hsiung** wrote a draft law for a Republic of Taiwan. In recent years, the term has been used to support Taiwan's permanent or legal independence from China. *See also* REPUBLIC OF CHINA.

RESEARCH, DEVELOPMENT, AND EVALUATION COMMISSION (YEN-CHIU FA-CHAN WEI-YUAN-HUI). An organ of the **Executive Yuan** responsible for data collection and the coordination of research and planning. It has five departments: research and development, overall planning, control and evaluation, information systems management, and documentation and publication. The commission has been well known for its research studies and opinion surveys, as well as for its role in advising the **premier**.

RESOLUTION 31 (SAN-YI CHUEH-YI-AN). A resolution proposed by U.S. senators Alan Cranston and Edward Kennedy during the congressional debates on the **Taiwan Relations Act** in 1979. It pledged actions, though unspecified, by the United States in the event of a threat to **Taiwan** or to America's interests in Taiwan. This resolution reflected a serious concern on the part of Congress about Taiwan's security in the wake of the United States breaking diplomatic relations with the **Republic of China**. Resolution 31 was also a reaction to President Jimmy Carter's concluding the **Normalization Agreement** with the People's Republic of China, which iterated an unequivocal **one-China** policy and declared that the **United States–Republic of China Defense Treaty** would be terminated after one year. The authors of the resolution sought to strengthen the U.S. commitment to Taiwan in this context. Competing resolutions at the time linked an attack on Taiwan to U.S. security interests, but less specifically. Vice President Walter Mondale and lobbyist Frank Moore convinced Congress to weaken provisions in this resolution, and as a result, somewhat less clear security provisions are found in the Taiwan Relations Act.

RETROCESSION DAY (KUANG-FU CHIEH). Formerly a national holiday to celebrate the return of **Taiwan** to China on 25 October 1945 after fifty years as a Japanese colony. On that date, General **Ch'en Yi** received the instrument of surrender from Japanese General **Rikichi Ando** in **Taipei**. Provision for Taiwan's return was made in the **Cairo Declaration** and was repeated in the **Potsdam Declaration**. Leaders of **pan-green**, however, argue that the transfer of Taiwan to the **Republic of China** was not a formal or legal agreement, pointing out that both were simply wartime statements and were not signed, and that no written agreement was reached at the time of Japan's surrender or in the subsequent formal treaty, the **San Francisco Treaty**. They thus say that Taiwan's legal status is undetermined—a view that bolsters their call for an independent Taiwan. The administration of President **Chen Shui-bian** thus canceled the holiday. In recent years, the holiday has been celebrated with fanfare in China and by both political camps in Taiwan, with different agendas.

REYERSZOON, CORNELIS. Dutch military leader who attacked Macao in 1622 and, after failing to hold it, retreated to the **Pescadores** and built a large fort there. He subsequently negotiated with Chinese officials and gave up the Pescadores in return for China giving **Taiwan** to Holland.

– S –

SAKUMA SAMATA. A Japanese Army general who became governor-general of **Taiwan** in 1906 and served until 1915. He was appointed after forty years of military service, mostly as a military policeman. His rule was characterized by policies to pacify the population and bring hostile aboriginal areas under the government's control. His tough and often brutal tactics engendered local opposition to Japanese rule.

SENIOR PARLIAMENTARIANS (TSE-SHEN MIN-YI TAI-PIAO). Also called elder parliamentarians, or "old thieves" by opposition politicians, they served as representatives or delegates to the **National Assembly**, the **Legislative Yuan**, and the **Control Yuan** prior to 1991, when they stepped down in advance of plenary elections to the National Assembly and the Legislative Yuan. The senior parliamentarians were delegates who were elected when the government was located on the mainland, and their replacements appointed thereafter. **Supplemental elections** were held to add to the local representation in the parliamentary bodies of government beginning in 1969, but they were insufficient to reduce the influence of the senior parliamentarians fast enough to suit many people in the context of the rapid democratization of the country in subsequent years.

By the 1980s, many of the senior parliamentarians were old and in bad health, and newly elected representatives often dominated debates. Still, they were seen as an impediment to democracy and were pressured by both the **Nationalist Party** and the **Democratic Progressive Party** to step down. They refused to give up their positions in spite of efforts to get them to leave because they felt they were in office constitutionally, because they reaffirmed the nation's **one-China** policy, and because of the reluctance of their critics to force them out due to respect for age in Taiwan. In January 1989, the Legislative Yuan passed a bill on their "voluntary retirement" to force them to step down, but few did. In June 1990, the **Council of Grand Justices** rendered an interpretation of the **Constitution** terminating their tenure in office, after which they retired.

SHAN, PAUL (1923–). Appointed cardinal by Pope John Paul II in January 1998, Shan was the first in **Taiwan** to have this rank since Cardinal Yu Pin died in 1978. He was also the only cardinal appointed in Asia in 1998 and was only the fifth Chinese cardinal ever. Shan was born in Hepei province. In 1979, he was chosen bishop of Hualien. In 1991, he became bishop of the **Kaohsiung** diocese. *See also* RELIGION.

SHANGHAI COMMUNIQUÉ (SHANG-HAI KUNG-PAO). Also called the Joint U.S.–China Communiqué or the First Shanghai Communiqué, this agreement was concluded during President Richard Nixon's visit to China. Signed on 28 February 1972, the communiqué signified a marked warming of relations between the United States and the People's Republic of China. While the document contains mostly statements of each side's views and reflects as much disagreement as agreement, it nevertheless mirrored a "meeting of the minds" and an effort to deal with the "**Taiwan** question." China's stated position was that the People's Republic of China is the sole legal government of China, that Taiwan is a province of China, that the liberation of Taiwan is an internal affair, and that U.S. forces and military installations must be withdrawn from Taiwan. The United States declared that the settlement of the Taiwan matter must be peaceful, a long-held policy of the United States.

Regarding Beijing's claim that Taiwan is part of China, the U.S. side said that it "does not challenge" this position—suggesting to some that it concurred and to others that it disagreed but did not want to make issue of Taiwan in the context of seeking a better relationship with China due to the rapidly increasing "Soviet threat" and an arms race with the Soviet Union that the United States was not winning due to the costs of the Vietnam War. Clearly the phrase "does not challenge" is ambiguous, probably purposely so. The U.S. side further stated, "All Chinese on either side of the **Taiwan Strait** maintain there is but one China and Taiwan is part of China." This use of incorrect English and the fact that the statement was only speculation, or was patently false, again suggests that the United States sought to create ambiguity.

In any event, the Shanghai Communiqué became one of the documents making up the formal basis of U.S.–China policy in subsequent years. The United States agreed in the Shanghai Communiqué to withdraw U.S. military forces and installations from Taiwan and did so. The Shanghai Communiqué was later said to be the basis for the United States to establish formal diplomatic relations, though some doubted this, especially in the way President Carter did it in 1979. **Taipei** was not happy with the Shanghai Communiqué at the time that it was signed and later. It was seen as very detrimental to Taiwan's national interests. U.S. officials, including top decision makers in both the Nixon administration and subsequent administrations, however, maintained that the agreement did not damage or threaten Taiwan's interests, because a better relationship between the United States and the People's Republic of China would make Taiwan more secure.

SHEN CHANG-HUAN (1913–1998). Sometimes called the "godfather" of **Taiwan**'s diplomacy, he was minister of foreign affairs from 1960 to 1966 and from 1972 to 1979, secretary of the **National Security Council** from 1979 to 1984, and after that secretary-general to the **president**. He was considered a hard-liner regarding relations with the Soviet Union and in other ways. He was not active politically after 1988. *See also* FOREIGN POLICY.

SHIEH TUNG-MIN (1907–2001). Governor of Taiwan Province from 1972 to 1978 and vice president from 1978 to 1984 under President **Chiang Ching-kuo**, for some time Shieh was the highest-ranking **Taiwanese** official in the government. Shieh was also one of the first Taiwanese to gain membership in the **Nationalist Party**'s **Central Standing Committee**. Shieh studied in China when he was young and returned to **Taiwan** after World War II. Many Taiwanese did not see him as a representative of their interests, and some viewed him as having "sold out" to the Nationalist Party. In 1966, Wang Sing-nan, an activist in the **Taiwan Independence Movement** (who subsequently became a **Democratic Progressive Party** legislator) sent a letter bomb to Shieh, which exploded when he opened it, injuring his hand and requiring its amputation.

SHIH CHI-YANG (1935–). Former president of the **Judicial Yuan**, Shih served as vice premier from 1988 to 1993, having served as minister of justice from 1984 to 1988. In 2004, Shih was appointed chairman of the **Truth Committee** to investigate the shooting of President **Chen Shui-bian** and Vice President **Annette Lu**.

SHIH MING (1918–). A noted **Taiwanese** historian who joined the Red Army during World War II and fought against the Japanese. He founded the **Association for Taiwan Independence** in 1967.

SHIH MING-TEH (1941–). A famous dissident known as "**Taiwan**'s Nelson Mandela" who was imprisoned from 1962 to 1977 for sedition and was later, in 1980, sentenced to death for his part—some said the key leadership role—in the **Kaohsiung Incident**. However, the sentence was commuted, after which he served another ten years in prison. After release, he became leader of the **Democratic Progressive Party**'s **New Tide faction**. He then became chairman of the party from 1993 to 1996. Shih was not radical after he became head of the party, nor did he seem to bear a grudge against the **Nationalist Party** or the government for his years in prison. In fact, Shih became a voice of moderation. He even proposed a "Greater Chinese Commonwealth," similar to the British Commonwealth, as a formula to deal with China or the issue of Taiwan's relationship with the People's Republic of China. In December 1998, he was elected to a seat in the **Legislative Yuan**. He later quit the Democratic Progressive Party or was pressured to leave because of his changed view on independence, and he departed from politics. In 2005, Shih took a position teaching at Taiwan University. In 2006, Shih organized a huge nationwide protest movement against President **Chen Shui-bian** and his relatives' and associates' corruption.

SHIMONOSEKI (TREATY OF) (MA-KUAN T'IAO-YUEH). Treaty signed in the Japanese city of that name on 17 April 1895, ending the Sino–Japanese War. Japan, the victor in the war, got from China payment of an indemnity for the war and the cession of territory, including **Taiwan** and the **Pescadores**, to Japan "in perpetuity." The Western powers viewed the treaty as legal and thus saw Taiwan's transfer to Japan as legitimate. Neither the Chinese administration on Taiwan nor the population was consulted at the time of the signing of the treaty. In Taiwan, there were forces both for and against the transfer. Two attempts to form a republic at this time, however, failed. *See* REPUBLIC OF TAIWAN.

SIDEWINDER MISSILE (HSIANG-WEI-SHE FEI-TAN). An air-to-air missile that the United States provided to the **Republic of China**'s Air Force in 1958, during the second **Offshore Islands** crisis. The transfer was intended to help **Taipei** defend the islands and preclude an invasion of Taiwan, which many at the time feared was Beijing's next objective after taking some or all of the Offshore Islands. Others, however, question whether Beijing actually had this intent. *See also* ARMED FORCES.

SIEW, VINCENT C. (1939–). **Lien Chan**'s vice presidential running mate in the 2000 election, Siew was **premier** from August 1997 to 2000, having served previously as director-general of the Board of Foreign Trade of the Ministry of Foreign Affairs, chairman of the **Mainland Affairs Council**, minister of economic affairs, and member of the **Legislative Yuan**. Siew was considered to be an economic expert, a diplomat (having represented the country at various economic conferences), and a man of the people (coming from a poor family and being a good politician—having defeated a strong **Democratic Progressive Party** incumbent in the 1996 Legislative Yuan election). Siew played a key role in the passage of constitutional amendments in 1997.

"SINGAPORE SOLUTION" (HSIN-CHIA-PO MO-SHIH). A model sometimes cited to resolve the "Taiwan issue." Advocates suggest that **Taiwan** should be regarded as a "Chinese nation-state," but with sovereignty and separate from China—as is the case of Singapore. *See also* GERMAN FORMULA.

SINO–AMERICAN MUTUAL DEFENSE TREATY (CHUNG-MEI KUNG-T'UNG FANG-YÜ TIAO-YUEH). *See* UNITED STATES–REPUBLIC OF CHINA DEFENSE TREATY.

SIX ASSURANCES (LIU-HSIANG PAO-CHENG). Provisions in a statement made by President Ronald Reagan through the **American Institute in Taiwan** to President **Chiang Ching-quo** on 14 July 1982, prior to the **August Communiqué** in which the United States agreed (with Beijing) to reduce and eventually end arms aid to Taiwan. The assurances were that the United States would not set a specific date to end arms sales to **Taiwan**, would not hold talks with the People's Republic of China regarding arms sales to Taiwan, would not play a mediating role between the two, would not revise the **Taiwan Relations Act**, would not change its position regarding the sovereignty of Taiwan, and would not pressure Taiwan to negotiate with China.

Although the Six Assurances were not conveyed in written form, U.S. officials have, in some formal settings, mentioned them. Early in the George W. Bush administration, Senator Jesse Helms, chairman of the Senate Foreign Relations committee, asked Secretary of State Colin Powell if the United States would consult China about arms sales to Taiwan; Powell assured him that would not happen. Later, in 2002, Assistant Secretary of State James Kelly noted that the six assurances had been mentioned frequently in congressional testimony and that the United States had no plan to develop a "model" for solving cross-strait problems and would not be a mediator. Some say the six assurances were stated only to control damage in U.S.–Taiwan relations after the August Communiqué. Others say they have had lasting significance and are a permanent or semipermanent part of U.S.–Taiwan policy.

SIX-POINT PROPOSAL (LI LIU-TIAN). Points made in a speech by President **Lee Teng-hui** to the **National Unification Council** in April 1995 in response to Jiang Zemin's **Eight-Point Proposal**. Lee spoke of unification, but in "gradual phases." He also said that Beijing must accept the "reality" of the government of the **Republic of China** and agree to equality in negotiations with **Taipei**. The People's Republic of China did not respond in a positive way to Lee's points.

SIX-POINT REJOINDER (LIU-TIAN HUI-YING). Announcement made by Premier **Sun Yun-suan** on 10 June 1982 in reply to the People's Republic of China's just-announced **Nine-Point Proposal**. He stated that Taiwan was unwilling to negotiate for the following reasons: the **Nationalist Party** had had a bad experience with the Chinese Communists in the past, the Chinese Communist Party had lost credibility by its handling of Tibetan unification in the 1950s and 1960s, the People's Republic of China continued to try to isolate the **Republic of China** in the world community, **Taiwan**'s domestic political situation would not allow the Nationalist Party to negotiate on such a highly publicized and controversial issue, Beijing's guarantees of Taiwan's autonomy after unification lacked credibility, and the People's Republic of China had a history of shifts and reversals in policy. Sun's statements were eventually accepted by most in Taiwan, including various opposition leaders.

SIX-POINT SUPPLEMENT (LIU-TIAN PU-CH'UNG). "Concessionary points" made by Deng Xiaoping to U.S. professor Winston Yang in June 1983, broadening Ye Jianying's earlier **Nine-Point Proposal**. Deng, however, still excluded autonomy for **Taiwan**'s **armed forces**, security, intelligence, and foreign affairs agencies. Taiwan did not consider the points meaningful because neither the original offer nor this one regarded the **Republic of China** as having sovereignty.

SIX-YEAR DEVELOPMENT PLAN (LIU-NIEN FA-CHAN CHI-HUA). A plan approved by the government in 1991 to improve the country's economic infrastructure during the six-year period to 1996. Over US$300 billion was allocated for 779 projects, including roads, rail and subway systems, petrochemical and other heavy industries, and pollution-control facilities. It was reported that the plan would put **Taiwan** in the top twenty countries in the world by per capita income before the year 2000.

SKY BOW MISSILE (T'IAN-KUNG FEI-TAN). A surface-to-air missile produced in **Taiwan** by the **Chungshan Institute of Science and Technology** to defend the country against invading aircraft from the People's Republic of China. It was successfully tested in March 1986. The **Tienkung II**, an upgraded version, was tested in 1998 and was said to be equivalent to the U.S. Patriot missile and would be used to defend the country against missile attacks. *See also* ARMED FORCES.

SKY SWORD MISSILE (T'IAN-CHIEN FEI-TAN). An air-to-air missile made in **Taiwan** and carried on locally built (under contract) **F-5E** jet fighter planes. It resembles the **Sidewinder missile**. It was test fired in April 1986.

SONK, MAARTEN. Dutch military leader who replaced **Cornelis Reyerszoon** in 1624 and finalized negotiations with China that involved trading the **Pescadores** for **Taiwan**. He subsequently became the first Dutch governor of Taiwan, though it was not until years later that Holland was the exclusive colonizer of the island.

SOONG, JAMES (1942–). Presidential candidate in 2000, vice presidential candidate in 2004, and chairman of the **People First Party**, Soong was secretary-general of the **Nationalist Party** from 1988 to 1993, having served as director-general of the **Government Information Office** from 1979 to 1984 and later as head of the party's Department of Cultural Affairs from 1984 to 1987. In January 1988, Soong took a strong stand in support of President **Lee Teng-hui** to head the Nationalist Party after **Chiang Ching-kuo**'s death, arguing that Lee should be made formal head of the party and that not doing so would send the wrong signal about Taiwan's democratization and would result in a divided government. At the time, Lee's opponents wanted to make him only temporarily head of the ruling party or make him only one of several party chairmen. Soong also strongly supported Lee during another challenge in early 1990 when Lee stood for reelection by the **National Assembly**.

In appreciation, Lee appointed Soong governor of Taiwan Province, after which, in 1994, Soong was elected governor of Taiwan (the office having been made an elective one) in a strong victory with President Lee's support. Soong's win, some said, indicated that ethnic identity could be overcome—Soong being **Mainland Chinese** while the majority of voters were **Taiwanese**. Soong and Lee subsequently became antagonists, the reasons being uncertain. Some said Lee did not want a Mainland Chinese successor. Others said Lee felt that Soong was too ambitious. They may have disagreed on relations with the People's Republic of China. Regardless, they came into serious and open disagreement over the issue of Lee proposing the elimination of the provincial government. In 1996, Soong resigned, creating a crisis in the government and the ruling party. Though his resignation was not accepted and he stayed on as governor until December 1998 when the position as an elected office was abolished, the crisis was not resolved amicably.

Their disagreement escalated in late 1999 when Soong sought the Nationalist Party's nomination for the 2000 presidential race, which Lee opposed. Soong argued that the opinion polls favored him. Lee didn't accept this argument and orchestrated that the nomination go to **Lien Chan**, saying that he was more experienced. Soong ran as an independent and in the early campaigning was way ahead in the opinion polls. Then party documents indicating that funds had been diverted into his personal accounts when he was secretary-general of the party were released, many said at Lee's behest. This hurt Soong's campaign. He did not relent, however, and this split the conservative vote between him and Lien and threw the election victory to **Chen Shui-bian**. Still, Soong received only slightly less of the popular vote than Chen and won a larger percentage in most of the districts in west, north, and east Taiwan and among women and minority voters. After the election, Soong and Lien cooperated, as did the Nationalist Party and Soong's newly formed **People First Party**, against Chen. The two in 2004 joined forces, with Soong running as vice president with Lien, but the two lost in a very close and controversial election. Soong and Lien challenged the results and led their followers to protest what they called a fraudulent election. In 2006, Soong registered as an independent candidate for **Taipei** mayor.

SOONG MAYLING (1898–2003). Also known as Madam **Chiang Kai-shek**, she held a number of political and extrapolitical positions and had considerable political influence in the Nationalist government and the **Nationalist Party**, both during her husband's life and after. At the time of World War II, she was one of only two foreigners ever to address a joint session of the U.S. Congress, appealing for help from the United States on behalf of the Nationalist cause at that time. In 1988, after **Chiang Ching-kuo** died, she sided with those who sought to prevent **Lee Teng-hui** from gaining leadership of the party. She subsequently became politically inactive and resided in the United States until her death. Her sister was married to **Sun Yat-sen**, but instead of leaving with the Nationalists in 1949, she stayed in

China and served in a high position in that government. Soong's brother, T. V. Soong, was minister of finance when the Nationalists ruled China but went to the United States in 1949. Soong had no children. She died on 23 October 2003 in the United States.

SOUTH (NAN). A "New left" Marxist-humanist magazine that began publication in 1986. Many of its articles criticized **Taiwan**'s capitalist economic development and what the magazine's editors regarded as resultant social problems in Taiwan.

SOUTHERN STRATEGY. *See* GO SOUTH POLICY.

SOUTHERN TAIWAN SCIENCE PARK (STSP) (NAN-PU K'E-HSUEH KUNG-YEH YUAN-CHU). **Taiwan**'s second science park, after the **Hsinchu Science Park**, which includes Tainan Science Park and Kaohsiung Science Park, established in 1996 and 2001 respectively. The park is research oriented, and research centers and universities have set up R & D centers there.

"SPIRIT OF 1992" (CHIU-ER CHING-SHEN). Term used to describe the agreement between **Taiwan** and the People's Republic of China in 1992 regarding the **one-China**, separate interpretations principle that lead to the **Koo-Wang talks** in 1993 in Singapore. After he became **president**, **Chen Shui-bian** cited the spirit of 1992, his critics said, to deny there was a consensus of opinions. *See also* 1992 CONSENSUS.

SPRATLY ISLANDS (NAN-SHA CHUN-TAO). Also known as Nan-sha (in Chinese) and located in the South China Sea, these small islands are territory claimed by the **Republic of China**. **Taipei** maintains a small military force on one of the islands. The islands are also claimed by the People's Republic of China, Vietnam, the Philippines, Malaysia, and Indonesia. They are considered strategically located in terms of controlling vital sea-lanes, and their ownership supports legal claim to undersea resources in the vicinity.

STATUTE ON THE VOLUNTARY RETIREMENT OF SENIOR PARLIAMENTARIANS (TSE-SHEN MIN-YI TAI-PIAO T'UI-CHIH T'IAO-LI). Passed in 1989 upon the initiative of the **Nation-**

alist Party, this law was intended to force members of the Control Yuan, the Legislative Yuan, and the National Assembly who were elected in the 1947 election or were subsequently appointed to positions in these parliamentary organs of government to resign. Most of the senior parliamentarians, however, refused to do so and stayed in office. It was not until the Council of Grand Justices subsequently ruled that they had to leave that they stepped down, although the Statute on the Voluntary Retirement of Senior Parliamentarians may have had some influence on their decisions.

STRAITS EXCHANGE FOUNDATION (SEF) (HAI-HSIA CH'IAO-LIU CHI-CHIN-HUI). A private organization established in early 1991 to manage contacts with the People's Republic of China. However, since it has ties with the Mainland Affairs Council and receives much of its budget from the government, it is considered quasi-official. On the other hand, being technically private, it has been able to deal with officials in China without such contacts being regarded as formal negotiations or government-to-government talks. For several years, the SEF was chaired by Koo Chen-fu. The SEF's counterpart organization is the Association for Relations across the Taiwan Strait (ARATS).

Talks were held between the two organizations in 1992, but little was accomplished because of differing definitions of "one China." Also, there were problems because Beijing treated the talks as a matter of domestic affairs while Taipei treated them as diplomatic in nature. In 1993, the SEF helped engineer the Koo-Wang talks that led to what many called a breakthrough in Taipei-Beijing relations. In 1995, however, following President Lee Teng-hui's visit to the United States, which angered leaders in Beijing, cross-strait meetings between the SEF and ARATS were suspended. Talks were resumed in October 1998 but produced no tangible results. The SEF remains active, though it has accomplished little in recent years. Chang Chun-hsiung became the chairman of the SEF upon Koo Chen-fu's death in mid-2005. See also NATIONAL UNIFICATION COUNCIL.

SU TSENG-CHANG (1947–). Chosen premier in early 2006, Su had just stepped down as chairman of the Democratic Progressive Party to take the blame for the party's setback in the December 2005 mayoral and city council elections. Before this, Su was secretary-general of the **Office of the President**. Early in his career, he was one of the lawyers that defended opposition dissidents following the **Kaohsiung Incident**. He was subsequently one of the founding members of the Democratic Progressive Party. He was elected magistrate in Pingtung County in 1989 and served to 1993. He served as a member of the **Legislative Yuan** from 1996 to 1997 and as magistrate of Taipei County from 1997 to 2004. He became party chairman in 2004 when **Chen Shui-bian** stepped down from that post to take responsibility for the party's poor showing in the December Legislative Yuan election. Su is considered one of the top leaders of his party and a possible presidential candidate in 2008. He is seen as close to Chen Shui-bian.

SUBSTANTIVE FOREIGN RELATIONS (SHIH-CHIH WAI-CH'IAO). A policy of the government of the **Republic of China** to promote bilateral or multilateral nondiplomatic relations, such as sports, culture, science, technology, **trade**, and **investment**, in lieu of formal diplomatic ties. This term came into common usage in the 1970s as a result of **Taipei**'s loss of diplomatic ties with a number of nations following its expulsion from the **United Nations** in 1971 and President Richard Nixon's trip to Beijing in 1972. *See also* FOREIGN POLICY.

SUN LI-JEN (1900–1990). A Nationalist general trained at the Virginia Military Institute in the United States, Sun served under General Joseph Stilwell in the Burma campaign during World War II. Later, he became commander in chief of Nationalist Chinese ground forces. In August 1955, **Chiang Ching-kuo** placed Sun under arrest for allegedly organizing a coup against the government. Sun had been critical of **Chiang Kai-shek** and Chiang Ching-kuo's commissar system and may have secretly sought support in the United States for replacing Chiang Kai-shek. He remained under detention or house arrest until 1988 even though the **Control Yuan** had exonerated him of any plot against Chiang Kai-shek or the government. He died two years later.

SUN YAT-SEN (1866–1925). Known as the father of the **Republic of China**, the founder of the **Nationalist Party**, and the most famous advocate of Chinese nationalism in the early part of the twentieth century, Sun was born in Kuangtung (or Canton) Province. At the age of thirteen, Sun went to Hawaii, where he attended middle school, high school, and college. He subsequently returned to China and then went to Hong Kong, where he graduated from Hong Kong Medical College in 1892. He practiced medicine briefly in Macao before he moved to Kuangchou. There he gave up medicine to devote his time and energy to the overthrow of the Manchu government in China. In 1894, following a failed uprising, he fled to Japan. In 1897, while in Japan, Sun gave a series of lectures, which were later published as the book *The Three Principles of the People*. Sun advocated revolution in contrast to most other Chinese intellectuals and officials of the time, who advocated political reform.

During his early career as a revolutionary, Sun spent most of his time abroad seeking support for the cause of overthrowing the Manchu government and establishing a democratic system of government in China, while his followers in China sought actively and aggressively to spark a revolution. In 1894, he founded the Hsing Chung Hui (Revive China Society) in Hawaii, and in 1905 the Tung Meng Hui (Revolutionary Alliance) in Japan. On 10 October 1911, Sun's supporters finally succeeded in sparking revolution and ended Manchu rule of China.

In January 1912, Sun was inaugurated the provisional **president** of the Republic of China. However, he subsequently abdicated in order to prevent a civil war in China. (Yuan Shih-kai in the meantime had consolidated power in Peking and had won the allegiance and support of the Western powers.) Subsequently Sun, because of disappointment with the West, invited Soviet representatives to China who advised him on party organization and other matters, thus accounting for the fact that the Nationalist Party has a Leninist organizational structure. In the 1920s, Sun made still other attempts to establish a democratic government in China but failed.

During his lifetime, Sun wrote about politics, political philosophy, and political development. His political ideals or political philosophy are summarized in his *San Min Chu I*, or *Three Principles of the*

People—his most famous treatise. Sun's "Principles" became the ideological basis of the Nationalist Party and the government of the Republic of China when it ruled China and later, after it moved to **Taiwan**. Sun's thinking and writings were highly influenced by American democracy and political thought.

Sun visited Taiwan for the first time in 1900 and built a base of support there, though this did not survive the Japanese colonial period very well. His political thinking and writings, however, had a strong influence in Taiwan after it became part of the Republic of China in 1945, and even more after the government moved to Taiwan in 1949. His teachings and writings were taught in schools in Taiwan at all levels, and his works were widely read by government and Nationalist Party officials. Some also say that Sun's writings about economic and political development, and the interrelationship between the two, are the first of their kind and that they provided the design or framework for Taiwan's economic and political modernization. Sun's status and his teachings have been demoted in importance since **Chen Shui-bian** became president, with President Chen even calling him a "foreigner" on one occasion.

SUN YAT-SEN'S BIRTHDAY (KUO-FU YEN-CHEN CHI-NIEN-JIH). 12 November, an official holiday—though it is no longer a day when government offices are closed.

SUN YUN-SUAN (1913–2006). Premier from 1978 to 1984, having previously served in a number of top government positions and having a high rank in the **Nationalist Party**, he was minister of communications from 1967 to 1969 and minister of economic affairs from 1969 to 1978. Throughout 1983, Sun was thought to be **Chiang Ching-kuo**'s choice for vice president in 1984 and ultimately his successor. Chiang, however, picked **Lee Teng-hui**. In February 1984, Sun suffered from a serious stroke, effectively ending his political career. *See also* SIX-POINT REJOINDER.

SUPPLEMENTAL ELECTIONS (TSENG-PU HSÜAN-CHU). From 1969 to 1991, national elections for seats in the **Legislative Yuan** and the **National Assembly** were supplemental since the **Re-**

public of China claimed to represent all of China, and elections could not be held on the mainland as it was governed by the Communists. Before that, delegates to these two parliamentary bodies and also the **Control Yuan** were frozen in office, or their replacements were appointed. Some considered the supplemental elections to contribute to **Taiwan**'s democratization since more seats were added to represent Taiwan. Others felt that this process was at best incremental. Supplemental elections ended when the **senior parliamentarians** stepped down in 1991 and nonsupplemental elections were held in 1991 and 1992 for the National Assembly and the Legislative Yuan. *See also* SENIOR PARLIAMENTARIANS.

SWORN BROTHERHOODS (HSIUNG-TI-HUI). Secret alliances of friendship that became an important part of social life for many early Chinese settlers on **Taiwan**. Members were usually males in their late teens and early twenties and came from all walks of life: soldiers, merchants, vagabonds, peasants, and even scholars. Gambling, banditry, and fighting were common activities among the members. Beginning in 1683, the Ch'ing government tried generally unsuccessfully to suppress these groups. The brotherhoods had become powerful elements by the mid-1800s in both the rural and the urban areas of Taiwan.

– T –

TAICHUNG. Meaning "stage of the center" in Chinese and located in the middle of Taiwan, Taichung is one of Taiwan's five largest cities. It is located near Taichung Harbor, which is the site of many of the projects associated with Taiwan's effort to become a regional business hub. Taichung's population is close to one million; the population of Taichung county is a million and a half.

TAIHOKU IMPERIAL UNIVERSITY (T'AI-WAN T'I-KUO TA-HSUEH). The first university established in **Taiwan** (in **Taipei**) in 1927 and generally regarded as its best. After 1945, it was renamed **National Taiwan University**.

TAINAN. Meaning "stage of the south" in Chinese and located in the southern part of the island, it is one of **Taiwan**'s five largest cities. An-ping, very close to Taiwan, was the capital of Taiwan when it was under Dutch colonial rule; Tainan became the capital when Taiwan was ruled by **Cheng Ch'eng-kung**. It is known today as having the most Buddhist and Confucian temples of any city in Taiwan. Its population is around three-quarters of a million.

TAIPEI (TAI-PEI). Meaning "stage of the north" in Chinese, it is the largest city in **Taiwan**. There is little or no historical record of the area, however, before it was settled in the 1700s. It became a major river-port city on the **Tamsui River** in the 1800s, bringing prosperity to the city and increasing its population markedly. In 1875, it became an administrative district under the jurisdiction of the government in Peking, and in 1892, walls around the city were completed. When Taiwan became part of the Japanese Empire, Taipei was the administrative center of Taiwan. In 1945, it became the capital of Taiwan Province under the jurisdiction of the **Republic of China**, and in 1949 it became the provisional capital of the Republic of China. In 1967, it was given the status of special municipality under the jurisdiction of the **Executive Yuan**. Taipei's population is near three million; the population of greater Taipei or Taipei County is close to six million.

TAIPEI 101 (T'AI-PEI YI-LING-YI). Skyscraper located in the Hsinyi district of **Taipei** that was completed in December 2004 and became the tallest building in the world. It is 507 meters high (1671 feet) and has 101 floors, thus the name Taipei 101. It is unique for its very fast elevators, the fastest in the world, and its Chinese-style construction.

TAIPEI CITY COUNCIL (T'AI-PEI SHIH-YI-HUI). Established in 1946 as a provisional legislative organ, it became a formal body after the institutionalization of local self-government in 1950. There were six elections of members from 1950 to 1967, at which time **Taipei** was made a special municipality. The next election was held in 1969, following which there have been elections at four-year intervals. There are forty seats for the first one million residents and one additional seat for each additional one hundred thousand people. Elections are conducted in five precincts, and one woman is required for each seven members. In 1994, fifty-two members were elected, including many from the **Democratic Progressive Party** and the **New Party**, causing the **Nationalist Party** to lose control of the council. It regained control after the 1998 election.

TAIPEI CITY GOVERNMENT (T'AI-PEI SHIH-CHENG-FU). Established in 1945 as an executive organ when **Taipei** was designated a city under provincial jurisdiction, it governed ten administrative districts (*chu*). In 1967, Taipei, because of its growth and importance, was made a special municipality under the **Executive Yuan**—although critics said this was to preclude the mayorship from becoming a springboard for a popular **Taiwanese** leader. In 1968, six suburbs were incorporated: Chingmei, Mucha, Nankang, Neihu, Shihlin, and Peitou. In 1994, the mayor once again became an elected official, at which time **Chen Shui-bian** was elected. **Ma Ying-jeou** was elected in 1998 and reelected in 2002.

TAIPEI ECONOMIC AND CULTURAL REPRESENTATIVE OFFICE (TECRO) (T'AI-PEI CHING-CHI WEN-HUA TAI-PIAO-CH'U). Representing a name change in 1994 from the former **Coordination Council for North American Affairs**, TECRO represents the **Republic of China** in the realms of diplomatic, cultural, economic, and military affairs in Washington, D.C. Local offices are referred to as Taipei Economic and Cultural Offices (TECO). The name change was seen by some to mirror an upgrading of **Taiwan**'s status by the United States following a "review" of U.S. Taiwan policy by the Clinton administration, which came after considerable pressure was felt from the Republican-controlled Congress that perceived that Taiwan was not being treated well. *See* TAIWAN POLICY REVIEW.

TAIPEI INTERNATIONAL CONVENTION CENTER (T'AI-PEI KUO-CHI HUI-YI CHUNG-HSIN). Large facility in **Taipei** that opened in 1991 for conferences and exhibits and is considered one of the best of its kind in the world. The **China External Trade Development Council** operates it. It operates the adjoining World Trade Center, which promotes business in **Taiwan**, especially trade.

TAIPEI SOCIETY (BEI SHE). An organization founded in 1989 by a group of scholars, mainly from universities in the **Taipei** area and from **Academic Sinica**, to monitor government activities and act as a critical voice about **Taiwan** politics. Many of their papers and reports have been widely read and have stirred political debate. In 2004, the organization gave the Chen administration a "failing report card" in terms of constitutional, educational, and environmental reforms, as well as cross-strait relations, social welfare, **media**, and academic development. In early 2006, the group suggested that legislators demonstrate their integrity and put their private money in trusts.

TAIPEI TIMES **(T'AI-PEI SHIH-PAO).** One of **Taiwan**'s three English-language **newspapers**. It is **pan-green** in its leanings. *See also* MEDIA.

TAIWAN (T'AI-WAN). Literally "terraced bay," the origin of the term is uncertain, though in the seventeenth century it referred to a small islet where the Dutch established their early colonial base. The Dutch subsequently used the word to designate what is now the island of Taiwan. *Taiwan* currently refers—depending on one's point of view—to simply the island of Taiwan, a Chinese province (belonging either to the **Republic of China** or to the People's Republic of China), a territory constituting most of the Republic of China, or a nation-state (meaning that it should be synonymous with or substituted for the term "Republic of China"). *See also* DAN WAN; FORMOSA.

TAIWAN CAUCUS. *See* CONGRESSIONAL TAIWAN CAUCUS.

TAIWAN CHURCH NEWS **(T'AI-WAN CH'IAO-HUI-PAO).** A publication of the **Presbyterian Church in Taiwan**, it was **Taiwan**'s first newspaper. It publishes both religious and political news.

TAIWAN COMMUNIST PARTY (TCP) (T'AI-WAN KUNG-CHAN-TANG). Formed in 1928, the TCP existed until 1931 as a local branch of the Japan Communist Party. At that time, it supported the creation of an independent, socialist Taiwan, reflecting the positions of both the Japan Communist Party and the Chinese Communist Party. It subsequently became inactive and was suppressed during the subsequent era of militarism in Japan. It has been reported that President **Lee Teng-hui** was once a member, and his opponents have on a number of occasions publicly accused him of this, including during the 1996 election campaign. Lee denies the charge and says that his age and place of birth do not fit the person they described. After **martial law** was lifted, there were some attempts to form a party called the Taiwan Communist Party, but the government did not allow this. In some subsequent election campaigns, the name and even banners appeared in public, but few paid much notice. The Chinese Communist Party (in China) has not made any serious effort to establish a branch or a brother party in Taiwan.

TAIWAN DEMOCRATIC MOVEMENT OVERSEAS (HAI-WAI T'AI-WAN MIN-CHU YUN-TUNG). An organization started by **Hsu Hsin-liang** when the **Democratic Progressive Party** rebuffed Hsu in his attempt to represent the party abroad and decided not to establish overseas units.

TAIWAN DEMOCRATIC SELF-GOVERNMENT LEAGUE (T'AI-WAN MIN-CHU TSE-CHIH CHENG-FU LIEN-MENG). Established in Shanghai in 1947 by Ms. Hsieh Hsueh-hong and other **Taiwanese** Communists in China, in 1949 it became one of the "satellite parties" that worked with the Chinese Communist Party. It established branches in Japan that opposed **Liao Wen-yi**'s work there, especially his call for a **United Nations**–sponsored plebiscite to decide Taiwan's future. The league's position, like the Chinese Communist Party, was that American and Japanese "imperialists" sought to keep Taiwan independent, and the **Taiwan Independence Movement** was their tool.

TAIWAN DEVELOPMENT COMPANY (T'AI-WAN K'AI-FA KUNG-SZU). The largest landholder in **Taiwan** before the end of World War II, it held 230,000 acres of land. It was Japanese owned. In the 1950s, this land was sold to tiller-farmers by the Nationalist government to conform to provisions in the **land reform** program.

TAIWAN ECONOMIC MIRACLE. *See* ECONOMIC MIRACLE.

TAIWAN ENVIRONMENTAL PROTECTION AGENCY (T'AI-WAN HUAN-CHING PAO-HU-CHU). Established in 1987 by local environmental groups, it became affiliated with the U.S.-based International Environmental Protection Association. This organization, in contrast to the official government agency, focused its attention primarily on nuclear power, the petrochemical industry, forest ecology, and land use. *See also* ENVIRONMENTAL PROTECTION ADMINISTRATION.

"TAIWAN EXPERIENCE" (T'AI-WAN CHING-YEN). A term used frequently in recent years to refer to **Taiwan**'s successful economic, social, and political modernization and the lessons that might be adopted by other countries, including the People's Republic of China. The term has specifically been used by the government in Taipei to refer to efforts to promote democracy on the mainland. *See also* ECONOMIC MIRACLE; POLITICAL MIRACLE.

TAIWAN GARRISON COMMAND GENERAL HEADQUARTERS. *See* GARRISON COMMAND.

TAIWAN HISTORICA (KUO-SHIH-KUAN TAI-WAN WEN-HSIEN-KUAN). Previously the Historical Research Commission of **Taiwan** Province, it became part of the central government after the streamlining of the provincial government. It was attached to the **Office of the President** in 2002. It is responsible for keeping historical works and records on Taiwan.

TAIWAN HUMAN RIGHTS ASSOCIATION (T'AI-WAN JEN-CH'UAN HSIEH-HUI). A human rights organization founded in **Taiwan** in the 1970s. It is concerned with local human rights problems and has generally reflected the views of opposition political candidates. After **Chen Shui-bian** was elected **president** in 2000, it became a much more important organization and received support from the government. *See also* CHINESE ASSOCIATION FOR HUMAN RIGHTS.

TAIWAN INDEPENDENCE CLAUSE (T'AI-TU TANG-KANG). A provision put into the **Democratic Progressive Party**'s charter in late 1991 that called for a **"Republic of Taiwan"** and a new "Taiwan Constitution." The **New Tide faction** supported the clause, as did **Chen Shui-bian**.

TAIWAN INDEPENDENCE MOVEMENT (TIM) (T'AI-WAN TU-LI YUN-TUNG). A term that during the Japanese colonial period referred to organizations that sought greater autonomy, democracy, or separation from Japan. In the late 1950s, it mainly meant the provisional government of the Republic of Formosa founded in 1956 by **Liao Wen-yi**. But as that organization faded in importance and others were established, the term came to be generic to mean organizations that supported a separate nation (from China), disagreeing with the government's position that **Taiwan** was part of China. The various organizations, however, disagreed about how to attain "independence" or even whether that should be considered a goal in view of the fact that some perceived that Taiwan was already independent, given that it was generally considered to have sovereignty in the name of the **Republic of China**. Many of those that espoused the latter view sought to end **Nationalist Party** rule or felt that Taiwan should be ruled by **Taiwanese**, not **Mainland Chinese**. They also differed in opinion about what to do with approximately 15 percent of the population, or the three million Mainland Chinese living in Taiwan: whether they should be forced to leave, assimilated, or simply made to share political power. In any case, all of the TIM groups were illegal in Taiwan for some time, and advocating an independent Taiwan was considered treason. In fact, numerous supporters of independence were imprisoned. Thus no specific TIM organization operated in the open in Taiwan.

They did operate openly in some other countries, especially the United States and Japan. However, several of the groups, especially those that were most active in the United States, were antagonistic toward other groups. And also their relationships with politicians and groups with similar views in Taiwan were not always cordial. Some supported opposition candidates in Taiwan, but this was not as frequent as might have been expected since many politicians in Taiwan kept their distance from these groups.

World United Formosans for Independence and the **Formosan Association for Public Affairs** were the most active of the groups supporting Taiwan independence.

In the 1980s and 1990s, due to democratization, independence (at first self-determination, which usually meant the same thing) was discussed and even advocated in political debates and in election campaigns in Taiwan. Thus independence lost its conspiratorial aura. Meanwhile, with Taiwanization (bringing more Taiwanese into the government and the Nationalist Party under **Chiang Ching-kuo** and **Lee Teng-hui**), the term came to mean more independence from China than from the Nationalist Party. An independent Taiwan was favored and openly advocated (in fact it was in the party platform) by the **Democratic Progressive Party**, though there were disagreements within the DPP as to whether it should prevail over other objectives, whether it was a short-term or long-term goal, and whether it was a prerequisite to democracy. (*See* FORMOSA FACTION; NEW TIDE FACTION.)

In 1996, some Democratic Progressive Party members felt that the party was abandoning the cause and formed the **Taiwan Independence Party**. The **New Party**, when it was formed, took a position strongly opposing Taiwan's independence and still does. The Nationalist Party technically opposed independence, but critics of President Lee Teng-hui, especially those in the party's **Non-Mainstream faction**, said he secretly supported it. When **Chen Shui-bian** was elected **president**, the term no longer referred to Nationalist rule and came to mean solely separation from China. For President Chen, it became a difficult issue since his base supported it but the United States and many other nations opposed Taiwan's formal or legal independence. Also, Taiwan was moving closer to China through various commercial ties. Immediately after his election, President Chen promised not to declare independence to placate the United States, so when he advocated it or acted to promote it, Washington responded. Beijing, of course, opposed the idea and has regularly promised to use military force against Taiwan if the government officially proclaims independence. *See also* ANTI-SUCCESSION LAW.

TAIWAN INDEPENDENCE PARTY (TAIP) (CHIEN-KUO-TANG). A **political party** formed in October 1996 by a splinter group from the **Democratic Progressive Party** (DPP) that was disappointed with what it considered the Democratic Progressive Party's watered-down stand on **Taiwan independence**. More specifically, the TAIP grew out of the Nation Building Association, founded by **Peng Ming-min** immediately after his defeat in the March 1996 presidential election. For a while, some called the TAIP **Taiwan**'s "fourth force" or fourth meaningful political party. However, it did not gain much political influence and suffered from internal disagreements and later ceased to function. *See also* FORMOSA PARTY.

TAIWAN INSTITUTE OF ECONOMIC RESEARCH (TAI-WAN CHING-CHI YEN-CHIU-YUAN). Established in 1976 by **Koo Chen-fu** to study macroeconomic issues, it was also the first private think tank in **Taiwan**.

***TAIWAN JOURNAL* (T'AI-WAN CH'I-KAN).** A weekly newspaper-style English publication of the **Government Information Office** in **Taipei** published before 1964 under the name *Free China Weekly* and later as the *Free China Journal*. *See also* MEDIA.

***TAIWAN NEWS* (YING-WEN T'AI-WAN JIH-PAO).** One of **Taiwan**'s three major English-language **newspapers**. It was formerly called *China News*. *See also* MEDIA.

TAIWAN POLICY REVIEW (T'AI-WAN CHENG-TSE HUI-KU). A process set in motion in the United States in 1994 as a result of the new Republican Congress aggressively calling on the White House to upgrade relations with **Taiwan**, which the Bill Clinton administration did, though some say very reluctantly. It provided for more direct contacts between high officials from the United States and the **Republic of China**, supported **Taipei**'s entry into the **World Trade Organization**, and brought about the use of the term "Taipei" in the name of the Republic of China's representative offices in the United States. *See also* TAIPEI ECONOMIC AND CULTURAL REPRESENTATIVE OFFICE.

TAIWAN POLITICAL MIRACLE. *See* POLITICAL MIRACLE.

***TAIWAN POLITICAL REVIEW* (T'AI-WAN CHENG-CHIH HUI-KU).** An opposition publication started by **Kang Ning-hsiang** in

1975. Though it published only five issues before it was closed by the government, it had considerable impact for a while and served as a model for other publications that followed. In fact, after it was closed, Kang launched the magazine *The Eighties*. *See also* MEDIA.

TAIWAN POWER COMPANY (T'AI-WAN TIAN-LI KUNG-SZU). A state corporation founded in 1946 and owned mainly by the central government, the provincial government, and the **Taipei** municipal government, plus financial institutions and individuals in **Taiwan**, Taipower is responsible for developing, generating, supplying, and marketing electric power throughout the country. In the 1950s and 1960s, the cheap electricity it supplied, much of which was generated by hydropower, helped spur Taiwan's industrialization and its economic growth. Now hydropower makes up less than 10 percent of Taiwan's total usage; coal, oil, and nuclear plants each account for about a third of electricity generated. All three of these have been controversial because they have to be imported, and because the first two cause air pollution. Nuclear power has provoked serious political controversy and protest in recent years. In late 2003, Taipower had sixty-two plants, including forty-two hydropower plants, seventeen thermal plants, three nuclear plants, and 1 wind facility. The power sources of electricity were 5 percent hydro, 43 percent coal, 10 percent oil, 15 percent natural gas, and 17 percent nuclear. *See also* ENERGY.

TAIWAN PRODUCTION BOARD (T'AI-WAN CHIH-TSAO-CHU). Established in 1949 by the **Taiwan Provincial Government** to stabilize the **economy**, reduce inflation, and develop various companies and enterprises, it was absorbed by the **Economic Stabilization Board** in 1953.

TAIWAN PROVINCIAL ASSEMBLY (T'AI-WAN SHENG-YI-HUI). A "local" representative legislative body in **Taiwan** that, because the government of the **Republic of China** controlled only Taiwan plus some outlying islands, paralleled or duplicated in large part the functions of the **Legislative Yuan**. It was established by law in 1959, its predecessors being the Provincial People's Political Council (1946–1951) and the Taiwan Provisional Provincial Assembly (1951–1959).

The Taiwan Provincial Assembly was long considered more democratic than the Legislative Yuan because voters in Taiwan elected all of its members. Members also were involved much more than Legislative Yuan members in serving their constituents and in legislative work (which in the case of the Legislative Yuan was frequently done in caucuses of **Nationalist Party** members in advance). On the other hand, the Nationalist Party held a majority in the assembly and thus controlled most debates and votes. The assembly, moreover, was not allowed to encroach on the duties and powers of the Legislative Yuan.

Members of the Taiwan Provincial Assembly were elected to four-year terms and were eligible to be reelected. Sessions lasted for no more than eighty days in a six-month period, though extensions were possible. The assembly elected a speaker who maintained order on the floor and led debates and proceedings. This position was considered a powerful and important political position. There were five speakers: Huang Ch'ao-ch'in (1946–1963), **Shieh Tung-min** (1963–1970), Ts'ai Hung-wen (1970–1981), **Kao Yu-jen** (1981–1990), and Huang Chen-yueh (1990–1998). The Taiwan Provincial Assembly had six standing committees: **agriculture** and forestry, civil affairs, **education**, finance, reconstruction, and transportation. The last three dealt with large amounts of funds and were generally considered more important.

With the downsizing of the provincial government in 1998, the Provincial Assembly was abolished. Many of its members ran successfully for positions in the Legislative Yuan.

TAIWAN PROVINCIAL GOVERNMENT (T'AI-WAN SHENG-CHENG-FU). Established in May 1947 to replace the Office of the Governor-General, the Taiwan Provincial Government was for many years the highest organ of local government. It had jurisdiction in over sixteen counties and five cities and comprised nineteen departments. It employed more than three hundred thousand people. It also controlled more than thirty businesses. The Taiwan Provincial Government Council was its policy-making body, which consisted of twenty-three members. Its executive head was the governor of Taiwan.

In 1988, with democratization, the Provincial Assembly was required to approve of the person nominated by the **premier** to be governor. After 1994, and until 1998, it was headed by an elected governor. (*See* SOONG, JAMES.)

In 1996, the **National Development Conference** recommended that the provincial government be abolished or drastically downsized. Subsequently, the **National Assembly** passed a constitutional amendment to this effect.

TAIWAN RECOVERY TRAINING CORPS (T'AI-WAN KUANG-FU HSUN-LIEN-T'UAN). An organization established in China shortly after Mao Zedong came to power in 1949 to reeducate **Taiwanese** living in China and to train them for use in an invasion of **Taiwan**. Ms. Chu Chen-tse was the director. Members of the corps were sent to Taiwan in the 1950s as infiltrators and spies.

TAIWAN RELATIONS ACT (TRA) (T'AI-WAN KUAN-HSI-FA). Legislation passed by the U.S. Congress in March 1979 and signed into law by President Jimmy Carter on 10 April 1979, the TRA reconstituted relations between the United States and Taiwan in the absence of formal diplomatic relations. Draft legislation was submitted to the Congress by the White House after President Carter announced that the United States would derecognize the **Republic of China** and establish formal diplomatic relations with the People's Republic of China, effective 1 January 1979. Congress viewed the draft legislation as inadequate and, in January and February, wrote the quite detailed TRA. Democrats led the effort, but it had strong bipartisan support and passed in the Senate by a majority of 85 to 4, and in the House by 339 to 50.

The TRA contains five sets of provisions regarding **Taiwan**'s sovereignty or nation-state status; Taiwan's security; Taiwan's economic health; human rights and democracy in Taiwan; and congressional oversight. Unlike the **Normalization Agreement**, which states that there is one China and that Taiwan is a part of China, the TRA suggests that Taiwan is an independent, sovereign nation. For example, it states that laws of the United States that apply to other foreign countries also apply to Taiwan, and it mandates that treaties concluded with the government of the Republic of China remain in force. It provides for Taiwan's security by declaring that threats, including boycotts or embargoes, are of "grave concern to the United States."

It furthermore commits the United States to maintaining military forces in the region to back up this provision. Though some say the defense clauses are ambiguous, others say they are better than those in the **United States–Republic of China Defense Treaty** that was canceled on 1 January 1980, because they cite boycotts and actions less serious than an invasion requiring U.S. concern. Taiwan was allowed special economic advantages under the TRA, including Overseas Private Investment Corporation guarantees. The human rights provision has been interpreted to place a burden on the government in Taiwan to democratize and to allow the people to decide their future. The act contained a provision requiring that Congress review it.

The TRA is unique in that it is the only instance of congressional legislation that regulates U.S. foreign relations with another country. It is important for its providing the foundation of U.S. relations with Taiwan. Along with the **Shanghai Communiqué**, the **Normalization Agreement**, and the **August Communiqué**, it is one of the four formal documents frequently cited in discussing U.S.–China policy. Unlike the other documents, however, which have less legal standing, the TRA is a law. Notably it contradicts the other documents in various ways, especially the latter two, causing some to say that U.S.–China policy is unclear.

The TRA was not received happily in **Taipei** at the time because it referred throughout to Taiwan or the people of Taiwan, instead of to the Republic of China. Since then, however, it has had strong support from Taipei. Officials of the government of the People's Republic of China did not express serious opposition at the time of its passage by the Congress, probably because they were distracted by China's conflict with Vietnam, and Deng Xiaoping did not want to provoke the United States at the time. Later, Beijing expressed strong opposition to the TRA. Beijing wanted, and still does, to see it abolished, diluted, or overshadowed by the communiqués. But that is unlikely to happen; in fact, the TRA has gained acceptance and significance in the United States and elsewhere with the passing of time, though some say this may change with China getting stronger and more important. *See also* FOREIGN POLICY.

TAIWAN RESEARCH INSTITUTE (TAI-WAN TSUNG-HO YEN-CHIU-YUAN). Founded in 1994 as a multidisciplinary think tank, it assesses national policy matters. Former president **Lee Teng-hui** is its honorary chairman.

TAIWAN REVIEW **(T'AI-WAN YUE-K'AN).** A monthly magazine published by the **Government Information Office** in **Taipei** in English and several other languages. It was formerly the *Free China Review*. *See also* MEDIA.

TAIWAN REVOLUTIONARY PARTY (T'AI-WAN K'E-MING-TANG). A political organization established in the United States by **Hsu Hsin-liang** in 1986, made up largely of the political left of the **World United Formosans for Independence**. It soon became known as a radical organization that advocated revolutionary change in **Taiwan**. It was eclipsed in 1986 when Hsu announced the formation of the Taiwan Democratic Party and subsequently said he would return to Taiwan.

TAIWAN SECURITY ENHANCEMENT ACT (TSEA) (T'AI-WAN AN-CHUAN CHIA-CH'IANG FA-AN). A bill introduced by the U.S. Senate in March 1999 and by the House of Representatives in May of that year. The U.S. House later passed it, though it never became law. The TSEA stated that the United States is obliged to provide arms to **Taiwan** according to the **Taiwan Relations Act** and that doing so should be based solely on the judgment of the United States regarding Taiwan's needs, not upon Beijing's opinion or reaction. The bill sought to ensure that the United States would fulfill its obligations under the Taiwan Relations Act and that Washington would establish closer military ties with Taiwan. It was proposed in the context of President Bill Clinton's moving toward closer ties with China and a Pentagon report on the threat to Taiwan caused by China placing an increasing number of missiles near the **Taiwan Strait** aimed at Taiwan. It became stalled in the Senate and then became moot when George W. Bush was elected president. *See also* FOREIGN POLICY.

TAIWAN SEMICONDUCTOR MANUFACTURING COMPANY, LTD. (TSMC) (CHI-T'I TIEN-LU CHIH-TSAO KU-FEN YU-HSIEN KUNG-SZU). Founded in 1987, TSMC is one of **Taiwan's**

largest and most highly regarded companies and its largest semiconductor producer. It was the first purely integrated circuit foundry in the world. In 1997, it became the first Taiwan company to be listed on the New York Stock Exchange.

TAIWAN STRAIT (T'AI-WAN HAI-HSIA). The body of water west of **Taiwan**, separating Taiwan from the Asia mainland. It is 137 kilometers (85 miles) wide at its narrowest point. It is also called the **Formosa Strait**.

TAIWAN TELEVISION ENTERPRISE (TTV) (T'AI-WAN TIAN-SHIH KUNG-SZU). Established in 1962 as a joint venture between the **Taiwan Provincial Government** and several Japanese corporations, it was the first television network in **Taiwan** and remains the largest. *See also* MEDIA.

TAIWAN TOBACCO AND WINE MONOPOLY (T'AI-WAN-SHENG YEN-CHIU KUNG-MAI-CHU). A state-owned enterprise that sells tobacco and alcoholic beverages and which had a monopoly on these products until 1995. Earlier in **Taiwan**'s history, it accounted for a large share of government revenues. The monopoly system was abolished in 2000 in order to comply with Taiwan's agreements on free trade.

TAIWAN WHITE PAPER (T'AI-WAN BAI-PI-SHU). Also called the second white paper or the February 2000 white paper, it was entitled "The One China Principle and the Taiwan Issue." The Chinese government issued it during the presidential election campaign in Taiwan that year in response to their view that the **Democratic Progressive Party**'s candidate, **Chen Shui-bian**, was an advocate of **Taiwan**'s independence. It stated a new condition, or the so-called third if—meaning that China would take military action if Taiwan refused to negotiate unification within a certain but unspecified time. It stated that the People's Republic of China is the sole legal government exercising sovereignty over all of China, including Taiwan. It declared that the government of Taiwan is a local government. It warned against foreign interference in China's "internal affairs" and against foreign countries forming military alliances with Taiwan or selling it weapons. It was especially critical of the U.S. plan to build theater missile defense in East Asia.

The paper blamed former president **Lee Teng-hui** for a deterioration in cross-strait ties, calling him a "representative of Taiwan's separatist forces" and a "saboteur of stability in the **Taiwan Strait**." Some said its main theme was contradicting and condemning Lee's two-states theory advanced in 1999. The Taiwan White Paper, on the other hand, proposed that Taipei and Beijing resume the cross-strait dialogue, on an equal footing and with a flexible agenda. In this sense, China seemed to be making major concessions. Issuing the paper was counterproductive inasmuch as it caused a backlash in Taiwan and helped Chen Shui-bian get elected. *See also* THREE IFS; WHITE PAPER ON TAIWAN.

TAIWAN YOUTH ASSOCIATION (T'AI-WAN CH'ING-NIEN-HUI). Also known as the Formosan Association, it was established by **Taiwanese** in Japan, some formally associated with **Liao Wen-yi**'s organizations. It later overshadowed Liao's organizations and for some time was the major representative of independence activities among Taiwanese in Japan. Wang Yu-teh was its first chairman.

TAIWANESE (TAI-WAN-JEN). A term used to refer to the Chinese who inhabited **Taiwan** before 1945, as opposed to the **Mainland Chinese** or Mainlanders who took up residence there after World War II and the original inhabitants or **aborigines**. Taiwanese are sometimes called the "older Chinese" or "early-arrival Chinese." They came from two parts of China: Fukien Province, just across the **Taiwan Strait**, and Kuangtung (or Canton) Province further south. The Fukien Taiwanese, or **Hoklo**, are the larger of the two groups. The **Hakka** hail mostly from Kuangtung. The two groups of Taiwanese make up around 85 percent of Taiwan's population. *Taiwanese* also connotes the language of the Fukien Taiwanese, which originates from the southern part of Fukien Province south of the Min River.

There has been a heated debate in recent years concerning whether **Taiwanese** are Chinese. Advocates of Taiwan's independence say they are not because the government of China banned women from going to Taiwan, and the men intermarried with the **aborigines**, creating a "new race." DNA studies indicate that possibly over 80 percent of Taiwanese have some aborigine blood.

TAIWANESE AMERICAN CITIZENS LEAGUE (T'AI-MEI KUNG-MIN HSUEH-HUI). An organization established in the United States in the early 1980s to try to influence U.S. elections and thus U.S. policy toward **Taiwan**. It was reported to have given financial support to Senator Edward Kennedy's 1980 presidential primary campaign in California and donations to Senator Clayborn Pell and Congressman Stephen Solarz. It was also involved in organizing **Taiwanese** to help support Matthew Martinez for a congressional seat from southern California in 1988 against Taiwan-born, but **Mainland Chinese**, Lilly Chen, causing her defeat. The league succeeded in getting U.S. census forms changed to distinguish between Taiwanese and Chinese.

TAIWANESE ASSOCIATION OF AMERICA (MEI-KUO-CH'U T'AI-WAN TUNG-HSIANG-HUI). Formed in the United States in the early 1960s from the Formosan Clubs in America, its membership was mainly **Taiwanese** living in the United States. It advocated self-determination, Taiwanese identity, and some other positions but was not politically radical. It was said to be made up of fifteen thousand to twenty thousand families. In 1974, it joined with similar groups in Japan, Canada, Western Europe, and Brazil to form the World Federation of Taiwanese Associations.

TAIWANESE HOME RULE MOVEMENT (T'AI-WAN TZU-CHIH YUN-TUNG). A movement in **Taiwan** active during the Japanese period that advocated autonomy. In 1914, **Sun Yat-sen** supported the organization's objectives. In 1944, in the face of defeat, Japan declared Taiwan a full prefecture of Japan, as this organization had demanded.

TAKASAGO. A major Japanese settlement on **Taiwan** before the Dutch established a presence nearby. It was a term used in Japanese records and maps for some time after to refer to Taiwan.

TAMSUI RIVER (TAN-SHUI HE). A river that flows past **Taipei** and to the **Taiwan Strait**. Taipei is a river port on the Tamsui River, though it is not currently of much commercial importance. The Tamsui is **Taiwan**'s only navigable river.

T'ANG CHING-SUNG. Governor of Taiwan at the time China transferred **Taiwan** to Japan via provisions in the **Treaty of Shimonoseki**. T'ang led the movement to establish the short-lived **Republic of Taiwan** expecting that he would become **president**.

TANGWAI. Literally meaning "outside the party" (party meaning the **Nationalist Party**), the term refers to a group of opposition politicians, mostly **Taiwanese**, who formed this informal or pseudo–political party in the mid-1970s. In 1977, members won twenty-one of seventy-seven seats in the **Taiwan Provincial Assembly**, as well as some other fairly important elective offices. Though the formation of new **political parties** was illegal, *tangwai* became for all intents and purposes an opposition party and campaigned against the Nationalist Party in the 1980 national election. Most *tangwai* politicians joined the **Democratic Progressive Party** in 1986.

TANGWAI CAMPAIGN ASSISTANCE GROUP (TANG-WAI CHING-HSUEN HOU-YUAN-HUI). Founded in 1978 by **Huang Hsin-chieh**, it sought to plan a coordinated election strategy and help *tangwai* candidates. **Shih Ming-teh** was its executive director. It indicated that the *tangwai* had become more organized and was more like a political party.

TANGWAI RESEARCH ASSOCIATION FOR PUBLIC POLICY (TRAPP) (KUNG-KUNG CHENG-TSE TANG-WAI YEN-CHIU HSIEH-HUI). An organization formed in 1984 by moderate *tangwai* politicians associated with **Kang Ning-hsiang**, it became what many called a proto–political party. Members subsequently negotiated with **Nationalist Party** leaders concerning their right to open local offices and become a de facto party. In September 1986, leaders of TRAPP were instrumental in forming the **Democratic Progressive Party**.

TEACHERS' DAY (CHIAO-SHIH-CHIEH). A national holiday in **Taiwan** honoring teachers and celebrating Confucius's birthday on

28 September. The administration of **Chen Shui-bian** changed the status of the holiday to one that did not allow government employees time off, ostensibly because of the link it made between China and Taiwan.

TEMPORARY PROVISIONS. *See* PROVISIONAL AMEND-MENTS FOR THE PERIOD OF MOBILIZATION FOR THE SUP-PRESSION OF COMMUNIST REBELLION.

TEN PROJECTS (SHIH-TA CHIEN-SHE). Major infrastructure projects launched by the government in 1973. They were completed in 1980, some ahead of schedule, at a cost of US$5 billion. They included the following: the Sun Yat-sen Freeway (362 kilometers or 225 miles in length extending from **Keelung** in the north to **Kaohsiung** in the south), the North Link Railroad, railroad electrification, the **Chiang Kai-shek International Airport**, Taichung Harbor, Suao Harbor, an integrated steel mill, the Kaohsiung Shipyard, Taiwan's petrochemical industry, and a nuclear power plant. These projects underscored the government's role in facilitating economic development in what many considered an important exception to a laissez-faire approach by the government toward the **economy**. Some of the projects were not immediately successful, such as the steel mill and the shipyard, due to global competition. The Ten Projects were followed by the **Twelve Projects** and the **Fourteen Projects**.

TENG, TERESA (1953–1995). Teng Li-jun in Chinese, she was born in Yunlin County in Taiwan. She became **Taiwan**'s most noted singing star, producing 1,500 songs and 150 albums. Early in her career, she entertained troops in Taiwan. Later she became famous throughout Asia, including the People's Republic of China, where many people reportedly spent a month's salary for one of her tapes. Some said she was, and remains, the most heard singer in the world.

TENGPU. An island located near **Quemoy**. It was the site of a major battle between Nationalist and Communist forces on 3 November 1949—a week after the **Battle of Kuningtou**. Nationalist forces won the battle, killing 3,700 Communist soldiers while losing 2,800 of their own.

THREE ACKNOWLEDGMENTS AND FOUR SUGGESTIONS (SAN-KE JEN-SHIH SZU-KE CHIEN-YI). Proposed in lieu of accepting the **1992 consensus** on **one China**, in 2000 President **Chen Shui-bian** broached the idea of acknowledging that cross-strait problems come from history, that neither side represents the other, and that any change in the situation should be approved by the people of **Taiwan**. His specific suggestions were that efforts should be made to improve cross-strait relations; create a new mechanism to coordinate different opinions; appeal to China to respect Taiwan's "space"; and declare to the world that Taiwan wants peace, democracy, and prosperity. China criticized the proposal; Taiwan's opposition parties called it a "conclusion without conclusions."

THREE EMPTIES (SAN K'UNG). A strategy pursued, according to the Foreign Ministry in **Taipei**, by the People's Republic of China to restrict **Taiwan**'s diplomatic space. The "empties" refer to measures taken by Beijing to reduce the **Republic of China**'s diplomatic ties, to block its efforts to join international organizations, and to eliminate bargaining chips that Taiwan has used to seek an equal relationship with Beijing. Supposedly when Taiwan is empty of these, then it will negotiate reunification with Beijing. *See also* FOREIGN POLICY; THREE NOES POLICY.

THREE IFS (SAN-KU RU-KUO). A statement of China's conditions that it imposes on **Taiwan** and which if not met will result in China using military force against Taiwan or invading the island. The first is "if Taiwan is separated from China in any name," the second is "if Taiwan is occupied by a foreign country," and the third is "if Taiwan refuses reunification through negotiations over a long period of time." The last one was stated late during the presidential election campaign of 2000 and was aimed at the **Democratic Progressive Party**'s candidate, **Chen Shui-bian**. China has not been consistent about its conditions and has also said it will take military action against Taiwan if it builds nuclear weapons or if there is serious chaos in Taiwan. *See also* TAIWAN WHITE PAPER.

THREE LINKS (SAN T'UNG). A proposal made in the early 1980s by the People's Republic of China that mail, **trade**, and transportation ties be established between China and **Taiwan**. In 1986, Deng Xiaoping suggested that the United States help in this effort. President **Lee Teng-hui** opposed the idea or at least its full implementation and stated that his **no haste policy** applied not only to **investment** in the mainland but also to the three links. Some businesspeople, including **Chang Yung-fa**, did not agree with President Lee on this issue and stated so publicly. Many businesspeople in Taiwan supported the three links. The **Democratic Progressive Party** initially opposed the three links but later moderated its stance. An agreement on transportation ties was reached in 1997 when Beijing accepted a proposal on direct shipping, and vessels then went from port to port across the **Taiwan Strait**. Other agreements still needed to be worked out, however.

When **Chen Shui-bian** became **president**, he promised better cross-strait relations and talked about fully implementing the three links. But many in his party opposed. Meanwhile, many businesses, including a lot that supported the DPP, favored the three links. This made the matter of the links very sensitive and controversial. Subsequently, even though the idea was originally proposed by China, Chinese leaders became less enthusiastic about pushing the contacts, thinking that Taiwan needed the links more than China and that the Taiwan government would have to eventually agree to the **one-China** principle in order to negotiate highly beneficial economic ties with China. Beijing has, on the other hand, made some concessions, including promising that the three links would not be political. Still, China's position that they are a domestic matter contradicts Chen Shui-bian's **one country on each side** of the Taiwan Strait position. *See also* MINI-THREE LINKS.

THREE MINILINKS. *See* MINI-THREE LINKS.

THREE NOES (SAN-BU). Provisions in a controversial public statement by President Bill Clinton when he visited the People's Republic of China in 1998. The three noes were the following: no independent Taiwan; no **two Chinas** or one China, one **Taiwan**; and no admission of Taiwan to international organizations that required nationhood for admission. Though all three had been U.S. policy, the president stating them, especially in the context that he did, caused considerable consternation in Taiwan. In fact, Clinton's statement was loudly condemned in Taiwan and may have provoked President **Lee Teng-hui** to advance his **two states theory** in 1999. Many observers thought that the Chinese government had asked President Clinton to make the statement.

THREE NOES POLICY (SAN PU CHENG-TSE). A policy of no contact, no negotiations, and no compromises, enunciated by President **Chiang Ching-kuo** at the **Nationalist Party**'s Twelfth Party Congress in 1981 in response to Beijing's "reunification negotiation offensive." (*See* NINE-POINT PROPOSAL.) The government subsequently said it would abandon the Three Noes when the People's Republic of China ends its threats of military action against **Taiwan**, its efforts to isolate Taiwan, and its "Four Cardinal Principles."

THREE PRINCIPLES OF THE PEOPLE (SAN-MIN-CHU-YI). Sometimes called the official ideology of the **Republic of China**, the principles were advocated by **Sun Yat-sen** in a work of that title. The three principles are nationalism, democracy, and people's livelihood. The first refers to nation building, since Sun thought China was a cultural entity more than a nation. The second represents Sun's advocacy of a republican form of government. And the third stresses economic development that would benefit the entire population. Sun, however, knew that democracy could not be realized quickly and advocated its development in stages: a military stage, a tutelage stage, and full democracy. For some years, the Nationalist government kept the democratization process at a slow pace based on the concept of tutelage. Antigovernment opposition groups for the most part did not attack the Three Principles of the People; rather, they criticized officials of the government and the **Nationalist Party** for not living up to these ideals.

TIAOYUTAI (TIAO-YU-T'AI). A group of small uninhabited islets, called Senkakus in Japanese and spelled "Diaoyutai" in the People's Republic of China, 120 nautical miles northeast of **Taiwan**. They were controlled by the United States after World War II. In 1972, they were returned to Japan along with Okinawa and the rest of the

Ryukyu Islands, but not before provoking the first campus demonstrations in Taiwan in more than twenty years. Some described the student demonstrations as spontaneous; others said the **Nationalist Party** staged them.

Taipei claimed the islands based on use by fishermen from Taiwan and its claim to China (inasmuch as the islands are geologically part of China's continental shelf). Beijing also laid claim to them. The fact that in the late 1960s there was speculation, based on a **United Nations** report, about large deposits of undersea oil in the area made them more important than they would otherwise have been. Japan's ownership of the islands in subsequent years was disputed periodically by both Taipei and Beijing.

In the fall of 1996, following Tokyo's declaration of a twelve-nautical-mile exclusion zone around the islands and patriotic groups in Japan putting a beacon and a flag on one of the islands, protestors from Hong Kong and Taiwan organized a mission to tear down the symbols. One protester from Hong Kong was killed, drawing world attention to the dispute. However, the governments in both Beijing and Taipei sought to prevent a crisis regarding the islands. The **Republic of China**, in 1997, nevertheless reiterated its territorial claim to the islands. The dispute between China and Japan over the islands has been intense in recent years but has involved Taiwan less.

TIENKUNG. *See* SKY BOW MISSILE.

TING CHIH-CHANG (ca. 1830s–1882). Sent to govern **Taiwan** in 1875 when, because of Western interests in the island, Peking dropped its ban on immigration to Taiwan and made some efforts to help Taiwan's economic development. Ting led these efforts plus other reform measures, but they were short lived. On the other hand, Ting's reforms helped lay the groundwork for a period of change and progress under **Liu Ming-ch'uan**.

TOMBSWEEPING DAY (MIN-TZU SAO-MU-CHIEH). A holiday when people clean the graves of their ancestors. It falls on 5 April (4 April in Leap Year). Some also view the holiday as commemorating the death of **Chiang Kai-shek**.

TOURISM (KUAN-KUANG SHIH-YEH). Tourism has been enhanced in **Taiwan** by its scenic beauty, its moderate climate, and its trove of Chinese **art** and historic treasures. The industry, however, was not promoted strongly in the past or in the years following World War II due to security and related concerns. In 1956, **Chiang Kai-shek** ordered a change in policy, and almost fifteen thousand tourists came that year. In the 1970s, after the government made further efforts to promote tourism, the number of visitors to the island increased by more than two and a half times in ten years. In 1976, more than a million tourists visited Taiwan. By the end of the decade, tourists brought US$800 million to the country, exceeding most categories of exports.

In the 1980s, the growth of tourism declined due to higher prices in Taiwan and competition from China and other countries in the area, though two million visited in 1988. In 2003, the number of tourists visiting dropped markedly due to the SARS epidemic that hit the island; there was a recovery the next year. The government expects tourism to continue to grow, but at a slower rate. The largest number of visitors come from Japan—about one-third. Hong Kong and the United States follow. Singapore, Indonesia, and the Philippines are a more recent source of tourists. The **National Palace Museum**, **Lungshan Temple**, and **Jade Mountain** are favorite tourist spots.

TRADE (MAO YI). **Taiwan** engaged in trade, though intermittent, with other areas in East Asia even before the arrival of Chinese on the island and before the period of Dutch colonization, though both contributed to that process. Under Japanese rule, Taiwan engaged in considerable commerce with Japan, mainly exporting food products (especially rice and sugar) and importing machinery and consumer goods.

Trade became much more important, though, in the late 1950s when the government scrapped its import substitution policy in favor of export promotion. Taiwan's main exports were textiles, processed food products, leather goods, wood, and paper products. All were labor-intensive industries. As the **economy** grew and labor costs increased, exports became more manufactured goods, such as electrical products, car parts, small appliances, and so on. More recently, Taiwan has exported electronic products, cameras and calculators, and computer parts and accessories. In the early 1960s, trade grew at a rate of more than 20 percent a year, reaching US$3 billion in 1970. By 1985, it had increased to US$52.4 billion, making Taiwan the tenth-largest exporting nation in the world. At this time, imports and exports equaled 80 percent of the gross national product, compared to 30 percent in Japan. In the 1990s, Taiwan became the largest exporter in the world of computer parts, accounting for more than half of the world's trade in a number of items.

Taiwan's trade has been in large part with Western capitalist countries, especially the United States and Japan, leading some to cite **dependency theory** and the possible dangers for Taiwan. This did not prove true though. In the 1980s, Taiwan began trading with Communist countries, including, most importantly, China (though most commerce passed through Hong Kong). In fact, trade boomed with China, facilitated by large Taiwan **investments** there. Early in this decade, China passed the United States to become Taiwan's largest export market; now it is nearly double the United States. Europe and the Association of Southeast Asian Nations countries follow the United States as a destination of Taiwan's exports. The biggest portion of imports are from Japan, the United States, Europe, ASEAN, and China. Taiwan has a large trade surplus with China, and surpluses with the United States, Europe, and ASEAN, and trade deficits with Japan and the oil-exporting countries.

TREATY OF SHIMONOSEKI. *See* SHIMONOSEKI (TREATY OF).

TRUTH COMMITTEE (CHEN-TIAO-HUI). Known officially as the Special Commission for the Investigation of the Truth about the March 19 Shooting, it was formed by the **Legislative Yuan** shortly after President **Chen Shui-bian** and Vice President **Annette Lu** were shot while campaigning for reelection in 2004. It is widely believed that the shooting generated a sympathy vote that enabled them to win reelection. **Pan-blue** said the shooting had been staged and were angry over losing the election. Thinking that President Chen would flaunt the commission, they made it an "act," which he had to sign, and they put provisions in the act that were questionable legally. Chen signed the act but wrote an unprecedented "aside" saying that it was unconstitutional and urged governmental "conscientious objection." The **president** then refused to appoint members to the commission and publicly condemned it as lawless. He also tried to block its working by refusing to appropriate funds for it.

TS'AI PEI-HO (1891–1986). An associate of **Lin Hsien-t'ang** and the editor of *Taiwan Youth*. He later established the League for the Establishment of a Formosan Parliament.

TSAI WAN-TSAI (1924–). The patriarch of the Tsai family, which is considered one of the richest in **Taiwan**. He inherited Fubon Financial Holding Co. and made it grow. His sons Daniel and Richard now run much of the business. Tsai (and family) was listed in the *Forbes* list of the richest people in the world in 2006, ranking number 207 in the world and number 3 in Taiwan.

TSIANG YIEN-SI (1915–1998). Also known as Y. S. Tsiang, he held a number of high posts in the government and the **Nationalist Party** over an extended period of time. These include secretary-general of the **Executive Yuan** from 1967 to 1972, minister of **education** from 1972 to 1977, secretary-general of the **Office of the President** in 1978, foreign minister from 1978 to 1979, secretary-general of the **Central Committee** of the Nationalist Party from 1979 to 1985, national policy adviser to the **president** from 1985 to 1989, and secretary-general in the Office of the President from 1990 to 1994. Tsiang was regarded as a powerful insider.

TUNGSHA ISLANDS. *See* PRATAS ISLANDS.

TVBS. A cable television station launched in 1993 that is now **Taiwan**'s leading cable station. In 1994, it started its Golden Channel, which specializes in popular entertainment. In 1995, it started Newsnet, which carries around-the-clock news. *See also* MEDIA.

TWELVE PROJECTS (SHIH-ER-HSIANG CHIEN-SHE). Infrastructure and development projects started in 1978 as a sequel to the **Ten Projects**. They included the following: an around-the-island railroad, the New Cross-Island Highway, Kaohsiung-Pingtung regional traffic improvement, **China Steel Corporation** expansion, a nuclear power project, Taichung Harbor expansion, new towns and housing, regional drainage, dike and levee construction, the Pingtung-Olanpi Highway Widening Project, farm mechanization, and cultural centers. *See also* FOURTEEN PROJECTS.

TWIN OAKS ESTATE. An estate in Washington, D.C., owned by **Taiwan** that has been the ambassador's residence (representative or minister after the United States derecognized the **Republic of China** in 1979) and the site of frequent parties and other social events. It is the largest private estate in the District of Columbia at 0.07 square kilometers (17.61 acres). Uriah Forrest, an American Revolutionary War general and later a member of the first continental congress and Maryland's first delegate to the U.S. Congress, originally owned the estate. In 1947, Ambassador Wellington Koo purchased the property for the Republic of China. In December 1978, when President Jimmy Carter decided to grant diplomatic recognition to the People's Republic of China, the estate was sold to a private organization, the Friends of Free China, which was cochaired by Senator Barry Goldwater, to prevent Beijing from making claim to it. The **Taiwan Relations Act**, subsequently passed by Congress, contained a provision in it that protected property owned by the Republic of China prior to December 1978, and the property was sold back.

TWO CHINAS (LIANGKE CHUNGKUO). The view that the **Republic of China** and the People's Republic of China are both sovereign Chinese nations, or should be, though some argue this is only temporary. The view was long opposed by both governments in Beijing and Taipei. It is still opposed, very strongly, by Chinese leaders who see it as a plot to split China. They have, in fact, often accused the United States of espousing this policy though official U.S. policy is to support **One China**. Advocates of Taiwan's independence say that it is a myth because, they say, Taiwan is not the same as the **Republic of China** or at least should not be. *See also* ONE CHINA; ONE CHINA, ONE TAIWAN; ONE COUNTRY, TWO AREAS; ONE COUNTRY, TWO ENTITIES; ONE COUNTRY ON EACH SIDE; ONE COUNTRY, TWO GOVERNMENTS.

TWO STATES THEORY (LIANGKUO LUN). The idea advanced by President **Lee Teng-hui** in 1999 in an interview with a German radio station during which he referred to Taiwan's relations with China as being relations between two countries or at least special relations between two countries. It was said that Lee was responding to the view Beijing was advancing that Taiwan was a renegade province, which he could not accept; alternatively he was angry about President Clinton's **three noes** declaration in 1998. After Lee's statement Taipei stopped using the term *two political entities*. Later the government adopted the terms *two states of one nation* and *special state-to-state relations*.

China was very upset with Lee's statement, labeling it a call for independence and an effort to split China's territory. In 2000, President **Chen Shui-bian** pledged, in his **five noes** statement, not to adopt this position, though many saw his subsequent actions and statements as suggesting otherwise.

TWO TWO EIGHT. *See ER ER BA.*

– U –

UCHIDA KAKICHI. A civil administrator of **Taiwan** under Governor-General **Sakuma Samata** from 1910 to 1915. He later became governor-general but was removed in 1924, after serving less than a year, for shielding illegal narcotic trafficking.

UNITED DAILY NEWS **(LIEN-HO PAO).** One of the three largest **newspapers** in **Taiwan**, with a circulation of over one million. The *United Daily News* operates several other papers including the *World Journal*, the largest Chinese newspaper in North America. It is politically more conservative than its rivals, the *China Times* and the *Liberty Times*. *See also* MEDIA.

UNITED FORMOSANS FOR INDEPENDENCE (T'AI-WAN TU-LI LIEN-MENG). A proindependence group formed from the group Formosans for a Free Formosa in 1960. At that point, it became a national organization in the United States. It was led by Chen I-te and advocated a **United Nations** trusteeship over **Taiwan**. It later evolved into the **United Formosans in America for Independence**.

UNITED FORMOSANS IN AMERICA FOR INDEPENDENCE (T'AI-WAN TU-LI LIEN-MENG MEI-KUO FEN-HUI). A proindependence group that evolved from the **United Formosans for Independence**. Like its predecessor organization, it was also led by Chen I-te and advocated a **United Nations** trusteeship over **Taiwan** in the late 1960s. It merged with some other similar groups in 1970 to become the **World United Formosans for Independence**.

UNITED MICROELECTRONICS CORPORATION (LIEN TIEN). One of **Taiwan**'s best-known and most highly regarded companies and its second-largest producer of semiconductors.

UNITED NATIONS (LIEN-HO-KUO). In 1945, the **Republic of China**, then ruling the mainland as well as Taiwan, was a founding member of the UN. It was also a permanent member of the Security Council. When the Communist military conquered the mainland (except the **Offshore Islands**), and the People's Republic of China was established, it did not assume the China seat in the United Nations. Subsequently, Chinese forces fought United Nations troops in Korea, and the United Nations placed an embargo against the People's Republic of China. In ensuing years, it seems that Beijing did not wish to join the United Nations and that the Soviet Union did not want this either, even though it said differently. The United States opposed Beijing taking the China seat and supported **Taipei** holding it. Taipei voted with the Western bloc when it was a UN member.

U.S. policy gradually changed about Beijing being a UN member as it became apparent that the Communist regime ruling China was permanent, and especially after 1969 when President Richard Nixon sought rapprochement with Beijing, perceiving that the Soviet Union was the biggest threat to the United States. Meanwhile, China also came to see the Soviet Union as its enemy and changed its position about UN membership. In 1971, the vote was taken on whether Beijing's admission constituted an important question (requiring a two-thirds majority in the General Assembly), and it was decided it did not. A vote was then taken on the issue of China's representation in the UN, and Beijing was admitted.

It is often said that **Taiwan** was expelled. Actually Taipei promised to withdraw if it lost the vote; it could have used its veto. It promised not to do this though, since it would have precipitated a constitutional crisis in the UN in which Taipei eventually would have lost anyway, and it did not want to create hostile international public opinion. After Taipei left the UN, it lost diplomatic ties with a number of countries and became isolated from the international community, Beijing having adopted a policy of forcing other international organizations to expel Taiwan while it refused to deal with countries that maintained diplomatic ties with Taipei. The Republic of China thus became isolated, and its sovereignty was brought into question. In fact, Taipei's withdrawal from the United Nations is said to have been the turning point in its efforts to maintain a credible diplomacy. Taipei certainly no longer represented China in international affairs. It is also said to have constituted a major reason for the opposition in Taiwan becoming more aggressive in demanding democratization, inasmuch as they argued persuasively that the international community would not support Taiwan's self-determination or right to choose its future if it were a dictatorship as China was. When Japan broke diplomatic ties with Taipei the next year, and the United States did so in 1979, this added to Taipei's difficulties.

The opposition had early on advocated that Taiwan should apply for membership in the United Nations as the **Republic of Taiwan**, or as just Taiwan. In 1986, this became a plank in the **Democratic Progressive Party**'s platform. It seemed unrealistic, however, as Beijing would surely use its veto to block this. In 1993, President **Lee Teng-hui** nevertheless accepted the DPP's position, and the government made application through the support of several countries that maintained diplomatic ties with Taipei. But the effort did not succeed. Lee and other Taiwan leaders said the defeat did not matter since it underscored Taiwan's moral position, namely that the UN, being a universal organization, should not discriminate against Taiwan, and that Taiwan, as a democratic nation, should be treated better. Lee and others also pointed to Taiwan's economic performance, saying that Taiwan had a lot to contribute to global financial stability and economic prosperity. The policy of making application to join the United Nations has been continued under the **Chen Shui-bian** administration but has still not succeeded and is unlikely to, though many people and countries are sympathetic to Taiwan's situation. The Chen administration's policy has shifted in favor of applying as a new country and for representation in the "United Nations system." As part of the latter policy, Taipei has made a strong pitch for participation in UN agencies, such as the World Health Organization (WHO). The SARS epidemic, which hit Taiwan, gave considerable resonance to this argument, as China's blocking of WHO involvement in Taiwan, according to most observers, impeded controlling the disease. Taipei meanwhile abides by International Atomic Energy Agency guidelines even though it is not a member, cooperates with Interpol without membership, and tries to cooperate with other UN-affiliate organizations as much as possible.

UNITED STATES (MEI KUO). The United States is the most important country in the world to the **Republic of China**, arguably more important than all other nations combined. The U.S. promise to defend **Taiwan** is essential to its very existence; Taiwan would no doubt otherwise be attacked by the Chinese People's Liberation Army and incorporated into the People's Republic of China. The United States is important to **Taipei** as well for many other reasons, including supporting its economic development and democratization. Leaders in Taiwan recognize this reality.

The United States had meaningful contacts with China before the Nationalist government came into being. These ties were commercial, religious (converting Chinese to Christianity), and strategic, in that chronological order. As the United States became a Pacific power, it saw foreign control, especially the colonization of China, as against its national interest and endeavored to keep China territorially intact. Thus evolved the Open Door Policy. However, the United States was a lesser world power at this time, and U.S. policy was not effective in controlling China's internal politics—upon which so much depended.

The United States was supportive of **Chiang Kai-shek** when he rose to power and unified China. This support grew as the United States became increasingly hostile toward Japan, and the two countries headed for war. American volunteers, the Flying Tigers, helped

China in spite of U.S. neutrality legislation. After Pearl Harbor, the United States openly aided China. It was Washington's strategy to keep China in the war against Japan to tie down large numbers of Japanese troops. Chiang Kai-shek helped, rejecting Japanese overtures to join Tokyo in "making Asia for Asians" through the East Asia Co-prosperity Sphere. **Madam Chiang Kai-shek**, having attended college in the United States, speaking impeccable English, and understanding American culture, served as her husband's spokesperson and public relations person—and she did the jobs well. America rendered vital support to Chiang and considered him, and China, an important strategic ally.

There were dissenting voices however. America's allies did not view China as a world power. And some Americans, most noteworthy among them General Joseph Stillwell, viewed Chiang as less than a loyal ally against Japan because of his preoccupation with fighting the Communists.

When World War II ended, the United States continued to support Chiang, helping him fight Mao and the Red Army. But American aid was sometimes restrained and was even at times counterproductive. General George Marshall went to China to mediate between the Nationalists and the Communists, but he had no leverage over the latter. His mission failed. Soon after, Communist forces prevailed over the Nationalists, and Chiang and his government, the **Nationalist Party**, along with the military, fled to Taiwan.

Meanwhile, the United States had had little contact with Taiwan since the 1800s, when Washington was interested in Taiwan as a coaling station and there had even been proposals that the United States colonize Taiwan. U.S. ties with Taiwan diminished during the period of Japanese colonial control (1895 to 1945), especially in the later years. Washington briefly considered invading Taiwan toward the end of World War II but gave up the idea after reckoning that the **Taiwanese** would help the Japanese defend the island rather than rising up against their colonial rule. After the war, the United States sent consular officials to Taiwan and expressed some objection to **Ch'en Yi**'s rule, but the United States did little in view of its preoccupation with what was happening on the mainland of China.

Following the "fall" of China to the Communists, the Democratic and Republican parties became very divided over the issue of the world's largest country joining the Communist bloc. Republicans blamed Democrats for the loss of China. The Truman administration purged alleged Communists and fellow travelers from the State Department and elsewhere in the government in response. Democrats then blamed Chiang Kai-shek for corruption and for losing the support of the masses, accounting for America's so-called defeat this way. Truman then "washed his hands" of the Nationalists, who, with Mao planning an invasion of Taiwan in the spring of 1950, were about to be annihilated. However, the invasion was delayed. At that critical juncture, the Korean War changed U.S. policy, and Truman sent the Seventh Fleet to shield Taiwan from an invasion.

As the world divided into democratic and Communist camps, Chiang became an ally once again. The United States, on the other hand, did not want Chiang to launch a war with China (Mao having signed a defense treaty with the Soviet Union in early 1950) that might drag America into a nuclear war with Russia. Washington thus sent Chiang considerable economic aid, and also military aid, but not offensive weapons.

In 1954, when Mao ordered an attack on the **Offshore Islands**, the United States came to Taipei's rescue. Washington then signed a defense treaty with Chiang—the **U.S.–Republic of China Defense Treaty**. The treaty did not cover the Offshore Islands, but the Congress changed that shortly through the **Formosa Resolution**. Another assault occurred in 1958, and the United States again acted to help Chiang Kai-shek. The result was a stalemate.

The United States supported Taipei representing China in the **United Nations** and tacitly sanctioned Chiang's plan to overthrow Mao and return to rule China. But it gave more help to Taiwan's economic and political modernization. The U.S. military used bases on Taiwan during the Vietnam War but did not fly B-52 bombing missions from Taiwan, even though Taipei made this offer.

Richard Nixon, elected president in 1968, saw China differently than previous presidents—as leverage and as a possible ally against the Soviet Union, rejecting the notion that there was unity between these two Communist countries. China now viewed the Soviet Union as a threat if not an enemy—thus a U.S.–China rapprochement.

Taiwan had to be sacrificed to some extent, though Nixon said he would not abandon Taiwan. It is not possible to know how this might have unfolded, as foreign policy under Nixon was given a lower priority with Watergate paralyzing the government and leading to Nixon's resignation in 1974, followed shortly after by Mao's death in 1976.

President Jimmy Carter put U.S.–China relations on the front burner in 1978, having ignored China for more than a year. This happened as a result of failing to build better relations with the Soviet Union. Carter's foreign policy had also been seen increasingly as poorly managed. The United States and China decided on diplomatic recognition, which was announced in December, to be effective 1 January 1979. This was formalized in the **Normalization Agreement**. Congress was unhappy over not being consulted and, moreover, felt that Taiwan had been treated badly. In a bipartisan effort, led by Democrats who were in a majority, Congress wrote the **Taiwan Relations Act** to restore a working relationship with Taiwan. The act viewed Taiwan as having sovereignty (which the Normalization Agreement seemed to deny) while ensuring that economic and other ties remained on track while asking Taiwan to democratize.

Under President Ronald Reagan, the United States seemed to undermine Taiwan's security when it agreed in the **August Communiqué** of 1982 to reduce and eventually end arms sales to Taiwan. However, Reagan gave Taiwan **Six Assurances**, and a loophole allowed the transfer of military technology that helped Taiwan produce its own fighter plane. President George H. W. Bush assured that Taiwan could defend itself by selling **F-16** fighters to Taiwan in 1992.

In 1989, the Tiananmen Massacre; a watershed election in Taiwan (in which the opposition made major gains, giving most observers the impression that a two-party system and democracy were evolving); and the pending fall of the Soviet Union all changed U.S. relations with China and with Taiwan—favoring the latter. There had been some feeling that China, with the help of supporters in the United States, might weaken and eventually nullify the Taiwan Relations Act, but no more.

President Bill Clinton was initially hostile toward China for its human rights record and was friendly toward Taiwan. But this changed when Clinton became attracted to the growing China market. In 1998, when President Clinton visited China, he announced a U.S. policy that he called the **Three Noes**, which rejected Taiwan's legal independence and its participating in international organizations as a nation-state. Congress, friendly toward Taiwan and not toward China, reacted to help Taiwan. It had already pressured Clinton to implement the **Taiwan Policy Review** that had upgraded U.S. relations with Taiwan a bit. Now Congress advanced the **Taiwan Security Enhancement Act** and made demands on the White House and State Department that gave the Taiwan Relations Act a higher status.

This all became moot when George W. Bush was elected president in 2000, Bush having taken a distinctly pro-Taiwan stance during the campaign. In fact, U.S.–Taiwan relations improved markedly. But due to the fact that the **Chen Shui-bian** administration was hinging its domestic political success on policies of ethnic discrimination and was provoking China (especially after 11 September, when Beijing joined the U.S. war on terrorism), attitudes in Washington changed, and Chen became seen as a troublemaker and even (later) as dangerous, not minding if he started a war between the United States and China. The United States still regarded Taiwan as a friend and probably saw its separate (from China) status as being in the U.S. national interest, but it also sought to avoid a crisis with China and thus remained cool toward President Chen.

UNITED STATES MUTUAL SECURITY AGENCY (MSA) (CHUNG-MEI KUNG-T'UNG AN-CHUAN TAI-PIAO-HSU). An American government agency with an office in **Taipei** through which U.S. decisions regarding **Taiwan** were articulated in the early post–World War II period. Its mission was to assist Nationalist forces to develop their military capabilities, but it often went far beyond that. The MSA mission in Taiwan was later divided into two parts: the **Military Aid and Advisory Group** and the Agency for International Development mission.

UNITED STATES–REPUBLIC OF CHINA DEFENSE TREATY (CHUNG-MEI FANG-YU HSIEH-TING). Signed by the two countries on 2 December 1954, it committed each to assist the other in the event of war or the threat of war. The treaty was part of a number of treaties and alliances concluded by the United States to surround and contain the People's Republic of China. The treaty, however, was the direct outcome of an attack by Chinese Communist forces on Nationalist-held **Quemoy** in September 1954. Though the treaty mentioned U.S. commitments to only **Taiwan** and the **Pescadores**, it was subsequently extended to include the **Offshore Islands** via the **Formosa Resolution**. In December 1978, President Jimmy Carter gave notification of the U.S. intent to terminate the treaty, and that happened on 1 January 1980. Some say security provisions in the **Taiwan Relations Act** replaced it.

UNSINKABLE AIRCRAFT CARRIER (YUNG-PU-CH'EN-MO-DI HANG-K'UNG-MU-CHIEN). A term used by the Japanese to underscore **Taiwan**'s geopolitical importance before and during World War II. General Douglas MacArthur used the same appellation in the early 1950s when the importance of Taiwan came up in debates over whether to aid Nationalist forces on Taiwan and keep the island from falling to Mao's forces. The term was mentioned during the Vietnam War because of America's use of bases there. It has been mentioned in recent years by military leaders in China who see obtaining Taiwan as constituting a significant military advantage to China.

– V –

VACATION DIPLOMACY (CHIA-JIH WAI-CH'IAO). A term used to describe golfing and other trips taken by President **Lee Teng-hui**, Premier **Lien Chan**, and other high **Republic of China** officials to other countries, especially in Southeast Asia, with which Taipei does not have formal diplomatic ties, for the purpose of countering Beijing's efforts to isolate **Taiwan**. Some of the trips have been regarded by the Western media as quasi-official and have enhanced **Taipei**'s diplomatic status. The trips have been assailed by officials in the People's Republic of China, and Beijing has sometimes been able to get the inviting country to cancel them. President Lee made notable trips to Indonesia, the Philippines, and Thailand in 1994. Other important trips have been made to Singapore and Malaysia. Vacation diplomacy has been linked to Taiwan's **Go South policy**. *See also* FLEXIBLE DIPLOMACY; PRAGMATIC DIPLOMACY.

VIENNA CONVENTION ON TREATIES (1969) (ER-NAI-WA HUI-YI). One of the most frequently cited conventions defining the legal basis of treaties, it has been cited by the People's Republic of China when arguing that the **Taiwan Relations Act** cannot be viewed as superior to or stronger legally than the **Normalization Agreement**, which established formal diplomatic relations between the United States and the People's Republic of China.

– W –

WANG, YUNG-CHING (1917–). The chairman of **Formosa Plastics Group** and one of **Taiwan**'s richest individuals, Wang has been called the "god of business management" in Taiwan. He became controversial in the 1990s after announcing plans to build a plant in China that would involve an **investment** of several billion dollars. In August 1996, he announced that his company would build offshore near **Chiayi** instead. Wang supported **Chen Shui-bian** for **president** but was soon at odds with him and his administration regarding **trade** with and **investment** in China. Wang is the third recipient of the **Republic of China**'s Order of Brilliant Star with Grand Cordon. The *Forbes* 2006 list of the world's richest people ranked Wang as 107, and number 1 in Taiwan, with a net worth of US$5.4 billion.

WANG CHIEN-SHIEN (1938–). A former **Nationalist Party** member who served as vice minister of economic affairs from 1989 to 1990 and subsequently as finance minister. He resigned from the latter office after proposing an increase in the value-added tax on property that had appreciated by a large amount. The increase did not receive the support of President **Lee Teng-hui** and thus was not enacted. He ran for a **Legislative Yuan** seat in 1992, winning big without the Nationalist Party's nomination. Wang was a member of the **New KMT Alliance**, and in 1993 he became one of the main advocates behind the creation of the **New Party** and was considered one of its founders. In 1997, the New Party nominated Wang as its presidential candidate but later shifted its support to **Lin Yang-kang**. In 1998, Wang ran very unsuccessfully for mayor of **Taipei** representing the

NP. In 2001, he ran for Taipei county magistrate as a candidate representing **pan-blue**, with the support of the Nationalist Party, the **People First Party**, and the **New Party**, but he did not win.

WANG CHING-FENG (1952–). The vice presidential candidate in 1996 on the ticket with **Chen Li-an**, Wang was the first woman to attempt to win such a high office. In 2004, Wang served as a spokesperson for the **Truth Committee** and called for the **Legislative Yuan** not to confirm the reelection victories of **Chen Shui-bian** and **Annette Lu**.

WANG DAOHAN (1915–2005). Mayor of Shanghai from 1980 to 1985 and mentor and close associate of China's top leader, Jiang Zemin, Wang was head of the **Association for Relations across the Taiwan Strait** when the **Koo-Wang talks** (for **Koo Chen-fu** and Wang) were held in Singapore in April 1993. The two met again in Shanghai in 1998, at which time Koo invited him to **Taiwan**. Due to Chinese anger with Taiwan over the issue of Taiwan's independence, he did not make the trip, and his subsequent efforts to get talks back on track did not succeed. Officials from Taiwan went to China after his death to attend his funeral.

WANG JYN-PYNG (1941–). President or speaker of the **Legislative Yuan** since 1999 and vice chairman of the **Nationalist Party** from 2000 to the present, Wang held local office in **Kaohsiung** before becoming a member of the Legislative Yuan in 1976. In 2002, he was reelected speaker even though the **Nationalist Party** was no longer the largest party in the legislature. Wang was a candidate for the position of chairman of the Nationalist Party in 2005 but lost to **Ma Ying-jeou**. He is considered a possible presidential or vice presidential candidate in 2008. Wang is **Taiwanese**.

WANG SHENG (1917–2002). An army general and one of the highest-ranking members of the **Nationalist Party** until he was "purged" in 1983 after President **Chiang Ching-kuo** felt that he was conspiring to become his successor. Chiang appointed him the **Republic of China**'s ambassador to Paraguay to get him out of the country. It was also reported that Wang set up the situation that led to the **Kaohsiung**

Incident without telling the **president**. Wang had a long and distinguished military career and had been close to the center of political power for many years. In mid-1992, Wang traveled to Beijing on what the press called a mission to improve cross-strait relations.

WEI TAO-MING (1901–1978). The second post–World War II governor of **Taiwan**, Wei was appointed in April 1947 to deal with the bad situation on Taiwan created by his predecessor, **Ch'en Yi**. Wei had previously served as ambassador to the United States. Wei subsequently suggested that the United States support him in separating Taiwan from the mainland so that the island could be governed effectively; for that, he was dismissed from his post by **Chiang Kai-shek** in December 1948.

WHITE PAPER ON CHINA (CHUNG-KUO PAI-P'I-SHU). A report issued by the U.S. Department of State in August 1949 critical of **Chiang Kai-shek** and the **Nationalist Party** for failures in China, indicting both for losing the civil war with the Communists. Corruption, lack of public support, and other problems were mentioned as the reasons. This report influenced President Harry Truman to announce the following January that the United States "would not pursue a policy that will lead to involvement in the civil conflict in China." Truman also declared that the United States would not provide military aid to Nationalist Chinese forces on **Taiwan**, indicating, some said, that he was giving the Chinese Communists a free hand to invade Taiwan.

WHITE PAPER ON TAIWAN (T'AI-WAN BAI-PI-SHU). A major policy statement published by the Taiwan Affairs Office of the State Council in the People's Republic of China in August 1993 called "The Taiwan Question and the Reunification of China." This report set forth Beijing's views on **Taiwan**'s history and why Taiwan is to be considered part of China. It also discussed Taiwan's legal status, relations across the **Taiwan Strait**, questions about Taiwan in international relations, and other issues. The authors, not named, also explained why China could not accept the **German formula** to deal with the Taiwan issue. The document seemed to reflect Beijing's concerns about Taiwan's status in a changing international situation, especially its efforts to join the **United Nations** and its **pragmatic diplomacy**. *See also* TAIWAN WHITE PAPER.

WHITE TERROR (PAI-SE K'UNG-PU). Term used to describe government oppression and the denial of basic freedoms prior to the end of **martial law**. The **Garrison Command** is often cited for its actions during this period. In 1998, the cabinet announced that it would establish a foundation to find and compensate approximately ten thousand people who were sentenced unjustly under martial law. *See also* GREEN TERROR.

WISDOM COALITION (CHI-SHIH-HUI). A group of members of the **Nationalist Party**, sometimes referred to as a caucus, faction, or subfaction of the party, that was formed in 1988 by a number of Nationalist Party legislators. Wisdom Coalition members were dissatisfied with the pace of democratic reform and Taiwan's growing isolation in the world community. They advanced the "Taiwanization" of the party and supported the idea of "**one China, one Taiwan**." In 1991, the Wisdom Coalition advocated the direct election of the **president** and the abolition of the **National Assembly** and the **Control Yuan**. The Wisdom Coalition was aligned with the Mainstream faction of the party and supported **Lee Teng-hui**.

WOMEN (NU JEN). The status and role of women in **Taiwan** was not in the past, and is not now, as low as many in the West have assumed and is higher than it is in most Asian countries. It varies among the ethnic groups, with women having a higher status among **Mainland Chinese** than **Taiwanese** (partly because of the influence of Japanese culture on the latter). **Hakka** women often engaged in physical work that many considered men's work. There are considerable differences in the status of women among the various **aborigine** groups, some of which were matriarchal in the past. Among the Chinese groups in Taiwan, all were and remain patriarchal and patrilineal.

Traditionally women played an important role in the family, and their status increased with age. Arranged marriages and the practice of inheritance going only to male heirs, however, continued later than in the West. Compared to the West, about the same percentage of women work (almost half), and compared to the United States, they own a larger percent of the national wealth, travel alone more, and are far less often the victims of crime, abuse, and physical harm. There are more female than male students in college and university. Also, more women in Taiwan have been elected to the national legislature and hold cabinet or other high office than in the United States. **Annette Lu** was elected vice president in 2000.

The most frequent complaints of women in Taiwan are as follows: working but yet still having most of the responsibility for child care and for maintaining the family, discrimination in the business world and in politics, and being hurt by divorce (finding remarriage difficult). They also report that they suffer from stress and depression due to social change. The feminist movement and movements to attain gender equality have had an impact but are not so aggressive as in the West, some say because equality is considered less an ideal in Chinese society and because of the harmful impact that promoting it had on the society in China under Communism, and also due to the fact that women play a dominant role in family affairs in many ways and in managing the family's money.

Still there have been a number of laws passed in recent years to advance women's rights, such as the Sexual Assault Prevention Act in 1997, the Domestic Violence Prevention Act in 1998, the Gender Equality in Employment Act in 2002, the Gender Equity Education Act in 2004, and the Sexual Harassment Prevention Act in 2005.

WORLD ANTI-COMMUNIST LEAGUE (WACL) (SHIH-CHIEH FAN-KUNG LIEN-MENG). The successor to the **Asian People's Anti-Communist League**, it was categorized as a nongovernmental organization, or NGO, and was headed by **Ku Cheng-kang**. It later took the name World Freedom League.

WORLD TAIWANESE ASSOCIATION (SHIH-CHIEH T'AI-WAN HUI). An organization operating abroad, mainly in the United States and Japan, which advocates **Taiwan**'s independence. In 1988, the organization held its annual meeting in Taiwan for the first time, and many of its members returned at the time. The movement's leader, Li Hsien-tung, who resides in Tokyo, did not return.

WORLD TRADE CENTER. *See* TAIPEI INTERNATIONAL CONVENTION CENTER.

WORLD TRADE ORGANIZATION (WTO) (SHIH-MAO TZU-CHIH). The most important international organization to which **Taiwan** has membership. The **Republic of China** was one of twenty-three nations that signed the Final Act of Geneva in 1947 that created the General Agreement on Tariffs and Trade (GATT), the WTO's predecessor organization, and became a founding member of GATT the next year. However, in 1950, after the government fled to Taiwan, it withdrew. It became an observer in 1965 but lost that position in 1971 when the People's Republic of China joined the **United Nations**. In 1990, Taiwan applied for membership, which was subsequently transferred to an application to the WTO.

In 2001, Taiwan was finally granted membership shortly after the People's Republic of China was admitted. Membership has had some economic shock effect on Taiwan, especially on its **agriculture** sector. But it has been a political victory and also offers Taiwan other economic advantages. Many felt that Taiwan, being the seventeenth-largest economy in the world, a major trading nation, and important in the realms of foreign aid and **investment** at the time it was admitted, should not and could not be excluded. Moreover, since Hong Kong was a member, it could hardly be argued that sovereignty was at issue.

WORLD UNITED FORMOSANS FOR INDEPENDENCE (WUFI) (SHIH-CHIEH T'AI-WAN TU-LI LIEN-MENG). Founded in 1970 by Trong R. Chai, WUFI was more radical than its predecessor organizations, refusing to rule out armed struggle as a means of establishing a free, democratic, and independent **Republic of Taiwan**, while advocating the use of violence against the **Nationalist Party**. Shortly after its founding, **Peter Huang** and Cheng Tzu-tai, WUFI's executive secretary, were indicted on charges of attempted murder for trying to assassinate **Chiang Ching-kuo** when he was in New York City. Because of this and subsequent bombing attacks attributed to the organization, including one that blew the hand off of the Taiwan provincial governor **Shieh Tung-min**, WUFI was labeled a terrorist organization by the State of California. Subsequently, a number of WUFI leaders left the organization to form other groups. WUFI continues to take a hard line on the issue of Taiwan's independence and advocates cutting all links, economic and otherwise, between Taiwan and the People's Republic of China. WUFI has been associated with the **New Tide faction** of the **Democratic Progressive Party**. *See also* FORMOSAN ASSOCIATION FOR PUBLIC AFFAIRS.

WU, K. C. (1903–1984). The fourth governor of **Taiwan**, appointed in December 1949. He received his education at Princeton University and was at one time mayor of Shanghai. He resigned from his position under protest in 1953 and went to the **United States**.

WU POH-HSIUNG (1939–). Secretary-general of the **Nationalist Party** from 1996 to 1998, Wu served as mayor of **Taipei** from 1988 to 1990, minister of state from 1990 to 1991, minister of the interior in 1994, and secretary-general in the **Office of the President** from 1994 to 1996. Wu, who is **Hakka**, has long been considered one of Taiwan's leading politicians.

– Y –

YAMI (YA-MEI). A tribe of **aborigines** that inhabits **Orchid Island**. Tribal legend tells of kinship ties with tribes in the Batanes Archipelago in the Philippines, which, in addition to language and other strong similarities, supports the theory that **Taiwan**'s native population hails from Southeast Asia.

YANG, C. K. (1933–). An **aborigine** known as the Iron Man of Asia, Yang broke the world's record in the decathlon at the Olympic Games in Rome in 1960.

YANGCHOW. The name used for **Taiwan** in early Chinese records— before the Han Dynasty.

YAO CHIA-WEN (1938–). Currently president of the **Examination Yuan**, Yao was one of the pioneers in the **Taiwan** independence movement and was a founding member of the **Democratic Progressive Party**. In November 1987, he was elected the second chairman of the party. Yao had been a participant in the **Kaohsiung Incident** and was jailed, but he was released in January 1987. In 1992, he was elected to the **Legislative Yuan**, but he failed in another bid in December 1998.

YEH KUNG-CH'IAO (1904–1981). Minister of foreign affairs from 1949 to 1958 and ambassador to the United States from 1958 to 1962, Yeh (also known as George Yeh) was involved in creating the **Republic of China**'s **foreign policy**, especially regarding its relations with the **United States**, during very critical times. **Chiang Kai-shek** disciplined him over the matter of Outer Mongolia's representation in the **United Nations** and considered him too pro-U.S.

YEN CHIA-KAN (1905–). Born in Kiangsu Province, Yen rose to prominence in the government and the **Nationalist Party** on the mainland. In 1950, he became minister of economic affairs and subsequently held a number of other important posts including the position of governor of Taiwan from 1954 to 1957. From 1963 to 1972, he was **premier**, and from 1966 to 1975 vice president. He became **president** upon the death of **Chiang Kai-shek** in 1975 and held that post until 1978. As president, however, he did not exercise vast political authority or influence; **Chiang Ching-kuo**, who was head of the ruling Nationalist Party and premier at the time he was president, wielded more political power than he did. He did not run for reelection in 1978.

YEN YUN-NIEN (1874–1923). Born in the **Keelung** area, Yen served as translator and intermediary to the Japanese in northern **Taiwan** in the late 1800s. Established in mining, Yen later signed an agreement with Fujita Gumi Company and developed mining in the area. In 1918, Mitsui, a large Japanese combine, developed a relationship with Yen to establish Keelung Coal Mining Company, helping to make Yen one of Taiwan's richest individuals. Yen was later appointed to the governor-general's advisory council and helped in the development of Taiwan's railroads, forestry, retail stores, and credit institutions.

YINGCHOW. The name used for **Taiwan** in Chinese records during the Han Dynasty and for some years later.

YOU CHING (1942–). A lawyer and legal scholar who served as **Shih Ming-teh**'s attorney during his trial after the **Kaohsiung Incident**. You was subsequently elected to the **Control Yuan** and in 1989 was elected magistrate of Taipei County—one of the most important victories for the **Democratic Progressive Party** in that election. In December 1998, he lost a bid for the **Legislative Yuan**, but he later won election and remains a DPP representative in the legislature. You is chairman of the Exchange Association of Taiwanese and European Legislators in the Legislative Yuan.

YOUNG CHINA PARTY (CHUNG-KUO CH'ING-NIEN-TANG). A political party formed in Paris in 1923 and subsequently active in Chinese politics before the Nationalist government moved to **Taiwan**. After 1949, the party broke many of its connections with the government and the **Nationalist Party** in order to become a real opposition party, but it never really succeeded in this effort. It maintained an anti-Communist stance and also opposed separatism. It had approximately twenty thousand members. Its head was Li Huang, one of the original founders and a delegate to the San Francisco Conference in 1945. Following the formation of the **Democratic Progressive Party**, the Young China Party lost support and faded from Taiwan's political scene.

YOUTH CORPS. *See* CHINA YOUTH CORPS.

YOUTH DAY (CH'ING-NIEN-CHIEH). 29 March, formerly an official holiday in the **Republic of China**. However, government offices are not closed on this day.

YU SHAN. Also called Jade Mountain, it is **Taiwan**'s highest peak at 3,997 meters (13,114 feet) above sea level.

YU SHYI-KUN (1948–). Elected chairman of the **Democratic Progressive Party** (DPP) in early 2006, Yu was **premier** from January 2002 to 2005, and before that he was secretary-general of the **Office**

of the President. Yu started his career at fifteen working for **Kuo Yu-hsin**, an opposition veteran who challenged KMT authoritarian rule. He was secretary-general of the *tangwai* from 1983 to 1984 and was one of the first members of the Democratic Progressive Party—in fact, chairing its founding meeting. He served as a magistrate of Ilan County, his home, and from 1989 to 1997 as a member of the **Taiwan Provincial Assembly**. In May 2000, before he was named vice premier, he was briefly secretary-general of the DPP, but he resigned, taking blame for four workers being swept away in a flood after waiting hours for rescue. Yu organized a "combat cabinet" upon his becoming premier. In September 2004, Yu caused a controversy when he publicly called for massive retaliation if China attacks **Taiwan**.

YUPIN, PAUL (1901–1978). The only Chinese cardinal of the Catholic Church when he died, he had been archbishop of Nanking before he fled China and went to the United States in 1949. He was very outspoken about religious persecution in the People's Republic of China, and he opposed the Vatican establishing diplomatic relations with Beijing. Because of his views and actions, he was on a list of "war criminals" in China. In 1960, he moved to **Taiwan**, where he headed Fu Jen University. *See also* RELIGION.

– Z –

ZEELANDIA (AN-P'ING KU-PAO). A fort and town established in 1624 by the Dutch on the northern end of a small islet off the coast of southwest **Taiwan** near what is now the city of Anping. The islet at the time was named Taiwan. It was the main Dutch settlement on Taiwan during its period of colonial rule of the island. Zeelandia was also the site of considerable trade between Taiwan and both China and Japan, as well as other cities in the region. In 1662, the fort was besieged by **Cheng Ch'eng-kung**'s forces and fell, marking the end of the period of Dutch colonial rule of Taiwan. *See also* PROVINTIA.

ZHENG HE. *See* CHENG HO.

Appendix A
Presidents, Vice Presidents, and Premiers since 1949

Presidents	Years
Chiang Kai-shek	1949–1975*
Yen Chia-kan	1975–1978
Chiang Ching-kuo	1978–1988
Lee Teng-hui	1988–2000
Chen Shui-bian	2000–

*Li Tsung-jen formally acted as president from January 1949 to 1 March 1950. President Chiang Kai-shek had resigned due to heavy losses in the Chinese Civil War with the Communists, but later it was said this was temporary.

Vice Presidents	Years
Li Tsung-jen	1948–1954
Chen Cheng	1954–1965
Yen Chia-kan	1966–1975
Shieh Tung-min	1978–1984
Lee Teng-hui	1984–1988
Li Yuan-zu	1990–1996
Lien Chan	1996–2000
Annette Lu	2000–

Premiers	Years
Yen Hsi-shan	1949–1950
Chen Cheng	1950–1954
Yu Hung-chun	1954–1958
Chen Cheng	1958–1963
Yen Chia-kan	1963–1972
Chiang Ching-kuo	1972–1978

Sun Yun-suan	1978–1984
Yu Kuo-hua	1984–1989
Lee Huan	1989–1990
Hau Pei-tsun	1990–1993
Lien Chan	1993–1997
Vincent Siew	1997–2000
Tang Fei	2000–2000
Chang Chun-hsiung	2000–2002
Yu Shyi-kun	2002–2005
Frank Hsieh	2005–2006
Su Tseng-chang	2006–

Appendix B
Selected Statistical Data

Population	23,036,000[1]
Crude birthrate (per 1,000)	11.25[2]
Infant mortality rate	0.54 percent[3]
Education (attendance rate)	99.5 percent[4]
Literacy	97.0 percent[5]
Life expectancy	77.43[6]
Labor force	10,600,000[7]
Unemployment	3.8 percent[8]
Gross domestic product	US$631.2 billion[9]
Growth in GDP	4.31 percent[10]
Inflation rate	1.8 percent (consumer prices), 1.4 percent (wholesale prices)[11]
GDP per capita	US$27,600[12]
Foreign trade	US$371 billion[13]
Foreign exchange reserves	US$257.0 billion[14]

NOTES

1. *The World Factbook*, CIA. Estimate is for July 2006. Taiwan ranks number fifty in the world in population.

2. Executive Yuan, *Statistical Data on the Republic of China*. Figure is for December 2003.

3. Background Note, U.S. Department of State (at www.state.gov). Figure is for 2004.

4. Background Note, U.S. Department of State (at www.state.gov). Figure is for 2003. Nine years of schooling is mandatory. Over 93 percent of students continue to high school or vocational school. There are more than 150 institutions of higher learning. Around fifteen thousand students go to the United States to study each year.

5. Background Note, U.S. Department of State (at www.state.gov). Figure is for 2003.

6. Online at www.indexmundi.com. Source cited is *The World Factbook*, CIA. Figure is for 1 January 2006. Life expectancy for males is 74.67 years; for females it is 80.47 years.

7. *The World Factbook*, CIA. Estimate is for 2005. Taiwan ranks number forty-three in the world.

8. *Invest in Taiwan*, Department of Investment Services. Figure is for January 2006. For those with less than a high school education, the rate was 4.07 percent; for those with a vocational education or higher, it was 3.8 percent. For those age fifteen to twenty-four, the rate was 9.46; for those twenty-five to forty-four, the rate was 3.67; for those forty-five to sixty-four, the rate was 2.41 percent. Note: the rate of unemployment at this time was lower than any time since March 2001.

9. *The World Factbook*, CIA. Estimate is for 2005 based on purchasing power parity. Taiwan ranks number nineteen among nations of the world.

10. *China Post*, 17 May 2006. Estimate is for 2006.

11. *China Post*, 17 May 2006. Estimate is for 2006.

12. *The World Factbook*, CIA. Figure is estimate for 2005. Taiwan ranks number thirty-three in the world.

13. Background Note, U.S. Department of State (at www.state.gov). Figure is for 2005. Exports were US$189 billion; imports were US$182 billion. Major export products were electronics, optical and precision instruments, information and communications products, textiles, plastics, and rubber products. Destinations were China (including Hong Kong), US$72 billion; United States, US$28 billion; and Japan, US$14 billion. Major imports include many of the items exported plus machinery, chemicals, basic metals, transportation equipment, and crude oil. Major sources were Japan, US$42 billion; China, US$22 billion; and United States, US$21 billion.

14. *Taipei Times*, 3 May 2006. Figure is for March 2006.

Bibliography

Much has been written on Taiwan given its size: books, monographs, scholarly articles, and magazine and newspaper pieces. The areas best covered are its economic development, political modernization, and foreign relations. This comports with what Taiwan has accomplished and where it stands in international politics: its economic miracle, its very successful democratization (it being a model in both realms), and its status as a vortex country, the Taiwan Strait being the world's most dangerous flashpoint. Scholars and news analysts have done most of the writing on Taiwan. English or Chinese are the languages most used. Some historical works on the Dutch period are written in Dutch, and the Japanese period in Japanese.

However, almost nothing can be found about Taiwan in the publications of the United Nations and other international organizations since Taiwan is not a member of the former and few of the latter. In addition, China demands that information (even economic, demographic, and other data) on Taiwan not be included in these publications. Government agencies in Taiwan fill this void and provide numerous (many free) publications in English and some other foreign languages about Taiwan. Many provide good up-to-date statistical and other data on Taiwan.

The Hoover Institution at Stanford University has an outstanding collection on the Republic of China, both historical and current. The Asian collections at Harvard, Yale, Princeton, and the University of California at Berkeley are also excellent for works on Taiwan.

For general and update information on Taiwan, *Asian Survey* publishes a summary article on all Asian countries in its January issue. The pieces on Taiwan have provided a good analysis on Taiwan. The yearbooks published by the Government Information Office in Taipei are very useful, and its chapters list Internet sources.

The Internet is a very good source of information on Taiwan. Below is a list of some helpful sites:

www.taipei.org: This is the site of the Government Information Office, New York branch. It is an official government source but provides information on a variety of topics.

http://ait.org.tw: This is the site of the American Institute in Taiwan, the U.S. "pseudo-embassy" in Taipei. You will get information here from the United States government about Taiwan.

http://cna.com: This is the site of Taiwan's main news agency. It is updated many times each day.

http://taipeitimes.com: This is the site of Taiwan's major English-language newspaper. It leans toward pan-green or supports the ruling Democratic Progressive Party and its ally the Taiwan Solidarity Union.

www.chinapost.com.tw: This is the site of Taiwan's second (in the past, first) most-read English-language newspaper. It favors the policies of pan-blue or the Nationalist Party, People First Party, and the New Party.

www.dpp.org.tw: This is the site of the ruling Democratic Progressive Party.

www.kmt.org.tw: This is the site of the Nationalist Party or Kuomintang (KMT).

www.pfp.org.tw: This is the site of the People First Party.

www.tsu.org.tw: This is the site of the Taiwan Solidarity Union.

CONTENTS

GENERAL WORKS

Aspalter, Christian. *Understanding Modern Taiwan: Essays in Economics, Politics, and Social Policy*. Burlington, VT: Ashgate, 2003.

Chaffee, Frederic H. *Area Handbook for the Republic of China*. Washington, DC: U.S. Government Printing Office, 1983.

Chang, Cecilia, ed. *The Republic of China on Taiwan, 1949–1988*. New York: St. John's University Press, 1991.

Chien, Frederick F. *Opportunity and Challenge*. Tempe: Arizona Historical Foundation, Arizona State University, 1995.

Clough, Ralph N. *Island China*. Cambridge, MA: Harvard University Press, 1978.

Cohen, Marc J. *Taiwan at the Crossroads: Human Rights, Political Development and Social Change on the Beautiful Island*. Washington, DC: Asia Resource Center, 1988.

Copper, John F. *Taiwan: Nation-State or Province?* 4th ed. Boulder, CO: Westview Press, 2003.

Edmonds, L. G. *Taiwan—the Other China*. New York: Bobbs-Merrill, 1971.

Furuya, Keiji. *Chiang Kai-Shek: His Life and Times*. New York: St. John's University Press, 1981.

Gates, Hill. *Chinese Working-Class Lives: Getting By in Taiwan*. Ithaca, NY: Cornell University Press, 1987.

Han, Lih-wu. *Taiwan Today*. Taipei: Institute of International Relations, 1974.

Hsiung, James, ed. *Contemporary Republic of China: The Taiwan Experience, 1950–1980*. New York: Praeger, 1981.

Jo, Yung-hwan, ed. *Taiwan's Future*. Tempe: Arizona State University, 1974.

Kubek, Anthony. *Modernizing China: A Comparative Analysis of the Two Chinas*. Washington, DC: Regency Gateway, 1987.

Lee, Wei-chin. *Taiwan in Perspective*. Boston: Brill, 2000.

Li, Victor C., ed. *The Future of Taiwan: A Difference of Opinion*. Armonk, NY: M. E. Sharpe, 1980.

Li, Xiaobing, and Zuohong Pan. *Taiwan in the Twenty-first Century*. Lanham, MD: University Press of America, 2003.

Liu, Alan P. L. *Phoenix and the Lame Lion*. Stanford, CA: Hoover Institution Press, 1987.

The Republic of China on Taiwan Today: Views from Abroad. Taipei: Kwang Hwa Publishing Company, 1989.

Sutter, Robert G. *Taiwan: Entering the 21st Century.* Lanham, MD: University Press of America, 1988.

Taiwan 2005 Yearbook. Taipei: Government Information Office, 2005.

BIBLIOGRAPHIES

Berton, Peter, and Eugene Wu. *Contemporary China: A Research Guide.* Stanford, CA: Hoover Institution Press, 1967.

Jacobs, Bruce, et al. *Taiwan: A Comprehensive Bibliography of English-Language Publications.* New York: Columbia University East Asian Institute, 1984.

Lee, Wei-chin, ed. *Taiwan.* Santa Barbara: ABC-CLIO, 1990.

GEOGRAPHY

Knapp, Ronald G., ed. *China's Island Frontier: Studies in the Historical Geography of Taiwan.* Honolulu: University of Hawaii Press, 1980.

Lanier, Alison. *Update-Taiwan.* Yarmouth, ME: Intercultural Press, 1982.

HISTORY

Bing, Su. *Taiwan's 400 Year History: The Origins and Continuing Development of the Taiwanese Society and People.* Washington, DC: Taiwanese Cultural Grassroots Association, 1986.

Campbell, William. *Formosa under the Dutch.* New York: AMS Press, 1967.

Chen, Theodore H. E. "Taiwan after Chiang Kai-shek." *Current History*, September 1975.

———. "Taiwan's Future." *Current History*, September 1979.

Chiu, Hungdah, and Shao-Chuan Leng, eds. *China, Seventy Years after the 1911 Hsin-Hai Revolution.* Charlottesville: University of Virginia Press, 1984.

Crozier, Ralph C. *Koxinga and Chinese Nationalism: History, Myth and the Hero.* Cambridge, MA: Harvard University Press, 1977.

Davidson, James W. *The Island of Formosa Past and Present.* London: Oxford University Press, 1990.

Davison, Gary Marvin. *A Short History of Taiwan: The Case for Independence.* Westport, CT: Praeger, 2003.

Goddard, W. G. *Formosa: A Study in Chinese History*. East Lansing: Michigan State University Press, 1966.

Gordon, Leonard H., ed. *Taiwan: Studies in Chinese Local History*. New York: Columbia University Press, 1970.

Green, Robert. *Taiwan*. San Diego, CA: Lucent Books, 2001.

Hsiung, James, ed. *The Taiwan Experience, 1950–1980*. New York: American Association for Chinese Studies, 1981.

Hung Chien-chao. *A History of Taiwan*. Rimini, Italy: Il Cerchio, 2000.

Hutsebaut, Marc, ed. *The Authentic Story of Taiwan: An Illustrated History*. Taipei: SMC Publishers, 1991.

Kerr, George. *Formosa Betrayed*. New York: Da Capo Press, 1976.

———. *Formosa: Licensed Revolution and the Home Rule Movement*. Honolulu: University of Hawaii Press, 1974.

Kierman, Frank Algerton. *The Fluke That Saved Formosa*. Cambridge: Massachusetts Institute of Technology, Center for International Studies, 1954.

Lai, Tse-han, et al. *A Tragic Beginning: The Taiwan Uprising of February 28, 1947*. Stanford, CA: Stanford University Press, 1991.

Li, Victor H., ed. *The Future of Taiwan: A Difference of Opinion*. Armonk, NY: M. E. Sharpe, 1980.

Lou, Tsu-K'uang. *Personal Legends of Formosa*. Pasadena, CA: Oriental Book Store, 1975.

Lumley, F. A. *The Republic of China under Chiang Kai-shek*. London: Barrie & Jenkins, 1976.

MacKay, George L. *From Far Formosa: The Island, Its People, and Missions*. San Francisco: Chinese Materials Center, 1972.

Mancall, Mark, ed. *Formosa Today*. New York: Praeger, 1964.

Manthorpe, Jonathan. *Forbidden Nation: A History of Taiwan*. New York: Palgrave MacMillan, 2005.

Plummer, Mark. "Taiwan: The Other China." *Current History*, September 1966.

———. "Taiwan's Chinese Nationalist Government." *Current History*, September 1971.

Roy, Denny. *Taiwan: A Political History*. Ithaca, NY: Cornell University Press, 2003.

Rubinstein, Murray A., ed. *Taiwan: A New History*. Armonk, NY: M. E. Sharpe, 1999.

Shieh, Milton J. T. *The Kuomintang: Selected Historical Documents, 1894–1969*. New York: Center of Asian Studies, St. John's University, 1970.

Sih, Paul K. T. ed. *Sun Yat-sen and China*. New York: St. John's University Press, 1974.

———. *Taiwan: A History*. Armonk, NY: M. E. Sharpe, 1998.

Takekoshi, Yosaburo. *Japanese Rule in Formosa*. Pasadena, CA: Oriental Book Store, 1978.

Wen, John L. *Elephant Embraces Dragon*. New York: Vantage Press, 1984.

CULTURE

Brown, Melissa J. *Is Taiwan Chinese? The Impact of Culture, Power, and Migration on Changing Identities*. Berkeley: University of California Press, 2004.

Chang, Sung-sheng. *Literary Culture in Taiwan: Martial Law to Market Law*. New York: Columbia University Press, 2004.

Chen, Chi-lu. *Material Culture of the Formosan Aborigines*. Taipei: Taiwan Museum, 1968.

Chen, Chung-min. *Ancestor Worship and Clan Organization in a Rural Village of Taiwan*. Nankang, Taipei: Academia Sinica, Bulletin of the Institute of Ethnology, 1967.

Chen, Yu-Ching. "Chinese Culture vs. Anti-Chinese Culture—Declaration of the Kuomintang on Its 80th Founding Anniversary." *Chinese Culture*, March 1975.

———. "President Chiang Kai-shek and Chinese Cultural Renaissance." *Asian Culture Quarterly*, Spring 1975.

Chia, Sylvia Shih Heng. "The World of Classical Poets in Taiwan, R.O.C. in the 1950s." *American Journal of Chinese Studies*, October 1998.

Chiu, Ming-chung. *Two Types of Folk Piety: A Comparative Study of Two Folk Religions in Formosa*. Chicago: University of Chicago Press, 1970.

Chu, J. J. "Labor Militancy and Taiwan's Export-Led Industrialization." *Journal of Contemporary Asia*, 2003.

———. "Labor Militancy in Taiwan: Export Integration vs Authoritarian Transition." *Journal of Contemporary Asia*, 2001.

Chu, Pao-tang. "Buddhist Organization in Taiwan." *Chinese Culture*, June 1969.

———. "Dragon Boat Festival, May 8." *Asian Outlook*, June 1970.

———. "Festivals in the Republic of China." *Asian Outlook*, February 1970.

Cohen, Myron L. *House United, House Divided: The Chinese Family in Taiwan*. New York: Columbia University Press, 1976.

Diamond, Norma. *K'un Shen: A Taiwan Village*. New York: Holt, Rinehart & Winston, 1969.

Eberhard, Wolfram. *Studies in Taiwanese Folktales*. Taipei: Orient Cultural Service, 1974.

Elvin, Mark, and G. William Skinner, eds. *The Chinese City between Two Worlds*. Stanford, CA: Stanford University Press, 1974.

Freedman, Ronald, and John Y. Takeshita. *Family Planning in Taiwan*. Princeton, NJ: Princeton University Press, 1969.

Gallin, Bernard. *Hsin Hising, Taiwan: A Chinese Village in Change*. Berkeley: University of California Press, 1966.

Gates, Hill. "Money for the Gods." *Modern China*, July 1987.

Gold, T. B. "Go with Your Feelings: Hong Kong and Taiwan Popular Culture in Greater China." *China Quarterly*, December 1993.

Gordon, Leonard H. D., ed. *Taiwan: Studies in Chinese Local History*. New York: Columbia University Press, 1970.

Harrell, Steven, and Chun-chieh Huang. *Cultural Change in Postwar Taiwan*. Boulder, CO: Westview Press, 1994.

Hong, Keelung, and Stephen O. Murray. *Looking through Taiwan: American Anthropologists' Collusion with Ethnic Domination*. Lincoln: University of Nebraska Press, 2005.

Hsia, C. T. *A History of Modern Chinese Fiction*. 1st ed. New Haven, CT: Yale University Press, 1961.

Hung, Joe. "Religious Activities on Taiwan." *Asian Culture Quarterly*, Spring 1976.

Johnson, İrmgard. "Whatever Happened to Peking Opera?" *Asian Affairs*, July–August 1975.

Jordan, David K. *Gods, Ghosts, and Ancestors: The Folk Religion of a Taiwanese Village*. Berkeley: University of California Press, 1972.

———. "Language Choice and Interethnic Relations in Taiwan." *La Monda Lingro-Problemo*, 1973.

Jordan, David K., and Andrew D. Morris. *The Minor Arts of Daily Life: Popular Culture in Taiwan*. Honolulu: University of Hawaii Press, 2004.

Kallgren, Joyce K. "Nationalist China: The Continuing Dilemma of the 'Mainland' Philosophy." *Asian Survey*, January 1963.

Kuo, Jason C. *Art and Cultural Politics in Postwar Taiwan*. Seattle: University of Washington Press, 2000.

Lee, M. L, and T. H. Sun. "The Family and Demography in Contemporary Taiwan." *Journal of Contemporary Family Studies*, Spring 1995.

Lee, Wen-jer. "Taiwan and Dr. Sun's Revolution." *Free China Review*, November 1965.

Liao, David C. E. *The Unresponsive: Resistant or Neglected? The Hakka Chinese in Taiwan Illustrate a Common Mission Problem*. Chicago: Moody Press, 1972.

Long, Howard R. *The People of Musha: Life in a Taiwanese Village*. Columbia: University of Missouri Press, 1961.

Lu, L., and S. F. Kao. "Traditional and Modern Characteristics across the Generations: Similarities and Discrepancies." *The Journal of Social Psychology*, Fall 2002.

McBeath, Gerald A. "Roots of Regime Stability in the Taiwanese Family." *American Journal of Chinese Studies*, April 1987.

McCaghy, C. H., and C. Hou. "Family Affiliation and Prostitution in a Cultural Context: Career Onsets of Taiwanese Prostitutes." *Archives of Sexual Behavior*, June 1994.

Metzger, Thomas A. "On Chinese Political Culture." *Journal of Asian Studies*, November 1972.

O'Hara, Albert R. "A Factual Survey of Taipei's Temples and Their Functions." *Journal of Social Science*, July 1967.

Palandri, Angela Jung. "Current Trends in Taiwan Poetry: Creativeness versus Conformity." *Literature East and West*, 1971.

Pang-yuan, Chi. *An Anthology of Contemporary Chinese Literature Taiwan: 1949–1974*. Taipei: National Institute for Compilation and Translation, 1975.

Pazderic, N. "Recovering True Selves in the Electro-Spiritual Field of Universal Love." *Cultural Anthropology*, May 2004.

Plummer, Mark. "Taiwan: Toward a Second Generation of Mainland Life." *Asian Survey*, January 1970.

Ramos, J. M. "Futures Languages in Taiwan." *Futures*, September 2001.

Rubinstein, Murray A., ed. *The Protestant Community of Modern Taiwan: Mission, Seminary and Church*. Armonk, NY: M. E. Sharpe, 1990.

Sangren, P. S. "Power and Transcendence in the Ma Tsu Pilgrimages of Taiwan." *American Ethnologist*, August 1993.

Saso, Michael. "The Taoist Tradition in Taiwan." *China Quarterly*, January–March 1971.

Stafford, C. "Good Sons and Virtuous Mothers: Kinship and Chinese Nationalism in Taiwan." *Man*, June 1992.

Starr, Kenneth. "Cultural Problems on Nationalist Taiwan." *France-Asia*, 1962.

Swartz, Mark M., Victor W. Turner, and Arthur Tuden, eds. *Political Anthropology*. Chicago: Aldine Publishing, 1966.

Teng, Yuang Chung. "The Cultural Development of Taiwan, ROC during the Past Forty Years: A Study of Seven Chinese Views." *American Journal of Chinese Studies*, October 1992.

Thompson, Laurence G. *Chinese Religion: An Introduction*. 2nd ed. Encino, CA: Dickenson Publishing, 1975.

Tong, Hollington K. *Christianity in Taiwan: A History*. Taipei: Hollington Tong, 1961.

Tozer, Warren. "Taiwan's Cultural Renaissance: A Preliminary View." *China Quarterly*, July–September 1970.

Tsai, Wen-hui. "Folk Religion in Modernizing Taiwan." *American Asian Review*, Fall 1996.

Wang, Sung-hsing. "Family Structure and Economic Development in Taiwan." *Bulletin of the Institute of Ethnology*, Academia Sinica, Autumn 1977.

Wei, Yi-min (Henry), and Suzanne Coutanceau. *Wine for the Gods: An Account of the Religious Traditions and Beliefs of Taiwan*. Taipei: Ch'eng Wen Publishing, 1976.

Weller, R. P. "Bandits, Beggars, and Ghosts: The Failure of State Control over Religious Interpretation in Taiwan." *American Ethnologist*, February 1985.

———. "Social Contradiction and Symbolic Resolution: Practical and Idealized Affines in Taiwan." *Ethnology*, October 1984.

Wolf, Arthur P., ed. *Religion and Ritual in Chinese Society*. Stanford, CA: Stanford University Press, 1974.

Wolf, Margery. *The House of Lim: A Study of a Chinese Farm Family*. New York: Appleton-Century-Crofts, 1968.

———. *Women and the Family in Rural Taiwan*. Stanford, CA: Stanford University Press, 1972.

Yen, C. K. "Rotarianism and Confucianism." *Chinese Culture*, June 1975.

Yen, Yuan-shu. "Social Realism in Recent Chinese Fiction in Taiwan." In *Thirty Years of Turmoil in Asian Literature*. Taipei: Taipei Chinese Center, International P.E.N., 1976.

Yip, Wai-lim, ed. "Chinese Arts and Literature: A Survey of Recent Trends." Occasional Papers/Reprints Series in *Contemporary Asian Studies* 9 (1977).

Yu, Priscilla C. "Taiwan's International Exchange Program: A Study in Cultural Diplomacy." *Asian Affairs*, Summer 1985.

SOCIETY

Ahern, Emily M., and Hill Gates, eds. *The Anthropology of Taiwanese Society*. Stanford, CA: Stanford University Press, 1981.

Bessac, Frank B. *An Example of Social Change in Taiwan Related to Land Reform*. Missoula: Department of Anthropology, University of Montana, 1967.

Bosco, J. "Taiwan Factions: Guanxi, Patronage, and the State in Local Politics." *Ethnology*, April 1992.

Brinton, M. C., et al. "Married Women's Employment in Rapidly Industrializing Societies: Examples from East Asia." *American Journal of Sociology*, March 1995.

Brown, Melissa, ed. *Negotiating Ethnicities in China and Taiwan*. Berkeley: University of California, China Research Monographs, 1995.

Casterline, John B. *Nuptiality Transition and Its Causes: A Study of Taiwan, 1905–1976*. Boulder, CO: Westview Press, 1988.

Ch'en, Kou-Chun. *Studies in Marriage and Funerals of Taiwan Aborigines*. Pasadena, CA: Oriental Book Store, 1970 (Chinese).

Chen, D. S. "Taiwan's Social Changes in the Patterns of Social Solidarity in the 20th Century." *China Quarterly*, March 2001.

Chen, Shao-hsing. "Trend Report of Studies in Social Stratification and Social Mobility in Taiwan." *East Asian Culture Studies*, March 1965.

Chen, Y. C. J., et al. "A Six-Year Follow-up of Behavior and Activity Disorders in the Taiwan Yu-cheng Children." *American Journal of Public Health*, March 1994.

Chi, C., et al. "The Practice of Chinese Medicine in Taiwan." *Social Science and Medicine*, November 1996.

Chin, Ko-lin. *Heijin: Organized Crime, Business, and Politics in Taiwan*. Armonk, NY: M. E. Sharpe, 2003.

Chou, Bih-er, Cal Clark, and Janet Clark. "Differences in the Political Attitudes of Women and Men Legislators in Taiwan." *American Asian Review*, Fall 1993.

Chou, Bih-er, et al. *Women in Taiwanese Politics: Overcoming Barriers to Women's Participation in a Modernizing Society*. Boulder, CO: Lynne Rienner Publishers, 1989.

Chu, Godwin C. "Impact of Mass Media on a Gemeinschaft-Like Social Structure." *Rural Sociology*, June 1968.

Chu, J. J. "Nationalism and Self-Determination: The Identity Politics in Taiwan." *Journal of Asian and African Studies*, 2000.

Clark, Cal. *The Social and Political Bases for Women's Growing Political Power in Taiwan*. Baltimore: School of Law, University of Maryland, 2002.

——. "Successful Structural Adjustment and Evolving State-Society Relations in Taiwan." *American Journal of Chinese Studies*, October 1994.

Clark, Janet, Cal Clark, and Bih-er Chou. "Assemblywomen in Taiwan: A Surprising Equality." *American Journal of Chinese Studies*, April 1992.

Clart, Philip, and Charles Brewer Jones. *Religion in Modern Taiwan: Tradition and Innovation in a Changing Society*. Honolulu: University of Hawaii Press, 2003.

Corcuff, Stephane. *Memories of the Future: National Identity Issues and the Search for a New Taiwan*. Armonk, NY: M. E. Sharpe, 2002.

Davis, D. R., and M. D. Ward. "The Entrepreneurial State: Evidence from Taiwan." *Comparative Political Studies*, October 1990.

Diamond, Norma. "Women under the Kuomintang Rule—Variations on the Feminine Mystique." *Modern China*, January 1975.

Farris, Catherine S. "Women, Work, and Child Care in Taiwan: Changing Family Dynamics in a Chinese Society." *American Asian Review*, Fall 1993.

Farris, Catherine S., and Anru Lee. *Women in the New Taiwan: Gender Roles and Gender Consciousness in a Changing Society*. Armonk, NY: M. E. Sharp, 2004.

Gallin, R. S. "Women and Work in Rural Taiwan: Building a Contextual Model Linking Employment and Health." *Journal of Health and Social Behavior*, December 1989.

Gates, Hill. *Chinese Working-Class Lives: Getting by in Taiwan*. Ithaca, NY: Cornell University Press, 1987.

Gold, Thomas B. *State and Society in the Taiwan Miracle*. Armonk, NY: M. E. Sharpe, 1986.

——. "Taiwan Society at the Fin de Siecle." *China Quarterly*, December 1996.

Greenhalgh, S. "Networks and Their Nodes: Urban Society in Taiwan." *China Quarterly* 99, 1984.

Grichting, Wolfgang. *The Value System on Taiwan, 1970*. Taipei: Privately printed, 1971.

Harrell, Steven. *Ploughshare Village: Culture and Context in Taiwan*. Seattle: University of Washington Press, 1982.

Harremann, R. W. "Family Planning in Taiwan: The Conflict between Ideologues and Technocrats." *Modern China*, April 1990.

Ho, Samuel P. S. "Decentralized Industrialization and Rural Development: Evidence from Taiwan." *Economic Development and Cultural Change*, October 1979.

——. "Industrialization in Taiwan: Recent Trends and Problems." *Pacific Affairs*, Spring 1975.

Ho, Ting-Jui. *A Comparative Study of Myths and Legends of Formosan Aborigines*. Pasadena, CA: Oriental Book Store, 1972.

Hsieh, C. R., and S.-J. Lin. "Health Information and the Demand for Preventive Care among the Elderly in Taiwan." *Journal of Human Resources*, Spring 1997.

Hsieh, H. C. "Women's Studies in Taiwan." *Women's Studies Quarterly*, Fall–Winter 1994.

Hsu, M.-T. "Recovery through Reconnection: A Cultural Design for Family Bereavement in Taiwan." *Death Studies*, October 2004.

Ikeda, Toshio. *A Survey of Taiwanese Family-Life*. Pasadena, CA: Oriental Book Store, 1972.

Jochim, C. "Flowers, Fruit, and Incense Only: Elite versus Popular in Taiwan's Religion of the Yellow Emperor." *Modern China*, January 1990.

Kao, C., et al. "Male-Female Wage Differentials in Taiwan: A Human Capital Approach." *Economic Development and Cultural Change*, January 1994.

Keijiro, Marui. *Survey of Taiwanese Religions in 1919*. 2 vols. Pasadena, CA: Oriental Book Store, 1974.

Lavely, W. "Industrialization and Household Complexity in Rural Taiwan." *Social Forces*, September 1990.

Lee, Y. J., et al. "Sons, Daughters, and Intergenerational Support in Taiwan." *American Journal of Sociology*, January 1994.

Li, William D. H. *Housing in Taiwan: Agency or Structure?* Brookfield, VT: Ashgate, 1998.

Liao, Cheng-hung, and Martin C. Yang. *Socio-economic Change in Rural Taiwan, 1950–1978*. Taipei: Department of Agricultural Extension, National Taiwan University, 1979.

Lin, P. J., et al. "Category Typicality, Cultural Familiarity, and the Development of Category Knowledge." *Developmental Psychology*, September 1990.

Long, Howard R. *The People of Musha: Life in a Taiwanese Village*. Columbia, MO: University of Missouri Press, 1961.

Lu, Hsin-yi. *The Politics of Locality: Making a Nation of Communities in Taiwan*. New York: Routledge, 2002.

Ma, L. C., and K. B. Smith. "Education, Social Class, and Parental Values in Taiwan." *Journal of Social Psychology*, August 1993.

——. "Social Correlates of Confucian Ethics in Taiwan." *Journal of Social Psychology*, October 1992.

Makeham, John, and A-chin Hsiau. *Cultural, Ethnic, and Political Nationalism in Contemporary Taiwan: Bentuhua*. New York: Palgrave Macmillan, 2005.

Marsh, Robert M. *The Great Transformation: Social Change in Taipei, Taiwan since the 1960s*. Armonk, NY: M. E. Sharpe, 1996.

——. "Social Capital, Guanxi, and the Road to Democracy in Taiwan." *Comparative Sociology*, 2003.

——. "Social Class Identification and Class Interest in Taiwan." *Comparative Sociology*, 2002.

——. "The Taiwanese of Taipei: Some Major Aspects of Their Social Structure and Attitudes." *Journal of Asian Studies*, May 1968.

Marsh, R. M., and C.-K. Hsu. "Changes in Norms and Behavior Concerning Extended Kin in Taipei, Taiwan, 1963–1991." *Journal of Comparative Family Studies*, Autumn 1995.

Murry, Stephen O., and Hong Keelung. *Taiwanese Culture, Taiwanese Society: A Critical Review of Social Science Research Done on Taiwan*. Lanham, MD: University Press of America, 1994.

O'Hara, Albert. *Social Problems: Focus on Taiwan*. Beaverton: International Specialized Book Service, 1980.

Olsen, Nancy J. "Social Class and Rural-Urban Patterning of Socialization in Taiwan." *Journal of Asian Studies*, May 1975.

Parish, W. L., and R. J. Willis. "Daughters, Education, and Family Budgets: Taiwan Experiences." *Journal of Human Resources*, Fall 1993.

Pasternak, Burton. *Kinship and Community in Two Chinese Villages*. Stanford, CA: Stanford University Press, 1972.

Rawnsley, G. D. "Treading a Fine Line: Democratization and the Media in Taiwan." *Parliamentary Affairs*, January 2004.

Rawnsley, Gary D., and Ming-Yeh T. Rawnsley. *Critical Security, Democratization, and Television in Taiwan*. Burlington, VT: Ashgate, 2001.

———. "Public Television and Empowerment in Taiwan." *Pacific Affairs*, Spring 2005.

Schak, D. C. "Socio-economic Mobility and the Urban Poor in Taiwan." *Modern China*, July 1989.

Shaw, T. A. "'We Like to Have Fun': Leisure and the Discovery of the Self in Taiwan's 'New' Middle Class." *Modern China*, October 1994.

Shee, Amy H. L. *Legal Protection of Children against Sexual Exploitation in Taiwan*. Brookfield, VT: Ashgate, 1998.

Sih, Paul K. T. "Taiwan: A Modernizing Chinese Society." *Chinese Culture*, December, 1972.

Speare, Alden, Jr., et al. *Urbanization and Development: The Rural-Urban Transition in Taiwan*. Boulder, CO: Westview Press, 1987.

Strom, R., et al. "Grandparents in Taiwan: A Three-Generational Study." *International Journal of Aging and Human Development* 42, no. 1 (1996).

Thornton, Arland, and Hui-sheng Lin. *Social Change and the Family in Taiwan*. Chicago: University of Chicago Press, 1994.

Thornton, A., et al. "Social and Economic Change, Intergenerational Relationships, and Family Formation in Taiwan." *Demography*, November 1984.

Tien, Hung-mao. *The Great Transition: Political and Social Change in the Republic of China*. Stanford, CA: Hoover Institution Press, 1989.

Tsai, S. L., et al. "Schooling Taiwan's Women: Educational Attainment in the Mid-20th Century." *Sociology of Education*, October 1994.

Tsai, Wen-hui. "From Tradition to Modernity: Social Change in the Republic of China." *American Journal of Chinese Studies*, October 1992.

———. *Socio-economic Changes and Modernization in an Age of Uncertainty: Taiwan in the 1990s and Its Future Challenge*. Baltimore: School of Law, University of Maryland, 2001.

———. "Welfare Policies for the Aged on Both Sides of the Taiwan Straits: A Comparison." *American Asian Review*, Summer 1989.

Tu, E. J. C., et al. "Kinship and Family Support in Taiwan: A Micro-simulation Approach." *Research on Aging*, December 1993.

Tyson, James. "Christians and the Taiwanese Independence Movement: A Commentary." *Asian Affairs*, Fall 1987.

Wang, Charlotte Shiang-yun. "Social Mobility in Taiwan." *Papers in Social Sciences*, nos. 80–83. Taipei: Academia Sinica, 1980.

Wang, T. Y., and I.-C. Liu. "Contending Identities in Taiwan: Implications for Cross-Strait Relations." *Asian Survey*, July–August 2004.

Wei, Hsian-Chuen, and Uwe Reischl. "Impact of Industrialization on Attitude towards Parents and Children in Contemporary Taiwan." *Industry of Free China*, July 1983.

Weller, R. P. "Social Contradiction and Symbolic Resolution: Practical and Idealized Affines in Taiwan." *Ethnology*, October 1984.

Wilson, Richard W. "Some Rural-Urban Comparisons of Political Socialization in Taiwan." *Asian Studies*, April 1972.

Wilson, Richard W., Amy A. Wilson, and Sidney L. Greenblatt, eds. *Value Change in Chinese Society*. New York: Praeger, 1979.

Wolf, Margery. *A Thrice-Told Tale: Feminism, Postmodernism and Ethnographic Responsibility*. Stanford, CA: Stanford University Press, 1992.

——. "The Woman Who Didn't Become a Shaman." *American Ethnology*, August 1990.

Wong, Chun-kit J. *The Changing Chinese Family Pattern in Taiwan*. Pasadena, CA: Oriental Book Store, 1981.

Wright, T. "Student Mobilization in Taiwan: Civil Society and Its Discontents." *Asian Survey*, November–December 1999.

Wu, B. "The Declining Gender Difference in Crime: The Taiwanese Case." *International Journal of Offender Therapy and Comparative Criminality*, Winter 1995.

——. "The Impact of an Anti-amphetamine Law on Juvenile Delinquency on Taiwan." *International Journal of Offender Therapy and Comparative Criminality*, September 1996.

Wu, Tsong-shien. *Taiwan's Changing Rural Society*. 2 vols. Pasadena, CA: Oriental Book Store, 1972.

Yen, E. C., et al. "Cultural and Family Effects on Fertility Decisions in Taiwan, R.O.C.: Traditional Values and Family Structure Are as Relevant as Income Measures." *American Journal of Economics and Sociology*, October 1989.

Yi, C. C. "Studying Social Change: The Case of Taiwanese Family Sociologists." *Current Sociology*, Spring 1993.

——. "Urban Housing Satisfaction in a Transitional Society: A Case Study in Taichung, Taiwan." *Urban Studies*, February 1985.

Yuan, D. Y., and Edward G. Stockwell. "The Rural-Urban Continuum: A Case Study of Taiwan." *Rural Sociology*, September 1964.

Zveglich, J. E., Jr., et al. "The Persistence of Gender Earnings Inequality in Taiwan, 1978–1992." *Industrial Labor Relations Review*, July 1997.

EDUCATION

Appleton, S. "Regime Support among Taiwan High School Students." *Asian Studies*, August 1973.

——. "The Political Socialization of Taiwan's College Students." *Asian Survey*, October 1970.

——. "Silent Students and the Future of Taiwan." *Pacific Affairs*, Summer 1970.

——. "The Social and Political Impact of Education in Taiwan." *Asian Survey*, August 1976.

Barendsen, Robert Dale. *Higher Educational Institutions in Taiwan*. U.S. Office of Education, Bulletin No. 18. Washington, DC: Government Printing Office, 1966.

Guo, Yugui. *Asia's Educational Edge: Current Achievements in Japan, Korea, Taiwan, China, and India*. Lanham, MD: Lexington Books, 2005.

Hong, L. K. "Taiwanese Students in the U.S." *Social Psychology*, December 1978.

Hughes, C., and R. Stone. "Nation-Building and Curriculum Reform in Hong Kong and Taiwan." *China Quarterly*, December 1999.

Kao, Charles H. C. *Brain Drain: A Case Study of China*. Taipei: Mei Ya Publications, 1971.

——. "An Evaluation of the Republic of China's Policy on Tuition for Public Higher Education." *Industry of Free China*, May 1984.

Kaser, Davis. *Book Pirating in Taiwan*. Philadelphia: University of Pennsylvania Press, 1969.

Lew, William J. F. "Education in Taiwan." *Asian Affairs*, May–June 1978.

Martin, Roberta. "The Socialization of Children in China and Taiwan: An Analysis of Elementary School Textbooks." *China Quarterly*, June 1975.

Smith, Douglas C. *Middle Education in the Middle Kingdom: The Chinese Junior High School in Modern Taiwan*. Westport, CT: Greenwood Press, 1997.

Stevenson, H. W., et al. "Cognitive Performance and Academic Achievement of Japanese, Chinese, and American Children." *Child Development*, June 1985.

Synott, John P. *Teacher Unions, Social Movements, and the Politics of Education in Asia: South Korea, Taiwan, and the Philippines*. Burlington, VT: Ashgate 2002.

Tien, Flora F. "Higher Education Reform in Taiwan: History, Development and the University Act." *American Asian Review*, Fall 1996.

Tsurumi, E. Patricia. *Japanese Colonial Education in Taiwan, 1895–1945*. Cambridge, MA: Harvard University Press, 1977.

Wilson, Richard W. *Learning to Be Chinese: The Political Socialization of Children in Taiwan*. Cambridge: Massachusetts Institute of Technology Press, 1970.

ECONOMICS

Adams, D. W., et al. "Differences in Uses of Rural Financial Markets in Taiwan and the Philippines." *World Development*, April 1993.

Asian Business. "Economic Report: Taiwan's Great Leap Forward." December 1987.

Aw, B. Y., and A. R. Hwang. "Productivity and the Export Market: A Firm-Level Analysis." *Journal of Development Economics*, August 1995.

Berger, Suzanne, and Richard K. Lester. *Global Taiwan: Building Competitive Strengths in a New International Economy.* Armonk, NY: M. E. Sharpe, 2005.

Besley, T., and A. R. Levinson. "The Role of Informal Finance in Household Capital Accumulation: Evidence from Taiwan." *Economic Journal*, January 1996.

Brandt, K. "Economic Development: Lessons of Statecraft in Taiwan." *Orbis*, Winter 1968.

Caldwell, J. Alexander. "The Financial System in Taiwan: Structure, Functions, and Issues for the Future." *Asian Survey*, August 1976.

Chan, S. "Defense Burden and Economic Growth: Unraveling the Taiwanese Enigma." *American Political Science Review*, September 1988.

———. "The Mouse That Roared: Taiwan's Management of Trade Relations with the United States." *Comparative Political Studies*, October 1987.

Chan, S., and C. Clark. *Flexibility, Foresight, and Fortuna in Taiwan's Development: Navigating between Scylla and Charybdis.* London: Routledge, 1992.

Chan, S., et al. "State Entrepreneurship, Foreign Investment, Export Expansion, and Economic Growth: Grander Causality in Taiwan's Development." *Journal of Conflict Resolution*, March 1990.

Chan, V. L., et al. "External Economies in Taiwan's Manufacturing Industries." *Contemporary Economic Policy*, October 1995.

Chang, David W. "U.S. Aid and Economic Growth in Taiwan." *Asian Survey*, March 1965.

Chao, Chieh-chien. "Economic Growth, Trade Development and Foreign Investment in Taiwan, ROC." *Industry of Free China*, April 1985.

Chase, Michael, Kevin Pollpeter, and James C. Mulvenon. *Shanghaied?: The Economic and Political Implications of the Flow of Information Technology and Investment across the Taiwan Strait.* Santa Monica: Rand Corporation, 2004.

Chen, J. R. "The Effects of Land Reform on the Rice Sector and Economic Development in Taiwan." *World Development*, November 1994.

Chen, Shih-meng S., et al. *Disintegrating KMT-State Capitalism: A Closer Look at Privatizing Taiwan's State- and Party-Owned Enterprises.* Taipei: Taipei Society, 1991.

Chen, Shyh-Jer, and Koji Taira. "Industrial Democracy, Economic Growth, and Income Distribution in Taiwan." *American Asian Review*, Winter 1995.

Chen, T. J., and D. P. Tang. "Export Performance and Productivity Growth: The Case of Taiwan." *Economic Development and Cultural Change*, April 1990.

Chen, Thomas P., and K. Thomas Liaw. "Bank Deposit Insurance Policies: An International Overview and Recommendations for Taiwan." *American Asian Review*, Winter 1993.

Chen, X. "Taiwan Investments in China and Southeast Asia: 'Go West, but Also Go South.'" *Asian Survey*, May 1996.

Cheng, Chen. *Land Reform in Taiwan*. Taipei: China Publishing, 1961.

Cheng, Chu-yuan. "Economic Development in Taiwan and Mainland China: A Comparison of Strategies and Performance." *Asian Affairs*, Spring 1983.

———. "Economic Relations across the Taiwan Straits: Progress, Effects and Prospects." *American Asian Review*, Spring 1997.

———. "The Role of the ROC in International Economic and Financial Organizations." *American Asian Review*, Winter 1995.

———. "Taiwan's Economy in Transition: New Challenges and Prospects." *Asian Outlook*, July–August 1991.

———. "Taiwan's Economy in Transition: Structural Changes and Prospects." *American Asian Review*, Fall 1996.

———. "United States-Taiwan Economic Relations: Trade and Investment." *Columbia Journal of World Business*, Spring 1986.

Cheng, Linsun. "Modern Banks and Government Debts in the Republican China." *American Journal of Chinese Studies*, October 1998.

Cheng, Peter P. "Taiwan: Protective Adjustment Economy." *Asian Survey*, January 1975.

Cheng, T. J. "Transforming Taiwan's Economic Structure in the 20th Century." *China Quarterly*, March 2001.

Chi, Schive. *The Foreign Factor: The Multinational Corporation's Contribution to the Economic Modernization of the Republic of China*. Stanford, CA: Hoover Institution Press, 1990.

Chow, Peter C. Y. "Money Market Segmentation and Financial Liberalization: A Revised Financial Repression Thesis in Taiwan." *American Journal of Chinese Studies*, April 1987.

———. "The Role of Taiwan's Economy in the International Economic Community: The ROC's Bid for Memberships in the IMF and World Bank." *American Asian Review*, Summer 1997.

———. *Taiwan in the Global Economy: From an Agrarian Economy to an Exporter of High-Tech Products*. Westport, CT: Praeger, 2002.

Chow, Peter C. Y., and Bates Gill. *Weathering the Storm: Taiwan, Its Neighbors, and the Asian Financial Crisis*. Washington, DC: Brookings Institution Press, 2000.

Chu, W. W. "Causes of Growth: A Study of Taiwan's Bicycle Industry." *Cambridge Journal of Economics*, January 1997.

———. "Export-Led Growth and Import Dependence: The Case of Taiwan, 1969–81." *Journal of Development Economics*, March 1988.

——. "Import Substitution and Export-Led Growth: A Study of Taiwan's Petrochemical Industry." *World Development*, May 1994.

Chu, Yun-peng. "Growth, Distribution, and Stability in Taiwan." *Industry of Free China*, October 1984.

Chuang, Chi-an. "Special Characteristics of Taiwanese Entrepreneurship." *American Journal of Chinese Studies*, April 1994.

Chuang, Y. C. "Identifying the Sources of Growth in Taiwan's Manufacturing Industry." *Journal of Development Studies*, February 1996.

Clark, Cal. "Dynamics of Development in Taiwan: Re-conceptualizing State and Market in National Competitiveness." *American Journal of Chinese Studies*, April 1994.

——. "Economic Development in Taiwan: A Model of a Political Economy." *Journal of Asian and African Studies*, January–April 1987.

——. *Taiwan's Development: Implications for Contending Political Economy Paradigms*. Westport, CT: Greenwood Press, 1989.

——. "The Taiwan Exception: Implications for Contending Political Economy Paradigms." *International Studies Quarterly*, September 1987.

Courtenay, P. "Taiwan's Hsinchu Science-Based Industrial Park." *Geography*, October 1993.

Cyr, Arthur I. *Taiwan: The Commercial State*. Baltimore: School of Law, University of Maryland, 2005.

DeGlopper, Donald R. *Lukang: Commerce and Community in a Chinese City*. New York: State University of New York Press, 1995.

De Melo, J., and L. A. Winters. "Do Exporters Gain from VERs?" *European Economic Review*, October 1993.

Deng, P. "Taiwan's Restriction of Investment in China in the 1990s: A Relative Gains Approach." *Asian Survey*, 2000.

Downen, Robert L. *To Bridge the Taiwan Strait*. Washington, DC: Council for Social and Economic Studies, 1982.

Etherington, D. M., and K. Foster. "The Structural Transformation of Taiwan's Tea Industry [1860 to the Present]." *World Development*, March 1992.

Fei, John, et al. *Growth with Equity: The Taiwan Case*. New York: Oxford University Press, 1979.

Ferdinand, Peter, ed. *Take-Off for Taiwan*. London: Pinter, 1996.

Fransman, Martin. "International Competitiveness, Technical Change, and the State: The Machine Tool Industry in Taiwan and Japan." *World Development*, December 1986.

Freeberne, Michael. "Lonely Taiwan Sows for the Future." *Geographical Magazine*, January 1972.

Futurist. "The De-farming of Taiwan." January–February 1995.

Galenson, Walter, ed. *Economic Growth and Structural Change in Taiwan: The Postwar Experience of the Republic of China*. Ithaca, NY: Cornell University Press, 1979.

Glass, Sheppard. "Some Effects of Formosa's Economic Growth." *China Quarterly*, July–September 1963.

Grad, Andrew J. *Formosa Today: An Analysis of the Economic Development and Strategic Importance of Japan's Tropical Colony*. New York: AMS Press, 1978.

Greenhalgh, Susan M., and Edwin A. Winkler. *Approaches to the Political Economy of Taiwan*. Armonk, NY: M. E. Sharpe, 1987.

Gregor, A. James. *Ideology and Development: Sun Yat-sen and the Economic History of Taiwan*. Berkeley, CA: Institute of East Asian Studies, 1982.

Gregor, A. James, and Maria H. Chang. *Essays on Sun Yat-sen and the Economic Development of Taiwan*. Baltimore: School of Law, University of Maryland, 1983.

He, Jia, and Christina Liu. "Predictability of Taiwan Stock Returns Using World, Pacific-Basin, and Country-Specific Macro Variables." *American Asian Review*, Winter 1993.

Ho, Chi-min. *Agricultural Development of Taiwan, 1903–1970*. Nashville, TN: Vanderbilt University Press, 1966.

Ho, Samuel P. S. "The Economic Development of Colonial Taiwan: Evidence and Interpretation." *Journal of Asian Studies*, February 1975.

———. *Economic Development of Taiwan, 1860–1970*. New Haven, CT: Yale University Press, 1978.

Howe, C. "The Taiwan Economy: The Transition to Maturity and the Political Economy of Its Changing International Status." *China Quarterly*, December 1996.

———. "Taiwan in the 20th Century: Model or Victim? Development Problems in a Small Asian Economy." *China Quarterly*, March 2001.

Hsieh, S. C., and T. H. Lee. *Agricultural Development and Its Contributions to Economic Growth in Taiwan—Input-Output and Productivity Analysis of Taiwan Agricultural Development*. Taipei: Joint Commission on Rural Construction, 1966.

Hsing, Mo-huan. *Taiwan: Industrialization and Trade Policies*. London: Oxford University Press, 1971.

Hsing, Y. "Blood, Thicker Than Water: Interpersonal Relations and Taiwanese Investment in Southern China." *Environment and Planning*, December 1996.

Hsu, D. Y. C., and J. T. Hwang. "Labor Shortage and Unutilized Labor Reserve in Taiwan." *Journal of Contemporary Asia* 22, no. 4 (1992).

Hu, J. C. "Taiwan: An Emerging Hub for the East Asian Regional Economy." *Journal of Social, Political, and Economic Studies*, Fall 1996.

Huang, C. "Joint Ventures between State Enterprises and Multinational Corporations in Taiwan." *International Studies Notes* 15 (1990).

Huang, S. W. "Structural Change in Taiwan's Agricultural Economy." *Economic Development and Cultural Change*, October 1993.

Hung, R. "The Great U-Turn in Taiwan: Economic Restructuring and a Surge in Inequality." *Journal of Contemporary Asia* 26, no. 2 (1996).

Hwang, Y. Dolly. *The Rise of a New World Economic Power: Postwar Taiwan.* Westport, CT: Greenwood Press, 1991.

Jacoby, Neil H. *U.S. Aid to Taiwan: A Study of Foreign Aid, Self-Help and Development.* New York: Praeger, 1966.

Jenkins, R. "The Political Economy of Industrial Policy: Automobile Manufacture in the Newly Industrializing Economies." *Cambridge Journal of Economics,* October 1995.

Ka, C. M., and M. Selden. "Original Accumulation Equity and Late Industrialization: The Cases of Socialist China and Capitalist Taiwan." *World Development,* October–November 1986.

Kau, Yin-mao. "The Power Structure in Taiwan's Political Economy." *Asian Survey,* March 1996.

Keefer, James F. *Taiwan's Agricultural Growth during the 1970's.* Washington, DC: Economic Research Service, U.S. Department of Agriculture, 1971.

Klatt, Werner. "An Asian Success Story: Peaceful Agricultural Revolution in Taiwan." *Issues and Studies,* April 1972.

Kleingartner, Archie, and Hsueh-yu Peng. "Taiwan: An Exploration of Labor Relations in Transition." *British Journal of Industrial Relations* 29, no. 3 (1991).

Koo, Anthony Y. C. *The Role of Land Reform in Economic Development: A Case Study of Taiwan.* New York: Praeger, 1968.

Kuo, Shirley W. Y. *The Taiwan Economy in Transition.* Boulder, CO: Westview Press, 1983.

——. *The Taiwan Success Story: Rapid Growth with Improved Distribution in the Republic of China, 1952–1979.* Boulder, CO: Westview Press, 1981.

Kuo, Wan Yong. "Technical Change, Foreign Investment and Growth in the Manufacturing Industries, 1952–1970." In *The Economic Development of East and Southeast Asia,* ed. Shinichi Ichimura. Honolulu: University of Hawaii Press, 1967.

Lavrencic, Karl. "Taiwan: Will Politics Spoil the Economic Miracle?" *World Today,* January 1985.

Lee, Teng-hui. *Intersectoral Capital Flows in the Economic Development of Taiwan, 1895–1960.* Ithaca, NY: Cornell University Press, 1971.

Leng, Tse-Kang. "State-Business Relations and Taiwan's Mainland Economic Policy." *American Journal of Chinese Studies,* April 1994.

Levenson, A. R., and T. Besley. "The Anatomy of an Informal Financial Market: Rosca Participation in Taiwan." *Journal of Development Economics,* October 1996.

Li, K. T. "Contributions of Women in the Labor Force to Economic Development in Taiwan, the Republic of China." *Industry of Free China,* August 1985.

———. "The State of the Economic Contest." *Industry of Free China*, October 1982.

Li, Kuo-ting. *The Evolution of Policy behind Taiwan's Development Success.* New Haven, CT: Yale University Press, 1988.

Li, Kwoh-ting, and Tzong-shian Yu, eds. *Experiences and Lessons of Economic Development on Taiwan.* Taipei: Academia Sinica, 1980.

Liang, K. S., and C. I. Hou Liang. "Development Policy Formation and Future Policy Priorities in the Republic of China." *Economic Development and Cultural Change*, April 1988.

Liang, Kuo-shu. "Financial Reforms Recommended by the Economic Reform Committee, Republic of China." *Industry of Free China*, March 1986.

Lin, Ching-yuan. *Industrialization in Taiwan, 1946–1972: Trade and Import Substitution Policies for Developing Countries.* New York: Praeger, 1973.

Lin, S. J., and Y. F. Chang. "Linkage Effects and Environmental Impacts from Oil Consumption Industries in Taiwan." *Journal of Environmental Management*, April 1997.

Linberger, Herbert F., and H. C. Chang. *Farm Information for Modernizing Agriculture: The Taiwan System.* New York: Praeger, 1973.

Liu, Fu-shan. "Agricultural Marketing Improvements in Taiwan." *Industry of Free China*, July 1983.

Liu, L. Y., and W. T. Woo. "Saving Behavior under Imperfect Financial Markets and the Current Account Consequences." *Economic Journal*, May 1994.

Liu, M. C. "Determinants of Taiwan's Trade Liberalization: The Case of a Newly Industrialized Country." *World Development*, June 2002.

Liu, Paul K. C. "Technological Progress, Employment Structure and Income Distribution in Taiwan." *Industry of Free China*, August 1984.

McBeath, Gerald A. *Wealth and Freedom: Taiwan's New Political Economy.* Brookfield, VT: Ashgate, 1998.

Metraux, Daniel E. *Taiwan's Political and Economic Growth in the Late Twentieth Century.* Lewiston, NY: Edwin Mellen Press, 1991.

Mosher, Steven W., ed. *The United States and the Republic of China: Democratic Friends, Economic Partners and Strategic Allies.* New Brunswick, NJ: Transaction Publishers, 1990.

Myers, Ramon H., and Norman Schroder. "America's Economic Stake in Taiwan." *Asian Affairs*, November–December 1975.

Negandhi, Anant R. *Management and Economic Development: The Case of Taiwan.* The Hague: Martinus Nijhoff, 1973.

Niehoff, Justin D. "The Villager as Industrialist: Ideologies of House-hold Manufacturing in Rural Taiwan." *Modern China*, July 1987.

Noble, G. W. "Contending Forces in Taiwan's Economic Policymaking: The Case of Hua Tung Heavy Trucks." *Asian Survey*, June 1987.

Pan, Lien-fan. "The Urban Land Reform in the Republic of China." *Chinese Culture*, March 1975.

Pang, C. K. "The State and Socioeconomic Development in Taiwan since 1949." *Issues and Studies* 26, no. 5 (1990).

Pannell, Clifton W. "Urban Land Consolidation and City Growth in Taiwan." *Pacific Viewpoint*, September 1974.

Pasternak, Burton. *Kinship and Community in Two Chinese Villages*. Stanford, CA: Stanford University Press, 1972.

Pomper, M. A. "The Economy of Taiwan: A Study in Development." *Asian Affairs*, July–August 1976.

——. "Taiwan's Economy and Economic Development." *American Asian Review*, Spring 1996.

Prybyla, Jan S. *The Societal Objective of Wealth, Growth, Stability and Equity in Taiwan*. Baltimore: School of Law, University of Maryland, 1978.

——. "Some Reflections on De-recognition and the Economy of Taiwan." In *Taiwan: One Year after United States-China Normalization*. Washington, DC: U.S. Government Printing Office, 1980.

Rabushka, Alvin. *The New China: Comparative Economic Development in Mainland China, Taiwan, and Hong Kong*. Boulder, CO: Westview Press, 1987.

Ranis, Gustav, Sheng Cheng Hu, and Yun-peng Chu, eds. *The Political Economy of Taiwan's Development into the 21st Century*. Vol. 2. Cheltenham, England: Edward Elgar Publishing, 1998.

Reisen, H., and H. Yeches. "Time-Varying Estimates on the Openness of the Capital Account in Korea and Taiwan." *Journal of Development Economics*, August 1993.

Rock, T. M. "Integrating Environmental and Economic Policy Making in China and Taiwan." *The American Behavioral Scientist*, May 2002.

Rodrik, D. "The 'Paradoxes' of the Successful State." *European Economic Review*, April 1997.

Rostow, W. W. *The World Economy: History and Prospects*. Austin: University of Texas Press, 1978.

Schive, C. *The Foreign Factor: The Multinational Corporation's Contribution to the Economic Modernization of the Republic of China*. Stanford, CA: Hoover Institution Press, 1990.

Seth, Rama, and Robert N. McCauley. "Taiwan's Current Surplus and International Financial Market Linkages." *American Journal of Chinese Studies*, April 1994.

Selya, Roger M. *The Industrialization of Taiwan*. New Brunswick: Transaction Publishers, 1974.

Shen, T. H. *The Sino–American Joint Commission on Rural Reconstruction*. Ithaca, NY: Cornell University Press, 1970.

Silin, R. H. *Leadership and Values: The Organization of Large-Scale Taiwanese Enterprises*. Cambridge, MA: Harvard University Press, 1976.

Simon, Denis F. "Charting Taiwan's Technological Future: The Impact of Globalization and Regionalization." *China Quarterly*, December 1996.

———. *Taiwan, Technology Transfer and Transnationalism: The Political Management of Dependency*. Boulder, CO: Westview Press, 1985.

Simon, Denis, and Michael Kau, eds. *Taiwan: Beyond the Economic Miracle*. Armonk, NY: M. E. Sharpe, 1992.

Steinhoff, Manfred. *Prestige and Profit: The Development of Entrepreneurial Abilities in Taiwan*. Miami, FL: Australian National University Press, 1980.

Tai, Hung-chao. *Land Reforms and Politics: A Comparative Analysis*. Berkeley: University of California Press, 1974.

The Taiwan Development Experience and Its Relevance to Other Countries. Taipei: Kwang Hwa Publishing, 1988.

Tang, S. Y. "Informal Credit Markets and Economic Development in Taiwan." *World Development*, May 1995.

Trindade, V. "The Big Push, Industrialization and International Trade: The Role of Exports." *Journal of Development Economics*, October 2005.

Tsai, M. C. "Dependency, the State and Class in the Neoliberal Transition of Taiwan." *Third World*, June 2001.

Tsay, C. L. "Industrial Restructuring and International Competition in Taiwan." *Environment and Planning* A, January 1993.

———. "Labor Recruitment in Taiwan: A Corporate Strategy in Industrial Restructuring." *Environment and Planning*, April 1994.

Tsiu, T. K. "Taiwan's Approach to Economic Development." *Industry of Free China*, October 1984.

von Gessel, Marinus. "American Businessmen's Views on the Investment Climate in Taiwan, ROC." *Industry of Free China*, April 1980.

Wade, Robert. "Asian Financial Systems as a Challenge to Economics: Lessons from Taiwan." *California Management Review*, Summer 1985.

———. "Managing Trade: Taiwan and South Korea as Challenges to Economics and Political Science." *Comparative Politics*, January 1993.

Wang, N. T., ed. *Taiwan's Enterprises in Global Perspective*. Armonk, NY: M. E. Sharpe, 1992.

Wang, P., and C. K. Yip. "Macroeconomic Effects of Factor Taxation with Endogenous Human Capital Evolution: Theory and Evidence." *Southern Economic Journal*, January 1995.

Wang, Ping, and Yuan-li Wu. "Learning from the EC: The Implications of European Economic Integration for China and Taiwan." *American Journal of Chinese Studies*, October 1996.

Wang, V. W. C. "Developing the Information Industry in Taiwan: Entrepreneurial State, Guerrilla Capitalists, and Accommodative Technologists." *Pacific Affairs*, Winter 1995–1996.

Wang, Yan, and Zhi Wang. "The Impact of Opening Direct Trade across the Taiwan Straits: A Quantitative Assessment." *American Journal of Chinese Studies*, October 1997.

Wang, Zhi, and Francis T. Tuan. "The Impact of China's and Taiwan's WTO Membership on World Trade—a Computable General Equilibrium Analysis." *American Journal of Chinese Studies*, October 1996.

Webb, L. "Taiwan: The Economic Prospects." *Australian Quarterly*, December 1956.

Wheeler, Jimmy W., and Perry L. Wood. *Beyond Recrimination: Perspectives on U.S.–Taiwan Trade Tensions*. Indianapolis: Hudson Institute, 1987.

Winckler, Edwin A., and Susan M. Greenhalgh, eds. *Contending Approaches to the Political Economy of Taiwan*. Armonk, NY: M. E. Sharpe, 1987.

Winn, J. K. "Relational Practices and the Marginalization of Law: Informal Financial Practices of Small Businesses in Taiwan." *Law and Society Review* 28, no. 2 (1994).

Wu, Chung-lih. "Some Measures to Promote a More Balanced Bilateral Trade Relationship between the ROC and the USA—Economic and Political Implications." *International Commerce Bank of China Economic Review*, January–February 1988.

Wu, Kuang-hua, and Chiao Wei-cheng, eds. *JCRR and Agricultural Development in Taiwan*. Taipei: Joint Commission on Rural Construction, 1978.

Wu, Rong-I. "The Survival of Development of Taiwan." *Asian Affairs*, September–October 1973.

———. "Taiwan's Success in Industrialization." Industry of Free China, November 1985.

———. "Trade Liberalization and Economic Development in Taiwan." *American Journal of Chinese Studies*, April 1987.

Wu, Yuan-li. *Becoming an Industrialized Nation: ROC's Development on Taiwan*. New York: Praeger, 1985.

Wu, Yuan-li, and Kung-chia Yeh, eds. *Growth, Distribution and Social Change: Essays on the Economics of the Republic of China*. Baltimore: School of Law, University of Maryland, 1978.

———. "Income Distribution in the Process of Economic Growth of the Republic of China." In *Growth Distribution, and Societal Change: Essays on the Economy of the Republic of China*, ed. Yuan-li Wu and Yeh Kung-chia. Baltimore: School of Law, University of Maryland, 1978.

Xu, D. "The KMT Party's Enterprises in Taiwan." *Modern Asian Studies*, May 1997.

Yang, Martin M. C. *Socio-economic Results of Land Reform in Taiwan*. Honolulu: East-West Center Press, 1970.

Yin, Jason Z., and Charles C. Yen. "An Assessment of the Economic Relations between Taiwan and Mainland China." *American Asian Review*, Winter 1992.

Yip, C. K., and P. Wang. "Taxation and Economic Growth: The Case of Taiwan." *The American Journal of Economics and Sociology*, July 1992.

Young, Frank J. "Problems of Manpower Development in Taiwan." *Asian Survey*, August 1976.

Yu, Tzong-shian. "The Relationship between the Government and the Private Sector in the Process of Economic Development in Taiwan, ROC." *Industry of Free China*, October 1985.

Yuan, Mei-ling. "The Study of Labor-Management Conference in Taiwan." *Quarterly Journal of Labor* 102 (1991).

Yum, Kwang Sup. *Successful Economic Development of the Republic of China in Taiwan*. New York: Vantage Press, 1968.

POLITICS

Aberbach, Joel, et al., eds. *The Role of the State in Taiwan's Development*. Armonk, NY: M. E. Sharpe, 1994.

Alagappa, Muthiah, ed. *Taiwan's Presidential Politics: Democratization and Cross Strait Relations in the Twenty-first Century*. Armonk, NY: M. E. Sharpe, 2001.

Appleton, S. C. "Taiwan: The Year It Finally Happened." *Asian Studies*, January 1972.

Aspalter, Christian. *Democratization and Welfare State Development in Taiwan*. Burlington, VT: Ashgate, 2002.

Bader, William B., and Jeffrey T. Bergner, eds. *The Taiwan Relations Act: A Decade of Implementation*. Indianapolis: Hudson Institute, 1989.

Bate, H. Maclear. *Report from Formosa*. Philadelphia: Century Bookbindery, 1952.

Bellows, Thomas J. *Taiwan and Mainland China: Democratization, Political Participation and Economic Development in the 1990s*. New York: Center for Asian Studies, St. John's University, 2000.

Bosco, J. "Faction vs. Ideology: Mobilization Strategies in Taiwan's Elections." *China Quarterly*, March 1994.

Brindley, Thomas A. "The China Youth Corps: Democratization in Progress." *American Journal of Chinese Studies*, October 1994.

Brodsgaard, Erik Kjeld, and Susan Young. *State Capacity in East Asia: Japan, Taiwan, China, and Vietnam*. New York: Oxford University Press, 2000.

Brown, Deborah A. "Democracy in the Republic of China on Taiwan." *American Asian Review*, Fall 1997.

Buxbaum, David C., ed. *Chinese Family Law and Social Change*. Seattle: University of Washington Press, 1978.

Cabestan, J. P. "Taiwan in 1999: A Difficult Year for the Island and the Kuomintang." *Asian Survey*, January–February 2000.

Chang, David W. "Minor Parties in Recent Chinese Political Development in the PRC and the ROC on Taiwan." *American Journal of Chinese Studies*, April 1987.

Chang, King-yuh, ed. *The Democratization of the Republic of China: Process, System, and Impact*. Taipei: Institute of International Relations, 1992.

Chang, Maria Hsia. "Political Succession in the Republic of China on Taiwan." *Asian Survey*, April 1984.

Chang, Ya-yun. "A Comparative Study between the Five-Power Constitution and Other Constitutions." *China Forum*, January 1975.

Chao, L., and R. H. Myers. "The First Chinese Democracy: Political Development of the Republic of China on Taiwan, 1986–1994." *Asian Survey*, March 1994.

Chao, L., et al. "Promoting Effective Democracy, Chinese Style: Taiwan's National Development Conference." *Asian Survey*, July 1997.

Chao, Linda, and Bruce J. Dickson. *Assessing the Lee Teng-hui Legacy in Taiwan's Politics: Democratic Consolidation and External Relations*. Armonk, NY: M. E. Sharpe, 2002.

Chao, Linda, and Ramon H. Myers. *Democracy's New Leaders in the Republic of China*. Stanford, CA: Hoover Institution Press, 1996.

———. *The First Chinese Democracy: Political Life in the Republic of China on Taiwan*. Baltimore, MD: Johns Hopkins University Press, 1998.

Chao, Linda, Ramon H. Myers, and Zhang Jialin. *Some Implications of the Turnover of Political Power in Taiwan*. Stanford, CA: Hoover Institution, 2002.

Chou, Y., and A. J. Nathan. "Democratizing Transition in Taiwan." *Asian Survey*, March 1987.

Cheng, L., and L. White. "Elite Transformation and Modern Change in Mainland China and Taiwan: Empirical Data and the Theory of Technocracy." *China Quarterly*, March 1990.

Cheng, Sheldon S. D. "A Study of the Temporary Provisions of the Constitution of the Republic of China." *Chinese Culture*, December 1972.

Cheng, T. J. "Democratizing the Quasi-Leninist Regime in Taiwan." *World Politics*, July 1989.

Cheng, T. J., and S. Haggard, eds. *Political Change in Taiwan*. Boulder, CO: Lynne Rienner Publishers, 1992.

Chiu, Hungdah, ed. *China and the Taiwan Issue*. New York: Praeger Publishers, 1979.

——. "Recent Constitutional Development in the Republic of China on Taiwan." *American Journal of Chinese Studies*, October 1992.

Chu, J. J. "Political Liberalization and the Rise of Taiwanese Labor Radicalism." *Journal of Contemporary Asia* 23, no. 2 (1993).

Chu, Y. H. "Political Development in 20th-Century Taiwan: State-Building, Regime Transformation and the Construction of National Identity." *China Quarterly*, March 2001.

——. "Taiwan's National Identity Politics and the Prospect of Cross-Strait Relations." *Asian Survey*, July–August 2004.

——. "Taiwan's Unique Challenges." *Journal of Democracy*, July 1996.

Chun, A. "Democracy as Hegemony, Globalization as Indigenization, or the 'Culture' in Taiwanese National Politics." *Journal of Asian and African Studies*, 2000.

Clark, Cal. "Taiwan's Democratization and Political Transformation: Toward the 21st Century and Beyond." *American Asian Review*, Spring 1998.

Cole, A. B. "Political Roles of Taiwanese Enterprise." *Asian Survey*, September 1967.

Copper, John F. *As Taiwan Approaches the New Millennium: Essays on Politics and Foreign Affairs.* Lanham, MD: University Press of America, 1999.

——. *Consolidating Taiwan's Democracy.* Lanham, MD: University Press of America, 2005.

——. "Ending Martial Law in Taiwan: Implications and Prospects." *Journal of Northeast Asian Studies*, Summer 1988.

——. "The KMT's 14th Party Congress: Toward Unity or Disunity." *American Journal of Chinese Studies*, October 1994.

——. "Politics in Taiwan." In *Survey of Recent Developments in China (Mainland and Taiwan), 1985–86*, ed. Hungdah Chiu. Baltimore: School of Law, University of Maryland, 1987.

——. *A Quiet Revolution: Political Development in the Republic of China.* Washington, DC: Ethics and Public Policy Center, 1988.

——. "Remembering President Chiang-kuo." *Asian Thought and Society*, January 1988.

——. "The Role of Minor Political Parties in Taiwan." *World Affairs*, Winter 1993.

——, ed. *Taiwan in Troubled Times: Essays on the Chen Shui-bian Presidency.* Singapore: World Scientific, 2002.

——. *Taiwan: Nation State or Province?* 4th ed. Boulder, CO: Westview Press, 2003.

——. "Taiwan: New Challenges to Development." *Current History*, April 1986.

——. *The Taiwan Political Miracle: Essays on Political Development, Elections and Foreign Relations.* Lanham, MD: University Press of America, 1997.

——. *Taiwan's Mid-1990s Elections: Taking the Final Steps to Democracy.* Westport, CT: Praeger Publisher, 1998.

——. "Taiwan's 1985 Elections." *Asian Affairs*, Spring 1986.

——. "Taiwan's 1986 National Election: Pushing Democracy Ahead." *Asian Thought and Society*, July 1987.

——. "Taiwan's 1989 Elections: Pushing Democracy Ahead." *Journal of Northeast Asian Studies*, Winter 1990.

——. *Taiwan's 1991 and 1992 Non-Supplemental Elections: Reaching a Higher State of Democracy.* Lanham, MD: University Press of America, 1994.

——. "Taiwan's 1991 National Assembly Election." *Journal of Northeast Asian Studies*, Spring 1991.

——. "Taiwan's 1992 Legislative Yuan Election." *World Affairs*, Fall 1992.

——. *Taiwan's Recent Elections: Fulfilling the Democratic Promise.* Baltimore: School of Law, University of Maryland, 1990.

Copper, John F., with George P. Chen. *Taiwan's Elections: Political Development and Democratization in the Republic of China.* Baltimore: School of Law, University of Maryland, 1985.

Cox, G. W. "Is the Single Nontransferable Vote Super proportional? Evidence from Japan and Taiwan." *American Journal of Political Science*, August 1996.

Cox, G. W., and E. M. S. Niou. "Seat Bonuses under the Single Nontransferable Vote System: Evidence from Japan and Taiwan." *Comparative Politics*, January 1994.

Dreyer, J. T. "Taiwan's December 1991 Election." *World Affairs*, Fall 1992.

Durdin, Tillman. "Chiang Ching-kuo and Taiwan: A Profile." *Orbis*, Winter 1975.

Fa, Jyh-pin. *A Comparative Study of Judicial Review under Nationalist Chinese and American Constitutional Law.* Baltimore: School of Law, University of Maryland, 1980.

Gregor, A. James, and Maria H. Chang. *The Republic of China and U.S. Policy: A Study in Human Rights.* Washington, DC: Ethics and Public Policy Center, 1983.

——. "The Taiwan Independence Movement: The Failure of Political Persuasion." *Political Communication and Persuasion*, 1985.

Gurtov, Melvin. "Recent Developments on Formosa." *China Quarterly*, July–September 1967.

——. "Taiwan in 1966: Political Rigidity, Economic Growth." *Asian Survey*, January 1967.

Guy, Nancy. *Peking Opera and Politics in Taiwan.* Urbana: University of Illinois Press, 2005.

Haggard, Stephan, and Mathew D. McCubbins. *Presidents, Parliaments, and Policy.* Cambridge: Cambridge University Press, 2001.

Harrison, Selig S. "Taiwan after Chiang Ching-kuo." *Foreign Affairs*, Spring 1988.

Hickman, John. "Constituency Magnitude as a Determinant of Seat/Vote Proportionality and Electoral Competition in Taiwan's 1992 and 1995 Legislative Yuan Elections." *American Asian Review*, Summer 1998.

Hicks, N. "A Tale of Two Chinas." *Geographic Magazine*, January 1993.

Hood, S. J. "Political Change in Taiwan: The Rise of Kuomintang Factions." *Asian Survey*, May 1996.

Hsieh, Erh-yi. "The System of Punishment of Public Officials." *Chinese Journal of Administration*, January 1965.

Hsieh, John Fuh-sheng, Dean P. Lacy, and Emerson M. S. Niou. "Economic Voting in the 1994 Elections." *American Asian Review*, Summer 1996.

Hsu, Cheng-hsi. "The American and Chinese Legislative Systems." *Sino–American Relations*, Winter 1975.

Hu, Jason C., ed. *Quiet Revolutions on Taiwan, Republic of China*. Taipei: Kwang Hwa Publishing Company, 1994.

Huang, Mab. *Intellectual Ferment for Political Reforms in Taiwan, 1971–1973*. Ann Arbor: University of Michigan Center for Chinese Studies, 1976 (Chinese).

Huang, Teh-fu. "Electoral Competition and the Evolution of the Kuomintang." *Issues and Studies*, May 1995.

Huang, Teh-fu, and Emerson M. S. Niou. "Democratic Consolidation and the Party System in Taiwan." *American Asian Review*, Fall 1996.

Huang, Y. H. "PRSA: Scale Development for Exploring the Impetus of Public Relations Strategies." *Journalism and Mass Communication Quarterly*, Summer 2004.

Hughes, Christopher. *Taiwan and Chinese Nationalism: National Identity and Status in International Society*. London: Routledge, 1997.

Ijiri, H. "Slighting Taiwan Is behind the Times." *Japan Quarterly*, January–March 1989.

Israel, John. "Politics on Formosa." *China Quarterly*, July–September 1963.

Jacobs, J. Bruce. "Paradoxes in the Politics of Taiwan: Lessons for Comparative Politics." *Politics*, November 1978.

———. "Recent Leadership and Political Trends in Taiwan." *China Quarterly*, January–March 1971.

———. "Taiwan's Press: Political Communication Link and Research Resource." *China Quarterly*, December 1976.

Kagan, Richard C. "Taiwan: Another Greece." *Dissent*, January–February 1969.

Kallgren, Joyce K. "Nationalist China: Political Inflexibility and Economic Accommodation." *Asian Survey*, January 1964.

———. "Nationalist China: Problems of a Modernizing Taiwan." *Asian Survey*, January 1965.

Kao, Ying-mao, and Hungdah Chiu. *The New Reforms ahead of the Republic of China*. Long Island, NY: China Times Cultural Foundation, 1989.

Kemenade, W. van. "Taiwan, Voting for Trouble?" *Washington Quarterly*, Spring 2000.

Kuo, C. T. "Taiwan's Distorted Democracy in Comparative Perspective." *Journal of Asian and African Studies*, 26 October 2000.

Kuo, P. "Taiwan's News Media: Its Role in Democratization." *World Affairs*, Winter 1993.

Lasater, Martin L. *Security of Taiwan: Unraveling the Dilemma*. Washington, DC: Center for Strategic and International Studies, 1982.

Lavrencic, K. "Taiwan: Will Politics Spoil the Economic Miracle?" *World Today*, January 1985.

Lee, Kwo-wei. "A Study of Social Background and Recruitment Process of Local Political Decision-Makers in Taiwan." *Indian Journal of Public Administration*, April–June 1972.

Lee, Wei-chin, and Te-Yu Wang. *Sayonara to the Lee Teng-hui Era: Politics in Taiwan, 1988–2000*. Lanham, MD: University Press of America, 2003.

Leng, S. C., and C. Y. Lin. "Political Change on Taiwan: Transition to Democracy." *China Quarterly*, December 1993.

Leng, Shao-chuan. *Chiang Ching-kuo's Leadership in the Development of the Republic of China on Taiwan*. Lanham, MD: University Press of America, 1993.

Lerman, Arthur J. "National Elite and Local Politicians in Taiwan." *American Political Science Review*, December 1977.

———. *Taiwan's Politics: The Provincial Assemblymen's World*. Washington, DC: University Press of America, 1978.

Li, Wen-lang. "Party Competition and Electoral Success in a Confucian State." *American Journal of Chinese Studies*, October 1992.

Lin, C. P., ed. "Democracy in Taiwan (symposium)." *World Affairs*, Winter 1993.

Lin, T. M., et al. "Conflict Displacement and Regime Transition in Taiwan: A Spatial Analysis." *World Politics*, July 1996.

Linebarger, Paul M. A. "The Republic of China on Taiwan: A Descriptive Appraisal." *World Affairs*, Spring 1963.

Ling, L. H. M., and C. Y. Shih. "Confucianism with a Liberal Face: The Meaning of Democratic Politics in Postcolonial Taiwan." *The Review of Politics*, Winter 1998.

Ling, T., and R. H. Myers. "Winds of Democracy: The 1989 Taiwan Elections." *Asian Survey*, April 1990.

———. "Surviving the Rough-and-Tumble of Presidential Politics in an Emerging Democracy: The 1990 Elections in the Republic of China on Taiwan." *China Quarterly*, March 1992.

Long, S. "Taiwan's National Assembly Elections." *China Quarterly*, March 1992.

Maguire, Keith, and Robert Gordon. *The Rise of Modern Taiwan: Government and Politics in the Republic of China*. Abington, England: Ashgate, 1998.

Mancall, Mark. "Succession and Myth in Taiwan." *Journal of International Affairs*, 1964.

Mason, Bruce B. *Local Government in Taiwan: Some Observations*. Tempe: Bureau of Government Research, Arizona State University, 1964.

McBeath, Gerald A. "Transformation of the Chinese Nationalist Party (KMT): Adjusting to Liberalization." *American Journal of Chinese Studies*, October 1997.

Meisner, Maurice. "The Development of Formosan Nationalism." *China Quarterly*, July–September 1963.

Mendel, Douglas. *The Politics of Formosan Nationalism*. Berkeley: University of California Press, 1970.

Moody, Peter R. *Opposition and Dissent in Contemporary China*. Stanford, CA: Hoover Institute Press, 1977.

———. *Political Change in Taiwan: A Study of Ruling Party Adaptability*. New York: Praeger, 1992.

Moon, E. P. "Single Non-transferable Vote Methods in Taiwan in 1996: Effects of an Electoral System." *Asian Survey*, July 1997.

Myers, R. H. "A New Chinese Civilization: The Evolution of the Republic of China on Taiwan." *China Quarterly*, December 1996.

———. "Political Theory and Recent Political Developments in the Republic of China." *Asian Survey*, September 1987.

Nathan, A. J. "The Legislative Yuan Elections in Taiwan: Consequences of the Electoral System." *Asian Survey*, April 1993.

Niou, E. M. S. "Understanding Taiwan Independence and Its Policy Implications." *Asian Survey*, July–August 2004.

Obeng, Samuel Gyasi, and Beverly Hartford. *Surviving through Obliqueness: Language of Politics in Emerging Democracies*. New York: Nova Science Publishers, 2002.

Omestad, T. "Dateline Taiwan: A Dynasty Ends." *Foreign Policy*, Summer 1988.

Ong, Joktik. "A Formosan's View of the Formosan Independence Movement." *China Quarterly*, July–September 1963.

Peng, Ming-min. "Political Offenses in Taiwan: Laws and Problems." *China Quarterly*, June–September 1971.

———. *A Taste of Freedom; Memoirs of a Formosan Independence Leader*. New York: Holt, Rinehart & Winston, 1972.

Rankin, Karl L. *China Assignment*. Seattle: University of Washington Press, 1967.

Ravenholt, A. "Formosa Today." *Foreign Affairs*, July 1952.

Rigger, S. "The Democratic Progressive Party in 2000: Obstacles and Opportunities." *China Quarterly*, December 2001.

Rigger, Shelley. *From Opposition to Power: Taiwan's Democratic Progressive Party*. Boulder, CO: Lynne Rienner, 2001.

——. *Politics in Taiwan: Voting for Democracy*. London: Routledge, 1999.

——. "The Risk of Reform: Factional Conflict in Taiwan's 1989 Local Elections." *American Journal of Chinese Studies*, October 1994.

——. "Taiwan's Lee Teng-hui Complex." *Current History*, September 1996.

Riggs, Fred W. *Formosa under Chinese Nationalist Rule*. New York: Octagon Books, 1972.

Robinson, J. A., and D. Brown. "Taiwan's 2000 Presidential Election." *Orbis*, Fall 2000.

Robinson, James A. "Domestic Politics in Taiwan's U.N. Aspirations." *American Asian Review*, Fall 1995.

——. "The KMT as a Leninist Regime: Prolegomenon to Devolutionary Leadership through Institutions." *Political Chronicle* 3, no. 1 (1991).

——. "Lee Teng-hui and Taiwan's Political Development." *American Asian Review*, Spring 1996.

——. "Local Elections in Taiwan, 1993–94: Appraising Steps in Democratization." *Political Chronicle* 6, no. 2 (1994).

——. "Myth and Taiwan Politics." *American Asian Review*, Summer 1996.

——. "Taiwan's 1995 Legislative Yuan Election: Appraising Steps in Democratization." *American Asian Review*, Fall 1996.

——. "Taiwan's 1996 National Assembly and Presidential Elections: Appraising Steps in Democratization." *American Asian Review*, Spring 1998.

Robinson, James A., and Julian Baum. "Party Primaries in Taiwan: Footnote or Text in Democratization." *Asian Affairs*, Summer 1993.

Rudolph, Jorg M. *Media Coverage on Taiwan in the People's Republic of China*. Baltimore: School of Law, University of Maryland, 1983.

Schafferer, Christian. *The Power of the Ballot Box: Political Development and Election Campaigning in Taiwan*. Lanham, MD: Lexington Books, 2003.

Shaw, Y. M. "Taiwan: A View from Taipei." *Foreign Affairs*, Summer 1985.

Shaw, Yu-ming. *Beyond the Economic Miracle: Reflections on the Developmental Experience of the Republic of China on Taiwan*. Taipei: Kwang Hwa Publishing, 1988.

Shin, D. C., and H. Shyu. "Political Ambivalence in South Korea and Taiwan." *Journal of Democracy*, July 1997.

Sicherman, H. "An Interview with President Lee Teng-hui of the Republic of China on Taiwan." *Orbis*, Fall 1995.

Simon, S. "Domestic and International Considerations of Taiwan's 2004 Presidential Election: An Interdisciplinary Roundtable." *Pacific Affairs*, Winter 2004–2005.

Solarz, Steven J. "Democracy and the Future of Taiwan." *Freedom at Issue*, March–April 1984.

Soong, J. C. Y. "Political Development in the Republic of China on Taiwan, 1985–1992: An Insider's View." *World Affairs*, Fall 1992.

Srinivasen, K. "Taiwan Is Confident of the Future." *Issues and Studies*, April 1972.

Tan, Q., et al. "Local Politics in Taiwan: Democratic Consolidation." *Asian Survey*, May 1996.

Tang, C. P. "Democratizing Urban Politics and Civic Environmentalism in Taiwan." *China Quarterly*, December 2003.

Teng-hui, Lee. "Chinese Culture and Political Renewal." *Journal of Democracy*, October 1995.

Tien, Hung-mao. *The Great Transition: Political and Social Change in the Republic of China*. Stanford, CA: Hoover Institution Press, 1989.

———. "Taiwan in 1986: Reforms under Adversity." In *China Briefing, 1987*, ed. John S. Major and Anthony J. Kane. Boulder, CO: Westview Press, 1987.

———, ed. *Taiwan's Electoral Politics and Democratic Transition: Riding the Third Wave*. Armonk, NY: M. E. Sharpe, 1995.

The Truth about the February 28, 1947 Incident in Taiwan. Taichung: Historical Research Commission of Taiwan Province, 1967.

Tsai, Wen-hui. *Bringing People Back In: Collected Essays on Major Elections in Taiwan at the Turn of the 21st Century*. Baltimore: School of Law, University of Maryland, 2003.

———. *Building a Democratic State in Modernizing Taiwan: The 2001 Legislative Election and the Push for Pluralism*. Baltimore: University of Maryland, 2001.

———. "A Giant Step Forward: The 1996 Presidential Election of the Republic of China on Taiwan." *American Asian Review*, Spring 1997.

Tsang, S. "High Stakes, High Risks." *World Today*, February 2004.

Tsang, Steve, ed. *In the Shadow of China: Political Developments in Taiwan since 1949*. Honolulu: University of Hawaii Press, 1993.

Tung, William L. *The Political Institutions of Modern China*. The Hague: Martinus Nijhoff, 1968.

Wachman, Alan M. *Taiwan: National Identity and Democratization*. Armonk, NY: M. E. Sharpe, 1994.

Wang, Gung-hsing. "Nationalist Government Policies, 1949–1951." *Annals of the American Academy of Political and Social Science*, September 1951.

Wang, J.-H. "World City Formation, Geopolitics, and Local Political Process: Taipei's Ambiguous Development." *International Journal of Urban and Regional Research*, June 2004.

Weiss, J. "'One Country, Two Systems': Beijing's Threat to the Republic of China." *Journal of Social, Political and Economic Studies*, Spring 1988.

Williams, Jack F. *The Taiwan Issue: Proceedings of the Symposium, November 6, 1975*. East Lansing: Asian Studies Center, Michigan State University, 1976.

Winckler, Edwin A. "Institutionalization and Participation in Taiwan: From Hard to Soft Authoritarianism." *China Quarterly*, September 1984.

Wong, J. "Deepening Democracy in Taiwan." *Pacific Affairs*, Summer 2003.

Wright, Teresa. *The Perils of Protest: State Repression and Student Activism in China and Taiwan*. Honolulu: University of Hawaii Press, 2001.

Wu, Jaushieh J. *Taiwan's Democratization: Forces behind the New Momentum*. Hong Kong: Oxford University Press, 1995.

Wu, Y. S. "Marketization of Politics: The Taiwan Experience." *Asian Survey*, April 1989.

Zhao, Suisheng. *Power by Design: Constitution-Making in Nationalist China*. Honolulu: University of Hawaii Press, 1996.

MILITARY AND SECURITY

General

Bellows, Thomas J. "Taiwan's Security and Foreign Affairs: Toward 2000 and Beyond." *American Asian Review*, Spring 1998.

Brands, H. W. "Testing Massive Retaliation: Credibility and Crisis Management in the Taiwan Strait." *International Security*, Spring 1988.

Bullard, Monte. *The Soldier and the Citizen: The Role of the Military in Taiwan's Development*. Armonk, NY: M. E. Sharpe, 1997.

Bush, Richard C. *Untying the Knot: Making Peace in the Taiwan Strait*. Washington, DC: Brookings Institution Press, 2005.

Chan, S. "Defense Burden and Economic Growth: Unraveling the Taiwanese Enigma." *American Political Science Review*, September 1988.

Chang, F. K. "Conventional War across the Taiwan Strait." *Orbis*, Fall 1996.

Chang, Parris, ed. *If China Crosses the Taiwan Strait: The International Response*. Lanham, MD: University Press of America, 1993.

Chang, Thomas. "Forum on Strategic Situation in the Western Pacific and Taiwan Strait." *Asian Outlook*, February 1986.

Chase, M. S. "Defense Reform in Taiwan: Problems and Prospects." *Asian Survey*, May–June 2005.

Chiang, Wei-kuo. *The Strategic Significance of Taiwan in the Global Strategic Picture*. Taipei: Li Min Cultural Publications, 1977.

Chiu, Hungdah. "Growth of the Chinese Military and Its Threat to Taiwan." *American Asian Review*, Spring 1996.

Christensen, T. J. "The Contemporary Security Dilemma: Deterring a Taiwan Conflict." *Washington Quarterly*, Autumn 2002.

Copper, John F. "Taiwan's Military Modernization." *National Security Studies Quarterly*, Winter 2001.

———. "Taiwan's State Security Law: Old Wine in New Bottles." *Journal of Defense and Diplomacy*, October 1987.

Davis, D. R., and S. Chan. "The Security-Welfare Relationship: Longitudinal Evidence from Taiwan." *Journal of Peace Research*, February 1990.

Dreyer, J. T. "Flashpoint in the Taiwan Strait." *Orbis*, Fall 2000.

———. "Regional Security Issues." *Journal of International Affairs*, Winter 1996.

———. "The Republic of China's National Defense." *American Asian Review*, Spring 1996.

———. "The Taiwan Strait Crisis and the R.O.C.'s National Security." *American Asian Review*, Fall 1997.

Edmonds, Martin, and Michael M. Tsai. *Defending Taiwan: The Future Vision of Taiwan's Defense Policy and Military Strategy*. New York: Routledge-Curzon, 2003.

Field, R. H. "Strategic Formosa." *Current History*, April 1949.

Fleming, D. F. "Our Brink of War Diplomacy in the Formosa Strait." *Western Political Quarterly*, September 1956.

Fraser, A. M. "Military Posture and Strategic Policy in the Republic of China." *Asian Affairs*, May–June 1974.

Fravel, M. T. "Towards Civilian Supremacy: Civil-Military Relations in Taiwan's Democratization." *Armed Forces and Society*, Fall 2002.

Frost, Michael S. *Taiwan's Security and United States Policy: Executive and Congressional Strategies*. Baltimore: School of Law, University of Maryland, 1982.

Fu, Jen-kun. *Taiwan and the Geopolitics of the Asian-American Dilemma*. Westport, CT: Greenwood Press, 1992.

Gregor, James, and Maria Hsia Chang. "The Military Defense of the Republic of China." In *Struggles for Change in Mainland China*. Taipei: Institute of International Relations, 1980.

Hearsley, H. J. "An Analysis of the Military Threats across the Taiwan Strait: Fact or Fiction." *Comparative Strategy*, April–June 2000.

Hickey, Dennis Van Vranken. *Taiwan's Security in the Changing International System*. Boulder, CO: Lynne Rienner Publishers, 1997.

———. *United States-Taiwan Security Ties: From Cold War to beyond Containment*. Westport, CT: Praeger, 1994.

Hua, V. "A Cross-Strait Battle Ten Thousand Miles Away." *SAIS Review*, Summer–Fall 2002.

Hughes, J. H. "China's Ballistic Missiles Threat." *Journal of Social, Political, and Economic Studies*, Spring 2002.

———. "The People's Republic of China Confronts Taiwan." *Journal of Social, Political, and Economic Studies*, Summer 2001.

Kallgren, Joyce. "Nationalist China's Armed Forces." *China Quarterly*, July–September 1963.

Kao, Ying-mao M. "Opportunities and Challenges: Taiwan's Diplomacy in the Globalization Era." *Journal of Third World Studies*, Spring 2003.

Kapur, Harish. *Taiwan in a Changing World: Search for Security*. Bloomington, IN: Authorhouse, 2004.

Lasater, Martin L. "The PRC's Force Modernization: Shadow over Taiwan and U.S. Policy." *Strategic Relations*, Winter 1984.

Lin, C. P. "The Military Balance in the Taiwan Straits." *China Quarterly*, June 1996.

Mowery, D. C. "The Taiwan Aerospace-McDonnell Douglas Agreement: A Modest Expansion of the Trend toward Globalization in Aerospace." *Journal of Policy Analysis and Management*, Summer 1992.

O'Hanlon, M. "Why China Cannot Conquer Taiwan." *International Security*, Fall 2000.

Pastor, R. A. "The Paradox of the Double Triangle: Preempting the Next Crises in Taiwan and Cuba." *World Policy Journal*, Spring 2000.

Prestowitz, C. V., Jr. "The McDonnell Douglas–Taiwan Aerospace Agreement: Selling off Our Birthright." *Journal of Policy Analysis and Management*, Summer 1992.

Quester, George H. "Taiwan and Nuclear Proliferation." *Orbis*, Spring 1974.

Ross, R. S. "The Stability of Deterrence in the Taiwan Strait." *National Interest*, Fall 2001.

Roucek, Joseph S. "The Geopolitics of Formosa." *United Asia*, April 1963.

Roy, D. "Tensions in the Taiwan Strait." *Survival*, Spring 2000.

Scobell, A. "Show of Force: Chinese Soldiers, Statesmen, and the 1995–1996 Taiwan Strait Crisis." *Political Science Quarterly*, Summer 2000.

Shambaugh, D. "A Matter of Time: Taiwan's Eroding Military Advantage." *Washington Quarterly*, Spring 2000.

——. "Taiwan's Security: Maintaining Deterrence amid Political Accountability." *China Quarterly*, December 1996.

Tsang, Steve Yui-Sang. *Peace and Security across the Taiwan Strait*. New York: Palgrave Macmillan, 2004.

Tucker, Nancy Bernkopf. *Dangerous Strait: The U.S.–Taiwan–China Crisis*. New York: Columbia University Press, 2005.

U.S. Office of Naval Operations. *Taiwan (Formosa)*. Washington, DC: Naval Department, 1944.

Wang, T. Y. "Taiwan and Theater Missile Defense." *Journal of Social, Political, and Economic Studies*, Fall 2000.

Wang, Y.-K. "Taiwan's Democratization and Cross-Strait Security." *Orbis*, Spring 2004.

Ward, D., et al. "Military Spending and Economic Growth in Taiwan." *Armed Forces and Society*, Summer 1993.

Wu Chen-tsai. "Role of the Republic of China in Collective Defense." In *Problems of Defense of South and East Asia*, ed. K. K. Sinha. Bombay, India: Manaktalas, 1969.

Security Relations with the United States

Campbell, K. M. and D. J. Mitchel. "Crisis in the Taiwan Strait." *Foreign Affairs*, August 2001.

Chan, S. "Extended Deterrence in the Taiwan Strait: Learning from Rationalist Explanations in International Relations." *World Affairs*, Fall 2003.

Chang, Jaw-Ling Joanne, and William W. Boyer. *United States-Taiwan Relations: Twenty Years after the Taiwan Relations Act*. Baltimore: School of Law, University of Maryland, 2000.

Chin, Chu-Kwang. "The U.S.–Japan Joint Declaration: Strategic Implications for Taiwan's Security." *World Affairs*, Winter 1998.

Chiu, Hungdah, Lee Hsing-wei, and Chih-Yu T. Wu. *Implementation of Taiwan Relations Act: An Examination after Twenty Years*. Baltimore: School of Law, University of Maryland, 2001.

Clubb, O. E. "Formosa and the Offshore Islands in American Policy, 1950–1955." *Political Science Quarterly*, December 1959.

Downen, Robert L. *Bridging the Taiwan Strait*. Washington, DC: Council on American Affairs, 1984.

Economist, The. "Keeping Their Balance: How Will China React to US Arms Sales to Taiwan?" 28 April 2001.

Friedberg, A. L. "Will We Abandon Taiwan?" *Commentary*, May 2000.

Frost, Michael S. *Taiwan's Security and United States Policy: Executive and Congressional Strategies*. Baltimore: School of Law, University of Maryland, 1982.

Gregor, A. J. "East Asian Stability and the Defense of the Republic of China on Taiwan." *Comparative Strategy*, October–December 1997.

———. "U.S. Interests in Northeast Asia and the Security of Taiwan." *Strategic Relations*, Winter 1985.

Hickey, Dennis. "U.S. Arms Sales to Taiwan: Institutionalized Ambiguity." *Asian Survey*, December 1986.

Hsu, King-yi. "Sino–American Relations and the Security of Taiwan." *Asian Affairs*, September–October 1978.

Hsu-hsiung, F. "The Transformation of U.S.–Taiwan Military Relations." *Orbis*, Summer 2004.

Ku, Joseph. "Furors over U.S. Decision Denying Sales of FX Fighters to ROC." *Asian Outlook*, February 1982.

Lasater, Martin L. "Future Fighter Sales to Taiwan." *Comparative Strategy*, 1985.

———. *The Taiwan Issue in Sino–American Strategic Relations*. Boulder, CO: Westview Press, 1984.

Lee, David Tawei. *The Making of the Taiwan Relations Act: Twenty Years in Retrospect*. New York: Oxford University Press, 2000.

McClaran, J. P. "U.S. Arms Sales to Taiwan: Implications for the Future of the Sino–U.S. Relationship." *Asian Survey*, July 2000.

Nathan, A. J. "What's Wrong with American Taiwan Policy?" *Washington Quarterly*, Spring 2000.

O'Hanlon, M. "Damn the Torpedoes: Debating Possible U.S. Navy Losses in a Taiwan Scenario." *International Security*, Fall 2004.

Pomper, M. A. "Administration Says House Vote to Shore up Taiwan Relations Endangers U.S. China Strategy." *CQ Weekly*, 5 February 2000.

Pomper, M. A., and L. Nitschke. "Clinton Rejects Taiwan Request for Four Aegis Destroyers." *CQ Weekly*, 22 April 2000.

Shlapak, David A., David T. Orletsky, and Barry Wilson. *Dire Strait? Military Aspects of the China–Taiwan Confrontation and Options for U.S. Policy*. Santa Monica: Rand, 2003.

Snyder, Edwin K., et al. *The Taiwan Relations Act and the Defense of the Republic of China*. Berkeley: Institute of International Studies, University of California, 1980.

Sutter, Robert. "U.S. Arms Sales to Taiwan: Implications for American Interests." *Journal of Northeast Asian Studies*, September 1982.

Towell, P. "U.S. Reduces Fleet off Taiwan." *Congressional Quarterly Weekly Report*, 30 March 1996.

Tsou, Tang. "The Quemoy Imbroglio: Chiang Kai-shek and the United States." *Western Political Quarterly*, December 1959.

Weidenbaum, M. L. "United States–China–Taiwan: A Precarious Triangle." *Challenge*, September–October 2000.

Wolfowitz, P. "Remembering the Future." *National Interest*, Spring 2000.

FOREIGN POLICY

Bellows, Thomas J. "The Republic of China's International Relations." *American Journal of Chinese Studies*, October 1992.

———. "The ROC's U.N. Strategy: Problems and Prospects." *American Asian Review*, Fall 1995.

———. "Taiwan's Foreign Policy in the 1970s: A Case Study of Adaptation and Viability." *Asian Survey*, July 1976.

Bremmer, I. "The Dragon Awakes." *National Interest*, Summer 2005.

Bueler, W. M. "Taiwan: A Problem of International Law or Politics?" *World Today*, June 1971.

Chan, G. "Taiwan as an Emerging Foreign Aid Donor: Developments, Problems, and Prospects." *Pacific Affairs*, Spring 1997.

Chang, David W., and Hung-chao Tai. "The Informal Diplomacy of the Republic of China, with a Case Study of ROC's Relations with Singapore." *American Journal of Chinese Studies*, October 1996.

Chang, Maria Hsia. "Taiwan's Mainland Policy and the Reunification of China." *Strategic Study Monograph*. Claremont Institute: Asian Studies Center, 1990.

Chang, Pao-min. "Choices for Taiwan." *World Today*, September 1978.

Chen, Chi-di. "On Its Own—the Republic of China (Recent Trends in Foreign Relations)." *Asian Affairs*, Fall 1983.

Chen, Frederick Tse-shyand, ed. *China Policy and National Security*. Dobbs Ferry, NY: Transnational Publishers, 1984.

Chen, Jie. *Foreign Policy of the New Taiwan: Pragmatic Diplomacy in Southeast Asia*. Northampton, MA: Edward Elgar, 2002.

Chen, Lung-chu, and W. M. Reisman. "Who Owns Taiwan? A Search for International Title." *Yale Law Journal*, March 1972.

Cheng, P. P. "Taiwan and the Two Chinas." *Current History*, September 1969.

Chien, F. F. "The Republic of China on Taiwan: Active Partner in the Pacific Rim." *Comparative Strategy*, January–March 1995.

Chien, Frederick. "A View from Taipei." *Foreign Affairs*, Winter 1991–1992.

Chien, Frederick F. *Faith and Residence: The Republic of China Forges Ahead*. Houston, TX: Kwang Hwa Publishing Company, 1988.

China Institute of International Affairs. *China and the United Nations*. New York: Carnegie Endowment for International Peace, 1959.

Ching, Frank. "Most Envied Province." *Foreign Policy*, Fall 1979.

Chiu, Hungdah. "The Outlook for Taiwan." *Asian Affairs*, January–February 1980.

——. "The U.N. Membership for Taiwan." *American Asian Review*, Winter 1995.

Chuang, Richard Y. "The International Standing of the Republic of China: Achievements, Image, and Prospects." *American Journal of Chinese Studies*, October 1996.

Clark, Cal. "Taiwan's Pragmatic Diplomacy and Campaign for UN Membership." *American Asian Review*, Spring 1996.

Clough, Ralph. "The ROC's International Participation: Obstacles and Strategies." *American Asian Review*, Fall 1995.

Copper, John F. "The Future of Taiwan: An Analysis of Its Legal and Political Status." *Asian Quarterly* 3 (1973).

——. "Taiwan's Options." *Asian Affairs*, May–June 1979.

——. "Taiwan's Strategy and America's China Policy." *Orbis*, Summer 1977.

——. *Words across the Taiwan Strait: A Critique of Beijing's "White Paper" on China's Reunification*. Lanham, MD: University Press of America, 1995.

Dent, C. M. "Taiwan's Foreign Economic Policy: The 'Liberalization Plus' Approach of an Evolving Developmental State." *Modern Asian Studies*, May 2003.

Doherty, C. J. "Lawmakers Press White House for Firm Defense of Taiwan." *Congressional Quarterly Weekly Report*, 16 March 1996.

Harkavy, Robert E. "The Pariah State Syndrome." *Orbis*, Fall 1977.

Hickey, D. V. "U.S. Policy and Taiwan's Bid to Rejoin the United Nations." *Asian Survey*, November 1997.

Hsieh, Chiao Chiao. *Strategy for Survival: The Foreign Policy and External Relations of the Republic of China on Taiwan, 1949–79*. London: Sherwood Press, 1985.

Keeton, G. W. "The Problem of Formosa." *World Affairs*, January 1951.

Klatt, W. "Taiwan and the Foreign Investor." *Pacific Affairs*, Winter 1977–1978.

Klein, Donald, and W. Levi. "Formosa's Diplomatic World." *China Quarterly*, July–September 1963.

Lee, David T., and Robert L. Pfaltzgraff, Jr., eds. *Taiwan in a Transformed Global Setting*. Brasseys, 1995.

Lee, Lai T. *The Reunification of China: Pro-Taiwan Relations in Flux*. Westport, CT: Greenwood Press, 1991.

Lee, T. H. "The Taiwan Experience and China's Future." *World Affairs*, Winter 1993.

Li, K. T. "Republic of China's Aid to Developing Nations." *Pacific Community*, July 1970.

Li, R. "Accidents Can Happen." *World Today*, May 2000.

Li, Thian-hok. "The China Impasse: A Formosan View." *Foreign Affairs*, April 1958.

Lieberthal, K. "Preventing a War over Taiwan." *Foreign Affairs*, March–April 2005.

Lin, C. Y. "Taiwan's South China Sea Policy." *Asian Survey*, April 1997.

Mosher, Steven W., ed. *The United States and the Republic of China: Democratic Friends, Strategic Allies and Economic Partners*. New Brunswick, NJ: Transaction Publishers, 1991.

Myers, Ramon H., ed. *A Unique Relationship: The United States and the Republic of China under the Taiwan Relations Act*. Stanford, CA: Hoover Institution Press, 1989.

Pacific Affairs. "Taiwan Strait." Winter 1999–2000.

Phillips, C. S., Jr. "International Legal Status of Formosa." *Western Political Quarterly*, June 1957.

Pillsbury, Michael. *Taiwan's Fate: Two Chinas but Not Forever*. Santa Monica: Rand Corporation, 1975.

Rigger, S. "Taiwan Rides the Democratic Dragon." *Washington Quarterly*, Spring 2000.

Robinson, James A. "Democratization and Taiwan's External Relations: Pragmatic Diplomacy, the UN, and Mainland Affairs." *American Asian Review*, Spring 1997.

———. "World Politics Confronts Respect: Implications of Taiwan's Democratization for China and the United States." *Journal of East Asian Affairs*, January 1996.

Rosen, Sumner M. "The Republic of China on Taiwan, the United Nations and the International Labor Organization." *American Asian Review*, Spring 1997.

Ross, R. S. "The 1995–1996 Taiwan Strait Confrontation: Coercion, Credibility, and the Use of Force." *International Security*, Fall 2000.

Rowe, David. "Republic of China: Post-United Nations." *Issues and Studies*, May 1972.

Saxena, J. N. "The Legal Status of Taiwan." *Indian Journal of International Law*, January 1972.

Seymour, James D. "Taiwan and the United Nations." *American Asian Review*, Winter 1995.

Shen, James C. H. *The View from Twin Oaks: A Collection of Selected Speeches, 1971–1978*. Vols. 1 and 2. Washington, DC: n.p., 1978.

Sicherman, H. "A Conversation with Chen Shui-bian." *Orbis*, Spring 2003.

Solomon, Richard H. "Thinking through the China Problem." *Foreign Affairs*, January 1978.

Sutter, Robert G., and William Johnson, eds. *Taiwan in World Affairs*. Boulder, CO: Westview Press, 1994.

Swaine, M. D. "Trouble in Taiwan." *Foreign Affairs*, March–April 2004.

Thompson, Thomas N. "Taiwan's Ambiguous Destiny." *Asian Survey*, July 1976.

Trager, Frank N. "A 'Willy Brandt' Solution for China?" *Asian Affairs*, September–October 1975.

Wachman, A. M. "Taiwan: Parent, Province, or Blackballed State?" *Journal of Asian and African Studies*, 2000.

Wang, F. L. "To Incorporate China: A New Policy for a New Era." *Washington Quarterly*, Winter 1998.

Wang, Yu S., ed. *Foreign Policy of the Republic of China on Taiwan: An Unorthodox Approach*. Westport, CT: Greenwood Press, 1990.

Weng, Byron S. J. "Taiwan–Hong Kong Relations, 1949–1997 and Beyond." *American Asian Review*, Winter 1997.

Wu, Chun-tsai. "Change in the World Situation and the Republic of China." *Pacific Community*, October 1970.

Wu, Y.-S. "Taiwanese Nationalism and Its Implications: Testing the Worst-Case Scenario." *Asian Survey*, July–August 2004.
Yu, Priscilla C. "Taiwan's International Exchange Program: A Study in Cultural Diplomacy." *Asian Affairs*, Summer 1985.

Relations with China

Arnold, T., and A. Donald. "The Unity of China (Lecture to the Royal Society for Asian Affairs)." *Asian Affairs*, October 1992.
Betts, R. K., and T. J. Christensen. "China: Getting the Questions Right." *National Interest*, Winter 2000–2001.
Biddick, T. V. "Diplomatic Rivalry in the South Pacific: The PRC and Taiwan." *Asian Survey*, August 1989.
Bo, Zhiyue. "Cross-Strait Relations, Part 2: From Talks to Diverging Views, 1993–1995." *China Law and Government,* China July–August 2002.
———. "Cross-Strait Relations, Part 3: Divergence and Confrontation, 1996–2000." *China Law and Government*, September–October 2002.
Bowles, C. "China Problem Reconsidered." *Foreign Affairs*, April 1960.
Brown, Deborah A. "Beijing and Taipei in Hong Kong: Confluence or Conflict." *American Asian Review*, Summer 1997.
Brzezinksi, Z. "Living with China." *National Interest*, Spring 2000.
Buruma, I. "Taiwan's New Nationalists." *Foreign Affairs*, July–August 1996.
Cabestan, J. P. "Taiwan's Mainland Policy: Normalization, Yes; Reunification, Later." *China Quarterly*, December 1996.
Chai, W. "Blueprints for War or Peace in Future China–Taiwan Relations: Two Important Documents." *Asian Affairs*, Fall 2004.
Chan, G. "Strait Talking." *World Today*, December 2004.
Chang, King-yuh. *A Framework for China's Reunification*. Taipei: Kwang Hwa Publishing, 1986.
Chao, C. M. "Will Economic Integration between Mainland China and Taiwan Lead to a Congenial Political Culture?" *Asian Survey*, March–April 2003.
Chao, Chien-min. "David and Goliath: A Comparison of Reunification Policies between Mainland China and Taiwan." *Issues & Studies*, July 1994.
———. "'One Country, Two Systems': A Theoretical Analysis." *Asian Affairs*, Summer 1987.
Chen, George P. "Taiwan's Relations with Mainland China: Three Major Issues between Taipei and Beijing." *American Asian Review*, Spring 1996.
Chen, Qimao. "The Taiwan Issue and Sino–U.S. Relations: A PRC View." *Asian Survey*, November 1987.
Cheng, Tun-jen, et al., eds. *Inherited Rivalry: Conflict across the Taiwan Straits*. Boulder, CO: Lynne Rienner Publishers, 1995.

Cheng, Y. S. and C. C. K. Tam. "The Taiwan Presidential Election and Its Implications for Cross-Strait Relations: A Political Cleavage Perspective." *Asian Affairs*, Spring 2005.

Chiou, C. L. "Dilemmas in China's Reunification Policy towards Taiwan." *Asian Survey*, April 1986.

Ch'iu, Ch'ui-liang, and Leong H. Liew. *Uncertain Future: Taiwan–Hong Kong–China Relations after Hong Kong's Return to Chinese Sovereignty*. Brookfield, VT: Ashgate 2000.

Chiu, Hungdah. *China and the Taiwan Issue*. New York: Praeger, 1979.

———. "The Current State of Divided China: New Perspectives and Policies on the Republic of China (Taiwan) Side." *American Journal of Chinese Studies*, April 1992.

———. "The Koo-Wang Talks and Intra-Chinese Relations." *American Journal of Chinese Studies*, October 1994.

———. "Koo-Wang Talks and the Prospect of Building Constructive and Stable Relations across the Taiwan Strait." *Issues and Studies*, August 1993.

———. "Normalizing Relations with China: Some Practical and Legal Problems." *Asian Affairs*, November–December 1977.

Chiu, Hungdah, and Karen Murphy. *The Chinese Connection and Normalization*. Baltimore: School of Law, University of Maryland, 1979.

Christensen, T. J. "Chinese Realpolitik." *Foreign Affairs*, September–October 1996.

Chu, Y.-H. "Power Transition and the Making of Beijing's Policy towards Taiwan." *China Quarterly*, December 2003.

Chu, Yu-han. "The Challenge of the 1997 Hong Kong Handover for Taiwan." *Pacific Affairs*, Winter 1999–2000.

Clark, C. "The China–Taiwan Relationship: Growing Cross-Strait Economic Integration." *Orbis*, Fall 2002.

Clarke, Adam W. *Taiwan–China: A Most Ticklish Standoff*. Huntington, NY: Novinka Books, 2001.

Clubb, O. E. "Sino–American Relations and the Future of Formosa." *Political Science Quarterly*, March 1965.

Cohen, Marc J. "One China or Two: Facing up to the Taiwan Question." *World Policy Journal*, Fall 1987.

Copper, John F. "Prospects for the Unification of Taiwan with China." *Pacific Community*, January 1976.

Crane, G. T. "China and Taiwan: Not Yet Greater China." *International Affairs*, October 1993.

DeLisle, J. "The China–Taiwan Relationship: Law's Spectral Answers to the Cross-Strait Sovereignty Question." *Orbis*, Fall 2002.

Dodge, P. "Circumventing Sea Power: Chinese Strategies to Deter U.S. Intervention in Taiwan." *Comparative Strategy*, October–December 2004.

Duncanson, Dennis. "What Is Taiwan to China?" *Asian Affairs*, October 1986.

Economist, The. "Separate Ways." 15 January 2005.

Gilbert, Lewis. "Peking and Taipei." *China Quarterly*, July–September 1963.

Glosny, M. A. "Strangulation from the Sea? A PRC Submarine Blockade of Taiwan." *International Security*, Spring 2004.

Gold, T. B. "The Status Quo Is Not Static: Mainland-Taiwan Relations." *Asian Survey*, March 1987.

Goldstein, L., and W. Murray. "Undersea Dragons: China's Maturing Submarine Force." *International Security*, Spring 2004.

Hairen, Zong. "Responding to the 'Two States Theory.'" *China Law and Government*, March–April 2002.

Halbach, Axel J. "Taiwan and the People's Republic of China, Foes or Partners?" *Intereconomics*, May–June 1979.

Hinton, Harold C. "Who Needs Peking? The Case against Normalization." *Korea and World Affairs*, Winter 1978.

Hsiao, Frank S. T., and Laurence R. Sullivan. "The Politics of Reunification: Beijing's Initiative on Taiwan." *Asian Survey*, August 1980.

Hsiung, James C. "The Hong Kong Settlement: Effects on Taiwan and Prospects for Peking's Reunification Bid." *Asian Affairs*, Summer 1985.

Hsu, King-yi. "Taiwan's Response to Peking's United Front Tactics." *Asian Affairs*, November–December 1980.

Hu, C. "Taipei's Approach to Unification with the Mainland." *Journal of Social, Political, and Economic Studies*, Spring 1992.

Hu, W. "China's Taiwan Policy and East Asian Security." *Journal of Contemporary Asia* 27, no. 3 (1997).

Hu, W. J. "In Search of National Security: Strategic Concepts of the Republic of China at a Crossroads." *Comparative Strategy*, April–June 1995.

Huan, Guo-cang. "Taiwan: A View from Beijing." *Foreign Affairs*, Summer 1985.

Huebner, J. W. "The Abortive Liberation of Taiwan." *China Quarterly*, June 1987.

Hughes, C. "Long Shadows." *World Today*, December 2001.

Jia, Qingguo. "Changing Relations across the Taiwan Strait." *Asian Survey*, March 1992.

Kenemade, W. van. "Taiwan: Domestic Gridlock, Cross-Strait Deadlock." *Washington Quarterly*, Autumn 2001.

Kraar, Louis. "Taiwan: Trading with the Enemy; Taiwan Has Become a Major Supplier of Goods to the Mainland, Just When Its Other Markets Were Beginning to Wane." *Fortune*, 17 February 1986.

Li, C. "China in 2000: A Year of Strategic Rethinking." *Asian Survey*, January–February, 2001.

Lin, C. P. "Beijing and Taipei: Dialectics in Post-Tiananmen Interactions." *China Quarterly*, December 1993.

Ma, Ying-jeou. "The Republic of China's Policy toward the Chinese Mainland." *Issues and Studies*, February 1992.

Master, G. "China, Taiwan, and the World Trade Organization." *Washington Quarterly*, Summer 2001.

Montaperto, Ronald N., James J. Przystup, and Gerald W. Faber. *"One China" and Relations across the Taiwan Strait.* Washington, DC: Institute for Strategic Studies, National Defense University, 2000.

Munro, R. H. "Giving Taipei a Place at the Table." *Foreign Affairs*, November–December 1994.

Murray, B. "Tiananmen: The View from Taipei." *Asian Survey*, April 1990.

O'Connell, D. P. "The Status of Formosa and the Chinese Recognition Problem." *American Journal of International Law*, April 1956.

Overholt, W. H. "Would Chiang Find Mao an Unacceptable Strange Bedfellow?" *Asian Survey*, August 1974.

Pomper, M. A., and L. Nitschke. "Debate over Trade Status Newly Stoked by China's Tough Stance on Taiwan." *CQ Weekly*, 26 February 2000.

Pye, L. W. "Taiwan's Development and Its Implications for Beijing and Washington." *Asian Survey*, June 1986.

Qimao, Chen. "The Taiwan Strait Crisis: Its Crux and Solutions." *Asian Survey*, November 1996.

Robinson, T. W. "America in Taiwan's Post–Cold War Foreign Relations." *China Quarterly*, December 1996.

Rudnick, D. "Business before Politics." *World Today*, February 2004.

Scobell, Andrew. "Taiwan: The Other China." *Brookings Review*, Fall 1988.

Shaw, Yu-ming. "Taiwan: A View from Taipei." *Foreign Affairs*, Summer 1985.

Sheng, Lijun. *China and Taiwan: Cross-Strait Relations under Chen Shui-bian.* New York: Palgrave, 2003.

——. *China's Dilemma: The Taiwan Issue.* London: I. B. Tauris Publishers, 2001.

Simmons, Robert T. "Taiwan and China: The Delicate Courtship." *Current History*, September 1973.

So, Alvin Y., and Nan Lin. *The Chinese Triangle of Mainland China, Taiwan, and Hong Kong: Comparative Institutional Analyses.* Westport, CT: Greenwood Press, 2001.

Tien, H. M. "Taiwan in 1995: Electoral Politics and Cross-Strait Relations." *Asian Survey*, January 1996.

Tsang, S. "Target Zhou Enlai: The 'Kashmir Princess' Incident of 1955." *China Quarterly*, September 1994.

Tucker, N. B. "War or Peace in the Taiwan Strait?" *Washington Quarterly*, Winter 1996.

Tung, C.-Y. "An Assessment of China's Taiwan Policy under the Third Generation Leadership." *Asian Survey*, May–June 2005.

Wachman, A. M. "The China–Taiwan Relationship: A Cold War of Words." *Orbis*, Fall 2002.

Wang, Shao-nan. "Why Did We Refuse the Chinese Communists' Peace Talks?" *Asian Outlook*, December 1981.

Wang, T. Y. "Cross-Strait Relations after the 2000 Election in Taiwan." *Asian Survey*, September–October 2002.

———. "One China, One Taiwan: An Analysis of the Democratic Progressive Party's China Policy." *Journal of Asian and African Studies*, 2000.

Wang, Yu San. *The China Question: Essays on Current Relations between Mainland China and Taiwan.* New York: Praeger Special Studies/Praeger Publishers, 1985.

Weiss, Julian. "'One Country, Two Systems': Beijing's Threat to the Republic of China." *Journal of Political and Economic Studies*, Spring 1988.

Weng, B. S. J. "One Country, Two Systems: From a Taiwan Perspective." *Orbis*, Fall 2002.

Whiting, A. S. "China's Use of Force, 1950–1996, and Taiwan." *International Security*, Fall 2001.

Wu, An-chia. "The ROC's Mainland Policy in the 1990s." *Issues and Studies*, September 1991.

Wu, Hsin-hsing. *Bridging the Strait: Taiwan, China and the Prospects for Reunification.* Hong Kong: Oxford University Press, 1994.

———. "Taiwan–Mainland China Relations under the Leadership of Lee Teng-hui." *American Asian Review*, Summer 1996.

Wu, Y. S. "Taiwan in 2000: Managing the Aftershocks from Power Transfer." *Asian Survey*, January–February 2001.

———. "Taiwan in 1994: Managing a Critical Relationship." *Asian Survey*, January 1995.

Yeh, Milton D. "Taiwan–Mainland Relations: An Analysis of International and Domestic Factors." *American Journal of Chinese Studies*, October 1992.

Yu, G. T., and D. J. Longenecker. "The Beijing–Taipei Struggle for International Recognition: From the Niger Affair to the U.N." *Asian Survey*, May 1994.

Yu, P. K. H. "Model of Democrats in Island China/Mainland Relations." *Journal of Contemporary Asia*, 1992.

Yu, T. "Taiwanese Democracy under Threat: Impact and Limit of Chinese Military Coercion." *Pacific Affairs*, Spring 1997.

Zagoria, Donald S., and Chris Fugarino. *Breaking the China–Taiwan Impasse.* Westport, CT: Praeger, 2003.

Relations with the United States

Acheson, Dean. "United States Foreign Policy and Formosa." *Foreign Affairs*, April 1955.

Bachrack, Stanley D. *The Committee of One Million*. New York: Columbia University Press, 1976.

Bader, William B., and Jeffrey T. Berger, eds. *The Taiwan Relations Act: A Decade of Implementation*. Indianapolis: Hudson Institute, 1989.

Barnett, A. Doak. *U.S. Arms Sales: The China–Taiwan Tangle*. Washington, DC: Brookings Institution, 1982.

Bellows, Thomas J. "Taiwan's U.N. Drive as an Issue between the U.S. Congress and the Administration." *American Asian Review*, Spring 1997.

Brands, H. W. "Testing Massive Retaliation: Credibility and Crisis Management in the Taiwan Strait." *International Security*, Spring 1988.

Bueler, William M. *U.S.–China Policy and the Problem of Taiwan*. Boulder, CO: Associated University Press, 1971.

Bush, Richard C. *At Cross Purposes: U.S.–Taiwan Relations Since 1942*. Armonk, NY: M. E. Sharpe, 2004.

Carpenter, William M. "The U.S., the R.O.C. and the P.R.C." *American Asian Review*, Spring 1997.

Chang, J. L. J. "How Clinton Bashed Taiwan—and Why." *Orbis*, Fall 1995.

Chiu, Hungdah, and David Simon, eds. *Legal Aspects of U.S.–Republic of China Trade and Investment—Proceedings of a Regional Conference of the American Society of International Law*. Baltimore: School of Law, University of Maryland, 1977.

Chow, Peter C. Y. *The U.S.–Taiwan Free Trade Agreement: A Bridge for Economic Integration in the Asia–Pacific Region*. Baltimore: School of Law, University of Maryland, 2003.

Cohen, Jerome Alan, et al. *Taiwan and American Policy, the Dilemma in U.S.–China Relations*. New York: Praeger, 1971.

Copper, John F. *China Diplomacy: The Washington–Taipei–Beijing Triangle*. Boulder, CO: Westview Press, 1991.

——. *Playing with Fire: The Looming War with China Over Taiwan*. New York: Praeger, 2006.

——. "'The Taiwan Relations Act' as Viewed from Beijing and Taipei." *American Asian Review*, Winter 1992.

Corson, T. "Bush Got One Right." *American Prospect*, 18 June 2001.

Cotton, J. "Redefining Taiwan: 'One Country, Two Governments.'" *World Today*, December 1989.

Downen, Robert L. *The Taiwan Pawn in the China Game: Congress to the Rescue*. Washington, DC: Center for Strategic and International Studies, Georgetown University, 1979.

Freeman, C. W., Jr. "Sino–American Relations: Back to Basics." *Foreign Policy*, Fall 1996.

Gable, Carl I. "Taiwan Relations Act: Legislative Recognition." *Vanderbilt Journal of Transnational Law*, Summer 1979.

Garver, John W. "Arms Sales, the Taiwan Question, and Sino–U.S. Relations." *Orbis*, Winter 1985.

Goldstein, S. M., and R. Schriver. "An Uncertain Relationship: The United States, Taiwan and the Taiwan Relations Act." *China Quarterly*, March 2001.

Goldwater, Barry M. *China and the Abrogation of Treaties*. Washington DC: Heritage Foundation, 1978.

Gong, Gerrit W. *Taiwan Strait Dilemmas: China–Taiwan–U.S. Policies in the New Century*. Washington, DC: Center for Strategic and International Studies, 2000.

Gregor, A. J., and Maria H. Chang. *The Republic of China and U.S. Policy: A Study in Human Rights*. Washington, DC: Ethics and Public Policy Center, 1983.

Harrison, S. S. "Taiwan after Chiang Ching-kuo." *Foreign Affairs*, Spring 1988.

Hickey, D. V. V. "America's Two-Point Policy and the Future of Taiwan." *Asian Survey*, August 1988.

Hoge, J. F., Jr. "A Test of Wills over Taiwan." *Foreign Affairs*, November–December 1997.

Hsiao, Gene T., ed. *Sino–American Detente*. New York: Praeger, 1974.

Hsiung, James C. "U.S. Relations with China in the Post-Kissingerian Era: A Sensible Policy for the 1980's." *Asian Survey*, August 1977.

Hsu, King-yi. "America's National Interests and Its Continued Support of the Republic of China." *Issues and Studies*, March 1974.

Iriye, Akira. "Dilemmas of American Policy towards Formosa." *China Quarterly*, July–September 1963.

Jensen, B. "Eisenhower's Full Powers for Formosa and Their Constitutional Basis." *International Politics*, 1955.

Kau, Michael Y. M., et al. "Public Opinion and Our China Policy." *Asian Affairs*, January–February 1978.

Kim, H. N., and J. L. Hammersmith. "U.S.–China Relations in the Post-Normalization Era, 1979–1985." *Pacific Affairs*, Spring 1986.

Kindermann, Gottfried-Karl. "Washington between Beijing and Taipei: The Restructured Triangle, 1978–1980." *Asian Survey*, May 1980.

Kintner, William, and John F. Copper. *A Matter of Two Chinas: The China–Taiwan Issues in U.S. Foreign Policy*. Philadelphia: Foreign Policy Research Institute, 1979.

Koenig, Louis W., et al. *Congress, the Presidency, and the Taiwan Relations Act*. New York: Praeger, 1985.

Lardy, Nicholas R., and Daniel H. Rosen. *Prospects for a US-Taiwan Free Trade Agreement*. Washington, DC: Institute for International Economics, 2004.

Lasater, Martin. *U.S. Policy toward China's Reunification.* Washington, DC: Heritage Foundation, 1988.

Lasater, Martin L. *Policy and Evolution: The U.S. Role in China's Reunification.* Boulder, CO: Westview Press, 1988.

———. *The Taiwan Conundrum in U.S. China Policy.* Boulder, CO: Westview, 2000.

———. "U.S. Interests in the New Taiwan." *Orbis,* Spring 1993.

Li, S. "What China Can Learn from Taiwan." *Orbis,* Summer 1989.

Li, Victor H. *De-recognizing Taiwan: The Legal Problems.* Washington, DC: Carnegie Endowment for International Peace, 1977.

Myers, Ramon H., ed. *Two Chinese States: U.S. Foreign Policy and Interests.* Stanford, CA: Hoover Institution Press, 1978.

Nerbonne, J. J. *A Foreign Correspondent Looks at Taiwan.* New York: W. S. Hein Imported Books, 1973.

Peterson, A. "Dangerous Games across the Taiwan Strait." *Washington Quarterly,* Spring 2004.

Pomper, M. A., and P. Towell. "Bush's Vow to Defend Taiwan Takes Lawmakers by Surprise." *CQ Weekly,* 28 April 2001.

———. "Tension with China May Revive Hill Debate over Trade, Taiwan." *CQ Weekly,* 7 April 2001.

Revenal, E. C. "Approaching China, Defending Taiwan." *Foreign Affairs,* October 1971.

Tierney, John, Jr., ed. *About Face: The China Decision and Its Consequences.* New Rochelle, NY: Arlington House, 1979.

Tucker, B. N. "If Taiwan Chooses Unification, Should the United States Care?" *Washington Quarterly,* Summer 2002.

Unger, L. "De-recognition Worked." *Foreign Policy,* Fall 1979.

Wachman, Alan M. "Carter's Constitutional Conundrum: An Examination of the President's Unilateral Termination of a Treaty." *Fletcher Forum,* Summer 1984.

Waldron, A. "Our Stake in Taiwan." *Commentary,* October 2004.

———. "Two Chinas?" *Commentary,* 16 January 2004.

Wang, Vincent Wei-cheng. "Rethinking U.S.–Taiwan Relations after the Cold War: Creative Ambiguity vs. Assertive Democratization." *American Asian Review,* Fall 1996.

Weiss, Thomas. "Taiwan and U.S. Policy." *Orbis,* Winter 1969.

Wheeler, Jimmy W., and Perry L. Wood. *Beyond Recrimination: Perspectives on U.S.–Taiwan Trade Tensions.* Indianapolis: Hudson Institute, 1987.

Wright, Quincy. "The Chinese Recognition Problem." *American Journal of International Law,* July 1955.

Zagoria, Donald S. "Normalizing Relations with China by 'Abandoning' Taiwan." *Pacific Community,* November 1977.

Relations with Other Countries

Ash, R. "Economic Relations between Taiwan and Europe." *China Quarterly*, March 2002.

Carpenter, W. M. "The Taiwan Strait Triangle." *Comparative Strategy*, December 2000.

Jui, Chen-kao. *An Assessment on the Development of Substantive and Formal Relations with African Countries by the Republic of China*. Taipei: Commission on Research and Development Evaluation of the Executive Yuan, 1991.

Leifer, M. "Taiwan and South-East Asia: The Limits To Pragmatic Diplomacy." *China Quarterly*, March 2001.

Mendel, D. H., Jr. "Japanese Policy and Views toward Formosa." *Journal of Asian Studies*, May 1969.

———. "Japanese Public Views on Taiwan's Future." *Asian Survey*, March 1975.

———. "Japan's Taiwan Tangle." *Asian Survey*, October 1964.

———. "Taiwan and Trade in Japan's Mainland Chinese Policy." *Asian Forum*, October–December 1972.

Mengin, F. "A Functional Relationship: Political Extensions to Europe–Taiwan Economic Ties." *China Quarterly*, March 2002.

Payne, R. J., and C. R. Veney. "Taiwan and Africa: Taipei's Continuing Search for International Recognition." *Journal of Asian and African Studies*, 2001.

Peng-Er, Lam. "Japan–Taiwan Relations: Between Affinity and Reality." *Asian Affairs*, Winter 2004.

Roy, D. "The Sources and Limits of Sino–Japanese Tensions." *Survival*, Summer 2005.

Slawecki, L. M. S. "The Two Chinas in Africa." *Foreign Affairs*, January 1963.

Stockwin, Harvey. "A Hong Kong–Macao–Taiwan Triangle?" *The Round Table*, January 1979.

Tsou, Tang. *Embroilment over Quemoy: Mao, Chiang, and Dulles*. Salt Lake City: University of Utah Press, 1959.

Tubilewicz, C. "The Baltic States in Taiwan's Post–Cold War 'Flexible Diplomacy.'" *Europe Asia Studies*, July 2002.

———. "Breaking the Ice: The Origins of Taiwan's Economic Diplomacy towards the Soviet Union and Its European Allies." *Europe–Asia Studies*, September 2004.

———. "Taiwan's Macedonian Project, 1999–2001." *China Quarterly*, September 2004.

Wang, Q. K. "Taiwan in Japan's Relations with China and the United States after the Cold War." *Pacific Affairs*, Fall 2000.

About the Author

John F. Copper is the Stanley J. Buckman Distinguished Professor of International Studies at Rhodes College in Memphis, Tennessee. He is the author of more than twenty books on China, Taiwan, and Asian affairs. His book *China's Global Role* (1980) won the Clarence Day Foundation Award for outstanding research and creative activity. Professor Copper's most recent books include *China Diplomacy: The Washington-Taipei-Beijing Triangle* (1992); *Words across the Taiwan Strait: A Critique of Beijing's "White Paper" on China's Reunification* (1995); *The Taiwan Political Miracle: Essays on Political Development, Elections and Foreign Relations* (1997); *Taiwan's Mid-1990s Elections: Taking the Final Steps to Democracy* (1998); *Taiwan: Nation-State or Province?* (3rd ed., 1999); *As Taiwan Approaches the New Millennium* (1999); *Taiwan in Troubled Times* (editor, 2001); *Taiwan: Nation-State or Province?* (4th ed., 2003); *Consolidating Taiwan's Democracy* (2005); and *Playing with Fire: The Looming War with China over Taiwan* (2006). Dr. Copper has also contributed to more than 40 other books and has published over 150 articles and pieces in scholarly journals and newspapers. Professor Copper has testified before the Senate Foreign Relations Committee and the House Foreign Affairs Committee, each several times. He is the recipient of the 1997 International Communications Award. Dr. Copper speaks Chinese and has lived in Asia for fifteen years.